Fictional Characters of Literature
(The Ultimate Quiz)

Introduction

Fictional Characters of Literature proves that the Classical novelists not only produced great plots and storylines that mirrored life, but that they also created haunting and memorable characters. The focus of this book is on these characters - the ones who inhabit this realm of fantasy and imagination. Every time you open up this book, you will instantly tumble, like Alice, into this fictional universe.

Fictional Characters of Literature offers students an exposure to the Classics that should lead to future literary pursuits or careers. To the curious, it will provide a handy reference with easy access to a three-way index of authors, titles, and characters. For everyone else, it offers an escape into a world where they will eventually say: I see *novel* characters.

Fictional Characters of Literature has a distinctive format. Six English literature periods are covered. The material presented within each of these periods progresses from easy to difficult. Against this frame of reference, other international classical novelists are examined. On each page the reader will find three characters from the chronological period under consideration. Immediately following the name of each of these characters will be the following information: the character's occupation, his or her participation in the plot or subplot, and the date of publication. Below this information, there are three different accurate titles with their respective authors. The reader must select the correct novel for this particular character. The correct numbers for the right answer is shown on the top of the following page. Where any given title would automatically give away the correct answer, titles are intentionally left out of the selection process and only a choice of authors is presented.

Fictional Characters of Literature was written with poetic license: form has been intentionally sacrificed for   content. The rules of correct grammar (particularly regarding different types of clauses) have been stretched - sometimes beyond the breaking point - in order to provide ample and abundant clues.

The Seventeenth and Eighteenth Centuries
(1600-1799)

Some of the noted novelists of this period are as follows: Daniel Defoe, Henry Fielding, Lawrence Sterne, Fanny Burney, Oliver Goldsmith, Voltaire, Jonathan Swift, John Bunyan, Dr. Samuel Johnson, Tobias George Smollett, Matthew Gregory Lewis, Mrs. Ann Radcliffe and Miguel Cervantes.

During the 17th century, the novel came into existence after novelists began drifting across the reality line into fantasy.   Unhappy with the everyday humdrum descriptions of previous writers, they decided to do some elaborating with regard to character and plot.   Where truth had ruled supreme in the prose that existed before their time such as essays, biographies, tracts, etc., they took flights of fancy which allowed fabrication to become the order of the day.

During the 17th century, the majority of novels were of a religious and moral nature like John Bunyan's <u>Grace Abounding</u> (1666) and <u>The Pilgrim's Progress</u> (1678).   Readers were also exposed to long sentimental stories based on heroism carried over from chivalric times.   The classic example of these earlier works is <u>Don Quixote</u>, written by Cervantes in 1605.

The early part of the 18th century ushered in novels like those of Daniel Defoe, Henry Fielding, and Samuel Richardson.   Defoe spruced up the lives of <u>Robinson Crusoe</u> and <u>Captain Singleton</u> in an attempt to doctor the truth about them and make it more interesting.   Fielding created memorable characters which are embodied in <u>Tom Jones</u> and <u>Amelia</u>.   Richardson's ethical dilemmas of young women focused on right conduct and manners: as exemplified in novels like <u>Pamela</u> and <u>Clarissa Harlowe</u>.

The novels of the latter part of the 18th century were divided into two genres: Sentimental novels and Gothic novels.   Each sought different reactions. Sentimental novels elicited sympathy by focusing on the emotional state of very sensitive men as exemplified by Oliver Goldsmith's <u>The Vicar of Wakefield</u> and Henry MacKenzie's <u>The Man of Feeling</u>.   The Gothic novel sought to evoke either horror or terror.   It is exemplified by Mrs. Ann Radcliffe's <u>The Mysteries of Udolpho</u> and Matthew Lewis's <u>The Monk</u>.

Dr. Pangloss - this character is the comical philosopher-tutor of metaphysico-theologico-cosmolonigology whose extensive travels with Cacambo, Mlle. Cunegonde, and his pupil encompasses myriad adventures in Europe and South America until they all settle down on a small farm in Constantinople; eventually, each of these characters gets their own little job to do making this farm work in this optimal utopian society in this eighteenth century novel (1759).

1   **Gil Blas** by Alain Rene Le Sage
2   **Candide** by Voltaire
3   **Madame Bovary** by Gustave Flaubert

Susannah - this character is the maid on an estate who interrupts one of her master's never-ending discussions and debates with Uncle Toby to inform them that her mistress needs a mid-wife; eventually, she confuses the child's chosen name while coming down stairs to the baptizing clergyman, Pastor Yorick, because she cannot remember the name of a philosopher named Trismegistus in this eighteenth century novel (1760-1767).

4   **The Vicar of Wakefield** by Oliver Goldsmith
5   **The Man of Feeling** by Henry Mackenzie
6   **Tristram Shandy** by Laurence Sterne

Squire Allworthy - this character is the retired childless widower who lives in the country at **Paradise Hall** with his sister, Bridget, her son, Blifil and a young adopted orphan that he found left in his bed; eventually, he disowns and disinherits Blifil after the lawyer, Scout, discloses that he gave a deathbed letter from Bridget to Blifil divulging that the orphan was really her illegitimate child with the late clergyman named Mr. Summers in this eighteenth century novel (1749).

7   **Candide** by Voltaire
8   **Tom Jones** by Henry Fielding
9   **Tristram Shandy** by Laurence Sterne

2-6-8

Rev. Arthur Villars - this character is the dedicated guardian of an attractive, spontaneous 17 year-old orphaned ward named Evelina Anville whose real father, Sir John Belmont, refuses to recognize her legitimacy; eventually, this caring clergyman learns to trust Lord Orville as his ward's love interest and ultimately gives them his blessing after Sir John realizes his error and accepts her as his real daughter in this eighteenth century novel (1778).

1	**Amelia** by Henry Fielding
2	**Pamela** by Samuel Richardson
3	**Evelina** by Fanny Burney

Squire William Thornhill - this character is the villainous landlord whose roguish behavior regarding the Primrose family entails slandering Olivia's name involving a mock marriage with a false priest, the courtship of George Primrose's ex-fiancé, Arabella Wilmot and having Dr. Primrose put in debtor's prison for nonpayment of rent; eventually, he is revealed to be the   nephew of Mr. Burchell and the Primrose family is allowed to return to their earlier idyllic state in this eighteenth century novel (1776).

4	**The Castle of Otranto** by Horace Walpole
5	**Sir Charles Grandison** by Samuel Richardson
6	**The Vicar of Wakefield** by Oliver Goldsmith

Robinson - this character is the self-willed son of a northern English family who rejects the security of middle class life and sets out on sea journeys that take him to the Moorish port of Sallee, Brazil, South America and China and finally on a caravan to Siberia; eventually, the longest period of his 54 years away from England which is interspersed with occasional trips home is spent living the life of a Puritan individualist where he challenges his ability to survive and develop his own ethic in this eighteenth century novel (1719).

7	**Captain Singleton** by Daniel Defoe
8	**Robinson Crusoe** by Daniel Defoe
9	**Caleb Williams** by William Godwin

<u>Jeremy E.</u> - this character is the Irish highwayman who becomes the 4th out of 5 husbands of a female adventurer after passing himself off as a wealthy gentleman from Lancashire while she pretended to be a woman of means; eventually, he is reunited with her in Newgate Prison where her death sentence is commuted and they are transported to the colonies where they prosper as elders who are repentant enough to return to England in this eighteenth century novel (1722).

1	<u>Moll Flanders</u> by Daniel Defoe
2	<u>Amelia</u> by Henry Fielding
3	<u>Pamela</u> by Samuel Richardson

<u>Mrs. Slipslop</u> - this character is the maid who protests when Lady Booby fires a 21 year-old pleasant-minded, handsome footman for resisting her advances because she also is attracted to him; eventually, she reneges taking this footman and Parson Adams on their journey to Somersetshire when she sees the footman's affection for his sweetheart, Fanny Goodwill, whom they met as they traveled in this eighteenth century novel (1742).

4	<u>Caleb Williams</u> by William Godwin
5	<u>Joseph Andrews</u> by Henry Fielding
6	<u>Humphrey Clinker</u> by Tobias George Smollett

<u>Mr. Burchell</u> - this character is the traveling stranger whose fortuitous meeting on horseback with Dr. Primrose and his family allows him to rescue the clergyman's daughter, Sophia, after she is thrown from her horse and lands in a stream; eventually, he marries her after rescuing her once again from a kidnaping while the Primrose family ends its downward spiral from idyllic existence to utter despair in this eighteenth century novel (1776).

7	<u>The Vicar of Wakefield</u> by Oliver Goldsmith
8	<u>The Man of Feeling</u> by Henry Mackenzie
9	<u>Tristram Shandy</u> by Laurence Sterne

1-5-7

Mlle. Cunegonde - this character is the daughter of Baron Thunderton-Tronckhwho whose extensive travels with Dr. Pangloss, Cacambo, and her love interest encompasses myriad adventures in Europe and South America until they all finally settle down on a small farm in Constantinople; eventually, each of these characters is assigned their own little job to do making this farm work in this optimal utopian society in this eighteenth century novel (1759).

1   <u>Gil Blas</u> by Alain Rene Le Sage
2   <u>Candide</u> by Voltaire
3   <u>Madame Bovary</u> by Gustave Flaubert

Strap - this character is the expatriate Englishman living in France who helps free his childhood companion from the army of King Luis XIV only to later join him in unsuccessful marriage swindles involving Miss Snapper and Miss Melinda Goosetrap; eventually, he lives to see his old friend rightfully claim his inheritance, marry his childhood sweetheart, Narcissa, and settle down to the life of a country squire in this eighteenth century novel (1748).

4   <u>Peregrine Pickle</u> by Tobias George Smollett
5   <u>Humphrey Clinker</u> by Tobias George Smollett
6   <u>Roderick Random</u> by Tobias George Smollett

Lady Booby - this character is the vindictive widow who fires a 21 year-old footman after he resists her advances in spite of the protests of her maid, Mrs. Slipslop who also is attracted to him; eventually, she relents after realizing that a strawberry mark on this footman's shoulder makes him the son of Squire Wilson while his sweetheart, Fanny Goodwill, is found to be Pamela's sister and her nephew's sister-in-law in this eighteenth century novel (1742).

7   <u>Humphrey Clinker</u> by Tobias George Smollett
8   <u>Joseph Andrews</u> by Henry Fielding
9   <u>Caleb Williams</u> by William Godwin

Jenny Jones - this character is the young maid-servant of Mr. and Mrs. Patridge who is bribed by Bridget Allworthy into falsely conceding that she is the mother of the illegitimate orphan who had been left in Squire Allworthy's bed at <u>Paradise Hall</u>; eventually, she is rescued from Ensign Northerton in her new identity as Lady Waters by this very same orphan and is finally exonerated after she is exposed by Mr. Partridge in this eighteenth century novel (1749).

1	<u>Candide</u> by Voltaire
2	<u>Tom Jones</u> by Henry Fielding
3	<u>Tristram Shandy</u> by Laurence Sterne

Dr. Primrose - this character is the benevolent clergyman whose eponymous name beclouds the Job-like fate that befalls him and his family in their downward spiral from idyllic existence to utter despair when he is put into debtor's prison by villainous landlord, Squire Thornhill; eventually, he and his family are returned to their earlier affluent state, justice is served on Squire Thornhill, his daughter, Sophia, marries Sir William Thornhill and his son, George, marries Arabella Wilmot in this eighteenth century novel (1776).

4	<u>Tristram Shandy</u> by Laurence Sterne
5	<u>The Man of Feeling</u> by Henry Mackenzie
6	<u>The Vicar of Wakefield</u> by Oliver Goldsmith

Tom Pipes - this character is the loyal companion and servant who is assigned by his master, Commodore Hawser Trunnion, the full-time chore of chaperoning the young rebellious son he has adopted and made his heir; eventually he becomes embroiled in a number of chaotic adventures with this reckless youth until the latter legitimately inherits his own estate, marries Emelia Gauntlet and settles down to the life of a country squire in this eighteenth century novel(1751).

7	<u>Roderick Random</u> by Tobias George Smollett
8	<u>Humphrey Clinker</u> by Tobias George Smollett
9	<u>Peregrine Pickle</u> by Tobias George Smollett

2-6-9

<u>Olivia</u> - this character is the daughter of a benevolent clergyman named Dr. George Primrose whose family's downward spiral from idyllic existence to utter despair bottoms out with him being put into debtor's prison by the villainous landlord, Squire Thornhill and she is kidnaped; eventually, her reputation is restored, Sophia marries Sir William Thornhill, George marries Arabella Wilmot and her father's fortune is restored in this eighteenth century novel (1776).

1	<u>Rasselas</u> by Dr. Samuel Johnson
2	<u>The Vicar of Wakefield</u> by Oliver Goldsmith
3	<u>Humphrey Clinker</u> by Tobias George Smollett

<u>Miss Andrews</u> - this character is the young, virtuous servant girl in Bedford shire who enlists the help of a housekeeper named Mrs. Jervis and a village minister named Parson Williams is staving off the amorous advances of her rakish master, Mr. B.; eventually, she marries this young man after he relents kidnaping her by surreptitiously sending her to his caretaker, Mr. Jewkes in Lincoln shire in this epistolary 18th century novel (1740-1741).

4	<u>Amelia</u> by Henry Fielding
5	<u>Pamela</u> by Samuel Richardson
6	<u>Evelina</u> by Fanny Burney

<u>Parson Yorick</u> - this character is the country clergyman who is summoned to baptize a sickly newborn child after a delivery by Dr. Slop because the baby's father, Uncle Toby, and Corporal Trim are concerned about the child's survival; eventually, this curate is ecstatic when a servant named Susannah confuses the parson's first name for the baby's intended name because she forgot the father's choice of a philosopher named Trismegistus in this eighteenth century novel (1760-1767).

7	<u>Candide</u> by Voltaire
8	<u>Tom Jones</u> by Henry Fielding
9	<u>Tristram Shandy</u> by Laurence Sterne

2-5-9

<u>Arabella Wilmot</u> - this character is the fiancee and future daughter-in-law of a benevolent clergyman, Dr. George Primrose, whose family's downward spiral from idyllic existence to utter despair ends with him being put into debtor's prison by a villainous landlord, Squire Thornhill; eventually, she escapes Squire Thornhill's courtship and is married to George Primrose after he is exonerated from a death sentence regarding his attack on the villainous Squire Thornhill in this eighteenth century novel (1776).

1	<u>The Vicar of Wakefield</u> by Oliver Goldsmith
2	<u>Pamela</u> by Samuel Richardson
3	<u>The Castle of Otranto</u> by Horace Walpole

<u>Narcissa</u> - this character is the beautiful young woman whose sweetheart tries such jobs as chemist's helper, ship's surgeon's mate aboard British man-o-wars, footman, gigolo and French army private as he searches for the financial security to marry; eventually, she does marry him and they settle down on a Scottish estate after he secures his fortune with the help of his ex-Navy Lieutenant uncle, Tom Bowling, and his father, Don Rodrigo in this eighteenth century novel (1748).

4	<u>Roderick Random</u> by Tobias George Smollett
5	<u>Vathek</u> by William Beckford
6	<u>The Man of Feeling</u> by Henry Mackenzie

<u>Squire Western</u> - this character is the crude, uninformed Tory squire who holds harmless Jacobite political views which are in direct contrast to his metropolitan and firmly Whiggish sister and his cultivated, broad-minded neighbor, Squire Allworthy; eventually, he allows his daughter, Sophia, to marry Squire Allworthy's 21 year-old son after his true birthright is established in spite of Master Blifil's efforts to malign his step-brother in this eighteenth century novel (1749).

7	<u>Candide</u> by Voltaire
8	<u>Tom Jones</u> by Henry Fielding
9	<u>Tristram Shandy</u> by Laurence Sterne

1-4-8

<u>Matthew Bramble</u> - this character is the Welsh squire whose Pickwickian travels through England and Scotland with his sister, Tabitha, and their niece and nephew, Lydia and Jerry Melford, and a maid named Winifred Jenkins, happily concludes with a triple wedding ceremony; eventually, Lydia is married to George Dennison a/k/a George Wilson, Tabitha is wed to Lt. Obidiah Lismahago, and their maid, Winifred Jenkins, is united with a poor stableboy turned preacher in this epistolary 18th century novel   (1771).

1	<u>Roderick Random</u> by Tobias George Smollett
2	<u>Humphrey Clinker</u> by Tobias George Smollett
3	<u>Peregrine Pickle</u> by Tobias George Smollett

<u>Sophia</u> - this character is the daughter of a benevolent clergyman named Dr. Primrose whose family's downward spiral from idyllic existence to utter despair ends with him being put into debtor's prison by a villainous landlord, Squire Thornhill; eventually she is rescued by her future husband, Sir William Thornhill, Olivia's reputation is restored, George marries Arabella Wilmot and her father's fortune is recovered in this eighteenth century novel (1776).

4	<u>The Castle of Otranto</u> by Horace Walpole
5	<u>The Vicar of Wakefield</u> by Oliver Goldsmith
6	<u>Pamela</u> by Samuel Richardson

<u>Ferdinando Falkland</u> - this character is the rich, gloomy Squire whose secretary pays dearly for prying into his questionable past which includes heroic rescues of Emily Melville from harm along with being accused of the murder of her cousin, Barnabas Tyrrel, eventhough someone else had been tried and executed for the crime; eventually, he is summoned to court by a magistrate where he is so moved by his secretary's plight that just before dying of ill-health he finally confesses to Barnabas's murder which ultimately clears his secretary's reputation in this eighteenth century novel (1794).

7	<u>Rasselas</u> by Dr. Samuel Johnson
8	<u>Caleb Williams</u> by William Godwin
9	<u>Vathek</u> by William Beckford

2-5-8

<u>Jonathan Wild</u> - this character is the professional criminal who is baptized by another criminal named Titus Oates, joins up at 17 with the criminal, Count La Ruse and marries another   criminal named Laetitia Snap who later betrays him; eventually, he is hanged along with his wife and friends without La Ruse while justice is served when a good man, Mr. Heartfree, is exonerated after a missing jewel is returned by his wife in this eighteenth century novel (1743).

1	**Daniel Defoe**
2	**Henry Fielding**
3	**John Bunyan**

<u>Nekayah</u> - this character is the young princess who joins her brother, a 26 year-old Abyssian prince, a philosopher/poet named Imlac and her attendant/maid named Pekuah on a forbidden trek beyond an Eden-like valley between towering mountains so they can explore the outside world; eventually, she grasps that her desires will never be realized and joins the others in anticipating a return to the Abyssian valley from which they had escaped in this eighteenth century novel (1759).

4	<u>The Mysteries of Udolpho</u> by Mrs. Anne Radcliffe
5	<u>Rasselas</u> by Dr. Samuel Johnson
6	<u>Vathek</u> by William Beckford

<u>Commodore Hawser Trunnion</u> - this character is the crusty, well-meaning seafarer whose rural life with his retired companion, Lt. Hatchway, and his servant, Tom Pipes, is changed when he marries his neighbor, Grizzle, and adopts her nephew as his son and heir; eventually, his death leaves this rebellious young man enough money to survive until he legitimately inherits his own estate, marries Emelia Gauntlet and settles down to the life of a country squire in this eighteenth century novel (1751).

7	<u>Peregrine Pickle</u> by Tobias George Smollett
8	<u>Captain Avery</u> by Daniel Defoe
9	<u>Caleb Williams</u> by William Godwin

2-5-7

<u>Cacambo</u> - this character is the faithful servant whose extensive travels with Dr. Pangloss, Mlle. Cunegonde and his master encompasses myriad adventures in Europe and South America until they all settle down on a small farm in Constantinople; eventually, each of these characters is assigned their own little job to do making this farm work in this optimal utopian society in this eighteenth century novel (1759).

1   <u>Gil Blas</u> by Alain Le Sage
2   <u>Candide</u> by Voltaire
3   <u>Madame Bovary</u> by Gustave Flaubert

<u>Lt. Obadiah Lismahago</u> - this character is the quixotic Indian fighter and sportsman who encounters a Welsh squire named Matthew Bramble, his sister, Tabitha, a niece and nephew named Lydia and Jerry Melford and a maid named Winifred Jenkins as they travel across England and Scotland on a Pickwickian journey that happily concludes in a triple wedding ceremony; eventually, he marries Tabitha while Lydia is wed to George Dennison and Winifred is united with a stableboy turned preacher in this epistolary 18th century novel (1771).

4   <u>Humphrey Clinker</u> by Tobias George Smollett
5   <u>Roderick Random</u> by Tobias George Smollett
6   <u>Peregrine Pickle</u> by Tobias George Smollett

<u>Emily St. Aubert</u> - this character is the beautiful young French aristocrat whose marriage to a young nobleman named Valancourt is sabotaged by the villainous Signor Montoni who has married her aunt because he wants to rob both their estates; eventually, her engagement to a Venetian fiend named Count Morano is prevented when she flees from an eerie, Gothic Italian castle and is reunited with her sweetheart in this eighteenth century Gothic novel (1794).

7   <u>The Castle of Otranto</u> by Horace Walpole
8   <u>Vathek</u> by William Beckford
<u>9</u>   <u>The Mysteries of Udolpho</u> by Mrs. Ann Radcliffe

2-4-9

<u>Lady Clementina della Porretta</u> - this character is the neurotic Italian noblewoman who vies with another Italian noblewoman named Lady Olivia for the affections of an upstanding English baronet who is on visit to Italy from London, England; eventually, she jilts this baronet over differences in their religious affiliations which frees him to marry a vivacious and virtuous orphan named Harriet Byron from rural north England in this epistolary 18th century novel   (1753-1754).

1	<u>Sir Charles Grandison</u> by Samuel Richardson
2	<u>Tristram Shandy</u> by Laurence Sterne
3	<u>Joseph Andrews</u> by Henry Fielding

<u>Mr. Harley</u> - this character is the rural, naive, young upright English farmer whose modest income from a small estate takes him to London to secure an adjacent property that will increase his chances to marry an heiress named Miss Walton; eventually, his failure to secure the property and loss of Miss Walton's hand in marriage after her father betroths her to another results in his death from a broken heart in this eighteenth century Sentimental novel (1771).

4	<u>Caleb Williams</u> by William Godwin
5	<u>Joseph Andrews</u> by Henry Fielding
6	<u>The Man of Feeling</u> by Henry Mackenzie

<u>Vathek</u> - this character is the corrupt caliph whose insatiable curiosity leads him to renounce the Moslem creed and go on a pilgrimage with his court in search of the domains of Elbis and the secrets of the dark world; eventually, his unquenchable appetites for power compel him to seduce the Emir Fakreddin's young daughter, Nouronihar, and take her along to their eternal damnation in this eighteenth century Gothic novel (1786).

7	Mrs. Ann Radcliffe
8	William Beckford
9	Fanny Burney

1-6-8

Father Ambrosio - this character is the erudite Spanish holy man whose extreme virtuousness compels his intolerance of sinners such as Agnes who became pregnant by the Marquis Raymond De Las Cisternas; eventually, he is arrested with Mother St. Agatha, tortured by the Inquisition, and informed of his heritage regarding his sister, Antonia, and mother, Elvira, before being put to death by Lucifer in this eighteenth century Gothic novel (1795).

1   The Castle of Otranto by Horace Walpole
2   The Mysteries of Udolpho by Mrs. Ann Radcliffe
3   The Monk by Matthew Gregory Lewis

Arabella - this character is the spurned older sister who loses her handsome beau, Robert Lovelace, to her younger sister while this younger woman refuses to marry a repulsive, old rich man named Roger Solmes; eventually, she outlives her younger sister to hear how their cousin, Colonel William Morden, fatally avenged her death in a duel after a contrite Robert's marriage proposal was refused   in this epistolary 18th century novel (1747-1748).

4   Amelia by Henry Fielding
5   Clarissa Harlowe by Samuel Richardson
6   Cecilia by Fanny Burney

Miss Anville - this character is the attractive, spontaneous 17 year old orphaned ward of Rev. Arthur Villars and the one whose love is impeded when her real father, Sir John Belmont, fails to recognize her legitimacy; eventually, she is warmly accepted by Sir John as his daughter and her marriage to Lord Orville is allowed once she shows him that a scheming, indigent nurse switched the babies at birth in this epistolary 18th century novel   (1778).

7   Evelina by Fanny Burney
8   Pamela by Samuel Richardson
9   Amelia by Henry Fielding

3-5-7

Robin - this character is the first of five husbands of a future rogue who had been seduced by his older brother after she is taken by his family at the age of 14 when she is homeless; eventually, he dies after five years of marriage which compels his widow to enters a life of crime that ends with a commuted death sentence at Newgate Prison, reuniting with her fourth husband, Jeremy E., and a quiester life as a repentant, prosperous 70 year-old woman in this eighteenth century novel (1722).

1   **Far From the Madding Crowd** by Thomas Hardy
2   **Under Two Flags** by Ouida
3   **Moll Flanders** by Daniel Defoe

Aldonza Lorenzo - this character is the shapely, crass country girl   named Dulcinea del Toboso by a man named Alonso Quijano and the one known regionally for her expertise in salting pork; eventually, her inability as to why Alonzo is putting her up on a pedestal leaves her oblivious to his choice of her as his patroness and inspiration for his gallant deeds in this seventeenth century novel (1605).

4   **Don Quixote** by Miguel Cervantes
5   **The Man of Feeling** by Henry Mackenzie
6   **The Castle of Otranto** by Horace Walpole

Captain Booth - this character is the poor English soldier whose marriage to a amiable, young woman named Miss Harris is continually interrupted by short prison sentences for gambling and bankruptcy that are usually resolved by a wise and kindly curate named Dr. Harrison; eventually, his financial plight is finally resolved when Dr. Harrison's written confession from a dying clerk named Robinson revealing a forged will by an attorney named Murphy that illegally gave his wife's inheritance to her older sister Elizabeth in this eighteenth century novel (1751).

7   **Moll Flanders** by Daniel Defoe
8   **Amelia** by Henry Fielding
9   **Roxana** by Daniel Defoe

3-4-8

Miss Beverley - this character is the compassionate and captivating heiress whose uncle stipulates she become the ward of three different suitors and marry someone who will take the family name if she is to receive her inheritance; eventually, her endurance of indignity, privation and a nervous breakdown finally lead her to marital bliss with the once wishy-washy, delicate and impractical Mortimer Delvile in this eighteenth century novel (1782).

1	<u>Cecelia</u> by Fanny Burney
2	<u>Evelina</u> by Fanny Burney
3	<u>Clarissa Harlowe</u> by Samuel Richardson

Parson Adams - this character is the erudite, lovable clergyman and single-minded Christian whose naive trust in humanity's goodness guides his actions during his travels along an English road accompanying a 21 year-old former pupil who has set out from London to see his sweetheart, Fanny Goodwill; eventually, he puts the young couple up at his Somersetshire parsonage until the young man's sister, Pamela, her husband, Squire Booby and his aunt, Lady Booby, are satisfied that the young couple are secure in their social positions in this eighteenth century novel (1742).

4	<u>Humphrey Clinker</u> by Tobias George Smollett
5	<u>Joseph Andrews</u> by Henry Fielding
6	<u>Caleb Williams</u> by William Godwin

Conrad - this character is the young 15 year-old successor to Prince Manfred's throne who is supposed to provide his father with an heir after his marriage to 15 year-old Isabel has been performed by Father Jerome; eventually, he is killed before the wedding and the young peasant, Theodore, who is blamed later marries Isabel and assumes the throne himself in this eighteenth century novel (1764).

7	<u>The Castle of Otranto</u> by Horace Walpole
8	<u>Vathek</u> by William Beckford
9	<u>The Monk</u> by Matthew Gregory Lewis

1-5-7

<u>Fathom</u> - this character is the despicable young man who taken in and raised by an Austrian nobleman, Count Melville, along with the Count's daughter and son, Renaldo, because the Count mistakenly believed that his life had been saved by the boy's dissolute mother; eventually, this incorrigible young man's perfidy takes him through Europe and a number of occupations until he sincerely repents after being freed from prison by Renaldo who never waivers in his belief that Fathom's redemption was still possible in this eighteenth century novel (1752).

1   Tobias George Smollett
2   Henry Fielding
3   Henry Mackenzie

<u>Mortimer Delvile</u> - this character is the possessive lover and adoring husband of a kind, compassionate heiress named Miss   Beverley whose precarious inheritance hinged on her unconventional uncle's three demanding stipulations; eventually, he freed himself of his own paternal dependence, dealt with his jealousy of Cecilia's admirers and learned to become self-reliant in this eighteenth century novel (1782).

4   <u>Cecilia</u> by Fanny Burney
5   <u>Clarissa Harlowe</u> by Samuel Richardson
6   <u>Amelia</u> by Henry Fielding

<u>Amy</u> - this character is the faithful servant of a French adventurer whose chaotic life experiences while traveling from England to Paris and then Holland entails having ten children while being married twice and the mistress of three different men; eventually, this servant disappears after allegedly killing her mistress' legitimate daughter, Susan, because she feared that this daughter was going to expose her mother's checkered background in this eighteenth century novel (1724).

7   <u>Moll Flanders</u> by Daniel Defoe
8   <u>Amelia</u> by Henry Fielding
9   <u>Roxana</u> by Daniel Defoe

1
-4-9

Sophia Western - this character is the daughter of a west-county Tory squire whose innocuous political Jacobite views are in direct contrast with his sister who is metropolitan and firmly Whiggish in her ways; eventually, she marries a 21 year-old good-natured rascal after his true birthright and identity as Bridget Allworthy's son is established and he is welcomed home to Paradise Hall by Squire Allworthy despite Master Blifil's duplicity to malign him in this eighteenth century novel (1749).

1   Candide by Voltaire
2   Tom Jones by Henry Fielding
3   Tristram Shandy by Laurence Sterne

Count Morano - this character is the fiendish Venetian nobleman whose plans to marry a young, beautiful French aristocrat named Emily St. Aubert are thwarted by the equally sinister Signor Montoni who has married her aunt because he wants to rob both of their estates; eventually, his attempt to kidnap Emily from an eerie, Gothic Italian castle is prevented when he is severely wounded by Signor Montoni which allows Emily to finally marry a nobleman named Valancourt in this eighteenth century Gothic novel (1794).

4   The Castle of Otranto by Horace Walpole
5   Vathek by William Beckford
6   The Mysteries of Udolpho by Mrs. Ann Radcliffe

Captain Bob Singleton - this character is the roguish, pirate whose early childhood kidnaping and subsequent rearing by gypsies prepares him at 12 for voyages and wandering adventures he sails from Africa to the Indian Ocean during which he befriends a Quaker surgeon named William Walters; eventually, his pained conscience, suicidal tendency and sincere counsel from the peace-loving William, help him repent in England, marry William's sister and performs good deeds in this eighteenth century novel (1720).

7   Henry Fielding
8   Samuel Richardson
9   Daniel Defoe

2-6-9

<u>Tabitha Bramble</u> - this character is the sister of a Welsh squire whose Pickwickian journey through England and Scotland with his niece and nephew, Lydia and Jerry Melford, along with a maid named Winifred Jenkins happily concludes with a triple wedding ceremony; eventually, she marries Lt. Obidiah Lismahago while Lydia weds George Dennison and Winifred Jenkins is united with a stableboy turned preacher in this epistolary 18th century novel (1771).

1	<u>Peregrine Pickle</u> by Tobias George Smollett
2	<u>Roderick Random</u> by Tobias George Smollett
3	<u>Humphrey Clinker</u> by Tobias George Smollett

<u>Lady Bellaston</u> - this character is the London friend of Mrs. Western and the future hostess for Sophia Western and Mrs. Fitzpatrick when Sophia travels from the country to avoid a marriage with Master Blifil that has been arranged by Squire Western and Squire Allworthy; eventually, her scheme to compromise Sophia with Lord Fellamar backfires which allows Sophia to finally marry a good-natured 21 year-old after his birthright and true identity have been established in this eighteenth century novel (1749).

4	<u>Candide</u> by Voltaire
5	<u>Tristram Shandy</u> by Laurence Sterne
6	<u>Tom Jones</u> by Henry Fielding

<u>Widow Wadman</u> - this character is the old spinster who is determined to marry a retired army hero named Uncle Toby who lives on his brother's country estate along with his loyal servant, Corporal Trim, while spending his time playing made-up battles on model fortifications; eventually, her efforts are permanently thwarted when the Corporal reveals to his naive master that she is more interested in touching his exact war wound rather than a spot on the map where he was wounded in this eighteenth century novel (1760-1767).

7	<u>Tristram Shandy</u> by Laurence Sterne
8	<u>Joseph Andrews</u> by Henry Fielding
9	<u>Rasselas</u> by Dr. Samuel Johnson

3-6-7

<u>Mr. Partridge</u> - this character is the schoolmaster turned barber/amateur surgeon in the new identity of Little Benjamin and the one who loses his school, income and wife after being accused by Squire Allworthy of having an illegitimate son with his servant-maid, Jenny Jones; eventually, he reveals Lady Waters real identity as Jenny Jones when he visits a good-natured 21 year-old who has been unjustly imprisoned in this eighteenth century novel (1749).

1   <u>Tom Jones</u> by Henry Fielding
2   <u>Candide</u> by Voltaire
3   <u>Tristram Shandy</u> by Laurence Sterne

<u>Miss Snapper</u> - this character is the rich, young and physically challenged heiress who is unsuccessfully targeted when a ship's surgeon's mate and his boyhood companion, Strap, decide to swindle her money through marriage so they can better their finances; eventually; she is jilted by him which frees this surgeon's mate to later claim his rightful inheritance, marry his childhood sweetheart, Narcissa, and settle down to the life of a country squire in this eighteenth century novel (1748).

4   <u>Peregrine Pickle</u> by Tobias George Smollett
5   <u>Roderick Random</u> by Tobias George Smollett
6   <u>Humphrey Clinker</u> by Tobias George Smollett

<u>Lemuel</u> - this character is the surgeon/sea captain who relates a number of sea tales about how his voyages took him to countries such as Lilliput, Brobdingnag, Laputa, Balnibari, Glubbdibdrig, and Luggnagg where he encounters a group of immortals called the Struldbrugs; eventually, he speaks of his final voyage to the land of the Houyhnhmms where his contact with the Yahoos compels him to finally return to England in this eighteenth century novel (1726).

7   <u>Candide</u> by Voltaire
8   <u>Gulliver's Travels</u> by Jonathan Swift
9   <u>Rasselas</u> by Dr. Samuel Johnson

1-5-8

<u>Dr. Harrison</u> - this character is the wise, kindly curate who reconciles the young amiable Miss Harris with her mother after the former elopes with a poor soldier named Captain Booth while remaining his benefactor after imprisonments and bankruptcy due to gambling; eventually, he gets a written confession from a dying clerk named Robinson about a forged will that illegally gave Miss Harris's inheritance to her diabolic older sister in this eighteenth century novel (1751).

1	<u>Roxana</u> by Daniel Defoe
2	<u>Amelia</u> by Henry Fielding
3	<u>Moll Flanders</u> by Daniel Defoe

<u>George Dennison</u> - this character is the rich young gentleman who encounters a Welsh squire named Matthew Bramble, his sister, Tabitha, a niece and nephew named Lydia and Jerry Melford and a maid named Winifred Jenkins as they travel across England and Scotland on a Pickwickian journey that happily concludes with a triple wedding ceremony; eventually, he marries Lydia while Tabitha is wed to Lt. Obidiah Lismahago and Winifred is united with a stableboy turned preacher in this epistolary 18th century novel (1771).

4	<u>Roderick Random</u> by Tobias George Smollett
5	<u>Humphrey Clinker</u> by Tobias George Smollett
6	<u>Peregrine Pickle</u> by Tobias George Smollett

<u>Uncle Toby</u> - this character is the old retired soldier whose life centers around never-ending discussions and debates with his brother and playing military games on model fortifications with his loyal servant, Corporal Trim; eventually, he dispels any plans of marriage held by the neighboring spinster, Widow Wadman, after Corporal Trim reveals that she wants to touch his actual wound instead of the spot on the map where he was wounded in this eighteenth century novel (1760-1767).

7	<u>Joseph Andrews</u> by Henry Fielding
8	<u>Tristram Shandy</u> by Laurence Sterne
9	<u>Sir Charles Grandison</u> by Samuel Richardson

2-5-8

Fanny Goodwill - - this character is the young sweetheart for whom a 21 year-old footman sets out from London to meet after being fired by Lady Booby because of her spurned advances despite her maid Mrs Slipslop's pleas; eventually, her new higher social position makes her acceptable to Squire Booby and his aunt, Lady Booby, after a traveling peddler reveals that she is really Pamela's sister and the Squire's sister-in-law in this eighteenth century novel (1742).

1   **Caleb Williams** by William Godwin
2   **Humphrey Clinker** by Tobias George Smollett
3   **Joseph Andrews** by Henry Fielding

Miss Melinda Goosetrap - - this character is the wealthy woman who is targeted when a ship's surgeon's mate joins his boyhood companion, Strap, in a marriage swindle for her money so they can both improve their finances; eventually, she refuses marriage which frees up this surgeon's mate to later claim his rightful inheritance, marry his childhood sweetheart, Narcissa, and settle down to the life of a country squire in this eighteenth century novel (1748).

4   **Peregrine Pickle** by Tobias George Smollett
5   **Humphrey Clinker** by Tobias George Smollett
6   **Roderick Random** by Tobias George Smollett

Dr. Slop - this character is the klutzy country estate physician who is summoned as a backup for a midwife because the estate's master is impressed with the fact that he wrote a book on midwifery; eventually, his misuse of large forceps flattens the baby's nose for life is not witnessed by the baby's father who is downstairs speaking to Uncle Toby and Corporal Trim in this eighteenth century novel (1760).

7   **The Vicar of Wakefield** by Oliver Goldsmith
8   **The Man of Feeling** by Henry Mackenzie
9   **Tristram Shandy** by Laurence Sterne

3-6-9

<u>Miss Walton</u> - this character is the rural, young English heiress who is betrothed to a rich man while a young, naive, upright farmer named Mr. Harley travels to London to secure an adjacent property which will help him financially in his pursuit of her hand in marriage; eventually, she remains single after this young farmer returns from London unsuccessful, professes his love for her and then dies of a broken heart in this eighteenth century Sentimental novel (1771).

1	<u>Calib Williams</u> by William Godwin
2	<u>Joseph Andrews</u> by Henry Fielding
3	<u>The Man of Feeling</u> by Henry Mackenzie

<u>Squire Wilson</u> - this character is the kind, country gentleman who confesses to Parson Adams, a 21 year-old footman and the footman's sweetheart, Fanny Goodhill. about his London imprisonment for bankruptcy from excessive drinking and gambling; eventually, he finds this footman is his long lost son due to a strawberry mark on his shoulder and that his sweetheart is really Squire Booby's sister-in-law and Pamela's sister in this eighteenth century novel (1742).

4	<u>Caleb Williams</u> by William Godwin
5	<u>Joseph Andrews</u> by Henry Fielding
6	<u>Roderick Random</u> by Tobias George Smollett

<u>Corporal Trim</u> - this character is the ex-military loyal servant who convinces his master, Uncle Toby, that he should have model fortifications built on his brother's estate where he can re-enact old battles to pass the time; eventually, he relates to his naive master that the marriage-seeking spinster, Widow Wadman, really wants to touch his actual war wound and not the spot on the map which shows where he was wounded in this eighteenth century novel (1760).

7	<u>Caleb Williams</u> by William Godwin
8	<u>The Mysteries of Udolpho</u> by Mrs. Ann Radcliffe
9	<u>Tristram Shandy</u> by Laurence Sterne

3-5-9

<u>Elizabeth Matthews</u> - this character is the woman of the evening in a London prison who bribes her keepers into giving her a private room where she entertains a destitute soldier named Captain Booth after his unjust plight; eventually, she averts a duel between Captain Booth's and his former officer, Colonel James, which allows Captain Booth a future serene life with his wife, Dr. Harrison and the Atkinsons in this eighteenth century novel (1751).

1   <u>**Amelia**</u> **by Henry Fielding**
2   <u>**Moll Flanders**</u> **by Daniel Defoe**
3   <u>**Roxana**</u> **by Daniel Defoe**

<u>Lydia Melford</u> - this character is the niece who accompanies her uncle, Matthew Bramble, his sister, Tabitha, and her own brother, Jerry, along with a maid named Winifred Jenkins on a journey across England and Scotland that happily concludes with a triple wedding ceremony; eventually, she marries George Dennison while Lydia is wedded to Lt. Obidiah Lismahago and Winifred Jenkins is united with a stableboy turned preacher in this epistolary 18th century novel (1771).

4   <u>**Humphrey Clinker**</u> **by Tobias George Smollett**
5   <u>**Captain Singleton**</u> **by Daniel Defoe**
6   <u>**Peregrine Pickle**</u> **by Tobias George Smollett**

<u>Tom Bowling</u> - this character is the ex-Navy Lieutenant who helps his nephew reunite with his father, Don Rodrigo, after this brother-in-law had been banished from a Scottish estate for marrying a servant; eventually, he joins his fortune with that of Don Rodrigo's thereby allowing his young nephew to marry his sweetheart, Narcissa, and settle down on that very same estate in Scotland in this eighteenth century novel (1748).

7   <u>**Peregrine Pickle**</u> **by Tobias George Smollett**
8   <u>**Humphrey Clinker**</u> **by Tobias George Smollett**
9   <u>**Roderick Random**</u> **by Tobias George Smollett**

1-4-9

<u>Elizabeth Harris</u> - this character is the older, diabolic sister who joins a clerk named Robinson and a lawyer named Murphy in forging a will excluding her younger sister and her degenerate gambling husband, Captain Booth, from their mother's inheritance; eventually, she receives an annual allowance from her forgiving sister while the latter lives a comfortable life with her husband, Dr. Harrison and the Atkinsons in this eighteenth century novel (1751).

1	<u>Roxana</u> by Daniel Defoe
2	<u>Amelia</u> by Henry Fielding
3	<u>Moll Flanders</u> by Daniel Defoe

<u>Lady Howard</u> - this character is the mistress of <u>Howard Grove</u> who confronts Sir John Belmont with the legitimacy of an attractive, spontaneous 17 year old orphaned ward of Rev. Arthur Villars named   Miss Anville; eventually, written proof that a scheming, indigent nurse had switched her daughter, Polly Green, at birth for Miss Anville which allows this young ward the legitimacy to marry Lord Orville in this epistolary 18th century novel (1778).

4	Fanny Burney
5	Samuel Richardson
6	Henry Fielding

<u>Mr. Walton</u> - this character is the rich, rural land owner who betroths his daughter to a rich man while a young naive upright farmer named Mr. Harley travels to London to secure an adjacent property that would help in his pursuit of Miss Walton's hand in marriage; eventually, his meddling proves unsuccessful when his daughter remains single following this young farmer's profession of love and ensuring death from a broken heart in this eighteenth century novel (1771).

7	<u>Caleb Williams</u> by William Godwin
8	<u>Joseph Andrews</u> by Henry Fielding
9	<u>The Man of Feeling</u> by Henry Mackenzie

2-4-9

<u>Sir John Belmont</u> - this character is the true father of an attractive, spontaneous 17 year old orphan named Miss Anville and the one who lets her remain the ward of Rev, Arthur Villars because he won't acknowledge her; eventually, he accepts her as his real daughter and this new legitimacy allows her to marry Lord Orville in this epistolary 18th century novel (1778).

1   <u>Amelia</u> by Henry Fielding
2   <u>Pamela</u> by Samuel Richardson
3   <u>Evelina</u> by Fanny Burney

<u>Giaour</u> - this character is the horrible, old, ugly conjurer whose mystifying appearance allows a corrupt caliph to get an initial reading on the writings on some sabers that he possessed; eventually, this ghoul reappears and pressures this depraved caliph into brutally murdering fifty young children so that the dark powers will be satisfied in this eighteenth century Gothic novel (1786).

4   <u>The Castle of Otranto</u> by Horace Walpole
5   <u>Vathek</u> by William Beckford
6   <u>The Mysteries of Udolpho</u> by Mrs. Ann Radcliffe

<u>Signor Montoni</u> - this character is the sinister Italian who marries the aunt of a young beautiful French aristocrat named Emily St. Aubert because he wants to rob both of their estates; eventually, his plan to prevent this young girl's marriage to a nobleman named Valancourt so that he can marry her to a Venetian fiend named Count Morano is thwarted when she escapes from an eerie Italian castle in this eighteenth century Gothic novel (1794).

7   <u>The Castle of Otranto</u> by Horace Walpole
8   <u>Vathek</u> by William Beckford
9   <u>The Mysteries of Udolpho</u> by Mrs. Ann Radcliffe

3-5-9

<u>Sir Clement Willoughby</u> - this character is the annoying wooer of an attractive, spontaneous 17 year-old orphaned ward named Miss Anville who upsets her when he detains her needlessly in his coach; eventually, he loses her hand in marriage to a young nobleman of good stock named Lord Orville after she is finally accepted as the legitimate daughter of Sir John Belmont in this epistolary 18th century novel (1778).

1   <u>Evelina</u> by Fanny Burney
2   <u>Pamela</u> by Samuel Richardson
3   <u>Amelia</u> by Henry Fielding

<u>Carathis</u> - this character is the evil mother of a corrupt, depraved caliph and the one who not only assists her son in his fiendish ambitions but outdoes him in her devotion to the dark side; eventually, she arrives in the domain of Elbis on the back of a monster where she joins her son and the young princess, Nouronihar, in eternal punishment for the transgressions they all committed in this eighteenth century Gothic novel (1786).

4   <u>The Castle of Otranto</u> by Horace Wadpole
5   <u>The Mysteries of Udolpho</u> by Mrs. Ann Radcliffe
6   <u>Vathek</u> by William Beckford

<u>Parson Williams</u> - this character is the village minister in Bedford shire whose growing love for a young virtuous servant girl, Miss Andrews, occurs when he joins a housekeeper named Mrs. Jervis in preventing her from being compromised by her rakish master, Mr. B.; eventually, he watches as Miss Andrews marries her master after the latter relents and releases her from the strict control of his Lincoln shire caretaker, Mr. Jewkes in this epistolary 18th century novel (1740-1741).

7   <u>Evelina</u> by Fanny Burney
8   <u>Pamela</u> by Samuel Richardson
9   <u>Amelia</u> by Henry Fielding

Lord Orville - this character is a young London nobleman whose love interest is the attractive, spontaneous 17 year-old orphaned ward of Rev. Arthur Villars who is waiting to be recognized as the legitimate daughter of Sir John Belmont; eventually, he marries this ward, Miss Anville, after she presents proof that she really is Sir John's legitimate offspring in this epistolary 18th century novel (1778).

1   **Evelina** by Fanny Burney
2   **Pamela** by Samuel Richardson
3   **Amelia** by Henry Fielding

Elbis - this character is the lord of darkness who rules from below the mountains of Istakhar in a realm where grotesque extravagance and bizarre wealth abound; eventually, this fiend who is seen in the form of a young man with an eerie appearance witnesses as a corrupt caliph and a depraved princess named Nouronihar meet their eternal damnation in this eighteenth century Gothic novel (1786).

4   **Vathek** by William Beckford
5   **The Mysteries of Udolpho** by Mrs. Ann Radcliffe
6   **The Castle of Otranto** by Horace Wadpole

Lieutenant Hatchway - this character is the one-legged veteran mariner who lives with an ex-seafaring servant as companions in the household of Commodore Hawser Trunnion when a woman named Grizzle becomes the Commodore's new wife; eventually, he is asked to find the Commodore's reckless adopted son and heir when the latter disappears from the Winchester school in search of his new found love, Emelia Gauntlet, in this eighteenth century novel (1748).

7   **Roderick Random** by Tobias George Smollett
8   **Tom Jones** by Henry Fielding
9   **Rasselas** by Dr. Samuel Johnson

1-4-7

Don Rodrigo - this character is the rich Englishman whose journey to America to secure his fortune follows a disinheritance by his father for having married a servant in his family's household; eventually, he is reunited with his brother-in-law, who is an ex-Navy Lieutenant named Tom Bowling and is given a chance to help his son secure his fortune, marry his sweetheart named Narcissa and settle down on that very estate in Scotland in this eighteenth century novel (1748).

1	<u>Roderick Random</u> by Tobias George Smollett
<u>2</u>	<u>Sir Charles Grandison</u> by Samuel Richardson
3	<u>Tom Jones</u> by Henry Fielding

Harriet Byron - this character is the vivacious and virtuous young orphaned woman whose journey from rural northern England to 18th century London exposes her to libertines such as Sir Hargrave Pollexfen from whose clutches she is rescued by a virtuous nobleman; eventually, she marries this English baronet after his engagement to an Italian noblewoman named Lady Clementina della Porretta goes awry when she jilts him over their differing religious views in this epistolary 18th century novel (1753-1754).

4	<u>Roderick Random</u> by Tobias George Smollett
5	<u>Sir Charles Grandison</u> by Samuel Richardson
6	<u>Tom Jones</u> by Henry Fielding

Valancourt - this character is the young French nobleman whose plans to marry a beautiful young French aristocrat named Emily St. Aubert are sabotaged when a sinister Italian named Signor Montoni marries her aunt because he wants to rob both their estates; eventually, he is able to marry Emily after she flees from an eerie Italian castle and escapes marrying a villainous Italian nobleman named Count Morano in this epistolary 18th century novel (1794).

7	<u>The Castle of Otranto</u> by Horace Walpole
8	<u>Vathek</u> by William Beckford
9	<u>The Mysteries of Udolpho</u> by Mrs. Ann Radcliffe

1-5-9

<u>Colonel William Morden</u> - this character is the cousin of a young woman who refuses to marry a repulsive old rich man named Roger Solmes, only to be kidnaped, drugged and raped by a young, good-looking suitor of her older sister, Arabella, named Robert Lovelace; eventually, he avenges her suicide when he fatally wounds this contrite nobleman who had unsuccessfully professed his love and offered marriage to her before her death in this epistolary 18th century novel (1747-1748).

1	<u>Amelia</u> by Henry Fielding
2	<u>Clarissa Harlowe</u> by Samuel Richardson
3	<u>Cecilia</u> by Fanny Burney

<u>Father Jerome</u> - this character is the priest who denies Prince Manfred a divorce from his wife to marry 15 year-old Isabel so he can produce an heir to his usurped throne after his 15 year-old, Conrad, is crushed to death in the courtyard just prior to a marriage to Isabel; eventually, he sees his son, Theodore, marry Isabel, rightfully assume the throne after Prince Manfred and his wife retire once Manfred mistakenly stabs his daughter, Matilda, to death in this eighteenth century novel (1764).

4	<u>The Castle of Otranto</u> by Horace Walpole
5	<u>Vathek</u> by William Beckford
6	<u>Joseph Andrews</u> by Henry Fielding

<u>Jerry Melford</u> - this character is the nephew of a Welsh squire, Matthew Bramble, who accompanies his uncle along with his uncle's sister, and his own sister, Lydia, on a Pickwickian journey across England and Scotland that happily concludes in a triple wedding ceremony; eventually, he witnesses Lydia marry George Dennison while Tabitha weds Lt. Obidiah Lismahago and Winifred is united with a stableboy turned preacher in this epistolary 18th century novel (1771).

7	<u>The Monk</u> by Matthew Gregory Lewis
8	<u>Pamela</u> by Samuel Richardson
9	<u>Humphrey Clinker</u> by Tobias George Smollett

2-4-9

Roger Solmes - this character is the repulsive, old wealthy suitor chosen for a young woman by her siblings, James and Arabella, with the approval of their parents when her real love interest was discovered to be the ex-suitor of Arabella named Robert Lovelace; eventually, he is rejected by this young woman and a contrite Robert Lovelace is fatally wounded by Colonel Willaim Morden for causing the kidnaping, rape and ultimate suicide of this young woman in this epistolary 18th century novel (1747-1748).

1	**Amelia** by Henry Fielding
2	**Clarissa Harlowe** by Samuel Richardson
3	**Evelina** by Fanny Burney

Winifred Jenkins - this character is the maid of Matthew and Tabitha Bramble who travels with this Welsh family on a Pickwickian journey through the British Isles; eventually, she meets and falls in love with a poor stable boy turned preacher (after whom this novel is titled) and becomes his wife in a triple wedding ceremony in this epistolary 18th century novel (1771).

4	**Roderick Random** by Tobias George Smollett
5	**Peregrine Pickle** by Tobias George Smollett
6	**Humphrey Clinker** by Tobias George Smollett

Theodore - this character is the young peasant who is accused of murdering Prince Manfred's son and successor to the throne, 15 year-old Conrad, in the courtyard just prior to Conrad wedding ceremony with 15 year-old Isabella to be performed by Father Jerome; eventually, he marries Isabel and rightfully assumes the throne when Manfred and his wife retire to neighboring convents after Manfred stabs his daughter, Matilda, to death in error in this eighteenth century Gothic novel (1764).

7	**The Castle of Otranto** by Horace Walpole
8	**Vathek** by William Beckford
9	**The Monk** by Matthew Gregory Lewis

2-6-7

<u>Robert Lovelace</u> - this character is the young, good-looking nobleman who fraudulently lures a young woman away from the family that has ostracized her for not marrying a repulsive old rich man named Roger Solmes only to drug and rape her; eventually, his actions are avenged by her cousin, Colonel William Morden, when he is fatally wounded in a duel after unsuccessfully professing his love to her and offering her marriage before she died in this epistolary 18th century novel (1747-1748).

1	<u>Clarissa Harlowe</u> by Samuel Richardson
2	<u>Evelina</u> by Fanny Burney
3	<u>Cecelia</u> by Fanny Burney

<u>Isabella</u> - this character is the 15 year-old young woman whose marriage to 15 year-old Conrad is ends when Conrad is fatally crushed to death which prompts his father, Prince Manfred, to unsuccessfully divorce his wife and seek her hand in marriage is blocked by Father Jerome; eventually, she marries a young peasant named Theodore who rightfully assumes the throne after Manfred retires to a convent following the fatal stabbing in error of his daughter, Matilda in this eighteenth century novel (1764).

4	<u>Vathek</u> by William Beckford
5	<u>The Monk</u> by Matthew Gregory Lewis
6	<u>The Castle of Otranto</u> by Horace Walpole

<u>Nouronihar</u> - this character is the attractive, young princess daughter of Emir Fakreddin and the one who has a long standing engagement to her look-alike cousin, Gulchenrouz; eventually, she is seduced by a corrupt caliph and joins him on his pilgrimage to the domains of Elbis where they hope to learn the secrets of the dark side in this eighteenth century Gothic novel (1786).

7	<u>The Castle of Otranto</u> by Horace Walpole
8	<u>Vathek</u> by William Beckford
9	<u>The Mysteries of Udolpho</u> by Mrs. Ann Radcliffe

1-6-8

<u>Master Blifil</u> - this character is the perverse, scheming son of Bridget Allworthy, nephew of Squire Allworthy who lives as a childless widower at <u>Paradise Hall</u> and the step-brother of a good-natured adopted orphan who had been left in the Squire's bed; eventually, he is disowned and disinherited by his uncle after the lawyer Scout discloses that he gave a deathbed letter from Bridget to him divulging that the orphan was really her child with a late clergyman named Mr. Summers in this eighteenth century novel (1749).

1	<u>Candide</u> by Voltaire
2	<u>Tom Jones</u> by Henry Fielding
3	<u>Tristram Shandy</u> by Laurence Sterne

<u>Matilda (Rosario)</u> - this character is the evil sorcerer working for Lucifer and the one who disguises herself as a novice in order to lustfully seduce an erudite Spanish holy man named Father Ambrosio; eventually, she is tortured by the Inquisition along with Father Ambrosio, manages to gain her freedom from Lucifer, and is successful in convincing Father Ambrosio to sell his soul to Lucifer rather than face further tortures by the Inquisition in this eighteenth century novel (1795).

4	Tobias George Smollett
5	Samuel Richardson
6	Matthew Gregory Lewis

<u>Gulchenerouz</u> - this character is the young nephew of Emir Fakreddin and the long standing fiancé of this devout prince's daughter, Nouronihar; eventually, he is jilted by this princess when she is seduced by a corrupt caliph who convinces her to join his pilgrimage to the domains of Elbis where they hope to learn the secrets of the dark side in this eighteenth century Gothic novel (1786).

7	<u>The Mysteries of Udolpho</u> by Mrs. Ann Radcliffe
8	<u>The Castle of Otranto</u> by Horace Walpole
9	<u>Vathek</u> by William Beckford

2-6-9

<u>Gil Blas</u> - this character is the only son of a retired soldier and a chambermaid and the one who experiences a number of wild adventures while traveling to Salamanca, Spain to study divinity after being educated by his overweight, clergyman uncle; eventually, he settles down with his second wife, Dorothea, after a hectic life with the expectation of enjoying his old age in the comfort of his children   in this eighteenth century novel (1715).

1   Stendhl
2   Victor Hugo
3   Alan Rene LeSage

<u>Edwards</u> - the character is an elderly soldier and former farmer whom the young, sensitive, and gullible main character, Mr. Harley, had known from childhood; eventually, the main character,   a "bleeding heart," - promises this character and his two orphaned grandchildren a farm on his own estates in this eighteenth century novel (1771).

4   <u>Joseph Andrews</u> by Henry Fielding
5   <u>Caleb Williams</u> by William Godwin
6   <u>The Man of Feeling</u> by Henry Mackenzie

<u>Miss Emilia</u> - this character is the young woman whose visit to Winchester sparks her infatuation with a wild and reckless schoolboy whose subsequent disappearance from school in order to pursue her results in his adopted father, Commodore Hawser Trunnion, sending his one-legged live-in companion, Lieutenant Hatchway, to find him; eventually, she marries this young man after he inherits his legitimate fortune and settles down to the life of a country squire in this eighteenth century novel (1748).

7   <u>Roderick Random</u> by Tobias George Smollett
8   <u>Sir Charles Grandison</u> by Samuel Richardson
9   <u>Tom Jones</u> by Henry Fielding

3-6-7

Sir Hargrave Pollexfen - this character is the English scoundrel who kidnaps a virtuous orphan named Harriet Byron from a London masquerade ball with the intentions of psychologically coercing her to marry him; eventually, he is bested when an upstanding English baronet rescues her, unsuccessfully challenges him to a duel which he refuse to partake of, and ends up marrying her after being jilted by an Italian noblewoman named Lady Clementina della Porretta in this epistolary 18th century novel (1753-1754).

1	**Roderick Random** by Tobias George Smollett
2	**Sir Charles Grandison** by Samuel Richardson
3	**Tom Jones** by Henry Fielding

Emir Fakreddin - this character is the devout prince whose future plans of marriage between his pretty princess daughter, Nouronihar, and his handsome nephew, Gulchenrouz, are undermined when his daughter is seduced by a visiting depraved caliph; eventually, he is abandoned by his daughter when she decides to join this caliph on his pilgrimage to the domains of Elbis to learn the secrets of the dark side in this eighteenth century Gothic novel (1786).

4	**Vathek** by William Beckford
5	**The Mysteries of Udolpho** by Mrs. Ann Radcliffe
6	**The Castle of Otranto** by Horace Walpole

Grizzle - this character is the rural neighbor who marries a crusty old retired seafarer named Commodore Hawser Trunnion and joins his live-in companions who include a one-legged veteran mariner named Lieutenant Hatchway and an ex-seaman servant named Tom Pipes; eventually, she dies before her wild and reckless nephew finally realizes his legitimate fortune and marries Emelia Gauntlet to and settle down to the life of a country squire in this eighteenth century novel (1748).

7	**Roderick Random** by Tobias George Smollett
8	**Sir Charles Grandison** by Samuel Richardson
9	**Tom Jones** by Henry Fielding

2-4-7

Mrs. Jervis - this character is the Bedford shire housekeeper who joins the village minister, Parson Williams, in defending a young virtuous servant girl named Miss Andrews from her master Mr. B.'s amorous advances to compromise her; eventually, she watches as the servant girl becomes her mistress after Mr. B. relents and releases the latter from the strict control of his Lincoln shire caretaker, Mr. Jewkes in this epistolary 18th century novel (1740-1741).

1	**Pamela** by Samuel Richardson
2	**Cecilia** by Fanny Burney
3	**Amelia** by Henry Fielding

Manfred - this character is the usurping prince whose decision to divorce his wife and marry 15 year-old Isabel is blocked by Father Jerome eventhough he is seeking an heir after his 15 year-old son, Conrad, has been killed; eventually, he and his wife retire to neighboring convents after he fatally stabs his daughter, Matilda, in error just before a peasant named Theodore marries Isabel and rightfully claims the throne in this eighteenth century novel (1764).

4	**Vathek** by William Beckford
5	**The Man of Feeling** by Henry Mackenzie
6	**The Castle of Otranto** by Horace Walpole

Lorenzo de Medina - this character is the young, Spanish nobleman who discovers that his love, Antonia, has been seduced and killed by Father Ambrosio who was unaware that she was really his sister and that he is Elvira's son; eventually, he assists the Marquis Raymond de las Cisternas in rescuing his sister Agnes and their baby from Father Ambrosio and ends up marrying the beautiful heiress, Virginia de Villa France in this eighteenth century novel (1795).

7	**The Castle of Otranto** by Horace Walpole
8	**The Monk** by Matthew Gregory Lewis
9	**The Man of Feeling** by Henry Mackenzie

1-6-8

<u>Emily Jervois</u> - this character is the impressionable 14 year-old ward living at the suburban London estate named Colnebrooke whose infatuation with her guardian is unrealistic due to this English baronet's engagement to an Italian noblewoman named Lady Clementina della Porretta; eventually, eventually, she is rescued indirectly by this baronet from a demeaning marriage to a scoundrel that was set up by her reformed mother and stepfather, Mr. O'Hara, in this epistolary 18th century novel (1753-1754).

1	<u>Roderick Random</u> by Tobias George Smollett
2	<u>Tom Jones</u> by Henry Fielding
3	<u>Sir Charles Grandison</u> by Samuel Richardson

<u>Matilda</u> - this character is the young girl who is offered by her father, Prince Manfred, in marriage to Marquis of Vicenza in exchange of marrying the Marquis's daughter, 15 year-old Isabel after her betrothed, 15 year-old, Conrad is killed prior to the wedding ceremony in the courtyard; eventually, her hand in marriage is refused and she is mistakenly stabbed to death by Manfred who then joins his wife in returning to neighboring convents in this eighteenth century novel (1764).

4	<u>Vathek</u> by William Beckford
5	<u>The Man of Feeling</u> by Henry Mackenzie
6	<u>The Castle of Otranto</u> by Horace Walpole

<u>Miss Atkins</u> - this character is the young, London woman whose seduction into prostitution ends when a young rural upright farmer named Mr. Harley returns her safely to her retired army officer; eventually, her rescuer dies at home of a broken heart after learning that a young heiress named Miss Walton whom he had intended to marry was betrothed by her father to a rich man in this eighteenth century novel (1771).

7	<u>Roderick Random</u> by Tobias George Smollett
8	<u>The Man of Feeling</u> by Henry Mackenzie
9	<u>Joseph Andrews</u> by Henry Fielding

3-6-8

<u>Christian</u> - this character is the innocent believer who leaves behind his family and disbelieving neighbors and travels the straight and narrow path from the City of Destruction to the City of Zion while passing through a number of valleys on the way; eventually, he reaches the River of Death accompanied by a young man named Hopeful, makes it across safely, and is led through the Gates of Heaven by shining angels in this seventeenth century novel (1678;1684).

1   <u>Grace Abounding to the Chief of Sinners</u> by John Bunyan
2   <u>Puritan's Progress</u> by M. Furlong
3   <u>The Pilgrim's Progress</u> by John Bunyan

The Romantic Period
(1800-1840)

Some of the noted novelists of this period are as follows: Charles Dickens, Victor Hugo, Sir Walter Scott, Stendal, Jane Austen, James Fenimore Cooper, Washington Irving, Honore de Balzac, Maria Edgeworth, Thomas Love Peacock, Jane Porter, Johann Rudolf Wyss, Johann Wolfgang Goethe and Mary Shelley.

Novelists from this period found themselves seeking a different goals than their predecessors. Earlier religious themes were put on the back burner while humanitarianism concerns took over. The novelists of earlier Sentimental and Gothic novels were replaced by such pivotal authors as Jane Austen, Thomas Hardy and the Bronte sisters. In time , the novelist's quest of this period merged with contemporary poets such as Byron, Shelley and Keats. Their new responsibility as writers was to defend the individual against society and protect the individual's personal freedoms.

Rebellion was everywhere. The targets of this insurrection were the traditional authorities and old conventions. Politics was in great turmoil during this time because of the French revolution. A tremendous upheaval existed because significant changes had arisen in both industry and agriculture.

This new revolt involved radical shifts. One such shift was emphasis away from what was manufactured or man-made to what was natural and uncontrolled. Nature was used as a backdrop for addressing the plight of man. Everyday interactions between people was being described in more down to earth details. Reality took precedence over improvisation. What had spontaneity and truth took precedence over what was contrived.

The medieval superstition of the Gothic novels was replaced with a new type of mysticism with a magical Oriental flavor. Awe and wonder replaced fear and horror. A re-enactment of the 15th Renaissance took place. A new examination of the Classics resulted in literary pursuits that led back to Greek and Roman times. The ancient myths and cultures were reexamined in order to get a new perspective with the future betterment of mankind as its ultimate goal.

3

Quasimodo - this character is the ugly, deaf deformed 21 year-old cripple who is chosen Prince of Fools in Paris on the same day that Flemish ambassadors are visiting Louis XI, King of France, in 1482; eventually, he avenges the hanging death for witchcraft of a beautiful, young gypsy named Esmerelda that was sought by a jealous minor poet named Gringoire and a sexually-deviant rebuffed priest named Clause Frollo in this Romantic Period novel (1831).

1   **Father Goriot** by Honore de Balzac
2   **The Hunchback of Notre Dame** by Victor Hugo
3   **The Red and the Black** by Stendhal

Wackford Squeers - this character is the cruel, greedy master of the Yorkshire boarding school known as **Dotheboy's Hall** where students such as Smike are beaten and emaciated from lack of food; eventually, his attempt to steal a will favoring Madelaine Bray's fortune is detected by Frank Cheeryble and Newman Noggs and his ensuing arrest leads to a 7 year sentence in this Romantic Period novel (1838-1839).

4   **A Tale of Two Cities** by Charles Dickens
5   **Nicholas Nickleby** by Charles Dickens
6   **Great Expectations** by Charles Dickens

Frank Osbaldistone - this character is the young Englishman who is recalled from the French branch of his father's mercantile firm for unsatisfactory performance only to be replaced by his unscrupulous cousin, Rashleigh Osbaldistone; eventually, his journey to Scotland to expose Rashleigh's embezzlement scheme results in his inheritance of everything and marriage to Diana Vernon while Rashleigh dies at the hand of a Scottish outlaw named Macgregor Campbell in this Romantic Period novel (1818).

7   **The Warden** by Anthony Trollope
8   **Rob Roy** by Sir Walter Scott
9   **Kidnapped** by Robert Louis Stevenson

Alfred Jingle - this character is the crafty confidence man who furtively joins Mr. Tracy Tupman, Mr. Augustus Snodgrass, Mr. Nathaniel Winkle and the founder and lifetime president of a London gentlemen's club as they tour the countryside accepting invitations while observing conduct and behavior;   eventually, he reforms his devious life to marry a rich woman after being rescued from Fleet Street Prison by the club's founder in this Romantic Period novel (1836-1837).

1	**Pickwick Papers** by Charles Dickens
2	**The Three Musketeers** by Alexander Dumas Sr.
3	**The Red and the Black** by Stendhal

Andrii - this character is the daring ,young Cossack warrior whose return home from seminary training in Kiev with his older brother, Ostap, is followed by a journey with his father to a large fortified encampment on the Dnieper River to learn the art of war; eventually, he is killed by his father after deserting and renouncing his country, religion and family because of his feelings for a young Polish girl during strife that existed between Poland and Russia in this Romantic Period novel (1835).

4	**Fathers and Sons** by Ivan Turgenev
5	**Taras Bulba** by Nikolai V. Gogol
6	**Thaddeus of Warsaw** by Jane Porter

Julien Sorel - this character is the gifted, immoral carpenter's son pretentious piety and opportunism lead to his appointment as a   tutor of a young boy named Stanislas and an affair with his employer's wife, Madame de Renal; eventually, his hypocrisy and illicit sexual liaisons which include the young Mathilde de la Mole bring about his sentence of death for the attempted murder of his first mistress, Madame de Renal, in this Romantic Period novel (1830).

7	**The Charterhouse of Parma** by Stendhal
8	**Father Goriot** by Honore de Balzac
9	**The Red and the Black** by Stendhal

1-5-9

Fagin - this character is the corrupt, close-fisted elderly gang leader who teaches young street urchins like Jack Dawkins a/k/a the Artful Dodger and Toby Crackit how to pickpocket and burglarize while assisted by the vicious Bill Sikes and his loyal girlfriend, Nancy; eventually, he is publicly hanged for murder at Newgate Prison while Bill Sikes inadvertently hangs himself after murdering Nancy in this Romantic Period novel (1837-1839).

1	The Heart of Midlothian by Sir Walter Scott
2	Kidnapped by Robert Louis Stevenson
3	Oliver Twist by Charles Dickens

Claude Frollo - this character is the sexually-deviant, rebuffed priest who joins a jealous minor poet named Grinoire in a plot to hang a beautiful, young gypsy named Esmerelda for witchcraft while the Flemish ambassadors are to visit Louis XI, King of France, in 1482; eventually, his warped treachery is avenged when he is thrown to his death by an ugly, deaf, 21 year-old deformed cripple in this Romantic Period novel (1831).

4	Father Goriot by Honore de Balzac
5	The Red and the Black by Stendhal
6	The Hunchback of Notre Dame by Victor Hugo

Uncas - - this character is the valiant Indian chief Chingchcook's son who joins his father and the frontier scout named Natty Bumppo with the nickname, Hawkeye, on a dangerous journey escorting Major Duncan Heyward and the Munro sisters, Alice and Cora, between 2 forts; eventually, he is killed by the Huron leader, Magua, while avenging Cora's death after her kidnaping by Magua's renegade band in this Leatherstocking Tale (1826).

7	The Pilot by James Fenimore Cooper
8	The Last of the Mohicans by James Fenimore Cooper
9	The Pathfinder by James Fenimore Cooper

3-6-8

Elizabeth Bennet - this character is the young, smart, vivacious rural girl of spirit who turns down Fitzwilliam Darcy's first proposal of marriage because she doubts his honor based on the false accusations of a new regimental officer named Mr. Wickham; eventually, she relents when she learns that he helped get a legal marriage for Mr. Wickham and her sister Lydia after they eloped while paying off Mr. Wickham's debts in this Romantic Period novel (1811).

1   **Sense and Sensibility** by Jane Austen
2   **Pride and Prejudice** by Jane Austen
3   **Mansfield Park** by Jane Austen

Bill Sikes - this character is the young, vicious accomplice of a corrupt, close-fisted elderly gang leader, Fagin, who teaches young street urchins like Jack Dawkins a/k/a the Artful Dodger and Toby Crackit to pickpocket and burglarize; eventually, he mistakenly murders his loyal girlfriend, Nancy, and dies when he inadvertently hangs himself with a rope intended for his escape in this Romantic Period novel (1837-1839).

4   **Treasure Island** by Robert Louis Stevenson
5   **Patronage** by Maria Edgeworth
6   **Oliver Twist** by Charles Dickens

Major Duncan Heywood - this character is the young English officer who joins 2 Delaware Indians, Chingchcook and Uncas, and a frontier scout, Natty Bumppo nicknamed Hawkeye, in escorting the Munro sisters, Alice and Cora, on a dangerous journey between 2 forts; eventually, he is able to rescue Alice from a renegade band of Huron Indians after witnessing Uncas killed by Magua while trying to avenge the murder of Cora in this **Leatherstocking Tale** (1826).

7   **The Pathfinder** by James Fenimore Cooper
8   **The Pilot** by James Fenimore Cooper
9   **The Last of the Mohicans** by James Fenimore Cooper

2-6-9

Macgregor Campbell - this character is the Scottish outlaw during the Jacobite rebellion of 1715 whose friendship with Frank Osbaldistone allows him to discover how Frank's cousin, Rashleigh, is embezzling funds from the former's mercantile firm; eventually, he kills Rashleigh in a fight after Rashleigh becomes a turncoat who arrives at <u>Osbaldistone Hall</u> with the goal of arresting Sir Frederick Vernon and his daughter, Diana, in this Romantic Period novel (1818).

1	<u>Rob Roy</u> by Sir Walter Scott
2	<u>The Pathfinder</u> by James Fenimore Cooper
3	<u>Persuasion</u> by Jane Austen

Judith - this character is the Dutch woman born along the Hudson River near the Catskill Mountains who is reunited with her father after he and his dog, Wolf, return home from playing ninepins with Hendrick Hudson and his crew; eventually, her revelation to him that his nagging wife had died after rupturing a blood vessel during an argument with a Yankee peddler allows him to finally come clean and identify himself as her real father in this Romantic Period novel (1819-1820).

4	<u>The Legend of Sleepy Hollow</u> by Washington Irving
5	<u>Headlong Hall</u> by Thomas Love Peacock
6	<u>Rip Van Winkle</u> by Washington Irving

Madelaine Bray - this character is the beautiful, young girl whose self-indulgent, debauched father, Walter, lives off her meager income from sewing and painting while plotting to marry her off to a stingy, 70 year-old undesirable wooer named Arthur Gride; eventually, her father's death just before the wedding and the discovery of a will that leaves her rich allows the Cheeryble brothers to assist her in a marriage to her true love in this Romantic Period novel (1838-1839).

7	<u>A Tale of Two Cities</u> by Charles Dickens
8	<u>Great Expectations</u> by Charles Dickens
9	<u>Nicholas Nickleby</u> by Charles Dickens

1-6-9

Toby Crackit - this character is the young street urchin who joins   the vicious Bill Sikes and a workhouse foundling turned reluctant pickpocket in burglarizing the home of Mrs. Maylie and her adopted daughter, Rose; eventually, he reports back to a corrupt, close-fisted gang leader, Fagin, that the young foundling had been wounded by gunshot during the caper crawled back into the victim's house in this Romantic Period novel (1837-1839).

1	__Great Expectations__ by Charles Dickens
2	__A Tale of Two Cities__ by Charles Dickens
3	__Oliver Twist__ by Charles Dickens

Lieutenant Price - this character is the benevolent, crude Lieutenant in the English Marines whose disability bans him from active duty while dooming him and his family of 10 to poverty; eventually, his shy, delicate 10 year-old daughter, Fanny, goes to live on the Bertram estate with her aunt and uncle, Lady and Sir Thomas, her meddlesome aunt, Mrs. Norris, and her 4 reckless cousins where her dauntless virtue has a lasting positive effect on all concerned in this Romantic Period novel (1814).

4	__Persuasion__ by Jane Austen
5	__Wuthering Heights__ by Emily Bronte
6	__Mansfield Park__ by Jane Austen

Chingachcook - this character is the valiant chief who accompanies his son, Uncas, Major Duncan and a frontier scout named Natty Bumppo with the nickname Hawkeye as they escort the Munro sisters, Alice and Cora, between 2 forts; eventually, he joins the others in pursuit of a band of renegade Huron Indians led by their leader, Magua, after they kidnap the Munro sisters this __Leatherstocking Tale__ (1826).

7	__The Pilot__ by James Fenimore Cooper
8	__Drums Along the Mohawk__ by Walter Edmonds
9	__The Last of the Mohicans__ by James Fenimore Cooper

3-6-9

<u>Wilfred</u> - this character is the heroic, disinherited Crusader who returns home to England disguised as a traveling pilgrim in the company of a Jewish man, Isaac of York, and the latter's younger daughter, Rebecca; eventually, his victory in a jousting tournament wins both the hand of an attractive ward, Lady Rowena, and the blessing of his father who is the master of <u>Rotherwood</u>,, Cedric the Saxon, after he reveals his true identity in this Romantic Period novel (1820).

1   <u>Ivanhoe</u> by Sir Walter Scott
2   <u>Kenilworth</u> by Sir Walter Scott
3   <u>The Heart of Midlothian</u> by Sir Walter Scott

<u>Smike</u> - this character is the mentally retarded, older schoolboy at the Yorkshire boarding school, <u>Dotheboy's Hall</u>, where he is consistently whipped and denied food by a cruel, greedy headmaster named Wackford Squeers; eventually, he runs away to seek his fortune with a friend who rescues him, joins a traveling theatrical group led by Vincent Crummles and dies of tuberculosis while pining away for a young girl named Kate in this Romantic Period novel (1837-1839).

4   <u>David Copperfield</u> by Charles Dickens
5   <u>Oliver Twist</u> by Charles Dickens
6   <u>Nicholas Nickleby</u> by Charles Dickens

<u>Mr. Wardle</u> - this character is the hearty, cheerful and volatile owner of <u>Manor Farm</u> who hosts Mr. Tracy Tupman, Mr. Nathaniel Winkle, Mr. Augustus Snodgrass and the founder and lifetime president of a London gentlemen's club as they tour the countryside observing behavior and conduct; eventually, he rescues his spinster sister, Rachel, from a confidence man named Alfred Jingle and gives his blessing to her and Mr. Snodgrass in this Romantic Period novel (1836-1837).

7   <u>Pickwick Papers</u> by Charles Dickens
8   <u>Great Expectations</u> by Charles Dickens
9   <u>A Tale of Two Cities</u> by Charles Dickens

Mr. Bingly - this character is the eligible, young London bachelor whose leasing of **Netherfield Park** makes him the target of a matchmaker named Mrs. Bennet who is the mother of 5 unmarried daughters; eventually, he proposes to the most beautiful daughter, Jane Bennet, despite the duplicity of his two scheming sisters, Caroline and Mrs. Hurst, and with the blessing of an affluent aristocrat named Fitzwilliam Darcy in this Romantic Period novel (1813).

1   **Wuthering Heights** by Emily Bronte
2   **Pride and Prejudice** by Jane Austen
3   **Jane Eyre** by Charlotte Bronte

Mr. Bumble - this character is the arrogant, tyrannical overseer of a workhouse of poor orphans who marries a widowed employee of the workhouse, Mrs. Corney, after evaluating her financial status and determining she is a fit prize for marriage; eventually, he and his wife go bankrupt and end up as inmates in the very workhouse where they previously worked and mistreated their wards in this Romantic Period novel (1837-1839).

4   **The Return of the Native** by Thomas Hardy
5   **Barchester Towers** by Anthony Trollope
6   **Oliver Twist** by Charles Dickens

M. de Renal - this character is the stingy, coarse and avaricious landowner and village aristocrat of a French town after Napoleon's fall who hires a carpenter's son by the name of Julien Sorrel to tutor his son, Stanilas; eventually, he sends Julien to a seminary after learning from an anonymous letter that an illicit affair had been going on between this young tutor and his wife, Madame de Renal, in this Romantic Period novel (1830).

7   **The Charterhouse of Parma** by Stendhal
8   **The Hunchback of Notre Dame** by Victor Hugo
9   **The Red and the Black** by Stendhal

2-6-9

Sir Mulberry Hawke - this character is the villainous gambler whose dishonorable attempts to seduce a young, refined pretty girl named Kate are thwarted when a compassionate, unconventional clerk named Newman Noggs alerts her brother who summarily administers him a brutal beating; eventually, he dies a brutal death after first killing his silly stooge, Lord Frederick Verisopht, in a duel in this Romantic Period novel (1838-1839).

1   A Tale of Two Cities by Charles Dickens
2   Nicholas Nickleby by Charles Dickens
3   Great Expectations by Charles Dickens

Old Sally - this character is the indigent, old woman who witnesses the unwed Agnes Fleming's birth of a future workhouse orphan and pawns a wedding ring and locket that will ultimately identify the true identity of the orphan; eventually, this evidence is bought from Mrs. Bumble nee Mrs. Corney by the orphan's vengeful stepbrother, Edward Leeford Jr. a/k/a Monks and summarily thrown in the river in this Romantic Period novel (1837-1839).

4   Great Expectations by Charles Dickens
5   Oliver Twist by Charles Dickens
6   A Tale of Two Cities by Charles Dickens

Catherine Morland - this character is the young, impressionable 17 year-old daughter of a village preacher who joins her brother, James, in accompanying the Allen family to Bath where they meet the Thorpe and Tilney families; eventually, she spurns John Thorpe's advances and pursues Henry Tilney to his estate where her Gothic imagination from reading leads her to falsely accuse his father, General Tilney, of murdering his first wife in this Romantic Period novel (1818).

7   Emma by Jane Austen
8   The Mysteries of Udolpho by Ann Radcliffe
9   Northanger Abbey by Jane Austen

Arthur Gride - this character is the 70 year-old skinflint who becomes the undesirable prospect of a young, pretty girl named Madelaine Bray when her debauched father promises him her hand in marriage; eventually, he is implicated in a plot to defraud Madelaine out of her fortune along with Ralph after Wackford Squeers makes a full confession in this Romantic Period novel (1838-1839).

1   **Nicholas Nickleby** by Charles Dickens
2   **A Tale of Two Cities** by Charles Dickens
3   **Great Expectations** by Charles Dickens

Fitzwilliam Darcy - this character is the affluent, aristocratic landowner whose attraction to a smart, vivacious rural girl named Elizabeth Bennet is rebuffed when she turns down his first marriage proposal; eventually, he is successful in his pursuit of her hand   after she hears about his help in securing a legal marriage for Mr. Wickham and her sister, Lydia, after their elopement and his assistance in assuming her new brother-in-law's debts in this Romantic Period novel (1811).

4   **Jane Eyre** by Charlotte Bronte
5   **Wuthering Heights** by Emily Bronte
6   **Pride and Prejudice** by Jane Austen

Widow Bardell - this character is the landlady who misreads her friendly tenant's question of advice regarding Sam Weller for a marriage proposal whereas she retains the unscrupulous lawyers Dodson and Fogg and has him put into Fleet Street Prison for breach of promise; eventually, she is rescued from Fleet Street Prison herself by this founder and lifetime president of a London gentlemen's club when he pays the damages asked for in this Romantic Period novel (1836-1837).

7   **Pickwick Papers** by Charles Dickens
8   **Great Expectation** by Charles Dickens
9   **A Tale of Two Cities** by Charles Dickens

Robert Walton - this character is the English explorer aboard a ship frozen in ice who is told a gruesome tale by a brilliant inventor named Victor about his pursuit of the murderer who killed his brother, William, his adopted sister, Elizabeth, his friend, Henry Clerval and the family servant, Justine; eventually, Victor dies from overexposure before he can avenge those heinous crimes in this Romantic Period novel (1817).

1   **Frankenstein** by Mary Shelley
2   **Murders in the Rue Morgue** by Edgar Allen Poe
3   **Penguin Island** by Anatole France

Miss Rachel Wardle - this character is the flirtatious spinster whose fickleness leads her to jilt the plump Mr. Tracy Tupman for a crafty confidence man named Mr. Alfred Jingle who was only interested in her assumed wealth; eventually, she is rescued during their elopement when her brother, Mr. Wardle, pays off this charlatan and allows her to return alone to **Manor Farm** in this Romantic Period novel (1836-1837).

4   **Pickwick Papers** by Charles Dickens
5   **Great Expectations** by Charles Dickens
6   **A Tale of Two Cities** by Charles Dickens

Gina Pietranera - this character is the beautiful, intelligent Italian woman whose patronage of her young, adventurous nephew, Fabrizio, after the latter's involvement with Napoleon's defeat at Waterloo, leads to his 3 years at a theological seminary upon the advice of her lover, Count Mosca; eventually, she enters a marriage of convenience with an old duke, conspires with the poet, Ferrante, to fatally poison a prince, and ultimately marries her lover, Count Mosca in this Romantic Period novel (1839).

7   **The Charterhouse of Parma** by Stendhal
8   **Melincourt** by Thomas Love Peacock
9   **The Old Curiosity Shop** by Charles Dickens

1-4-7

<u>Nancy</u> - this character is the loyal girlfriend of a young gang member named Bill Sikes who helps a corrupt, close-fisted thief named Fagin teach street urchins like Jack Dawkins a/k/a the Artful Dodger and Toby Crackit pickpocket and burglarize; eventually, she is mistakenly murdered by her vicious boyfriend who in turn dies by misadventure when he hangs himself with a rope intended for his escape in this Romantic Period novel (1837-1839).

1	<u>Great Expectations</u> by Charles Dickens
2	<u>The Return of the Native</u> by Thomas Hardy
3	<u>Oliver Twist</u> by Charles Dickens

<u>Eugene de Rastignac</u> - this character is the impoverished law student who becomes involved with the boarder at Madame Vauquer's boarding house who keeps moving upstairs each year to cheaper lodgings with increasingly less visits by his two daughters; eventually, he and a medical student are the only ones present at this pauper's funeral at which his two daughters, Anastasie and Delphine, were absent in this Romantic Period novel (1835).

4	<u>Pere Goriot</u> by Honore de Balzac
5	<u>The Red and the Black</u> by Stendhal
6	<u>Madame Bovary</u> by Gustave Flaubert

<u>Esmerelda</u> - this character is the beautiful, young, gypsy dancer who performs tricks with a trained goat in Paris while the   Flemish ambassadors are visiting Louis XI, King of France in 1482; eventually, her rescue by an ugly, deaf 21 year-old deformed, cripple only delays her hanging for sorcery and witchcraft which is sought by a jealous minor poet named Gringiore and a sexually-deviant, rebuffed priest named Claude Frollo in this Romantic Period novel (1831).

7	<u>Pere Goriot</u> by Honore de Balzac
8	<u>The Red and the Black</u> by Stendhal
9	<u>The Hunchback of Notre Dame</u> by Victor Hugo

3-4-9

Jack Dawkins, (the Artful Dodger) - this character is the shrewd, young slum pickpocket who recruits a weak, starving runaway workhouse orphan and takes him to his corrupt, close-fisted leader, Fagin, who works with a vicious accomplice named Bill Sikes; eventually, this young thief is apprehended for robbery while his mentor, Fagin, is publicly hanged for murder at Newgate Prison and Bill Sikes experiences death by misadventure after mistakenly killing his girlfriend, Nancy, in this Romantic Period novel (1837-1839).

1	Great Expectations by Charles Dickens
2	Return of the Native by Thomas Hardy
3	Oliver Twist by Charles Dickens

Donald Bean Lean - this character is the Scottish Highlander who remains loyal to Fergis MacIvor and Prince Charles Edward Stuart when the latter invades England from France in 1745 to regain the throne from the new Hanover king of England, George II; eventually, he rescues a young British Jacobite officer named Edward after having betrayed him to Colonel Gardiner as a traitor in this Romantic Period novel (1814).

4	Kidnapped by Robert Louis Stevenson
5	Waverly by Sir Walter Scott
6	The Return of the Native by Thomas Hardy

Dr. Slammer - this character is the volatile English army surgeon of the 97th Regiment who challenges Mr. Nathaniel Winkle to a duel with Mr. Augustus Snodgrass as his second because of an offensive, drunken remark passed in front of a woman the previous night; eventually, his inability to recognize Mr. Winkle leads to the realization that the real scoundrel was Mr. Alfred Jingle who had borrowed Mr. Winkle's suit for the ball in this Romantic Period novel (1836-1837).

7	A Tale of Two Cities by Charles Dickens
8	Great Expectations by Charles Dickens
9	Pickwick Papers by Charles Dickens

3-5-9

<u>Ostap</u> - this character is the daring, young Cossack whose return home from seminary training in Kiev with his younger brother, Andrii, is followed by a journey with his father to a large fortified encampment on the Dnieper River to learn the art of war; eventually, he is able to hear his father's voice just as he is being led out to be tortured and killed in the city of Warsaw during strife between Poland and Russia in this Romantic Period novel (1835).

1	<u>Taras Bulba</u> by Nikolai V. Gogol
2	<u>Fathers and Sons</u> by Ivan Turgenev
3	<u>Thaddeus of Warsaw</u> by Jane Porter

<u>Sir Walter Elliot</u> - this character is the conceited widower who reluctantly leases his estate, <u>Kellynch Hall</u> and moves to Bath with his daughter Elizabeth while daughters, Anne and Mary, stay home; eventually, he is saved by his villainous nephew, William Elliot, from the scheming fortune hunter, Mrs. Clay, while his daughter Anne reunites with a Naval Officer named Captain Frederick Wentworth in this Romantic Period novel (1818).

4	<u>Pride and Prejudice</u> by Jane Austen
5	<u>Persuasion</u> by Jane Austen
6	<u>Sense and Sensibility</u> by Jane Austen

<u>Sowerberry</u> - the character is the undertaker and casket maker who takes on an emaciated orphan as an apprentice and has him act as a mourner at children's funerals; eventually, this orphan's escape from servitude leads to 2 more of his young employees, Noah Claypole and Charlotte, escaping to a London public house where they meet up with Fagin and his gang of street pickpockets and burglars in this Romantic Period novel (1837-1839).

7	<u>Great Expectations</u> by Charles Dickens
8	<u>Oliver Twist</u> by Charles Dickens
9	<u>The Return of the Native</u> by Thomas Hardy

1-5-8

<u>Anne Elliot</u> - this character is the good-looking daughter of a vain and spendthrift Baronet named Sir Walter Elliot who owns <u>Kellynch Hall</u> and the one pursued by her cold, calculating and charming cousin, William Elliot; eventually, she is reunited with a Naval Officer named Captain Frederick Wentworth, R.N. after he ends his pursuit of Louisa Musgrove and proposes to her in this Romantic Period novel (1818).

1	<u>Pride and Prejudice</u> by Jane Austen
2	<u>Persuasion</u> by Jane Austen
3	<u>Sense and Sensibility</u> by Jane Austen

<u>Tracy Tupman</u> - this character is the plump member of a London gentlemen's club whose susceptibility to falling in love leads him into a disastrous relationship with Miss Rachel Wardle, the fickle spinster sister of the owner of <u>Manor Farm</u>; eventually, his suicide note over being jilted leads the magnanimous founder of the club to find him at the <u>Leathern Bottle</u> lost in profound melancholy in this Romantic Period novel (1836-1837).

4	<u>Great Expectations</u> by Charles Dickens
5	<u>A Tale of Two Cities</u> by Charles Dickens
6	<u>Pickwick Papers</u> by Charles Dickens

<u>Mrs. Norris</u> - this character is the meddlesome clergyman's widow whose sisters range from being a baronet's wife to being the poverty stricken wife of a disabled Lieutenant in the English Marines and the mother of 9 children; eventually, this spiteful instigator's ongoing snipes about her shy, young niece, Fanny Price, stop when she leaves the Bertram household to live with her favorite niece, Maria, in this Romantic Period novel (1814).

7	<u>Barchester Towers</u> by Anthony Trollope
8	<u>Mansfield Park</u> by Jane Austen
9	<u>The Return of the Native</u> by Thomas Hardy

2-6-8

Emily Montrose - this character is the young woman whose return trip from India to England aboard a different ship than her English officer widowed father is interrupted by a shipwreck that leaves her stranded in an island cave near a volcano; eventually, she is rescued by a young man named Fritz who finds her cave while canoeing which further leads to the start of marriage plans that will need the approval of her father who is back in England in this Romantic Period novel (1813).

1	The Count of Monte-Cristo by Alexander Dumas, Sr.
2	Swiss Family Robinson by Johann Rudolf Wyss
3	Twenty Thousand Leagues Under The Sea by Jules Verne

Edward Leeford (Monks) - this character is the vengeful, greedy young member of a gang of pickpockets and burglars made up of street urchins like Jack Dawkins a/k/a The Artful Dodger and Toby Crackit who are led by Fagin and his vicious accomplice, Bill Sikes; eventually, he confesses that he tried to prevent his stepbrother from justly receiving an inheritance, makes restitution and moves to America where he dies in prison in this Romantic Period novel (1837-1839).

4	Great Expectations by Charles Dickens
5	Return of the Native by Thomas Hardy
6	Oliver Twist by Charles Dickens

Gringiore - this character is the naive, poverty-stricken minor poet and playwright who orders the start of a morality play in Paris on the same day that Flemish ambassadors are visiting Louis XI, King of France, in 1482; eventually, he joins a sexually-deviant rebuffed priest named Claude Frollo in having a beautiful young gypsy girl, Esmerelda, finally hanged for witchcraft after she is initially rescued by an ugly, deaf, 21 year-old deformed cripple in this Romantic Period novel (1831).

7	The Red and the Black by Stendhal
8	The Hunchback of Notre Dame by Victor Hugo
9	Madame Bovary by Gustave Flaubert

2-6-8

<u>Newman Noggs</u> - this character is the unconventional, sympathetic London clerk who seeks revenge against his present employer, Ralph, because his dishonesty and fraud are responsible for this clerk's current plight; eventually, he joins Frank Cheeryble in nabbing Wackford Squeers just as he steals a will favoring Madelaine Bray which results in a confession implicating Arthur Gride and Ralph in a conspiracy in this Romantic Period novel (1838-1839).

1   <u>Nicholas Nickleby</u> by Charles Dickens
2   <u>A Tale of Two Cities</u> by Charles Dickens
3   <u>Great Expectations</u> by Charles Dickens

<u>Sir Thomas Bertram</u> - this character is the elderly, reserved baronet husband of one of the 3 Ward sisters, Lady Bertram, and the stern father of 4 distant and reckless children named Tom, Edmund, Maria and Julia; eventually, he accepts a shy, delicate,virtuous 10 year-old niece named Fanny Price into his household because his wife and meddlesome sister-in-law want to help their 3rd destitute sister in this Romantic Period novel (1814).

4   <u>Castle Rackrent</u> by Maria Edgeworth
5   <u>Mansfield Park</u> by Jane Austen
6   <u>Sense and Sensibility</u> by Jane Austen

<u>Lucy Steele</u> - this character is the vulgar, mercenary woman whose secret engagement to Edward Ferrars hinges on his inheritance despite Edward's true feelings of love for Elinor Dashwood and his mother's opposition to her; eventually, her new found affections for Edwards's brother, Robert, upon hearing that Mrs. Ferrars changed her will in favor of Robert allows Elinor and Edward to ultimately marry in this Romantic Period novel (1811).

7   <u>Wuthering Heights</u> by Emily Bronte
8   <u>Sense and Sensibility</u> by Jane Austen
9   <u>Jane Eyre</u> by Charlotte Bronte

1-5-8

<u>Mrs. Corney</u> - this character is the wife of the arrogant, tyrannical overseer named Mr. Bumble who runs the workhouse for poor orphans where he first met and married her only after he determined that she was a person of means; eventually, she joins him in an ironic twist of fate when bankruptcy makes them both inmates in the very same poorhouse where they were both employed and maltreated other inmates in this Romantic Period novel (1837-1839).

1   <u>Oliver Twist</u> by Charles Dickens
2   <u>Great Expectations</u> by Charles Dickens
3   <u>Return of the Native</u> by Thomas Hardy

<u>Marietta Valsera</u> - this character is the young no-talent actress who watches a mean and jealous bodyguard named Gilette inadvertently shot by a young, handsome Italian nobleman named Fabrizio after Fabrizio is attacked by this knife-wielding assailant; eventually, she is jilted by Fabrizio who ends up entering a Carthusian monastery after his lover, Clelia, and their illegitimate son, Sardino, meet untimely deaths in this Romantic Period novel (1839).

4   <u>Madame Bovery</u> by Gustave Flaubert
5   <u>The Charterhouse of Parma</u> by Stendhal
6   <u>The Red and the Black</u> by Stendhal

<u>Nathaniel Winkle</u> - this character is the bungling member of a London gentlemen's club who joins Mr. Tracy Tupman, Mr. Augustus Snodgrass along with the founder and lifetime president as they tour the countryside accepting invitations and observing conduct and behavior; eventually, he marries Arabella Allen over the objections of his father, her brother, Mr. Allen, and her intended, Mr. Bob Sawyer in this Romantic Period novel (1836-1837).

7   <u>A Tale of Two Cities</u> by Charles Dickens
8   <u>Great Expectations</u> by Charles Dickens
9   <u>Pickwick Papers</u> by Charles Dickens

1-5-9

<u>Richard Varney</u> - this character is the Earl of Leicester, Robert Dudley's unprincipled squire who fakes a marriage to Amy Robart so that the Earl can seek favor with Queen Elizabeth over his rival the Earl of Sussex; eventually, power-hungry squire commits suicide in prison after tricking Amy into fatally falling through a rigged trap door in this Romantic Period novel (1821).

1   <u>Sense and Sensibility</u> by Jane Austen
2   <u>Kenilwoth</u> by Sir Walter Scott
3   <u>The Charterhouse of Parma</u> by Stendhal

<u>Fanny Price</u> - this character is the shy and delicate 10 year-old who leaves her impoverished family of 10 in Portsmouth, England to live with her 4 reckless cousins, their titled parents and a meddlesome aunt named Mrs. Norris at the Bertram estate; eventually, her lengthy stay there confirms her dauntless virtue to the extent that Sir Thomas Bertram finally agrees with her decision not to marry the young, wealthy Henry Crawford in this Romantic Period novel (1814).

4   <u>Jane Eyre</u> by Charlotte Bronte
5   <u>Wuthering Heights</u> by Emily Bronte
6   <u>Mansfield Park</u> by Jane Austen

<u>Count Mosca</u> - this character is the prime minister under two heads of state whose jealousy of an adventurous young Italian nobleman named Fabrizio prompts him to recommend to this young man's aunt, Gina Pietranera, that this young man enter a theological seminary; eventually, this skilled diplomat and ambitious politician forsakes any monetary gain when he decides to marry Gina and accept a life of poverty in this Romantic Period novel (1839).

7   <u>The Charterhouse of Parma</u> by Stendhal
8   <u>The Hunchback of Notre Dame</u> by Victor Hugo
9   <u>Pere Goriot</u> by Honore de Balzac

Judge Marmaduke Temple - this character is the old hunter and landowner who joins a nosey sheriff named Richard Jones and a avaricious magistrate named Hiram Doolittle in harassing Oliver Edwards, Indian John a/k/a Chingachgook, and an old hunter, Natty Bumppo a/k/a Leatherstocking; eventually, he makes restitution to Oliver Edward Effingham and his grandfather, Major Effingham and gives his blessing to Oliver and his daughter on their impending marriage in this Romantic Period novel (1823).

1	**Nicholas Nickleby** by Charles Dickens
2	**The Heart of Midlothian** by Sir Walter Scott
3	**The Pioneers** by James Fenimore Cooper

Mr. Gray - this character is the mysterious stranger whose precarious rescue off the northeast coast of England to an American frigate is accomplished by Lt. Richard Barnstable along with a weathered whaler from Nantucket named Long Tom Coffin; eventually, this mariner who is suspected to be John Paul Jones saves the frigate in a sea battle with 3 enemy English ships and then witnesses a double marriage in this Romantic Period novel (1823).

4	**Omoo** by Herman Melville
5	**The Pilot** by James Fenimore Cooper
6	**Typee** by Herman Melville

Amy Robsart - this character is the attractive wife of the Earl of Leicester, Robert Dudley, whose marriage is kept secret so that her husband can seek the favor of Queen Elizabeth over his rival, the Earl of Sussex; eventually, her husband's duel with Edmund Tressilian cannot stop her fatal fall through a trap door that has been rigged by an unprincipled, power-hungry squire named Richard Varney in this Romantic Period novel (1821).

7	**The Pilot** by James Fenimore Cooper
8	**Thaddeus of Warsaw** by Jane Porter
9	**Kenilworth** by Sir Walter Scott

3-5-9

Edward Ferrars - this character is the young, eligible bachelor who is unable to court his true love, the young Elinor Dashwood, because he had already become secretly engaged to the fortune hunting Lucy Steele; eventually, he is able to marry Elinor Dashwood after being jilted by Lucy upon learning that he had been disinherited by his mother in this Romantic Period novel (1811).

1   Wuthering Heights by Emily Bronte
2   Sense and Sensibility by Jane Austen
3   Jane Eyre by Charlotte Bronte

Clelia Conti - this character is the beautiful young daughter of a traitorous Count who, by chance, becomes the jailor over her young lover, an Italian nobleman named Fabrizio who turns out to be an Archbishop and father of her illegitimate son, Sardino; eventually, her untimely death after the unexpected death of her son drives this Archbishop into a Carthusian monastery on the Po river where he lives a life of solitude in this Romantic Period novel (1839).

4   The Red and the Black by Stendhal
5   The Hunchback of Notre Dame by Victor Hugo
6   The Charterhouse of Parma by Stendhal

Mathilde de la Mole - this character is the haughty, astute and self-restrained young future duchess in Paris after Napoleon's fall whose seduction by her father's opportunistic secretary, Julien Sorel, leaves her pregnant with his baby; eventually, her unborn child remains illegitimate when Julien is convicted and sentenced to death for the attempted murder of his married lover and first mistress, Madame de Renal in this Romantic Period novel (1830).

7   The Hunchback of Notre Dame by Victor Hugo
8   The Red and the Black by Stendhal
9   The Charterhouse of Parma by Stendhal

2-6-8

<u>Edward Tressilian</u> - this character is the unsuccessful, indigent young Cornish gentleman whose attempts to rescue his former sweetheart, Amy Robsart, result in a duel with her real husband, Robert Dudley, over an illicit affair; eventually, his exoneration by Queen Elizabeth is in vain when an attractive Amy fatally falls through a trap door rigged by the unprincipled, power-hungry squire named Richard Varney in this Romantic Period novel (1821).

1	<u>Kenilworth</u> by Sir Walter Scott
2	<u>Crotchet Castle</u> by Thomas Love Peacock
3	<u>Rob Roy</u> by Sir Walter Scott

<u>George Knightly</u> - this character is the candid, astute landowner who becomes the amorous object of an impressionable 17 year-old orphan, Harriet Smith, who lives in the parlor of a boarding school; eventually, his earlier marriage proposals to a clever, pampered matchmaker named Miss Woodhouse are finally accepted which allows Harriet to marry an upright farmer named Robert Martin in this Romantic Period novel (1816).

4	<u>Emma</u> by Jane Austen
5	<u>Mansfield Park</u> by Jane Austen
6	<u>Sense and Sensibility</u> by Jane Austen

<u>Elinor Dashwood</u> - this character is the young woman whose strong attraction to a young bachelor, Edward Ferrars, compels her to secure him a cleric position on an estate eventhough he intends to marry Lucy Steele; eventually, her marriage to a jilted Edward and reconciliation with his petulant, overbearing mother gets Edward's inheritance back while his brother, Robert, remains in disfavor for marrying the fortune hunter, Lucy Steele, in this Romantic Period novel (1811).

7	<u>Sense and Sensibility</u> by Jane Austen
8	<u>The Red and the Black</u> by Stendhal
9	<u>Pride and Prejudice</u> by Jane Austen

1-4-7

Fabrizio - this character is the young, courageous nobleman whose aunt, Gina Pietranera, finances his fighting in the battle of Waterloo because his miserly and fanatic father hates Napoleon and the French; eventually, his picaresque adventures end in a Carthusian monastery with a life of meditation after his lover, Clelia Conti, and their illegitimate son, Sandrino, die untimely deaths in this Romantic Period novel (1839).

1	**The Charterhouse of Parma** by Stendhal
2	**Les Miserables** by Victor Hugo
3	**Madame Bovary** by Gustave Flaubert

Lady Rowena - this character is the attractive ward of the coarse, aggressive Saxon master of **Rotherwood** named Cedric who commands her to marry an indolent Saxon named Athelstane over his son, Wilfred, because his son had adopted Norman ways; eventually, she is named **Queen of Love and Beauty** by a chivalrous Crusader whose win of a jousting tournament allows him to reveal his true identity as Wilfred in this Romantic Period novel (1835).

4	**The Heart of Midlothian** by Sir Walter Scott
5	**Kenilworth** by Sir Walter Scott
6	**Ivanhoe** by Sir Walter Scott

Lovel - this character is the wealthy, illegitimate young man who joins with a beggar, Edie Ochiltree, in conning a charlatan named Dousterswivel while providing Sir Arthur Wardour and his daughter, Isabel, enough of a found treasure to allow them solvency; eventually, his identity is established as the long lost son of the Earl of Glenallan which permits him to marry Isabella Wardour in this Romantic Period novel (1816).

7	**Rob Roy** by Sir Walter Scott
8	**Ivanhoe** by Sir Walter Scott
9	**The Antiquary** by Sir Walter Scott

1-6-9

<u>T. Sobieski</u> - this character is the exiled Polish refugee working in London as a tutor under the alias of Mr. Constantine who looks after a sickly, exiled Polish hero named General Butzon until this old exile's death expenses land him in <u>Newgate Prison</u>; eventually, his debts are paid by Pembroke Somerset at the behest of Mary Beaufort without the knowledge that they both share war experiences and had the same father, Sackville, thereby making them half-brothers in this Romantic Period novel (1803).

1	<u>The Absentee</u> by Maria Edgeworth
2	<u>Persuasion</u> by Jane Austen
3	<u>Thaddeus of Warsaw</u> by Jane Porter

<u>Rashleigh Osbaldistone</u> - this character is the unscrupulous, young Englishman who is recruited into a mercantile firm when his cousin, Frank, is recalled from France and sent to the home of his uncle, Sir Hildebrand, during the Jacobite rebellion of 1715; eventually, his journey to Scotland to embezzle the firm results in his exposure and death at the hand of the Scottish outlaw, Macgregor Campbell, while Frank inherits everything and marries Diana Vernon in this Romantic Period novel (1815).

4	<u>Rob Roy</u> by Sir Walter Scott
5	<u>Lorna Doone</u> by Richard D. Blackmore
6	<u>Waverly</u> by Sir Walter Scott

<u>Arabella Allen</u> - this character is the beautiful sister of a medical student who tries to marry her off to another medical student named Bob Sawyer eventhough she is repulsed by him and becomes attracted to Mr. Nathaniel Winkle when his touring gentlemen's club arrives at Bath; eventually, she secretly marries this bungling sportsman over their objections and convinces the lifetime president of her husband's club to resolve all their problems in this Romantic Period novel (1836-1837).

7	<u>Great Expectations</u> by Charles Dickens
8	<u>Pickwick Papers</u> by Charles Dickens
9	<u>A Tale of Two Cities</u> by Charles Dickens

3-4-8

<u>Sam Weller</u> - this character is the carefree, humorous and loyal cockney valet whose hiring by a magnanimous founder of a gentlemen's club mistakenly leads to a breach of promise case with the latter's landlady, Mrs. Bardell, represented by Dodson and Fogg as her unscrupulous lawyers; eventually, he accompanies his new employer when the latter dissolves his club and retires to his home in the country in this Romantic Period novel (1836-1837).

1	<u>Great Expectations</u> by Charles Dickens
2	<u>Pickwick Papers</u> by Charles Dickens
3	<u>A Tale of Two Cities</u> by Charles Dickens

<u>Pembroke Somerset</u> - this character is the adventurous, London nobleman who complies with Mary Beaufort's request to free a Polish exiled tutor from <u>Newgate Prison</u> because of indebtedness over expenses that he incurred after General Butzon's death; eventually, he discovers that he and this exile who was living under the alias of Mr. Constantine shared war experiences in Poland's war with Russia and that they had the same father, Sackville, which made them half-brothers in this Romantic Period novel (1803).

4	<u>The Absentee</u> by Maria Edgeworth
5	<u>Persuasion</u> by Jane Austen
6	<u>Thaddeus of Warsaw</u> by Jane Porter

<u>Edie Ochiltree</u> - this character is the beggar whose knowledge of the Scottish countryside allows him to hide Lovel in a cave after the latter mistakenly thinks he has killed Oldbuck's hot-tempered nephew, Captain Hector M'Intyre, in a duel; eventually, he joins in assisting Lovel in a scheme to trick an evil magician named Dousterswivel and help Sir Arthur Wardour and his daughter, Isabella in this Romantic Period novel (1816).

7	<u>Nightmare Abbey</u> by Thomas Love Peacock
8	<u>The Pirate</u> by Sir Walter Scott
9	<u>The Antiquary</u> by Sir Walter Scott

Mary Beaufort - this character is the London aristocrat who seeks the release of an exiled Polish tutor living under the alias of Mr. Constantine from <u>Newgate Prison</u> for expenses incurred after burying a Polish hero named General Butzon; eventually, she convinces Pembroke Somerset to free this refugee by paying his debts unaware that these two men had shared war experiences as well as the same father, Sackville, which made them half-brothers in this Romantic Period novel (1803).

1	<u>Thaddeus of Warsaw</u> by Jane Porter
2	<u>Persuasion</u> by Jane Austen
3	<u>The Absentee</u> by Maria Edgeworth

Augustus Snodgrass - this character is the poetic member of a London gentlemen's club who joins Mr. Tracy Tupman, Mr. Nathaniel Winkle along with the founder and lifetime president as they tour the countryside accepting invitations and observing conduct and behavior; eventually, his numerous visits to an estate known as <u>Manor Farm</u> finally lead to his marriage to the owner's daughter, Emily Wardle, in this first published Romantic Period novel (1836-1837).

4	<u>Great Expectations</u> by Charles Dickens
5	<u>Pickwick Papers</u> by Charles Dickens
6	<u>A Tale of Two Cities</u> by Charles Dickens

Lord Clonbrony - this character is the henpecked landlord of Irish estate who allows his wife's extravagance to push him into debt with such creditors as the money lender, Mr. Mordicai; eventually, he is rescued from debt by his son, Lord Colambre, when the latter proves that Nicholas Garraghty is managing his father's estates in a shabby manner and is really the debtor after the accounts are examined in this Romantic Period novel (1812).

7	<u>The Absentee</u> by Maria Edgeworth
8	<u>Emma</u> by Jane Austen
9	<u>Agnes Grey</u> by Anne Bronte

1-5-7

<u>Ludovic Lesley (Le Balafre)</u> - this character is the French maternal uncle of a young, courageous Scottish cadet and a member of King Henry XI's Scottish Archers; eventually, he is instrumental in killing the brutal Flemish outlaw named William de la Marck (the Wild Boar of Ardennes), thereby allowing the engagement of his chivalrous nephew and Isabelle, the Countess of Croye in this Romantic Period novel (1823).

1	<u>Nightmare Abbey</u> by Thomas Love Peacock
2	<u>Quentin Durward</u> by Sir Walter Scott
3	<u>Tristram Shandy</u> by Laurence Sterne

<u>Countess Anastasie De Restaud</u> - this character is one of two ungrateful daughters of an indulgent father (after whom this novel is titled); eventually, she sells the de Restaud diamonds to help her lover pay off his debts and is discovered in the swindle by her husband in this Romantic Period novel (1835).

4	<u>A Sentimental Education</u> by Gustave Flaubert
5	<u>Toilers of the Sea</u> by Victor Hugo
6	<u>Pere Goriot</u> by Honore de Balzac

<u>Edward</u> - this character is the young British officer in the service of the new Hanover king of England, George II, in 1745 when the Pretender, Prince Charles Edward Stuart, invaded from France into Scotland to regain the throne; eventually, he is exonerated of treason after being stripped of his commission and chooses Rosa Bradwardine over Flora MacIvor for his future wife in this Romantic Period novel (1814).

7	<u>Waverly</u> by Sir Walter Scott
8	<u>The Heart of Midlothian</u> by Sir Walter Scott
9	<u>Rob Roy</u> by Sir Walter Scott

2-6-7

Robert Dudley - this character is the Earl of Leicester whose marriage to the attractive Amy Robsart is kept secret so he can seek the favor of Queen Elizabeth over his rival, the Earl of Sussex; eventually, his deal with Edmund Tressilian cannot stop Amy's death when an unprincipled and power-hungry squire named Richard Varney tricks her into falling through a rigged trap door in this Romantic Period novel (1821).

1   **Waverly** by Sir Walter Scott
2   **Kenilworth** by Sir Walter Scott
3   **The Heart of Midlothian** by Sir Walter Scott

Nicholas Garraghty - this character is the corrupt Irish estate manager who is assisted by his brother, Dennis, in treating Irish tenants shabbily while their employer, Lord Clonbrony, and his extravagant wife live frivolous lives in England; eventually, he is exposed as the debtor instead of a creditor when his employer's son, Lord Colanbre, starts to untangle all of the accounts in this Romantic Period novel (1812).

4   **Persuasion** by Jane Austen
5   **The Absentee** by Maria Edgeworth
6   **Thaddeus of Warsaw** by Jane Porter

Monsieur Grandet - this character is the miserly mayor of the provincial French town who treats his wife and daughter, Eugenie, in the most shabby manner; eventually, he and his wife die leaving his rich, surviving daughter is doomed to a lonely and loveless life where she is jilted by her cousin, Charles, who rejects her unselfish love and cons her out of some gold coins that help him marry a heiress in this Romantic Period novel (1833).

7   Victor Hugo
8   Stendhal
9   Honore de Balzac

Monsieur Vautrin - this character is a fellow boarder of a young impoverished student named Eugene De Rastignac at the Maison Vauquer; eventually, he is exposed as the famous criminal Trompe-la-Mort by an agent for the police posing as an old maid when she recognizes distinguishing marks on his back and drugs his coffee in this Romantic Period novel (1835).

1	**Pere Goriot** by Honore de Balzac
2	**The Red and the Black** by Stendhal
3	**Madame Bovary** by Gustave Flaubert

Miss Broadhurst - this character is the young heiress who becomes the target of matchmaking when her mother and Lady Clonbrony try to wed her with Lady Clonbrony's Cambridge son, Lord Colambre, to prevent bankruptcy eventhough the Clonbronys own estates in Ireland; eventually, she marries Lord Colambre's friend, Arthur Berryl, while Lord Colambre marries Grace Nugent after her true heritage is revealed in this Romantic Period novel (1812).

4	**Emma** by Jane Austen
5	**Thaddeus of Warsaw** by Jane Porter
6	**The Absentee** by Maria Edgeworth

Scythrop Glowry - this character is the sullen young man who vacillates between marrying his visiting cousin, Marionetta, or his father Christopher's choice of Mr. Toobad's daughter, Celinda, who had been studying abroad; eventually, he is compelled to remain a bachelor after Marionetta decides to marry a dandy named Listless and Celinda (Stella) decides to marry a poet of the supernatural named Mr. Flosky in this Romantic Period novel (1818).

7	**Nightmare Abbey** by Thomas Love Peacock
8	**Kenilworth** by Sir Walter Scott
9	**Waverly** by Sir Walter Scott

1-6-7

<u>Charles Grandet</u> -   - this character is the nephew of the rich, miserly mayor of a provincial French town and the scoundrel who cons his cousin, Eugenie, out of her gold coins with a pledge of love; eventually, his marriage to a heiress leaves his cousin living a lonely existence; eventually, his disregard for the unselfish love offered by his cousin leads him into a dissolute life of lechery and adultery in this Romantic Period novel (1833).

1	Stendhal
2	Honore de Balzac
3	Gustave Flaubert

<u>Listless</u> - this character is the English dandy who travels with his French valet, Fatout, to a house party at Christopher Growry's estate that is attended by a poet of the supernatural named Mr. Flosky and an ichthyologist, Mr. Asterious, who is searching for a mermaid in the area; eventually, he marries Mr. Growry's visiting niece, Marionetta, who had been the love interest of his vacillating sullen son, Scythrop, in this Romantic Period novel (1818).

4	<u>Nightmare Abbey</u> by Thomas Love Peacock
5	<u>Kenilworth</u> by Sir Walter Scott
6	<u>Waverly</u> by Sir Walter Scott

<u>Meg Merrilies</u> - this character is the old gypsy woman who is a co-conspirator with the Dutch smuggler, Dirk Hatteraick, and an evil lawyer, Gilbert Glossin, in the killing of a revenue officer and the kidnaping of Harry Bertram when he was 5 years old; eventually, she is fatally shot in the heart by Dirk in a showdown in a cave after confessing to her role in the plot to Harry Bertram a/k/a Captain Brown in this Romantic Period novel (1815).

7	<u>Guy Mannering</u> by Sir Walter Scott
8	<u>Robinson Crusoe</u> by Daniel Defoe
9	<u>Tom Jones</u> by Henry Fielding

Dousterswivel - this character is the charlatan whose continuous wresting of money from a nobleman named Sir Arthur Wardour under the pretext of finding valuable minerals on the latter's property leads Sir Arthur to borrow 100 pounds from Jonathan Oldbuck of Monkbarns; eventually, he is conned by a beggar named Edie Ochiltree and a wealthy illegitimate young man of questionable parentage named Lovel that such a treasure really exists in Sir Arthur's cave in this Romantic Period novel (1816).

1	**Rob Roy** by Sir Walter Scott
2	**Nightmare Abbey** by Thomas Love Peacock
3	**The Antiquary** by Sir Walter Scott

General Butzon - this character is the sickly, exiled Polish hero whose welfare in London becomes the concern of another Polish exile who works as a tutor under the alias of Mr. Constantine; eventually, the death of this refugee incurs such expenses that this tutor is put in **Newgate Prison** until he is released by Pembroke Somerset at Mary Beaufort's behest unaware that the men shared war experiences and had the same father, Sackville, which made them half-brothers in this Romantic Period novel (1803).

4	**The Absentee** by Maria Edgeworth
5	**Persuasion** by Jane Austen
6	**Thaddeus of Warsaw** by Jane Porter

Christopher Glowry - this character is the ichthyologist whose search for a mermaid brings him to a manor owned by Christopher Glowery; eventually, he fishes another character, Mr. Toobad, out of a moat with a landing net after the latter mistakes a window for a door in his frantic effort to escape a mysterious stranger in this Romantic Period novel (1818).

7	**Nightmare Abbey** by Thomas Love Peacock
8	**Kenilworth** by Sir Walter Scott
9	**Waverly** by Sir Walter Scott

3-6-7

<u>Jeanie Deans</u> - this character is the daughter of a stern, fairly wealthy Scottish dairyman named David Deans and the one who convinces the Duke of Argyle and the Queen of England that her younger sister, Effie, was framed by a vindictive old woman named Meg Murdockson; eventually, she gets Effie a pardon, marries the minister, Reuben Butler, and bears him 3 children in this Romantic Period novel (1818).

1   <u>Nightmare Abbey</u> by Thomas Love Peacock
2   <u>The Heart of Midlothian</u> by Sir Walter Scott
3   <u>Tristram Shandy</u> by Laurence Sterne

<u>Honest Thady Quirk</u> - this character is the Irish family servant who works simultaneously for Sir Patrick, Sir Murtagh, Sir Kit and Sir Condy; eventually, he feels heartbroken about his son's, Jason, complicity in forcing Sir Condy to sell all his property to satisfy his debts eventhough Sir Condy is still allowed to financially provide for his separated wife, Isabella in this Romantic Period novel (1800).

4   <u>Agnes Grey</u> by Anne Bronte
5   <u>Castle Rackrent</u> by Maria Edgeworth
6   <u>Emma</u> by Jane Austen

<u>Abriham White</u> - this character is the untrustworthy kidnapper of U. S. Army Captain Middleton's young wife, Inez, who receives frontier justice from Ishmael Bush as patriarch of the Bush family as they travel West; eventually, he chooses hanging over starvation after his guilt is exposed and an 82 year-old trapper, Natty Bumppo, is found not guilty in the murder of Ishmael Bush's son, Ase, in this Romantic Period novel (1827).

7   <u>The Pit</u> by Upton Sinclair
8   <u>Tom Sawyer</u> by Mark Twain
9   <u>The Prairie</u> by James Fenimore Cooper

2-5-9

<u>Jason</u> - this character is the financial planner who convinces a client to assume all the outstanding debts of Sir Condy eventhough the latter employs the former's father, Honest Thady Quirk, as his servant; eventually, he disowns his own father, allows Sir Condy to provide for his separated wife, Isabella, and forces Sir Condy to sell all his estates to satisfy his debts in this Romantic Period novel (1800).

1   <u>Castle Rackrent</u> by Maria Edgeworth
2   <u>Emma</u> by Jane Austen
3   <u>Agnes Grey</u> by Anne Bronte

<u>Meg Murdockson</u> - this character is the vindictive old woman who frames the young Effie Deans because she bore Geordie Robertson a/k/a George Staunton's illegitimate son after her own daughter, Madge Wildfire, had also been seduced and jilted by this hunted criminal; eventually, her unsuccessful attempt to kill Effie's older sister, Jeanie, is thwarted by her own daughter Madge and she is later executed as a witch by the courts in this Romantic Period novel (1818).

4   <u>Tom Jones</u> by Henry Fielding
5   <u>Nightmare Abbey</u> by Thomas Love Peacock
6   <u>The Heart of Midlothian</u> by Sir Walter Scott

<u>Hard-Heart</u> - this character is the princely, young Pawnee chief and warrior who informs Natty Bumppo's party that includes the newly freed Inez Middleton and Ellen Wade about how Ishmael Bush and his family have joined up with the Sioux against them; eventually, he challenges the bold, fierce Sioux chief, Mahatoree, to combat and his ensuing success guarantees the routing of the remaining Sioux band by his Pawnee braves in this Romantic Period novel (1827).

7   <u>The Pit</u> by Upton Sinclair
8   <u>The Prairie</u> by James Fenimore Cooper
9   <u>Tom Sawyer</u> by Mark Twain

Isabella - this character is the young woman who wins a coin toss by a neighbor, Sir Condy, that entitles her to become his wife eventhough he is really in love with his Irish servant's, Honest Thady Quirk, niece, Judy; eventually, she is generously willed a sum of money after he dies eventhough they have separated and he is compelled to sell his estates by Honest Thady Quirk's son, Jason, in order to satisfy the debts he has accrued in this Romantic Period novel (1800).

1	Castle Rackrent by Maria Edgeworth
2	Emma by Jane Austen
3	Agnes Grey by Anne Bronte

Ishmael Bush - this character is the massive and fierce patriarch of the Bush family whose travels West bring them into contact with an 82 year-old trapper named Natty Bumppo, a Pawnee Indian named Hard-Heart and a Sioux Indian chief named Mahtoree; eventually, his frontier justice allows Inez to be reunited with   Captain Middleton, Ellen Wade to marry Paul Hover and Abirham White to choose hanging for causing the death of his son Ase Bush in this Romantic Period novel (1827).

4	Tom Sawyer by Mark Twain
5	The Prairie by James Fenimore Cooper
6	The Pit by Upton Sinclair

Geordie Robertson - this character is the wild, young dissolute son of a minister whose seduction of Madge Wildfire leaves her mother, Meg Murdockson, bent on revenge when his seduction of Effie Deans results in an illegitimate son; eventually, he is killed by his own long lost illegitimate son during a robbery attempt while he is living the respectable life of a nobleman along with Effie in this Romantic Period novel (1818).

7	The Heart of Midlothian by Sir Walter Scott
8	Nightmare Abbey by Thomas Love Peacock
9	Tristram Shandy by Laurence Sterne

1-5-7

Fergus MacIvor - this character is the Scottish clan chieftain who supports the Pretender, Prince Charles Edward Stuart, when the latter invades England from France in 1745 to regain the throne from the new Hanover king of England, George I; eventually, he remains loyal to the cause and is executed along with Evan Dhu Macombich when the rebellion fails and the Pretender escapes to France in this Romantic Period novel (1814).

1	<u>Tom Jones</u> by Henry Fielding
2	<u>Waverly</u> by Sir Walter Scott
3	<u>Nightmare Abbey</u> by Thomas Love Peacock

Hayraddin Maugrabin - this character is the treacherous Bohemian who acts as a guide for a Scottish Archer as he escorts Isabelle, the Countess of de Croye, and her aunt, Lady Hamilton, into the protective custody of the   Bishop of Leige at the direction of King Louis XI;; eventually,   he is hanged by the Duke of Burgandy when his attempt to lead this group into an ambush by the Wild Boar of Ardennes is thwarted in this Romantic Period novel (1823).

4	<u>Tristram Shandy</u> by Laurence Sterne
5	<u>Joseph Andrews</u> by Henry Fielding
6	<u>Quentin Durward</u> by Sir Walter Scott

Dirk Hatteraick - this character is the Dutch smuggler who joins an evil lawyer named Gilbert Grossin and a vindictive gypsy named Meg Merrilies in the killing of a revenue officer and the kidnaping of a 5 year-old boy named Harry Bertram; eventually, he fatally shoots Meg through the heart, kills Grossin while they share a jail cell awaiting trial and then commits suicide rather than face the hangman in this Romantic Period novel (1815).

7	<u>Nightmare Abbey</u> by Thomas Love Peacock
8	<u>Tristram Shandy</u> by Laurence Sterne
9	<u>Guy Mannering</u> by Sir Walter Scott

Bailie Nichol Jarvie - this character is the Glasgow weaver and magistrate who is a business associate of the Osbaldistone mercantile firm which has branches in France and Scotland; eventually, he accompanies Frank Osbaldistone into Scotland in pursuit of a corrupt cousin named Rashleigh who has absconded with certain crucial documents of the company only to find that this scoundrel has died at the hand of a Scottish outlaw named McGregor Campbell in this Romantic Period novel (1824).

1   **Nightmare Abbey** by Thomas Love Peacock
2   **Rob Roy** by Sir Walter Scott
3   **Peregrine Pickle** by Tobias George Smollett

Cedric the Saxon - this character is the coarse, aggressive Master of **Rotherwood** who chooses a descendent of Saxon kings named Athelstane for future marriage to his ward, Lady Rowena, over his son, Winifred, because his son has adopted Norman ways; eventually, he reconciles himself to both Norman rule under King Richard I and accepting the marriage between Lady Rowena and his chivalrous son who has heroically returned from the Crusades in this Romantic Period novel (1821).

4   **Kidnapped** by Robert Louis Stevenson
5   **Ivanhoe** by Sir Walter Scott
6   **Nightmare Abbey** by Thomas Love Peacock

Harriet Smith - this character is the impressionable 17 year-old of unknown parentage who lives in a parlor of a boarding school and becomes the ward of a clever, pampered matchmaker named Miss Woodhouse; eventually, her amorous interest in an astute, candid landowner engenders such jealousy in Miss Woodhouse that she finally accepts George Knightly's marriage proposal while Harriet returns to and marries her old lover, an upright farmer named Robert Martin in this Romantic Period novel (1816).

7   **Agnes Grey** by Anne Bronte
8   **Emma** by Jane Austen
9   **Return of the Native** by Thomas Hardy

The Victorian Period
(1840-1890)

Some of the noted novelists of this period are as follows: The Bronte Sisters, Thomas Hardy, Fyodor Dostoevski, Charles Dickens, Mark Twain, George Eliot, Herman Melville, Nathaniel Hawthorne, Gustave Flaubert, Henry James and Robert Louis Stevenson.

Victorian readers were shaken awake from their fanciful   lethargy to be told of the harsher realities of life.   Unlike earlier fictitious portrayals, life was real and in earnest.   The energy that was expended on plot in the Romantic Period was now channeled into stricter concern for disciplined form.   Social reforms were needed now.   Advances had been made in industry and technology while shifts in population had occurred from rural to urban.   Charles Dickens arrived to champion social change with his numerous characters and novels.   His plots stressed such social ills as abuses in child labor, corrupt orphanages, and debtor's prison.

While Victorians became more prudish in their moral attitudes, the amount of Victorian readers was on the rise because of an increasing literacy rate.   These same Victorian readers were slowly being made more aware of their role in society as they awaited their monthly installments in popular magazines.

As the novel gained greater popularity, a blurring began to occur between the old distinction of romanticism and realism and the new distinction between realism and the novel of purpose.   The Victorian novel on a specific mission.   Because it took up the banner of social reform and championed causes, it upgraded the quality of the novel per se.   Now, the novel had a purpose other than that of escape.   Now, it was down to earth.   No longer would it be viewed as a frivolous pastime.   Now, its power bespoke sober thought.   Finally, the novel had achieved dignity.

The Victorian novel underwent expansion with regard to its area of analysis. With all restrictions now lifted in regard to type of story line acceptable, the range of plots was extended to coverage of all human experiences.   Plots were extended to such areas as crime, sports, the sea, the military, politics, etc.

Edward Rochester - this character is the 35 year-old arrogant, pensive owner of <u>Thornfield</u> who becomes the chief love interest of the young governess hired to teach his ward and illegitimate daughter, Adele Varens, art and music; eventually, he marries this governess after being temporarily blinded in a fire started by his deranged widow, Bertha Mason Rochester, when her strict keeper, Gracie Poole, drinks too much and neglects her duties in this Victorian Period novel (1847).

1	<u>Jane Eyre</u> by Charlotte Bronte
2	<u>Wuthering Heights</u> by Emily Bronte
3	<u>Agnes Grey</u> by Anne Bronte

Edgar Linton - this character is the easy-going, well-bred owner of <u>Thrushcross Grange</u> whose marriage to his Yorkshire moor neighbor, Catherine Earnshaw, ends when she dies a few hours after the premature birth of a daughter named Cathy; eventually, the takes in the ailing child, Linton, who was born of his departed sister, Isabella, and Heathcliff only to finally lose everything indirectly to Heathcliff in this Victorian Period novel (1847).

4	<u>Jane Eyre</u> by Charlotte Bronte
5	<u>Wuthering Heights</u> by Emily Bronte
6	<u>Agnes Grey</u> by Anne Bronte

Prince Myshkin - this character is the Russian epileptic whose return train trip to St. Petersberg from a four year stay in a Swiss sanatorium finds him tangled up in a love triangle involving the spoiled beauty, Aglaya Epanchin, and the attractive harlot, Natasya Filipovna; eventually, he returns to the Switzerland sanatorium after his rival for Natasya's hand, Parfen Rogozhin, kills her in a jealous rage in this Victorian Period novel (1868-1869).

7	<u>Fathers and Sons</u> by Ivan Turgenev
8	<u>The Idiot</u> by Fyodor Dostoevski
9	<u>Dead Souls</u> by Nikolai V. Gogol

Clym Yeobright - this character is the young, successful Parisian diamond merchant who returns home to gloomy Egdon Heath and marries the vivacious Eustacia Vye only to lose her to an illicit lover, Damon Wildeve; eventually, he stops teaching and woodcutting to become a traveling preacher after Eustacia's drowning causes the death by misadventure of Damon in this Victorian Period novel (1878).

1	**Great Expectations** by Charles Dickens
2	**The Return of the Native** by Thomas Hardy
3	**Vanity Fair** by William Makespeace Thackeray

Hester Prynne - this character is the young, unwed and widowed mother in 1650's Boston whose somewhat-grotesque, elderly husband, Roger Chillingworth, reappears to discover she has an illegitimate daughter named Paul; eventually, she stoically carries on after the real father, Rev. Arthur Dimmesdale, drops dead after confessing his complicity in the sin in this Victorian Period novel (1850).

4	**Silas Marner** by George Eliot
5	**The Scarlet Letter** by Nathaniel Hawthorne
6	**Ethan Frome** by Edith Wharton

Rodion Raskolnikov - this character is the penniless, young law student nicknamed Rodya who murders an old, miserly   pawnbroker named Alonya along with her sister, Lizaveta, with an axe to prove that he is above the law; eventually, he is forced into a confession by a gifted detective named Porfiry and spends eight years in Siberia accompanied by the ex-prostitute girlfriend, Sonia, in this Victorian Period novel (1866).

7	**Fathers and Sons** by Ivan Turgenev
8	**Crime and Punishment** by Fyodor Dostoevski
9	**Dead Souls** by Nikolai V. Gogol

2-5-8

<u>Natty Bumppo</u> - this character is the wilderness scout who waits along with his friend, Jasper Western, at the Oswego River for a rendevous with Mabel Dunham, her salt-water seaman uncle, Charles Cap, Arrowhead and Dew-of-June; eventually, he takes them down the river through dangerous Iroquois Indian territory to her father, Sergeant Dunham, at the Fort Oswego garrison in this <u>Leatherstocking Tale</u> by an American author (1840).

1   <u>Arrowsmith</u> by Sinclair Lewis
2   <u>The Call of the Wild</u> by Jack London
3   <u>The Pathfinder</u> by James Fenimore Cooper

<u>Count Vronsky</u> - this character is the young, gallant and rich Russian nobleman whose love affair with the attractive wife of a ruthless politician obsessed with public reputation and social status named Alexei Karenin results in her infidelity and subsequent birth of an illegitimate daughter; eventually, his despair after she commits suicide by jumping in front of an incoming train spurs him to join the Army where he hopes death will finally end his grief in this Victorian Period novel (1875-1897).

4   <u>Fathers and Sons</u> by Ivan Turgenev
5   <u>The Idiot</u> by Fyodor Dostoevski
6   <u>Anna Karenina</u> by Count Leo Tolstoy

<u>Aunt Polly</u> - this character is the caring, soft-hearted aunt of a young lad full of mischief whose night trip to the cemetery with the son of a town drunk named Pap Finn exposes them to knife murder involving three grave robbers named Dr. Robinson, Injun Joe and Muff Potter; eventually, she has to rely on the asides of this lad's half-brother, Sid, in order to know whether this lad is telling the truth or not in this Victorian Period novel (1876).

7   <u>Sister Carrie</u> by Theodore Drieser
8   <u>Tom Sawyer</u> by Mark Twain
9   <u>Adam Bede</u> by George Eliot

3-6-8

Richard - this character is the young 19 year-old whose medical withdrawal from Harvard University compels him to sign on the prig, the **Pilgrim**, which is bound from Boston round the Cape of Good Horn and up to California; eventually, this coming of age for this young religiously conservative Boston aristocrat forces him to rub elbows with older, coarse, uneducated seamen and perform perilous duties in this Victorian Period novel (1840).

1	**The Sea Wolf** by Jack London
2	**Two Years Before the Mast** by Richard Henry Dana, Jr.
3	**Captain Courageous** by Rudyard Kipling

Captain Ahab - this character is the deranged captain of the **Pequod** whose officers consist of 1st, 2nd, and 3rd mates Sawbuck, Stubb and Flask and whose crew includes Queequeg, Daggoo, and Fleece and Pip; eventually, his delusional fixation fulfills the prophesies of a Parsee servant named Fedallah with the loss of all aboard except Ishmael in this Victorian Period novel (1851).

4	**Two Years Before the Mast** by Richard Henry Dana, Jr.
5	**The Sea Wolf** by Jack London
6	**Moby Dick** by Herman Melville

Jean Valjean - this character is the fugitive ex-convict and elected mayor of a French town under the guise of Father Madelaine who looks after a young girl named Cosette when her   prostitute mother, Fantine, dies; eventually, he reveals his true identity to Cosette and her young lawyer husband, Marius Pontmercy, on his deathbed after years of being hounded by a police inspector named Javert whose obsession with the law drives him to suicide in this Victorian Period novel (1862).

7	**Madame Bovery** by Gustave Flaubert
8	**The Red and the Black** by Stendhal
9	**Les Miserables** by Victor Hugo

2-6-9

Heathcliff - this character is the destitute orphan brought home by old Mr. Earnshaw from Liverpool to join his wife, his son, Hindley and his daughter, Catherine; eventually, his ill-treatment by Hindley and Catherine results in a vendetta by him where he ends up with a fiendish power over everybody and everything immediately around him in this Victorian Period novel (1847).

1	Wuthering Heights by Emily Bronte
2	Jane Eyre by Charlotte Bronte
3	Pride and Prejudice by Jane Austen

Philip Pirrip - this character is the diffident orphan whose life with blacksmith brother-in-law, Joe Gargery, and censorious sister, Georgiana, is disrupted when he abets an escaped convict in a graveyard named Abel Magwitch; eventually, he is rewarded when this grateful convict becomes his benefactor under the alias of Mr. Provis and is successful in winning the hand of Estella despite the schemes of a sour spinster named Miss Havisham in this Victorian Period novel (1860-1861).

4	Treasure Island by Robert Louis Stevenson
5	Great Expectations by Charles Dickens
6	Middlemarch by George Eliot

Black Dog - this character is the wayfaring seaman who appears at the Admiral Benbow Inn in remote Black Hill Cove that is run by young Jim Hawkin's mother and critically ill father; eventually, he escapes with his life after a life and death struggle with another ruthless seaman named Bill Bones in the Inn's parlor in front of Jim and his mother in this Victorian Period novel (1883).

7	Captain Courageous by Rudyard Kipling
8	Treasure Island by Robert Louis Stevenson
9	The Return of the Native by Thomas Hardy

Nemo - this character is the mysterious boarder who lives in the attic above the dingy shop of a junkyard dealer named Krook and the one buried in Potters Field after being found dead of an opium overdose; eventually, an analysis of his handwriting reveals that he is really the rogue named Captain Hawson who fathered Lady Dedlock's illegitimate daughter, Esther Summerson, in this Victorian Period novel (1852-1853).

1   **Twenty Thousand Leagues Under the Sea** by Jules Verne
2   **The Return of the Native** by Thomas Hardy
3   **Bleak House** by Charles Dickens

Marmeladov - this character is the destitute, out of work clerk whose constant drunkenness causes him to die by misadventure when he is run over by a carriage in front of a young law student named Rodion Raskolnikov; eventually, his funeral expenses are paid for by this law student when the latter donates money to the prostitute, Sonia, who in turn follows him to Siberia for eight years while the latter pays for the axe murders he has committed in this Victorian Period novel (1866).

4   **Fathers and Sons** by Ivan Turgenev
5   **Crime and Punishment** by Fyodor Dostoevski
6   **Dead Souls** by Nikolai V. Gogol

Mealy Potatoes - this character is the young warehouse worker from the slums who joins Mick Walker in making the life of a sensitive 10 year-old miserable at an export concern owned by Edward Murdstone and his partner, Grinby; eventually, his cruel treatment drives this overworked, underfed 10 year-old to seek the protection of his unconventional great aunt and future benefactress, Miss Betsy Trotwood, in this Victorian Period novel (1849-1850).

7   **Great Expectations** by Charles Dickens
8   **A Tale of Two Cities** by Charles Dickens
9   **David Copperfield** by Charles Dickens

1-5-9

Gracie Poole - this character is the austere English seamstress with a stern countenance who is employed on Edward Rochester's estate, <u>Thornfield</u>, for the express purpose of guarding his deranged wife, Bertha Mason Rochester; eventually, her drinking and resulting neglect on her post causes her demented charge to die by misadventure after burning down the estate while   temporarily blinding her employer in this Victorian Period novel (1847).

1   <u>Jane Eyre</u> by Charlotte Bronte
2   <u>Wuthering Heights</u> by Emily Bronte
3   <u>Pride and Prejudice</u> by Jane Austen

Roger Chillingworth -this character is the somewhat-grotesque, elderly physician in 1650's Boston whose appearance after being reported dead finds his unwed wife, Hester Prynne, with an illegitimate daughter named Pearl; eventually, his hounding forces a paternity confession from the morally weak minister, Arthur Dimmesdale, just before he collapses and dies in this Victorian Period novel (1850).

4   <u>Babbitt</u> by Sinclair Lewis
5   <u>The Scarlet Letter</u> by Nathaniel Hawthorne
6   <u>Moby Dick</u> by Herman Melville

Seth Pecksniff - this character is the flim-flam architect/land surveying teacher who selfishly bilks his students like John Westlock by charging a large entrance fee along with excessive fees for room and board; eventually, his investment in the Anglo-Bengalee Disinterested Loan and Life Insurance Company leads to ruin, eviction, drunkenness and begging when the company secretary, David Crimple, absconds with the company funds in this Victorian Period novel (1843-1844).

7   <u>Martin Chuzzlewit</u> by Charles Dickens
8   <u>Jude the Obscure</u> by Thomas Hardy
9   <u>Barchester Towers</u> by Anthony Trollope

<u>Becky Sharp</u> - this character is the young orphan who becomes the best friend of Amelia Sedley after entering Miss Pinkerton's finishing school for girls where she ultimately develops into an attractive, narcissistic scheming woman; eventually, her first marriage to Rawdon Crawley ends when he discovers her with a rich, old Marquis named Lord Steyne and her second marriage to Jos Sedley ends when his inexplicable death leaves her a wealthy widow in this Victorian Period novel (1847-1848).

1	<u>Barchester Towers</u> by Anthony Trollope
2	<u>Jude the Obscure</u> by Thomas Hardy
3	<u>Vanity Fair</u> by William Thackeray

<u>Eustacia Vye</u> - this character is the young, passionate woman whose obsession to escape gloomy Egdon Heath leads her to betray her educated husband, Clym Yeobright, by having an affair with the owner of the <u>Quiet Woman Inn</u>, Damon Wildeve; eventually, her suicide by drowning in a lake causes Damon's death by misadventure when he tries to save her and results in her husband becoming a traveling preacher in this Victorian Period novel (1878).

4	<u>Martin Chuzzlewit</u> by Thomas Hardy
5	<u>Wuthering Heights</u> by Emily Bronte
6	<u>The Return of the Native</u> by Thomas Hardy

<u>Nell Trent (Little Nell)</u> - this character is the frail, 14 year-old orphan who is legally evicted along with her degenerate gambling grandfather from a second hand goods store by a deranged dwarf named Daniel Quilp; eventually, she dies an untimely young death after traveling across the countryside with her grandfather while working for a puppet show, the Jarley's Wax Work and tending graves in a churchyard in this Victorian Period novel (1848).

7	<u>Pride and Prejudice</u> by Jane Austen
8	<u>Middlemarch</u> by George Eliot
9	<u>The Old Curiosity Shop</u> by Charles Dickens

3-6-9

Arthur Dimmesdale - this character is the morally and physically weak minister in 1650's Boston who is responsible for an unwed, widowed young woman named Hester Prynne's illegitimate daughter, Pearl; eventually, he collapses and dies after Roger Chillingworth hounding him into a confession of his sin in this Victorian Period novel (1850).

1	The Portrait of a Lady by Henry James
2	Silas Marner by George Eliot
3	The Scarlet Letter by Nathaniel Hawthorne

Dmitri - this character is the oldest of four sons consisting of Ivan, Alexey and Smerdyakov who were fathered by a lecherous, shrewd old businessman named Fyodor who deserted each of them after their mother died while keeping Smerdyakov as his servant; eventually, he is sentenced to Siberia after being unjustly convicted of his father's death eventhough Smerdyakow has confessed to Ivan in this Victorian Period novel (1880).

4	Dead Souls by Nikolai V. Gogol
5	Fathers and Sons by Ivan Turgenev
6	The Brothers Karamazov by Fyodor Dostoevski

Philip Nolan - this character is the arrogant young Texas army officer whose conviction of treason as a member of Aaron Burr's conspiracy to overthrow President James Madison earns him a harsh sentence when his outburst as the end of his court martial shocks the no-nonsense presiding judge, Colonel Morgan; eventually, he is dressed in an army uniform with plain buttons and receives updates on past and current events only once in this Victorian Period novel (1863).

7	The Pathfinder by James Fenimore Cooper
8	The Man without a Country by Edward Everett Hale
9	Drums Along the Mohawk by Walter Edmonds

Simon Legree - this character is the alcoholic Northern-born Southern plantation owner living during the mis-19th century who limits the ration of food he serves to a good-hearted old slave to one pack of corn a week; eventually, his cruel and inhumane beatings of this docile old slave continue past when this old man can either stand or speak and ultimately prove fatal just a short time before this slave's former master, George Shelby, returns to buy him back in this Victorian Period novel (1852).

1   **Little Women** by Louisa Maria Alcott
2   **To the Lighthouse** by Virginia Woolf
3   **Uncle Tom's Cabin** by Harriet Beecher Stowe

Sidney Carton - this character is the diplomatic, misanthropic law clerk for a narcissistic lawyer named Mr. Stryver and the one whose pointless life is turned around when he falls in love with an attractive young French woman named Lucie Manette; eventually, he goes to his death after trading places with his look-alike rival, Charles Darnay, who is imprisoned in the Bastille awaiting death by the guillotine in this Victorian Period novel (1859).

4   **Barchester Towers** by Anthony Trollope
5   **Jude the Obscure** by Thomas Hardy
6   **A Tale of Two Cities** by Charles Dickens

Becky Thatcher - this character is the blue-eyed, blonde, young girl in St. Petersburg on the Mississippi River who quickly succeeds another young girl affections of an imaginative young lad who continues to pester his Aunt Polly with his mischief; eventually, her judicial father presides over the murder trial where her new boyfriend is an eyewitness to how Injun Joe really murdered Dr. Robinson instead of Muff Potter at a grave site robbery in this Victorian Period novel (1876).

7   **The House of the Seven Gables** by Nathaniel Hawthorne
8   **Adam Bede** by George Eliot
9   **Tom Sawyer** by Mark Twain

3-6-9

<u>Jim Hawkins</u> - this character is the young English boy who leaves the safety of the <u>Admiral Benbow Inn</u> and joins Squire Trelwney and Dr. Livesey as a cabin boy on the <u>Hispaniola</u> as it travels the Spanish Main in search of Captain Flint's buried treasure; eventually, his rite of passage to manhood involves his encounters with the mutinous one-legged cook named Long John Silver and his shooting of the buccaneer named Israel Hands in this Victorian Period novel (1883).

1   <u>Treasure Island</u> by Robert Louis Stevenson
2   <u>Captain Courageous</u> by Rudyard Kipling
3   <u>Two Years Before the Mast</u> by Richard Henry Dana, Jr.

<u>Miss Havisham</u> - this character is the soured spinster whose pain from being jilted by an evil rogue named Arthur Compeyson is exemplified by her untouched reception table with wedding cake and settings; eventually, she dies in a blaze at her gloomy mansion leaving young Pip estranged from Estella after the latter had married the petulant, rich boy, Bentley Drummle in this Victorian Period novel (1860-1861).

4   <u>Kidnapped</u> by Robert Louis Stevenson
5   <u>The Return of the Native</u> by Thomas Hardy
6   <u>Great Expectations</u> by Charles Dickens

<u>Edward Dantes</u> - this character is the young ship captain of the <u>Pharaoh</u> whose impending marriage to his sweetheart, Mercedes, is interrupted when he is falsely imprisoned for 14 years in a dungeon as a result of a conspiracy against him; eventually, his chance meeting with the Abbe Faria in prison affords him the opportunity to escape and seek revenge against M. Danglers, M. Villefort and Ferinand Mondego in this Victorian Period novel (1844).

7   <u>Les Miserables</u> by Victor Hugo
8   <u>The Red and the Black</u> by Stendhal
9   <u>The Count of Monte-Cristo</u> by Alexander Dumas Sr.

1-6-9

Estella - this character is the pitiless, hardhearted young ward of a soured old spinster named Miss Havisham and the one who toys with the feelings of a young diffident orphan named Philip Pirrip until finally marrying a petulant, rich boy named Bentley Drummle; eventually, she discovers she is the daughter of Mr. Jagger's housekeeper, Molly, divorces Bentley and reunites with Pip after his fortune is confiscated by the Crown in this Victorian Period novel (1860-1861).

1	The Return of the Native by Thomas Hardy
2	Great Expectations by Charles Dickens
3	Kidnapped by Robert Louis Stevenson

Pierre Bezuhov - this character is the awkward, heavy set and towering illegitimate wealthy son of a Russian count and the one who is widowed after his first marriage to the attractive and libertine Helene; eventually, his close encounters with death as a French prisoner of war produces the maturity necessary for his happy marriage with Andrey Bolkonsky's ex-finance, Natasha Rostov, bearing four children in this Victorian Period novel (1865-1869).

4	Crime and Punishment by Fyodor Dostoevski
5	War and Peace by Count Leo Tolstoy
6	Fathers and Sons by Ivan Turgenev

Hurry Harry March - this character is the good-looking, stout frontier scout whose joins an avaricious ex-pirate turned trapper named Thomas Hutter in collecting Indian scalps for money while unsuccessfully trying to marry the latter's adopted daughter, Judith; eventually, he atones for his wanton killing of an Indian girl when he rescues Natty Bumppo's life by leading Captain Warley and his troops on a timely raid of the Iroquois Indian camp in this Victorian Period novel (1841).

7	An American Tragedy by Theodore Drieser
8	Drums Along the Mohawk by Walter Edmonds
9	The Deerslayer by James Fenimore Cooper

Starbuck - this character is the lanky first mate over second and third mates, Stubb and Flask (King-Post), aboard the <u>Pequod</u> who superstitious nature compels him to consider killing Captain Abab because he feels the captain's delusional fixation will put the lives of the crew in jeopardy; eventually, he is impotent in his attempts to dissuade Abab which costs everyone his life except Ishmael in this Victorian Period novel (1851).

1	<u>Two Years Before the Mast</u> by Richard Henry Dana, Jr.
2	<u>Moby Dick</u> by Herman Melville
3	<u>Captain Courageous</u> by Rudyard Kipling

Wilkins Micawber - this character is the uneasy, mysterious   confidential secretary of Uriah Heep who finally exposes his villainous, scheming employer as the thief who accumulated his wealth by secretly stealing funds from Mr. Wickfield and embezzling Miss Betsy Trotwood's fortune; eventually, he and his family are assisted by Miss Trotwood in their emigration to Australia where he ultimately becomes a magistrate in this Victorian Period novel (1849-1850).

4	<u>David Copperfield</u> by Charles Dickens
5	<u>Barchester Towers</u> by Anthony Trollope
6	<u>Jude the Obscure</u> by Thomas Hardy

Diggory Venn - this character is the young, traveling, salesman on gloomy Egdon Heath whose pursuit of a young woman named Thomasin (Tasmin) Yeobright is thwarted when she marries Damon Wildeve, a former engineer and present owner of the <u>Quiet Woman Inn</u>; eventually, he stops selling red dye to sheep owners and wins Tasmin's hand after Damon and Eustacia Vye drown in a small lake in this Victorian Period novel (1878).

7	<u>Barchester Towers</u> by Anthony Trollope
8	<u>The Return of the Native</u> by Thomas Hardy
9	<u>The Prisoner of Zenda</u> by Anthony Hope

2-4-8

<u>Joe Gargery</u> - this character is the kind and thoughtful blacksmith whose life in a cottage on the marshes centers around a shrewish wife named Georgiana and her young, diffident orphan brother, Philip Pirrip; eventually, he is widowed and achieves happiness with a new devoted wife named Biddy while watching young Pip become a gentleman and reunites with Estella in this Victorian Period novel (1860-1861).

1   <u>The Return of the Native</u> by Thomas Hardy
2   <u>Great Expectations</u> by Charles Dickens
3   <u>Wuthering Heights</u> by Emily Bronte

<u>Blind Pew</u> - this character is the malformed, blind seaman who shows up at the <u>Admiral Benbow Inn</u> in remote Black Hill cove on the day of Jim Hawkins' father's funeral to serve Bill Bones a blind spot indicating his impending death once his hiding place had been discovered by Black Dog; eventually, he is trampled by horses during the response to a pirate attack in this Victorian Period novel (1883).

4   <u>Captain Courageous</u> by Rudyard Kipling
5   <u>Treasure Island</u> by Robert Louis Stevenson
6   <u>Jude the Obscure</u> by Thomas Hardy

<u>Ishmael</u> - this character is the reflective, New York City schoolmaster who joins a pragmatic veteran South Seas harpooner named Queequeg in signing aboard the <u>Pequod</u> which brings him in contact with the deranged Captain Abab who has a delusional fixation that endangers the entire crew; eventually, he clings to Queequeg's floating coffin before being rescued and becomes the only survivor in this Victorian Period novel (1851).

7   <u>Two Years Before the Mast</u> by Richard Henry Dana, Jr.
8   <u>Moby Dick</u> by Herman Melville
9   <u>Captain Courageous</u> by Rudyard Kipling

2-5-8

Injun Joe - this character is the half breed murderer who knifes a young doctor named Dr. Robinson over the proceeds of a grave robbery and puts the blame on another accomplice who owns the knife, Muff Potter; eventually, he appears as a witness at Muff Potter's trial to accuse the drunk of the killing and escapes through the courtroom window when a young boy who witnessed the killing finally speaks up and identifies him as the real murderer in this Victorian Period novel (1876).

1   **Tom Sawyer** by Mark Twain
2   **The Pathfinder** by James Fenimore Cooper
3   **Drums Along the Mohawk** by Walter Edmonds

Mrs. March (Marmee) - this character is the compassionate New England matriarch who cozy life her four daughters in a small house called **Plumfield** is interrupted when a telegram leads her to the bedside of her critically ill Army Chaplin husband during the Civil War; eventually, her sixtieth birthday is celebrated in the company of Meg, Jo and Amy without delicate Beth who had died from scarlet fever in this Victorian Period novel (1868-1869).

4   **Seventeen** by Booth Tarkington
5   **Consuelo** by George Sand
6   **Little Women** by Louisa May Alcott

Alexei Karenin - this character is the pitiless, disinterested Russian politician who values social position over facing up to his wife's infidelity with the wealthy, handsome Count Vronsky in spite of their young son, Sergey; eventually, his constituents view him as a steadfast husband and father after his wife abandons him to travel to Italy with the Count and their newborn daughter which brings about his suicide in front of an incoming train in this Victorian Period novel (1875).

7   **The Idiot** by Fyodor Dostoevski
8   **Anna Karenina** by Count Leo Tolstoy
9   **Fathers and Sons** by Ivan Turgenev

1-6-8

<u>The Duchess</u> - this character is the royal platitude quoting, moralizing, ugly old woman who sits in her small house with a cook who overuses pepper, assorted other weird types and a   sneezing baby on her lap; eventually, this mad woman who is deathly afraid of the Queen because she has been condemned to be beheaded waits while the sentence is never carried out in this Victorian Period novel (1865).

1   <u>Gullivers Travels</u> by Jonathan Swift
2   <u>Robinson Crusoe</u> by Daniel Defoe
3   <u>Alice in Wonderland</u> by Lewis Carroll

<u>Jarvis Lorry</u> - this character is the English agent of the Franco-British Banking House of Tellson & Co. who travels with Lucie Manette to Paris so she can reunite with her freed father, Dr. Manette; eventually, he returns to Paris later in order to assist a law clerk named Sidney Carton free Lucie's imprisoned husband, Charles Durnay, in this Victorian Period novel (1859).

4   <u>A Tale of Two Cities</u> by Charles Dickens
5   <u>The Prisoner of Zenda</u> by Anthony Hope
6   <u>Jude the Obscure</u> by Thomas Hardy

<u>Colonel Pyncheon</u> - this character is the austere, immoral 17th century Salem Judge who condemns an innocent man named Matthew Maule to death during the witchcraft trials so that he can confiscate his land; eventually, he and his heirs die by drowning in their own blood because of Matthew Maule's curse until the land is returned to its proper owner in this Victorian Period novel (1851).

7   <u>Silas Marner</u> by George Eliot
8   <u>Babbitt</u> by Sinclair Lewis
9   <u>The House of the Seven Gables</u> by Nathaniel Hawthorne

3-4-9

Isabel Archer - this character is the 23 year-old American heiress whose cultural trip through Europe with Mrs. Touchett results in marriage proposals from two expatriates named George Osmond and Caspar Goodwood and an English nobleman named Lord Warburton; eventually, her sister-in-law, Countess Femini, informs her that the latter's stepdaughter, Pansy, issued from an illicit affair between her husband, George, and Madame Merle in this Victorian Period novel (1881).

1	The Scarlet Letter by Nathaniel Hawthorne
2	The Portrait of a Lady by Henry James
3	Little Women by Louisa May Alcott

Lady Honoria Dedlock - this character is the wife who conceals her relationship and illegitimate daughter with a rogue named Captain hawson from her reputable, refined husband; eventually, her flight from a blackmailing lawyer named Mr. Tulkinghorn ends when she is found dead by this daughter, Esther Summerson, at the gate of the cemetery where Captain Hawson is buried under the alias Nemo in this Victorian Period novel (1852-1853).

4	Barchester Towers by Anthony Trollope
5	Bleak House by Charles Dickens
6	Jude the Obscure by Thomas Hardy

Amelia Sedley - this character is the young, sweet-tempered considerate girl who becomes best friends with Becky Sharp when they are schoolmates at Miss Pinkerton's finishing school for girls; eventually, her first marriage to a gallant young English army officer named George Osborne which ends when he is killed at Waterloo produces a son named George while her second marriage to Captain William Dobbin that produces a young girl named Jane in this Victorian Period novel (1847-1848).

7	The Return of the Native by Thomas Hardy
8	Vanity Fair by William Makepeace Thackeray
9	Barchester Towers by Anthony Trollope

2-5-8

Uriah Heep - this character is the cringing, deferential, villainous clerk who is finally exposed by his repentant confidential secretary, Wilkins Micawber, as the thief who had bankrupted Mr. Wickfield and embezzled Miss Betsy Trotwood's fortune; eventually, his restitution and escape from prosecution fail to prevent his future imprisonment when he is caught committing forgery in another part of the country in this Victorian Period novel (1849-1850).

1	David Copperfield by Charles Dickens
2	A Tale of Two Cities by Charles Dickens
3	Great Expectations by Charles Dickens

Eppie (Heplizibah) - this character is the adopted daughter of an epileptic miserly old weaver and the real daughter of a landowner named Godfrey Cass and a deceased drug addict named Molly Cass who had traveled from a distant hamlet only to die in a snow storm from an overdose of laudanum; eventually, she refuses the generous offer to reunite with her real father only to marry Aaron Winthrop and continue to care for the aging weaver who had adopted her in this Victorian Period novel (1861).

4	Wuthering Heights by Emily Bronte
5	Silas Marner by George Eliot
6	Agnes Grey by Anne Bronte

Hank Morgan - this character is the skilled mechanic who is knocked unconscious and suffers a head injury after being hit over the head by a fellow worker during an argument at a New England arms factory; eventually, he rises to the position of The Boss and marries Alisande a/k/a Sandy and has a daughter named Hello-Central in this Victorian Period novel (1889).

7	The Prince and the Pauper by Mark Twain
8	Captain Courageous by Rudyard Kipling
9	A Connecticut Yankee In King Arthur's Court by Mark Twain

1-5-9

<u>Ivan</u> - this character is the second oldest of four sons named Dmitri, Alexey and Smerdyakov who were fathered by a lecherous, shrewd old businessman named Fyodor who deserted each of them after their mothers died while keeping Smerdyakov as a servant; eventually, he fails to convince a court about Smerdyakov's confession which results in Dmitri's conviction and sentencing to Siberia in this Victorian Period novel (1880).

1	<u>Fathers and Sons</u> by Ivan Turgenev
2	<u>The Brothers Karamazov</u> by Fyodor Dostoevski
3	<u>Dead Souls</u> by Nikolai V. Gogol

<u>Damon Wildeve</u> - this character is the engineer turned proprietor of the <u>Quiet Woman Inn</u> on gloomy Egdon Heath who reacts to Eustacia Vye's marriage to Clym Yeobright by spitefully marrying Clym's cousin, Thomasin Yeobright; eventually, his death by misadventure occurs when he attempts to save Eustacia Vye from her successful suicide attempt in a small lake in this Victorian Period novel (1878).

4	<u>The Return of the Native</u> by Thomas Hardy
5	<u>Barchester Towers</u> by Anthony Hope
6	<u>Kidnapped</u> by Robert Louis Stevenson

<u>Mr. Lockwood</u> - this character is the tenant on an old farm, <u>Thrushcross Grange</u>, whose curiosity about his landlord is satisfied when a housekeeper named Nelly Dean begins recounting an amazing history of those who once lived there; eventually, her haunting stories of the Earnshaws, Lintons, and the Heathcliffs reveal the tragedy of the unrequited love that existed between the landlord named Heathcliff and his spirited stepsister named Catherine Earnshaw in this Victorian Period novel (1847).

7	<u>Barchester Towers</u> by Anthony Trollope
8	<u>Bleak House</u> by Charles Dickens
9	<u>Wuthering Heights</u> by Emily Bronte

2-4-9

Reverend Obadiah Slope - this character is the villainous chaplin for the new political appointment to the fictional cathedral town in the West of England who teams up with the driving, domineering wife of the Bishop in an attempt to establish Low Church ways; eventually, his scandalous behavior with the wealthy, widowed daughter of Rev. Septimus Harding, Mrs. Eleanor Bold, brings about his return to London after being dismissed by Mrs. Proudie in this Victorian Period novel (1857).

1   The Warden by Anthony Trollope
2   The Ordeal of Richard Feveral by George Meredith
3   Barchester Towers by Anthony Trollope

Fedallah - this character is the tall, eerie Parsee whose presence aboard the Pequod as a servant of the deranged Captain Abab portends what awaits the crew because of this captain's delusional fixation; eventually, his prophesies are fulfilled to the extent that the entire crew with the exception of Ishmael lost their lives in this Victorian Period novel (1851).

4   Captain Courageous by Rudyard Kipling
5   Two Years Before the Mast by Richard Henry Dana, Jr.
6   Moby Dick by Herman Melville

Judge Thatcher - this character is the trustee for two young boys after they discover a box of gold in a robber's cave and the one who wisely invests the found money so that each boy is able to receive a dollar a day; eventually, one of the boys persuades him to take his remaining share of the loot because the boy fears the actions of his drunken, violent father, Pap in this Victorian Period novel (1885).

7   A Connecticut Yankee in King Arthur's Court by Mark Twain
8   Huckleberry Finn by Mark Twain
9   The Prince and the Pauper by Mark Twain

<u>Porfiry</u> - this character is the troubled, gifted detective whose investigation of the axe murders of an old, miserly pawnbroker, Alonya, and her sister, Lizaveta, leads him to a penniless, law student named Rodion Raskolnikov; eventually, this inspector's cleverness and compassion in getting this young man to confess leads to Rodya's spending eight years in Siberia accompanied by his ex-prostitute girlfriend, Sonia, in this Victorian Period novel (1866).

1   <u>Fathers and Sons</u> by Ivan Turgenev
2   <u>Crime and Punishment</u> by Fyodor Dostoevski
3   <u>Dead Souls</u> by Nikolai V. Gogol

<u>Herbert Pocket</u> - this character is the merry and tolerant London roommate of a young, diffident orphan named Philip Pirrip and the one whose familial connection leads young Pip to believe Miss Havisham is his secret benefactor; eventually, his ceaseless drive to prosper in life is rewarded when Pip secretly buys him a partnership in a profitable business in this Victorian Period novel (1860-1861).

4   <u>Barnaby Rudge</u> by Charles Dickens
5   <u>Great Expectations</u> by Charles Dickens
6   <u>The Old Curiosity Shop</u> by Charles Dickens

<u>Agnes</u> - this character is the young, talented governess whose unsuccessful stints with the Bloomfield family at <u>Wellwood</u> and the Murray family at <u>Horton Lodge</u> leads her to start a school for young ladies along with her mother; eventually, she marries an earnest clergyman named Edward Weston after he fulfills his apprenticeship as a curate under an ambitious rector named Mr. Hatfield in this Victorian Period novel (1847).

7   <u>Wuthering Heights</u> by Emily Bronte
8   <u>Jane Eyre</u> by Charlotte Bronte
9   <u>Agnes Grey</u> by Anne Bronte

2-5-9

<u>Louis de Franchi</u> - this character is the highly principled, honorable Parisian law student whose family-felt depression stems from his secret, unrequited love for Emilie who is the beautiful, unfaithful wife left in his charge by an absentee sea-captain friend; eventually, he is killed in a gun deal by Emilie's lover, M. de Chateau-Renaud, when the latter soils her reputation over a wager involving her attendance at a dinner party in this Victorian Period novel (1845).

1	<u>The Corsican Brothers</u> by Alexander Dumas, Sr.
2	<u>The Red and the Black</u> by Stendhal
3	<u>Nana</u> by Emile Zola

<u>Walter Cay</u> - this character is the wee-bred young clerk whose mission to the West Indies temporarily interrupts his ensuing marriage to a compassionate woman named Florence; eventually, he achieves prosperity and helps his father-in-law recover from a downward spiral of destructive behavior that resulted from losing his son, Paul, and a bad marriage to Mrs. Edith Granger in this Victorian Period novel (1846-1848).

4	<u>Far From the Madding Crowd</u> by Thomas Hardy
5	<u>Dombey and Son</u> by Charles Dickens
6	<u>Pendennis</u> by William Makepeace Thackeray

<u>Nelly Dean</u> - this character is the housekeeper at <u>Thrushcross Grange</u> who satisfies Mr. Lockwood's curiosity about his tormented, outlandish landlord, Heathcliff, by relating the amazing history of the Earnshaws, Lintons, and Heathcliffs; eventually, these haunting stories reveal the tragedy of unrequited love between this landlord named Heathcliff and his spirited stepsister, Catherine, in this Victorian Period novel (1847).

7	<u>Barchester Towers</u> by Anthony Trollope
8	<u>Wuthering Heights</u> by Emily Bronte
9	<u>Pendennis</u> by William Makepeace Thackeray

1-5-8

<u>Stubb</u> - this character is the nonchalant pipe-smoking second mate under Sawbuck aboard the <u>Pequod</u> whose fatalistic stoicism toward peril vanishes when he learns of Captain Abab's delusional fixation; eventually, his worst fears are realized when the prophesies of a Parsee servant named Fedallah finally come true in this Victorian Period novel (1851).

1	<u>Captain Courageous</u> by Rudyard Kipling
2	<u>Two Years Before the Mast</u> by Richard Henry Dana, Jr.
3	<u>Moby Dick</u> by Herman Melville

<u>Florence</u> - this character is the 12 year old sister of a bright, frail boy named Paul who dies at 6 years-old and the daughter of an austere widowed father who remarries Mrs. Edith Granger; eventually, her marriage to a prosperous clerk named Walter Cay produces a son named Paul who cures the downward spiral of the father's destructive behavior in this Victorian Period novel (1846-1848).

4	<u>The Old Curiosity Shop</u> by Charles Dickens
5	<u>Martin Chuzzlewit</u> by Charles Dickens
6	<u>Dombey and Son</u> by Charles Dickens

<u>Matthew Maule</u> - this character is the innocent victim condemned to death by an austere, immoral 17th century Salem Judge named Colonel Pyncheon during the witchcraft trials because this magistrate wanted the latter's land; eventually, he makes his dying curse comes true when the Colonel and his heirs die by drowning in their own blood until the property is returned to its proper owners in this Victorian Period novel (1851).

7	<u>Daisy Miller</u> by Henry James
8	<u>The House of the Seven Gables</u> by Nathaniel Hawthorne
9	<u>Babbitt</u> by Sinclair Lewis

3-6-8

Jane - this character is the governess from <u>Gateshead Hall</u> and the <u>Lowood School</u> who is hired at <u>Thornfield</u> to teach Edward Rochester's illegitimate child and ward, Adele Varens, art and music; eventually, she marries the temporarily blinded Edward after Edward's deranged wife, Bertha Mason Rochester, burns down <u>Thornfield</u> and dies by misadventure in this fire caused by her in this Victorian Period novel (1847).

1	<u>Wuthering Heights</u> by Emily Bronte
2	<u>Jane Eyre</u> by Charlotte Bronte
3	<u>Agnes Grey</u> by Anne Bronte

Arthur Compeyson - this character is the evil rogue whose jilting of Miss Havisham on her wedding day leaves her a soured spinster who keeps the wedding reception intact for years to come and pits the young Estella against a younger boy named Pip; eventually, he betrays an escaped convict named Abel Magwitch which leads to his own demise at the hands of the same man under an assumed name, Mr. Provis, some years later in this Victorian Period novel (1860-1861).

4	<u>Great Expectations</u> by Charles Dickens
5	<u>The Mystery of Edwin Drood</u> by Charles Dickens
6	<u>Barnaby Rudge</u> by Charles Dickens

Dr. Vesey Stanhope - this character is the absentee, English clergyman in a fictional cathedral town in the West of England who is compelled to return from Italy with his children Charlotte, La Signora Madeline Vesey Neroni, and Ethelbert (Bertie) due to a policy change issued by the new political appointee, Dr. Proudie; eventually, he feels free to return to Italy after the Rev. Obadiah Slope travels to London after being dismissed by Mrs. Proudie in this Victorian Period novel (1857).

7	<u>Barchester Towers</u> by Anthony Trollope
8	<u>The Return of the Native</u> by Thomas Hardy
9	<u>Orley Farm</u> by Anthony Trollope

Flask (King-Post) - this character is the undersized, portly third mate under first and second mates, Sawbuck and Stubb, who is whimsical with the crew of the Pequod and obsequious in front of his deranged captain; eventually, his docility in not questioning Captain Abab's delusional fixation seals his fate along with all the crew except Ishmael in this Victorian Period novel (1851).

1   <u>Two Years Before the Mast</u> by Richard Henry Dana, Jr.
2   <u>Captain Courageous</u> by Rudyard Kipling
3   <u>Moby Dick</u> by Herman Melville

Mercy (Merry) Pecksniff - this character is the conceited, pretentious daughter of a flim-flam teacher of architecture, Seth, and the one whose brutal marriage to a coarse hustler named Jonas ends when the latter poisons himself on the way to prison; eventually, her welfare is provided for by her dead husband's rich, old uncle eventhough her husband, Jonas, had attempted to murder her benefactor's brother, Anthony, in this Victorian Period novel (1843-1844).

4   <u>Martin Chuzzlewit</u> by Charles Dickens
5   <u>Barnaby Rudge</u> by Charles Dickens
6   <u>Dombey and Son</u> by Charles Dickens

Bill Bones - this character is the old, weather-beaten seaman who intimidates everyone while hiding out at the <u>Admiral Benbow Inn</u> until Dr. David Livesey reproaches him because young Jim Hawkins' father is critically ill; eventually, the stroke he suffers after Black Dog discovers his hideout is followed b a fatal stroke when Blind Pew serves him with a black spot which indicates his impending death in this Victorian Period novel (1883).

7   <u>Kidnapped</u> by Robert Louis Stevenson
8   <u>The Black Arrow</u> by Robert Louis Stevenson
9   <u>Treasure Island</u> by Robert Louis Stevenson

Beth - this character is the mild, delicate daughter whose life with her mother and sisters in a house called Plumfield is interrupted when Marmee receives a telegram during the Civil War telling her that her Army Chaplin husband is critically ill; eventually, she contracts scarlet fever and dies after being reunited with her other sister, Jo, who has returned from New York City in this Victorian Period novel (1868-1869).

1   Little Women by Louisa May Alcott
2   Seventeen by Booth Tarkington
3   Consuelo by George Sand

Mr. Jaggers - this character is the criminal lawyer who is hired by Mr. Provis to secretly handle a trust fund set up by a coarse ex-convict named Abel Magwitch for an shy, orphan boy named Philip Pirrip to become a gentleman; eventually, this attorney's housekeeper, Molly, is discovered to be a murderess who was Magwitch's former mistress and Estella's real mother in this Victorian Period novel (1860-1861).

4   David Copperfield by Charles Dickens
5   Great Expectations by Charles Dickens
6   The Tale of Two Cities by Charles Dickens

Cosette - this character is the illegitimate daughter of a deceased prostitute named Fantine and the one who mistakenly believes that her father is the town's mayor, Father Madelaine, who is being constantly hounded by a police inspector named Javert; eventually, she and her young lawyer husband, Marius Pontmercy, discover that Father Madelaine is not her real father but a fugitive ex-con named Jean Valjean in this Victorian Period novel (1862).

7   Nana by Emil Zola
8   Madame Bovary by Gustave Flaubert
9   Les Miserables by Victor Hugo

1-5-9

Chastity (Cherry) Pecksniff - this character is the oldest, pretentious and conceited daughter of a flim-flam teacher of architecture named Seth and the one who is stood up by her fiancé, Augustus Noddle, while also losing the hand of Jonas to her equally conceited sister, Mercy; eventually, she becomes her father's carping companion in his later years in this Victorian Period novel (1843-1844).

1	**Martin Chuzzlewit** by Charles Dickens
2	**Barnaby Rudge** by Charles Dickens
3	**Dombey and Son** by Charles Dickens

Messala - this character is the arrogant and cruel Roman soldier who joins his superior in stripping his childhood friend of all his property, sentencing his friend to slavery and turning his friend's mother and beautiful sister, Tirzah, into lepers; eventually, he is crippled and ruined financially while competing in a race with the childhood friend he had betrayed and is ultimately killed by the Egyptian magistrate's daughter, Iras in this Victorian Period novel (1880).

4	**The Antiquary** by Sir Walter Scott
5	**Ben Hur: The Tale of the Christ** by Lew Wallace
6	**The Heart of Midlothian** by Sir Walter Scott

Madame Defarge - this character is the hard-hearted, merciless wife of a French wineshop keeper who was the former house servant of Dr. Manette and the woman who sits by knitting while people are guillotined; eventually, she is killed when her pistol goes off during a struggle with Lucie Manette' English maid, Miss Pross in this Victorian Period novel (1859).

7	**Dombey and Son** by Charles Dickens
8	**A Tale of Two Cities** by Charles Dickens
9	**The Mystery of Edwin Drood** by Charles Dickens

Claire de Cintre, nee Bellegarde - this character is the unconcerned Parisian artist whose copies of the painting in the Louvre attracts the attention of an American businessman named Christopher Newman while he is traveling Europe in search of a wife; eventually, she brings about the death of young Valentin Bellegarde when he enters a duel to defend her honor in this Victorian Period novel (1877).

1	**Daisy Miller** by Henry James
2	**The American** by Henry James
3	**Washington Square** by Henry James

Agnes Wickfield - this character is the young, unselfish, practical daughter of Miss Betsy Trotwood's London lawyer and the one who becomes the love object of a cringing, deferential clerk named Uriah Heep who works for her father; eventually, she marries an aspiring writer after caring for this young man's dying wife, Dora, until he becomes a widow and returns to England from the the Continent in this Victorian Period novel (1877).

4	**David Copperfield** by Charles Dickens
5	**Great Expectations** by Charles Dickens
6	**A Tale of Two Cities** by Charles Dickens

Mr. Tristram - this character is the boisterous, expatriate who has married a warm and perceptive French woman; eventually, his sympathetic wife explains to a young lovelorn American millionaire named Christopher Newman how the Bellegardes family second guessed his every mood regarding the revelation in a secret document in this Victorian Period novel (1877).

7	**Washington Square** by Henry James
8	**Daisy Miller** by Henry James
9	**The American** by Henry James

2-4-9

Abel Magwitch (Mr. Provis) - this character is the coarse, uncouth, escaped convict whose gratitude leads him to becomes the secret benefactor of young Philip Pirrip (Pip) in order to make the latter a gentleman; eventually, he wins a fatal fight with the scoundrel, Arthur Compeyson, who betrayed him and Miss Havisham only to later die in prison after he is recaptured in this Victorian Period novel (1860-1861).

1	Treasure Island by Robert Louis Stevenson
2	Great Expectations by Charles Dickens
3	The Return of the Native by Thomas Hardy

Tommy Traddles - this character is the student at an inferior school named Salem House run by the harsh headmaster, Mr. Creakle, who meets other students such as a wealthy scoundrel named James Steerforth and a young sensitive boy sent there by his sadistic stepfather, Mr. Murdstone; eventually, his position later in life as a judge allows him to assist Miss Betsy Trotwood who has been embezzled by Uriah Heep in this Victorian Period novel (1849-1850).

4	Great Expectations by Charles Dickens
5	A Tale of Two Cities by Charles Dickens
6	David Copperfield by Charles Dickens

Tom Pinch - this character is the shy, naive middle-aged draftsman who allows a flim-flam architect and land surveyor named Seth Pecksniff to take advantage of him by overworking him as his assistant in teaching others; eventually, he realizes his employer's villainy after hearing of his employer's advances toward   Mary Graham which sends him to London to seek new employment through John Westlock in this Victorian Period novel (1843-1844).

7	Martin Chuzzlewit by Charles Dickens
8	David Copperfield by Charles Dickens
9	Barnaby Rudge by Charles Dickens

2-6-7

<u>Sir Ensor Doone</u> - this character is the grandfather of his beautiful ward, Lorna Doone, and the leader of an outlaw decadent family gang whose killings had extended to the father of a robust farmer named John Ridd; eventually, he gives Lorna a diamond necklace on his deathbed that ultimately reveals her true identity as the noblewomen, Lady Dugal, while also giving his blessing of her union with John Ridd in this Victorian Period novel (1869).

1   Charles Dickens
2   Thomas Hardy
3   Richard D. Blackmore

<u>Steven Blackpool</u> - this character is the indigent but trustworthy worker in Josiah Bounderby's Coketown factory who loses his job because of his wife's drinking and his own indecisiveness during a labor dispute; eventually, he is exonerated of a bank theft really committed by the younger Tom Gradgrind after he is found at the bottom of a mine shaft by Louisa Gradgrind and Sissy Jupe in this Victorian Period novel (1854).

4   <u>Tom Jones</u> by Henry Fielding
5   <u>Hard Times</u> by Charles Dickens
6   <u>Treasure Island</u> by Robert Louis Stevenson

<u>Neville Landless</u> - this character is the orphaned Englishman who travels with his sister, Helena, from Ceylon to England where he becomes a student of Mr. Crisparkle; eventually, his affection for Helena's friend, Rosa Bud, drives an opium-addicted choirmaster named Jack Jasper into blackmailing Helena and causing him to be accused of the murder of Jack's mining engineering nephew in this unfinished Victorian Period novel (1870).

7   <u>Kidnapped</u> by Robert Louis Stevenson
8   <u>The Return of the Native</u> by Thomas Hardy
9   <u>The Mystery of Edwin Drood</u> by Charles Dickens

3-5-9

Mrs. Sparsit - this character is the elderly housekeeper of a rich banker named Josiah Bounderby and the one who is ousted from living in his house and relocated to sleeping quarters in his bank to make room for his new young wife, Louisa Gradgrind, and her brother, Tom Gradgrind;   eventually, she avenges this act by identifying his mother, Mrs. Pegler, and exposing his self-made man myth in this Victorian Period novel (1854).

1   Hard Times by Charles Dickens
2   Barchester towers by Anthony Trollope
3   Jude the Obscure by Thomas Hardy

Muff Potter - this character is the town drunk in St. Petersburg on the Mississippi River who goes on trial for the killing of young Dr. Robinson after helping him and a half-breed Injun Joe rob a grave; eventually, this good-for-nothing is acquitted of the charge when a teenager's conscience forces him to identify the real killer as Injun Joe who immediately escapes through the courthouse window only to later die of starvation in a cave in this Victorian Period novel (1876).

4   Main Street by Sinclair Lewis
5   The House of the Seven Gables by Nathaniel Hawthorne
6   Tom Sawyer by Mark Twain

James Steerforth - this character is the spoiled, wealthy widow's son who jilts Rosa Dartle by seducing Little Em'ly whom he later abandons after their elopement on the eve of her marriage to Ham Peggotty; eventually, this scoundrel's plans to marry Little Em'ly to his depraved servant and accomplice, Littimer, ends ironically when he and his attempted rescuer, Ham, drown together in this Victorian Period novel (1849-1850).

7   Great Expectations by Charles Dickens
8   A Tale of Two Cities by Charles Dickens
9   David Copperfield by Charles Dickens

1-6-9

Sir Pitt Crawley - this character is the surly, miserly old odd-ball baronet who lives at <u>Queens Crawley</u> who hires a scheming, attractive narcissistic governess named Becky Sharp to govern his two young daughters, Miss Rosalind and Miss Violet only to have his subsequent marriage proposal to her expose her secret marriage to Rawdon Crawley; eventually, his future senility draws him into an affair with his butler's daughter, Betsy Horrocks, in this Victorian Period novel (1847-1848).

1   **<u>Vanity Fair</u> by William Makepeace Thackeray**
2   **<u>Lorna Doone</u> by Richard D. Blackmore**
3   **<u>Barchester Towers</u> by Anthony Trollope**

Edward Murdstone - this character is the miserly, sadistic second husband of a young comely widow named Clara, the ill-tempered stepfather of a sensitive young boy and the brother of a grating, obstinate, paranoiac woman; eventually, he dismisses a corpulent, good-natured loyal servant named Clara Peggotty after his naive wife dies giving birth to their child in this Victorian Period novel (1849-1850).

4   **<u>Great Expectations</u> by Charles Dickens**
5   **<u>A Tale of Two Cities</u> by Charles Dickens**
6   **<u>David Copperfield</u> by Charles Dickens**

Leon Dupuis - this character is the immature law clerk who has an illicit affair with a fickle romantically inclined country housewife married to a vacuous mediocre country doctor named Charles; eventually, he joins another former paramour, a wealthy chateau owner named Rodophe Boulanger, in refusing this woman financial help for her debts which ultimately leads to her suicide by arsenic poisoning in this Victorian Period novel (1857).

7   **Victor Hugo**
8   **Stendhal**
9   **Gustave Flaubert**

1-6-9

Gabriel John Utterson - this character is the dour lawyer who is told an intriguing story by his walking partner, Richard Ensfield, about a doctor friend of the former named Henry and a somewhat hateful person named Edward; eventually, his head clerk, Mr. Guest, notices a similarity between Henry and Edward's handwriting which leads to 2 letters being read upon the deaths of Dr. Hastie Lanyon and then Edward in this Victorian Period novel (1886).

1	The Hunchback of Notre Dam e by Victor Hugo
2	Dr. Jekyll and Mr. Hyde by Robert Louis Stevenson
3	Frankenstein by Mary Shelley

Tobias Gregson - this character is the Scotland yard detective who collaborates with his colleague, Lestrade, and a perceptive private investigator to solve a twin murder involving two American Mormons; eventually, the motive for the dual murders is revealed to be the result of a transcontinental vendetta that involves a beautiful young Mormon woman named Lucy Ferrier in this Victorian Period novel (1887).

4	The Mystery of Edwin Drood by Charles Dickens
5	Far From the Madding Crowd by Thomas Hardy
6	A Study in Scarlet by Sir Arthur Conan Doyle

Thomas Gradgrind - this character is the owner of an innovative private school in Coketown who forces his own children, Tom and Louisa, and all his students to concentrate only on factual information at the expense of imagination and emotions; eventually, this curriculum leads his son commits a bank theft while Louisa enters into a loveless marriage with a rich old banker named Mr. Josiah Bounderby in this Victorian Period novel (1854).

7	Hard Times by Charles Dickens
8	The Return of the Native by Thomas Hardy
9	Goodbye, Mr. Chips by James Hilton

James Durie - this character is the older Scottish brother who constantly reappears in his younger brother Henry's life whom he blackmails financially and emotionally after having earlier ceded his birthright and claim to Alison Graeme's love; eventually, his faked death by Secundra Dass turns awry when the cold climate of the American wilderness inadvertently affects his trick of suspended animation in this Victorian Period novel (1889).

1	**Kidnapped** by Robert Louis Stevenson
2	**The Black Arrow** by Robert Louis Stevenson
3	**The Master of Ballantrae** by Robert Louis Stevenson

Emma Haredale - this character is the young Catholic niece of the country squire named Geoffrey who owns an estate named **The Warren** and the fiancee of a young Protestant gentleman, Edward Chester, despite the latter's father's and her uncle's objections; eventually, she is rescued from her abductors by Edward during the Gordon riots, marries him and moves into **The Warren** with him after he restores it in this Victorian Period novel (1841).

4	**Barnaby Rudge** by Charles Dickens
5	**Pride and Prejudice** by Jane Austen
6	**Vanity Fair** by William Makepeace Thackeray

John Ridd - this character is the gentle, robust farmer from Exmoor whose trysts with the young, beautiful ward of Sir Ensor Doone are double-edged because her outlaw decadent family murdered his father; eventually, he marries Lorna Doone after she is reinstated as the noblewomen, Lady Dugal, and he has revenged his father's death by killing his murderer, the brutal Carver Doone, at **Wizard's Slough** in this Victorian Period novel (1869).

7	**George Eliot**
8	**William Makepeace Thackeray**
9	**Richard D. Blackmore**

3-4-9

<u>Christopher Newman</u> - this character is the young American millionaire in Paris whose marriage proposal is rejected by an aristocratic woman named Claire de Cintre because her mother, Madame de Bellegarde, doesn't think he is worthy enough to join their family; eventually, his uprightness prevents him from blackmailing the Bellegarde family and Claire ultimately becomes a nun in this Victorian Period novel (1877).

1 <u>The Marble Faun</u> by Nathaniel Hawthorne
2 <u>The American</u> by Henry James
3 <u>An American Tragedy</u> by Theodore Drieser

<u>Adele Varens</u> - this character is the young illegitimate daughter   of the arrogant, pensive owner of an estate named <u>Thornfield</u> and a French opera singer who duped him; eventually, this adopted ward of Edward Rochester escapes when <u>Thornfield</u> is burned to the ground and lives to see her temporarily blinded father marry her private governess after his deranged wife had died by misadventure in this fire in this Victorian Period novel (1847).

4 <u>Agnes Grey</u> by Anne Bronte
5 <u>Wuthering Heights</u> by Emily Bronte
6 <u>Jane Eyre</u> by Charlotte Bronte

<u>Christopher (Kit) Nubbles</u> - this character is the ungraceful, unselfish and robust youngster who adores Little Nell and runs errands for her degenerate gambling grandfather; eventually, he is exonerated of theft by Mr. Garland and Dick Swiveller after being accused by the lawyer, Solomon Brass, at the behest of the dwarf, Daniel Quilp, in this Victorian Period novel (1848).

7 <u>Pendennis</u> by William Makepeace Thackeray
8 <u>Middlemarch</u> by George Eliot
9 <u>The Old Curiosity Shop</u> by Charles Dickens

2-6-9

Rodolphe Boulanger - this character is the ingenious, urbane wealthy owner of a Chateau who has an illicit affair with a fickle romantically inclined country housewife who is married to a mediocre country doctor named Charles; eventually, he joins another former paramour, a law clerk named Leon Dupuis, in refusing this improvident woman financial help which ultimately leads to her suicide by arsenic poisoning in this Victorian Period novel (1857).

1	Gustave Flaubert
2	Victor Hugo
3	Stendhal

Squire Trelawney - this character is the prosperous landowner who joins Dr. Livesey in commissioning the ship, the Hispaniola in Bristol, England, hires Jim Hawkins as cabin boy and Long John Silver as cook, and sets sail for the fictitious Spanish Main in the Caribbean Sea; eventually, he outwits a group of pirates, captures the prize and returns home with Ben Gunn and Long John in this Victorian Period novel (1883).

4	Captain Courageous by Rudyard Kipling
5	Lord Jim by Joseph Conrad
6	Treasure Island by Robert Louis Stevenson

Jack Jasper - this character is the opium-addicted choirmaster at Cloisterham Cathedral who blackmails a young woman named Rosa Bud because of his unrequited love for her and jealousy of her new lover, Neville Landless; eventually, he comes under the intense scrutiny of a surreptitious white-haired newcomer named Datchery over the disappearance of a young mining engineer who is his nephew in this unfinished Victorian Period novel (1870).

7	A Study in Scarlet by Sir Arthur Conan Doyle
8	The Mystery of Edwin Drood by Charles Dickens
9	Far From the Madding Crowd by Thomas Hardy

1-6-8

Jo March - this character is the young, above height, awkward tomboy whose artistic bent comes out when she writes and devises plays as entertainment for her mother and three sisters; eventually, she breaks a long intended engagement to a rich, lonesome neighbor named Laurie which allows her to marry a German tutor named Professor Bhaer and establish a boy's school in a small house named Plumfield in this Victorian Period novel (1868-1869).

1	Consuelo by George Sand
2	Seventeen by Booth Tarkington
3	Little Women by Louisa May Alcott

Dough-Boy - this character is the wan, slow-witted ship's cook whose panic in the presence of the ship's three harpooners Queequeg, Tashtego and Daggoo makes him seek their approval by using extra food to appease them; eventually, he perishes when the ship's deranged captain, Abab, allows his delusional fixation to ultimately cause the death of his entire crew with the exception of Ishmael in this Victorian Period novel (1851).

4	Two Years Before the Mast by Richard Henry Dana, Jr.
5	Victory by Joseph Conrad
6	Moby Dick by Herman Melville

Andrey Bolkonsky - this character is the proud, skeptical and well-healed Russian prince whose acceptance of an Army commission obliges him to depart his estate, Bleak Hills, and leave behind his strange father, his wife, Lise, and unborn son, Nikolushka; eventually, his initial wounding during a battle against Napoleon doesn't deter him from re-enlisting and receiving a fatal wound at a future battle that is tended to by his ex finance, Natasha Rostov, in this Victorian Period novel (1865).

7	The Brothers Karamozov by Fyodor Dostoevski
8	War and Peace by Count Leo Tolstoy
9	Fathers and Sons by Ivan Turgenev

Mrs. Sarah Gamp - this character is the obese, throaty cockney midwife and nurse whose partiality to drink leads her to frequently quote an unseen friend known as Mrs. 'Arris; eventually, her collaborating testimony along with that of a young surgeon named Lewsome helps Mr. Pecksniff's ex-apprentice, John Westlock, expose a scoundrel named Jonas in a plot to poison his father in this Victorian Period novel (1843-1844).

1   **Middlemarch** by George Eliot
2   **Pendennis** by William Makepeace Thackeray
3   **Martin Chuzzlewit** by Charles Dickens

Alan Breck Stewart - this character is the Scottish highlander with a price on his head for rebelling against King George and the one rescued from the sailing ship, the **Covenant**, after his small boat is cut in half off Scotland; eventually, he guides an orphaned teen, David Balfour, to Queens Ferry where the latter petitions a lawyer named Mr. Rankeillor to recover the inheritance stolen from him by his uncle Ebenezer Balfour of Shaw in this Victorian Period novel (1886).

4   **The Virginians** by William Makepeace Thackeray
5   **Rob Roy** by Sir Walter Scott
6   **Kidnapped** by Robert Louis Stevenson

Berta Mason Rochester - this character is the deranged, maniac who secretly occupies the third floor on an estate named **Thornfield** which is owned by her arrogant, pensive husband, Edward, and occupied by an elderly housekeeper, Mrs. Fairfax, Edward's ward, Adele Varens and Adele's governess; eventually, she dies by misadventure in a fire of her own causing when her guard, Gracie Poole, drinks too much and neglects her post in this Victorian Period novel (1847).

7   **Wuthering Heights** by Emily Bronte
8   **Jane Eyre** by Charlotte Bronte
9   **Agnes Grey** by Anne Bronte

3-6-8

Mr. Venus - this character is the good-hearted taxidermist who joins a conniving fruit seller named Silas Wegg in a blackmail scheme involving Nicodemus Boffin and the validity of a will regarding the Harmon fortune; eventually, he regrets being Silas's partner, divulges the conspiracy and has his numerous marriage proposals accepted by an unlicenced pawnbroker named Pleasant Riderhood in this Victorian Period novel (1864-1866).

1   Our Mutual Friend by Charles Dickens
2   The Warden by Anthony Trollope
3   Adam Bede by George Eliot

Monsieur The Marquis St. Evremonde - this character is the sadistic French aristocrat whose speeding coach carelessly kills a boy in the country side; eventually, this uncle of the anti-aristocrat, Charles Darnay, is knifed to death that evening in his chateau by the boy's father, Gaspard, who is in turn hanged for the assassination in this Victorian Period novel (1859).

4   Quentin Durward by Sir Walter Scott
5   A Tale of Two Cities by Charles Dickens
6   Romona by George Eliot

Dr. Strong - this character is the headmaster of a school at Canterbury who enrolls the 10 year-old orphan at the behest of his unconventional, outspoken and generous great aunt, Miss Betsy Trotwood, after she meets and dismisses Edward and Jane Murdstone; eventually, he hires this orphan when he older as a part-timer to compile a classical dictionary when Miss Trotwood has her fortune embezzled by Uriah Heep in this Victorian Period novel (1849-1850).

7   Great Expectations by Charles Dickens
8   A Tale of Two Cities by Charles Dickens
9   David Copperfield by Charles Dickens

1-5-9

<u>Jeremy Stickles</u> - this character is the King's messenger whose life is saved when a gentle farmer named John Ridd warns him of an ambush that the latter had overheard would take place when the former crossed the valley bridge; eventually, he reciprocates and prevents Ridd's execution after John had attempted to rescue a highwayman named Tom Faggus that John's good-natured sister, Annie, loves in this Victorian Period novel (1869).

1	<u>Adam Bede</u> by George Eliot
2	<u>Lorna Doone</u> by Richard D. Blackmore
3	<u>Pendennis</u> by William Makepeace Thackeray

<u>Mr. Tulkinghorn</u> - this character is the unscrupulous lawyer in the employment of Sir Leicester and Lady Dedlock and the one who tries to blackmail Lady Dedlock regarding her illicit affair with Captain Hawson and resulting illegitimate daughter, Esther Summerson; eventually, he is murdered by Lady Dedlock's French maid, Mademoiselle Hortense, when he refuses to pay her blackmailing demands in this Victorian Period novel (1852-1853).

4	<u>Bleak House</u> by Charles Dickens
5	<u>Great Expectations</u> by Charles Dickens
6	<u>A Tale of Two Cities</u> by Charles Dickens

<u>Mortimer Lightwood</u> - this character is the clever lawyer hired by Nicodemus Boffin (Noddy) to reward any information leading to the murderer of Young John Harmon on his homeward voyage from South Africa to marry Bella Wilfer; eventually, he recognizes John Harmon on a London street posing as Bella Wilfer's husband under the guise of John Rokesmith and exposes him in this Victorian Period novel (1864-1866).

7	<u>A Tale of Two Cities</u> by Charles Dickens
8	<u>Dombey and Son</u> by Charles Dickens
9	<u>Our Mutual Friend</u> by Charles Dickens

2-4-9

Mr. Stryver - this character is the narcissistic, arrogant lawyer who defends the anti-aristocratic French expatriate language teacher named Charles Darnay who has been accused by John Barsad of transporting seditious documents between France and England; eventually, he wins the case by showing a close resemblance between his client and a law assistant named Sidney Carton in this Victorian Period novel (1859).

1	Middlemarch by George Eliot
2	A Tale of Two Cities by Charles Dickens
3	The Virginians by William Makepeace Thackeray

Bessie Leaven - this character is the volatile nurse/governess at Gateshead Hall whose charges include Mrs. Reed's three spoiled children and an orphan named Jane who suffers ten years of abuse and deprivation there; eventually, she develops a certain fondness for this imaginative little girl and shows her compassion until Mrs. Reed sends her off to Lowood School followed by employment by Edward Rochester at the estate of Thornfield in this Victorian Period novel (1847).

4	Wuthering Heights by Emily Bronte
5	Jane Eyre by Charlotte Bronte
6	Agnes Grey by Anne Bronte

Mrs. Proudie - this character is the domineering wife of a political appointee and successor of the late Dr. Grantly whose bishopric encompasses a fictional cathedral town in the West of England; eventually, her Low Church inclinations and dealings with a conniving chaplin named Rev. Obadiah Slope are undermined when her husband indirectly appoints Mr. Quiverful to be the new Warden of Hiram Hospital over Reverend Septimus Harding in this Victorian Period novel (1857).

7	The Warden by Anthony Trollope
8	Orley Farm by Anthony Trollope
9	Barchester Towers by Anthony Trollope

2-5-9

<u>David Balfour</u> - this character is the Scottish orphan whose journey to see his diabolic uncle, Ebenezer Balfour of Shaw, is interrupted when he is shanghaied aboard the <u>Covenant</u> which sinks after hitting   coastal reefs; eventually, he is guided by a Scottish Highlander, Alan Breck Stewart, to petitions a lawyer, Mr. Rankeillor, so he can recover his stolen inheritance in this Victorian Period novel (1886).

1   <u>Kidnapped</u> by Robert Louis Stevenson
2   <u>Rob Roy</u> by Sir Walter Scott
3   <u>Far From the Madding Crowd</u> by Thomas Hardy

<u>Jerry Cruncher</u> - this character is the English porter who works during the day at the Franco-British banking house of Tellson and Company and robs graves at night; eventually, he assists a law clerk named Sidney Carton in threatening to expose a former English spy, Solomon Pross acting under the alias John Barsad, and helps free the imprisoned Charles Darnay from the Bastille in this Victorian Period novel (1859).

4   <u>Quentin Durward</u> by Sir Walter Scott
5   <u>Tess of the D'Umbervilles</u> by Thomas Hardy
6   <u>A Tale of Two Cities</u> by Charles Dickens

<u>Allan Quartermain</u> - this character is the practical, cost-conscious explorer, hunter and adventurer who joins retiree army captain John Good, and his friend, Sir Henry Curtis, in a search of the latter's missing brother, George, who had changed his name to Neville after a family argument over their father's will; eventually, his travels bring him into contact with a Hottentot named Ventuogel, Zulus named Umbopa and Khiva, and villains named Twala, Scragga and Gogool in this Victorian Period novel (1886).

7   <u>Consuelo</u> by George Sand
8   <u>Moonstone</u> by Wilkie Collins
9   <u>King Solomon's Mines</u> by H. Rider Haggard

1-6-9

<u>Clara Peggotty</u> - this character is the corpulent, good natured loyal servant and nurse for a young, naive, widow who is also named Clara and has a young sensitive boy who ultimately looked after by his grand aunt, Miss Betsy Trotwood after he is orphaned; eventually, her dismissal by the miserly, sadistic Edward Murdstone after her mistress dies results in her marriage to the bashful suitor and wagon driver, Mr. Barkis in this Victorian Period novel (1849-1850).

1   <u>Great Expectations</u> by Charles Dickens
2   <u>A Tale of Two Cities</u> by Charles Dickens
3   <u>David Copperfield</u> by Charles Dickens

<u>Professor Bhaer</u> - this character is the charming, unconventional   German tutor who meets a tall governess named Jo who is working for Mrs. Kirke in the New York City boarding house where he is staying; eventually, he marries her after she calls off her intended marriage with a rich neighbor named Laurie and they establish a boy's school in the small cozy house known as <u>Plumfield</u> which had been inherited from her mother, Marmee in this Victorian Period novel (1868-1869).

4   <u>Consuelo</u> by George Sand
5   <u>Little Women</u> by Louisa May Alcott
6   <u>Seventeen</u> by Booth Tarkington

<u>Tom Faggus</u> - this character is the handsome blacksmith whose ruination by a lawsuit that parallels the decadence of the Doone family results in his drinking and life as a daring highwayman who finally joins the rebels against the King of England; eventually, he is rescued by John Ridd and the King's messenger, Master Jeremy Stickles, and marries John's good-natured sister, Annie, and settles down to a life of sobriety and respectability in this Victorian Period novel (1869).

7   Thomas Hardy
8   George Eliot
9   Richard D. Blackmore

3-5-9

Dorothea Brooke (Dodo) - this character is the serious young Englishwoman who realizes too late that she is incompatible with her gloomy and severe, middle-aged scholarly, pompous husband, Rev. Edward Casaubon; eventually, she forgoes Casaubon's fortune, marrys a impulsive artist/political thinker named   Will Ladislaw, moves to London where her husband is elected to Parliament and reconciles with family after a son is born in this Victorian Period novel (1871-1872).

1   **Middlemarch** by George Eliot
2   **Romola** by George Eliot
3   **Adam Bede** by George Eliot

Marius Pontmercy - this character is the young destitute attorney whose exile from his Royalist grandfather's wealth stems from his liberal Napoleonic views leads him to an avaricious, greedy man named Trenardier; eventually, he learns from this scoundrel renamed Jondrette that it was Cosette's father through adoption, Jean Valjean, who had been his rescuer from sure death at the barricades in this Victorian Period novel (1862).

4   **Salammbo** by Gustave Flaubert
5   **Les Miserables** by Victor Hugo
6   **Under Two Flags** by Ouida (Marie Louise de la Ramee)

Nana - this character is the beautiful, young Parisian courtesan/actress who seduces rich and poor suitors such as the wealthy banker, Monsieur Steiner, George and Philippe, the brutal actor, Fontan, and the pious aristocrat, Comte Muffat de Blauville; eventually, her financial and sexual swings reduce her to from streetwalking to acquiring a new mansion, new lovers and then fatally contracting smallpox in this Victorian Period novel (1880).

7   Gustave Flaubert
8   Victor Hugo
9   Emile Zola

1-5-9

Laura Bell - this character is the bright orphaned daughter of Rev. Francis Bell who is adopted by a former suitor, Helen Thistlewood, after she has married an apothecary/surgeon and had a young son named Arthur; eventually, she watches Arthur get over his crush on an actress, Emily Costigan, twelve years his senior, undergoes academic and financial failure and then happily marries him in this Victorian Period novel (1848-1850).

1   The Mayor of Casterbridge by Thomas Hardy
2   Romola by George Eliot
3   Pendennis by William Makepeace Thackeray

Lord Warburton - this character is the young English nobleman whose visit to the Touchett's family estate, Gardencourt, allows him to meet a visiting 23 year-old American heiress, Isabel Archer; eventually, he joins Caspar Goodwood in losing her hand to a egotistical aesthete named George Osmond in this Victorian Period novel (1881).

4   Daisy Miller by Henry James
5   The Portrait of a Lady by Henry James
6   The American by Henry James

Quilp - this character is the grotesque-looking, deranged dwarf who lends money to Little Nell's degenerate gambler grandfather so that he can ultimately marry 14 year-old Little Nell; eventually, he drowns in the Thames River while fleeing the police after being warned by Sally Brass in this Victorian Period novel (1848).

7   The Moonstone by Wilkie Collins
8   The Old Curiosity Shop by Charles Dickens
9   Orley Farm by Anthony Trollope

3-5-8

<u>Solomon Pross</u> - this character is the villainous brother who bilks his sisters entire savings and abandons her while she continues to be the loyal servant of Doctor and Lucie Manette that she has been from the latter's childhood; eventually, he becomes the English spy, John Basard, who informs Madame Defarge that Charles Darnay has married Lucie Manette in this Victorian Period novel (1859).

1   <u>Pendennis</u> by William Makepeace Thackeray
2   <u>Far From the Madding Crowd</u> by Thomas Hardy
3   <u>A Tale of Two Cities</u> by Charles Dickens

<u>Natasha Rostov</u> - this character is the determined, self-sufficient Russian princess who is secretly engaged to Prince Audrey Bolkonsky until Helene's unsavory brother, Anatole, unsuccessfully attempts to have a defrocked priest perform a sham wedding as part of an elopement; eventually, she is forgiven by a fatally wounded Audrey and marries Pierre Bezhov in this Victorian Period novel (1865-1869).

4   <u>The Possessed</u> By Fyodor Dostoevski
5   <u>The Gambler</u> by Fyodor Dostoevski
6   <u>War and Peace</u> by Count Leo Tolstoy

<u>Simonides</u> - this character is the former servant of an eminent Jewish family and the one who becomes a prosperous merchant in Antioch while acting as an agent for his dead master; eventually, his daughter, Esther, marries his dead master's young son who had become rich again after being rewarded for saving the life of a Roman official named Quintus Arrius during a sea battle in this Victorian Period novel (1880).

7   <u>The Antiquary</u> by Sir Walter Scott
8   <u>Ben Hur: The Tale of the Christ</u> by Lew Wallace
9   <u>The Heart of Midlothian</u> by Sir Walter Scott

3-6-8

John Jarndyce - this character is the single, mellowing proprietor of an ancestral home and the charitable protector of two wards named Ada Clare and Richard Carstone alone with their orphaned companion, Esther Summerson; eventually, he releases Esther from her marriage promise so she can marry a humane surgeon named Allan Woodcourt in this Victorian Period novel (1852-1853).

1	Bleak House by Charles Dickens
2	Coningsby by Benjamin Disraeli
3	The Ordeal of Richard Feveral by George Meredith

Dounia - this character is the beautiful, discerning younger sister of the penniless, young law student named Rodion Raskolnikov who is finally tricked into confessing to the axe murders of two sisters; eventually, she marries her publishing partner, Razumihin, after thwarting the advances of Luzhin and receiving a large sum of money from Svidrigailov who ultimately commits suicide in this Victorian Period novel (1866).

4	Fathers and Sons by Ivan Turgenev
5	Crime and Punishment by Fyodor Dostoevski
6	Dead Souls by Nikolai V. Gogol

Miss Betsy Trotwood - this character is the unconventional, outspoken and generous great aunt who becomes the last resort of an impoverished 10 year-old orphan who has run away from being overworked and unfed; eventually, this benefactor provides for his education and lives to see him marry Agnes Wickfield and starting a literary career after burying his first wife Dora in this Victorian Period novel (1849-1850).

7	Great Expectations by Charles Dickens
8	Bleak House by Charles Dickens
9	David Copperfield by Charles Dickens

1-5-9

<u>Bazaroff</u> - this character is the young, nihilist doctor who goes home with a fellow graduate named Arkady to meet his father, Kirsanoff, his father's new mistress, Fenichka, and their son; eventually, this arrogant guest suffers the humiliation from Arkady's choice of Katya over Madame Odintzoff and dies after   contracting typhus from one of his patients in this Victorian Period novel (1862).

1   <u>The Brothers Karamazov</u> by Fyodor Dostoevski
2   <u>Dead Souls</u> by Nicholai V. Gogol
3   <u>Fathers and Sons</u> by Ivan Turgenev

<u>Mr. Holgrave</u> - this character is the progressive-minded, young boarder who lives with Hepzibah Clifford and young Phoebe Pyncheon until Judge Jafrey Pyncheon fulfills Matthew Maule's curse and dies drowning in his own blood; eventually, he reveals his true identity as a Maule descendent and marries his young vivacious distant cousin, Phoebe, who successfully runs the little cent-shop on the premises in this Victorian Period novel (1851).

4   <u>A Connecticut Yankee in King Arthur's Court</u> by Mark Twain
5   <u>The House of the Seven Gables</u> by Nathaniel Hawthorne
6   <u>Washington Square</u> by Henry James

<u>Johnny Nonsuch</u> - this character is the young boy from Egdon Heath who stays with Eustacia Vye and her holiday bonfire company on Mistover Knap until she keeps a secret rendevous with an engineer turned owner of the <u>Quiet Woman Inn</u>, Damon Wildeve; eventually, he tells Diggory Venn about this meeting and later informs Clym Yeobright's about his mother's dying words regarding his wife, Eustacia, in this Victorian Period novel (1878).

7   <u>Far From the Madding Crowd</u> by Thomas Hardy
8   <u>The Return of the Native</u> by Thomas Hardy
9   <u>Jude the Obscure</u> by Thomas Hardy

3-5-8

<u>Mr. Creakle</u> - this character is the harsh headmaster of an inferior school named <u>Salem House</u> where students Tom Traddles and James Steerforth are newly joined by a young sensitive boy sent there by his miserly, sadistic stepfather, Mr. Edward Murdstone; eventually, this bully leaves <u>Salem House</u> and takes a new position in a model prison where the forger Uriah Heep and the pervert, Littimer, are inmates in this Victorian Period novel (1849-1850).

1	<u>Great Expectations</u> by Charles Dickens
2	<u>Bleak House</u> by Charles Dickens
3	<u>David Copperfield</u> by Charles Dickens

<u>Godrey Cass</u> - this character is the wealthy, morally weak landowner who waits 16 years before telling his wife, Nancy, that he had married a drug addicted commoner named Molly in a faraway hamlet and she had died in the snow from an overdose leaving behind an unacknowledged daughter named Eppie; eventually, his generous offer to reunite with his daughter is rebuffed when she decides to marry Aaron Winthrop and care for the aging weaver who adopted her this Victorian Period novel (1861).

4	<u>Agnes Grey</u> by Anne Bronte
5	<u>Silas Marner</u> by George Eliot
6	<u>Consuelo</u> by George Sand

<u>Miss Pross</u> - this character is the loyal servant of Dr. Manette and his daughter Lucie and the victimized sister of a villain named Solomon who becomes an English spy with the alias, John Basard, after he bilks his sister's entire savings and abandons her; eventually, she kills Madame Defarge with her own pistol during a fight between them in this Victorian Period novel (1859).

7	<u>Les Miserables</u> by Victor Hugo
8	<u>Far From the Madding Crowd</u> by Thomas Hardy
9	<u>A Tale of Two Cities</u> by Charles Dickens

3-5-9

<u>Cardinal Richelieu</u> - this character is the Chief Minister of the timid French king, Louis XIII, and the one who wants to outs the king's Queen, Anne of Austria, by exposing her love affair with the English Duke of Buckingham; eventually, his employ of such sinister characters as Lady de Winter and Chevalier de Rochefort are no match for the bravery of Athos, Aramis, Porthos and D'Artagnan in this Victorian Period novel (1844).

1	<u>The Three Musketeers</u> by Alexander Dumas, Sr.
2	<u>The Count of Monte-Cristo</u> by Alexander Dumas, Sr.
3	<u>Camille</u> by Alexander Dumas, Jr.

<u>Ben Gunn</u> - this character is the half-crazed pirate whose marooning for three years by Captain Flint of the ship, the <u>Hispaniola</u>, is ended when the <u>Hispaniola</u> returns with Captain Smollett, Squire Trelawney, Dr. Livesey, Long John Silver, Jim Hawkins and seamen who are both loyal and mutineers; eventually, he escapes aboard the <u>Hispaniola</u> and returns to England in this Victorian Period novel (1883).

4	<u>Kidnapped</u> by Robert Louis Stevenson
5	<u>Treasure Island</u> Robert Louis Stevenson
6	<u>The Master of Ballantrae</u> by Robert Louis Stevenson

<u>Corilla</u> - this character is the lead singer at the theater of Count Zustiniani who is replaced by another student who also studied under the music teacher, Niccolo Antonio Porpora; eventually, the no-talent musician, Anzoleto, who secures her replacement position as lead singer finally impregnates her and deserts her after leaving her with an illegitimate child in this Victorian Period novel (1842).

7	<u>Under Two Flags</u> by Ouida
8	<u>Consuelo</u> by George Sand (Mme. Aurora Dudevant)
9	<u>Romola</u> by George Eliot (Mary Anne Evans)

Silas Wegg - this character is the conniving fruit seller who is hired by a confidential clerk named Nicodemus Boffin to read books to him after the Boffins inherit the Harmon fortune; eventually, his failure at blackmail of Nicodemus with a taxidermist named Mr. Venus has him summarily fired and dumped into a wagon filled with garbage by a household servant in this Victorian Period novel (1864-1866).

1	**Great Expectations** by Charles Dickens
2	**Our Mutual Friend** by Charles Dickens
3	**A Tale of Two Cities** by Charles Dickens

Emma Rouault - this character is the romantically fickle french peasant girl whose marriage to a mediocre country doctor drives her into illicit affairs with Rodolphe Bourlanger and Leon Dupuis; eventually, her indebtedness lead her into public disgrace to where she is found by her husband, Charles, dying from ingested arsenic from Justin at Homais's chemist shop in this Victorian Period novel (1857).

4	**Pere Goriot** by Honore de Balzac
5	**The Red and the Black** by Stendhal
6	**Madame Bovary** by Gustave Flaubert

Governor Bellingham - this character is the Governor of Boston who is visited by the main character under the pretext of delivering a pair of embroidered gloves; eventually, the true nature of her visit (to retain custody of her illegitimate daughter) is revealed in this Victorian Period novel (1850).

7	**Silas Marner** by George Eliot
8	**The Scarlet Letter** by Nathaniel Hawthorne
9	**The American** by Henry James

<u>Monsieur Homais</u> - this character is the pretentious, shallow town chemist who propounds a very superficial philosophy of life and constantly uses cliches in his speech while hypocritically sprouting cursory ideals; eventually, his reputation remains intact while a mediocre doctor named Charles loses patients when their attempt to cure a boy's clubfoot fails, gangrene sets in and the boy's leg must be amputated in this Victorian Period novel (1857).

<u>Madame Bovary</u> by Gustave Flaubert

2   <u>The Charterhouse of Parma</u> by Stendhal

3   <u>Salammbo</u> by Gustave Flaubert

<u>Master Reuben Huckabuck</u> - this character is the grand-uncle of a gentle, robust farmer named John Ridd and the one who escapes the fate of his dead brother after being attacked and robbed by the decadent outlaw family known as the Doones; eventually, his futile attempt of offering a gold mine to John Ridd upon his marriage to the former's granddaughter, Ruth, are met with John's marriage to Lorna Doone in this Victorian Period novel (1869).

4   George Eliot

5   William Makepeace Thackeray

6   Richard D. Blackmore

<u>Mrs. Fairfax</u> - this character is the elderly housekeeper at Edward Rochester's estate, <u>Thornfield</u>, and the one responsible for hiring a governess to teach art and music to the owner's illegitimate daughter and ward, Adele Varens; eventually, she lives long enough to see that governess marry her master, Edward, after his deranged wife, Bertha, dies by misadventure when she burns down <u>Thornfield</u> in this Victorian Period novel (1847).

7   <u>Wuthering Heights</u> by Emily Bronte

8   <u>Jane Eyre</u> by Charlotte Bronte

9   <u>Agnes Grey</u> by Anne Bronte

1-6-8

M. Nioche - this character is the aging French shopkeeper who meets an American businessman named Christopher Newman after the latter met his daughter, Mlle. Nioche, in the Louvre; eventually,   he gives French lessons to this American while his daughter provides a number of copies of works that she had painted at the Louvre in this Victorian Period novel (1877).

1	The Ambassadors by Henry James
2	Daisy Miller by Henry James
3	The American by Henry James

Thomasin Yeobright - this character is the guileless, young woman from Egdon Heath who marries the former engineer turned owner of the Quiet Woman Inn, Damon Wildeve, after he is rejected by Eustacia Vye for Clym Yeobright; eventually, she remarries a red dye salesman turned dairyman named Diggory Venn after Damon and Eustacia are found dead from drowning in a small lake in this Victorian Period novel (1875).

4	The Return of the Native by Thomas Hardy
5	Tess of the D'Umbervilles by Thomas Hardy
6	The Mayor of Casterbridge by Thomas Hardy

Grushenka - this character is the wild Russian seductress whose enticing extended beyond Katrina's Ivanovna's fiancé, Dimitri, and his lecherous, shrewd old father, Fyodor, to a 19 year-old future monk named Alexey; eventually, she joins Alexey at Dimitri's hospital bedside and witnesses Katrina's plea for Dmitri's forgiveness over the latter that convicted him in this Victorian Period novel (1880).

7	The Gambler by Fyodor Dostoevski
8	The Brothers Karamazov by Fyodor Dostoevski
9	The Possessed by Fyodor Dostoevski

3-4-8

<u>Colonel Morgan</u> - this character is the no-nonsense judge who imposes a harsh sentence against an arrogant Texas army officer named Philip Nolan who is convicted in a treasonous conspiracy fostered by Aaron Burr to overthrow President James Madison; eventually, his sentencing of this brash young man to unequivocal ostracization in an army uniform with plain buttons ends years later when a sympathetic ship's captain chooses to update him on past and current events in this Victorian Period novel (1863).

1   <u>The Red Badge of Courage</u> by Stephen Crane
2   <u>The Man Without A Country</u> by Edward Everett Hale
3   <u>Arrowsmith</u> by Sinclair Lewis

<u>Laurie</u> - this character is the rich, lonely neighbor who had grown up with the March family and had a long standing and implicit engagement with their tall, awkward and artistic tomboy daughter, Jo; eventually, he rebounds from Jo's jilting him and ends up marrying her younger sister, Amy, whom he had met in Europe while he was traveling with his grandfather and she was on vacation with a distant aunt named Carroll in this Victorian Period novel (1868-1869).

4   <u>Little Women</u> by Louisa May Alcott
5   <u>Consuelo</u> by George Sand
6   <u>Seventeen</u> by Booth Tarkington

<u>Jim</u> - this character is the superstitious, slave of Miss Watson whose chance encounter with a young boy on Jackson's Island leads to a number of adventures, one of which involves joining up with two confidence men known as the King and the Duke; eventually, he discovers the 50 year-old town drunk dead in a flooded boat on the Mississippi and ultimately receives his freedom in Miss Watson's will in this Victorian Period novel (1885).

7   <u>Huckleberry Finn</u> by Mark Twain
8   <u>Tobacco Road</u> by Erskine Caldwell
9   <u>Tom Sawyer</u> by Mark Twain

2-4-7

Smerdyakov - this character is the mocking, epileptic illegitimate son of a lecherous, shrewd old businessman named Fyodor and the moronic half-brother of Dmitri, Ivan and Alexey; eventually, his intense hate as this father's servant drives him to murder and rob his father, confess this murder to his step-brother Ivan and then commit suicide by hanging himself in this Victorian Period novel (1880).

1	The Brothers Karamazov by Fyodor Dostoevski
2	The Possessed by Fyodor Dostoevski
3	The Gambler by Fyodor Dostoevski

James Carker - this character is the villainous business manager whose intermediary exchanges between the austere, pretentious London merchant who employs him and the latter's disgusted second wife, the former Mrs. Edith Granger, results in a tryst; eventually, he is accidentally killed by a train while avoiding a confrontation with his ex-employer on a countryside train station in this Victorian Period novel (1846-1848).

4	Dombey and Son by Charles Dickens
5	Far From the Madding Crowd by Thomas Hardy
6	Adam Bede by George Eliot

Pyotr Verhovensky - this character is the utterly despicable, nihilistic revolutionary bent on destruction who is born of a one-time liberal university professor turned tutor named Stepan; eventually, his sinister and fanatical behavior allows him to corrupt his friend, Nikolay Stavrogin, undermine his father's relationship with Varvara Petrovna Stavrogin and stir up political local unrest and terrorism in this Victorian Period novel (1867).

7	The Brothers Karamazov by Fyodor Dostoevski
8	The Idiot by Fyodor Dostoevski
9	The Possessed by Fyodor Dostoevski

<u>Captain Cuttle</u> - this character is the old ship's captain and loyal partner of Sol Gills in a nautical instrument shop who recognizes young Florence when she seeks safe haven from an austere London merchant who is her father; eventually, his protection allows her to ultimately enter into marriage with a prosperous clerk named Walter Cay and have a son named Paul in this Victorian Period novel (1846-1848).

1	<u>Dombey and Son</u> by Charles Dickens
2	<u>The Virginians</u> by William Makepeace Thackeray
3	<u>Middlemarch</u> by George Eliot

<u>Doctor Livesey</u> - this character is the local physician in remote Black Hill Cove whose visit to the <u>Admiral Benbow Inn</u> to treat young Jim Hawkins' father leads him to reproach an old, intimidating seaman named Bill Bones; eventually, his adventures on the Spanish Main with Squire Trelawney, Jim and Long John Silver result in ultimate victory over a number of pirates in this Victorian Period novel (1883).

4	<u>Kidnapped</u> by Robert Louis Stevenson
5	<u>The Master of Ballantrae</u> by Robert Louis Stevenson
6	<u>Treasure Island</u> by Robert Louis Stevenson

<u>Alexey Ivanovitch</u> - this character is the young, insolvent Russian nobleman who tutors and ultimately falls in love with an aristocratic, decadent Russian General's step-daughter, Polina, in the German resort town of Roulteenburg; eventually, his degenerate gambling continues even afer his is fired by the General, discarded by a French adventuress named Mll. Blanche and told by the English businessman, Mr. Astley, that Polina forgives him while laying ill in Switzerland in this Victorian Period novel (1866).

7	Ivan Turgenev
8	Fyodor Dostoevski
9	Nikolai V. Gogol

1-6-8

<u>Prof. Pierre Aronimax</u> - this character is a professor at the Paris Museum of Natural History who heads an expedition aboard the American frigate, <u>Abraham Lincoln</u>, to track down a mysterious creature that has attacked and sank ships all over the world; eventually, his encounter with an unusual underwater craft of the future find him and his companions on a Norwegian island after a violent whirlpool almost kills them in this Victorian Period novel (1870).

1	<u>The Count of Monte-Cristo</u> by Alexander Dumas, Sr.
2	<u>Swiss Family Robinson</u> by Johann Rudolf Wyss
3	<u>Twenty Thousand Leagues Under The Sea</u> by Jules Verne

<u>Long John Silver</u> - this character is the one-legged, middle-aged proprietor of a pub ho owns a parrot named Captain Flint and <u>Hispaniola</u> the seaman who is hired as a cook aboard a ship known as the   commissioned by Squire Trelawney and Dr. Livesey; eventually, he becomes entangled in a number of adventures involving Jim Hawkins, Ben Gunn and a group of pirates while in a part of the Caribbean Sea known as the Spanish Main in this Victorian Period novel (1883).

4	<u>Kidnapped</u> by Robert Louis Stevenson
5	<u>Treasure Island</u> by Robert Louis Stevenson
6	<u>Kidnapped</u> by Robert Louis Stevenson

<u>Pap</u> - this character is the 50 year-old town drunk who visits his son's room at the Widow Douglas's house after he learns that his son had come into a large amount of found money; eventually, the slave, Jim, discovers him dead in a flooded boat sometime after his son had escaped being kidnapped, held and beaten in a cabin in the woods in this Victorian Period novel (1876).

7	<u>Babbitt</u> by Sinclair Lewis
8	<u>Huckleberry Finn</u> by Mark Twain
9	<u>Winesburg, Ohio</u> by Sherwood Anderson

3-5-8

<u>Rev. Edward Casaubon</u> - this character is the dull, scholarly middle-aged clergyman who marries an earnest, mannerly young Englishwoman named Dorothea Brooke (Dodo) who later falls in love with his cousin, Will Ladislaw; eventually, his suspicious nature prompts him to add a codicil to his will regarding his fortune which the two lovers dismiss when they finally marry in this Victorian Period novel (1871-1872).

1	<u>Esther Wathers</u> by George Moore
2	<u>Penguin Island</u> by Anatole France
3	<u>Middlemarch</u> by George Eliot

<u>Helena Landless</u> - this character is the English orphan who travels from Ceylon with her brother, Neville, to Cloisterham, England; eventually, she enters a finishing school, becomes friends with Rosa Bud and watches her brother fall in love with Rosa while he is suspected of murdering the opium-addicted choirmaster Jack Jasper's mining engineer nephew in this unfinished Victorian Period novel (1870).

4	<u>The Egoist</u> by George Meredith
5	<u>The Mystery of Edwin Drood</u> by Charles Dickens
6	<u>Adam Bede</u> by George Eliot

<u>Joseph (Jo) Sedley</u> - this character is the overweight, foppish English civil servant in India who meets his future wife, Becky Sharp, after his sweet-tempered sister, Amelia, becomes her schoolmate and best friend at Miss Pinkerton's finishing school for girls; eventually, his life insurance makes her a wealthy widow on the Continent after is death at Aix-la-Chapelle remains inexplicable in this Victorian Period novel (1847-1848).

7	<u>The Enormous Room</u> by E.E. Cummings
8	<u>The Moon and Sixpence</u> by William Somerset Maugham
9	<u>Vanity Fair</u> by William Makepeace Thackeray

137

Mr. Quiverful - this character is the amiable Low Churchman candidate by the newly appointed Bishop's wife, Mrs. Proudie, to be the next Warden at Hiram Hospital after the Reverend Septimus Harding in the fictional cathedral town in the West of England; eventually, this father of fourteen is appointed by Dr. Proudie while the Rev. Francis Arabin is appointed Dean of the Cathedral before marrying Mrs. Eleanor Bold in this Victorian Period novel (1857).

1	Barchester Towers by Anthony Trollope
2	Orley Farm by Anthony Trollope
3	The Warden by Anthony Trollope

Captain William Dobbin - this character is the English army officer whose relationship with George Osbourne, brings him in contact with two schoolmates from Miss Pinkerton's finishing school for girls, the sweet-tempered Amelia Sedley and the scheming, narcissistic Becky Sharp; eventually, his marriage to Amelia which produces a daughter named Jane occurs only after her first husband, George Osbourne, dies at Waterloo in this Victorian Period novel (1847-1848).

4	Pendennis by William Makepeace Thackeray
5	Vanity Fair by William Makepeace Thackeray
6	The Virginianss by William Makepeace Thackeray

John Harmon - this character is the young London aristocrat who is almost murdered by George Radfoot on his homeward voyage from South Africa and the one who disguises himself as Julius Handford until he assumes a the new identity of John Rokesmith when he becomes a secretary for the Boffins; eventually, his marriage to Bella Wifer and the birth of their child is exposed by the lawyer, Mortimer Lightwood in this Victorian Period novel (1864-1866).

7	Our Mutual Friend by Charles Dickens
8	The Forsythe Saga by John Galsworthy
9	The Man Who Was Thursday by G.K. Chesterson

The Marquis de Bellegarde (Urbain) - this character is the older son of the aristocrat, Madame de Bellegarde, and older brother of the widowed Claire de Cintre and Valentin; eventually, he joins forces with his mother in manipulating an American businessman named Christopher Newman into destroying damaging evidence of a murder in this Victorian Period novel (1877).

1	**A Portait of a Lady** by Henry James
2	**The Wings of the Dove** by Henry James
3	**The American** by Henry James

Natasya Filipovna - this character is the young, attractive Russian harlot whose part in a love triangle involving an epileptic named Prince Myshkin and a spoiled beauty named Aglaya Epanchin, is further complicated by Parfen Rogozhin's interest in her; eventually, she jilts Prince Myshkin on their wedding day only to be murdered in a jealous rage by her new lover, Parafen Rogozhin in this Victorian Period novel (1868).

4	**The Brothers Karamozov** by Fyodor Dostoevski
5	**The Idiot** by Fyodor Dostoevski
6	**The Possessed** by Fyodor Dostoevski

Mr. Crisparkle - this character is the minor official at Cloisterham Cathedral and tutor of Neville Landless and the one who attempts unsuccessfully to bond his new student with a mining engineer and the latter's opium-addicted choirmaster uncle, Jack Jasper; eventually, he helps his student to hide out in London after the latter is accused of the young engineer's murder in this unfinished English Victorian Period novel (1870).

7	**Goodbye Mr. Chips** by James Hilton
8	**The Mystery of Edwin Drood** by Charles Dickens
9	**Secret Agent** by Joseph Conrad

3-5-8

<u>Bathsheba Everdene</u> - this character is the young, capricious vain and beautiful inheritor of <u>Weatherbury Farm</u> who is pursued romantically with her farm manager, Gabriel Oak, a sergeant in the dragoons, Francis Troy and a well-to-do neighbor, William Boldwood; eventually, she marries Gabriel Oak after William Boldwood shoots Francis Troy in the chest at a Christmas party in this Victorian Period novel (1874).

1	<u>Far From the Madding Crowd</u> by Thomas Hardy
2	<u>Tess of the D'Umbervilles</u> by Thomas Hardy
3	<u>Jude the Obscure</u> by Thomas Hardy

<u>Rosa Bud</u> - this character is the young English woman whose release from a prearranged, parental engagement with a young engineer allows her to pursue her new love interest, Neville Landless; eventually, she is blackmailed by a an opium-addicted choirmaster named Jack Jasper because of his unrequited love for her and subsequent jealousy of her boyfriend, Neville Landless, in this unfinished English Victorian Period novel (1870).

4	<u>Nostromo</u> by Joseph Conrad
5	<u>The Time Machine</u> by H.G. Wells
6	<u>The Mystery of Edwin Drood</u> by Charles Dickens

<u>Mlle. Nioche</u> - this character is the unconcerned Parisian artist whose copies of the painting in the Louvre attracts the attention of an American businessman named Christopher Newman while he is traveling Europe in search of a wife; eventually, she brings about the death of young Valentin Bellegarde when he enters a duel to defend her honor in this Victorian Period novel (1877).

7	<u>Daisy Miller</u> by Henry James
8	<u>The American</u> by Henry James
9	<u>The Turn of the Screw</u> by Henry James

1-6-8

<u>Fanny Robin</u> - this character is the pretty, young maid working at Bathsheba Everdene's farm, <u>Weatherbury Farm</u>, who is jilted by a sergeant of the Dragoons named Francis Troy; eventually, she and her new baby die due to impoverished living conditions and their bodies are subsequently claimed by Bathsheba and returned to the farm in this Victorian Period novel (1874).

1	<u>Jude the Obscure</u> by Thomas Hardy
2	<u>The Return of the Native</u> by Thomas Hardy
3	<u>Far From the Madding Crowd</u> by Thomas Hardy

<u>Arthur</u> - this character is the 16 year-old young Englishman whose infatuation with an actress twelve years his senior, Emily Costigan with the stage name, Miss Foheringay, horrifies his permissive mother, Helen, to distraction; eventually, he recovers from this crush after his mother summons his returned English army namesake uncle from a London club and this guardian gets him elected to Parliament and a successful marriage with Laura Bell in this Victorian Period novel (1848-1850).

4	<u>Vanity Fair</u> by William Makepeace Thackeray
5	<u>Pendennis</u> by William Makepeace Thackeray
6	<u>The Virginians</u> by William Makepeace Thackeray

<u>Lady Dugal</u> - this character is the beautiful 17 year-old ward of Sir Ensor Doone whose affectionate disposition attracts the attention of a gentle, robust farmer from Exmoor named John Ridd eventhough her family is responsible for the death of his father; eventually, her wound during her wedding ceremony to John Ridd is avenged along with John's father's death when John kills the brutal and jealous Carver Doone at <u>Wizard's Slough</u> in this Victorian Period novel (1869).

7	Robert Louis Stevenson
8	William Makepeace Thackeray
9	Richard D. Blackmore

3-5-9

<u>Hester Sorrel (Hetty)</u> - this character is the young niece of Martin Poyser whose unrequited love for Captain Arthur Donnithorne leads to an engagement to a young, intelligent and robust carpenter and the murder of Arthur's illegitimate child; eventually, she dies returning home to Hayslope after fulfilling her deportation which replaced her public hanging after Arthur secured a pardon for her in this Victorian Period novel (1859).

1   <u>Adam Bede</u> by George Eliot
2   <u>Consuelo</u> by George Sand
3   <u>The Egoist</u> by George Meredith

<u>Secundra Dass</u> - this character is the servant acquired by a Scotsman named James Durie in India after the latter arrived there aboard a smuggler's ship and made his fortune; eventually, his attempted deception of James's younger brother, Henry, by burying his master in a shallow grave employing suspended animation backfires because of the cold climate of the American wilderness in this Victorian Period novel (1889).

4   <u>Kidnapped</u> by Robert Louis Stevenson
5   <u>Treasure Island</u> by Robert Louis Stevenson
6   <u>The Master of Ballantrae</u> by Robert Louis Stevenson

<u>Nadgett</u> - this character is the landlord of an unassuming tenant named Tom Pinch and the one who is hired by Montague Tigg to be a private investigator on the trail of a coarse hustler named Jonas; eventually, his discovery that his employer did not return from a countryside trip with Jonas leads him to surmise that Jonas had murdered Montague while they were away in this Victorian Period novel (1843-1844).

7   <u>A Tale of Two Cities</u> by Charles Dickens
8   <u>Martin Chuzzlewit</u> by Charles Dickens
9   <u>Great Expectations</u> by Charles Dickens

1-6-8

<u>Dr. Tertius Lydgate</u> - this character is the ambitious young doctor who arrives in an English town with goals to establish a new hospital and do scientific research only to have his idealistic plans ruined by debts due to spendthrift wife formerly known as Rosamond Vincy; eventually, his plight is salvaged when Nicholas Bulstrode gives him a loan, Dorothea Brooke supports his hospital and Rosamond watches her spending in this Victorian Period novel (1871-1872).

1   <u>Adam Bede</u> by George Eliot
2   <u>Middlemarch</u> by George Eliot
3   <u>Romola</u> by George Eliot

<u>Edith Granger</u> - this character is the young, cold disillusioned widow who is introduced by a retired officer named Major Bagstock to an austere, pretentious widowed London merchant with two children named Florence and Paul;   eventually, she avenges herself on her pompous husband by having a tryst with his villainous business manager, Mr. Carker, who has been sent as an intermediary by his employer in this Victorian Period novel (1846-1848).

4   <u>Dombey and Son</u> by Charles Dickens
5   <u>Great Expectations</u> by Charles Dickens
6   <u>A Tale of Two Cities</u> by Charles Dickens

<u>Anzoleto</u> - this character is the no-talent musician who secures a lead singer position for his betrothed at the theater of Count Zustiniani at the expense of lead singer, Corilla; eventually, he impregnates this former lead singer and student of Niccolo Antonia Porpora, and deserts her after leaving her with an illegitimate child in this Victorian Period novel (1842).

7   <u>Consuelo</u> by George Sand (Mme. Aurora Dudevant)
8   <u>Silas Marner</u> by George Eliot (Mary Anne Evans)
9   <u>Under Two Flags</u> by Ouida

2-4-7

<u>Rosa Dartle</u> - this character is the older companion and obsessive lover of a good-looking scoundrel named James Steerforth whose past hot temper leaves her with a lifetime scar along with memories of other humiliations after he jilts her for Little Em'ly; eventually, her jilting by this rogue is avenged when his plans to marry Little Em'ly off to his depraved servant and accomplice, Littimer, ends when he and his attempted rescuer, Ham Peggotty, drown together in a shipwreck off Yarmouth, England in this Victorian Period novel (1849-1850).

1	<u>Great Expectations</u> by Charles Dickens
2	<u>A Tale of Two Cities</u> by Charles Dickens
3	<u>David Copperfield</u> by Charles Dickens

<u>Parfen Rogozhin</u> - this character is the nouveau rich Russian who befriends an impoverished epileptic prince on a train ride between Switzerland and St. Petersberg and ends up vying with him over the affections of beautiful harlot named Natasya Filipovna; eventually, he flees with Natasya Filipovna after she jilts Prince Myshkin on their wedding day and ends up murdering her in a fit of jealous rage in this Victorian Period novel (1868).

4	<u>The Idiot</u> by Fyodor Dostoevski
5	<u>Fathers and Sons</u> by Ivan Turgenev
6	<u>Dead Souls</u> by Nickolai V. Gogol

<u>Bardo</u> - this character is the blind scholar who lives in late 15th century Post Medici Florence and hires a young, good-looking Greek named Tito Melema as his secretary; eventually, he dies before his son-in-law's crimes are revealed and his widowed, childless daughter takes in Tito's mistress, Tessa, and her two illegitimate children in this Victorian Period novel (1863).

7	<u>The Ordeal of Richard Feveral</u> by George Meredith
8	<u>Under Two Flags</u> by Ouida (Marie Louise de la Ramee)
9	<u>Romola</u> by George Eliot

Frederic Moreau - this character is the young law student who has affairs with the faithful wife of the unfaithful businessman, M. Arnoux, the attractive young Louise Roque and a mistress of man named Rosanette; eventually, his reunites at age fifty with Mme. Arnoux with both agreeing that love and life are capricious in this Victorian Period novel (1868).

1	**A Sentimental Education** by Gustave Flaubert
2	**The Temptation of Saint Anthony** by Gustave Flaubert
3	**Madame Bovary** by Gustave Flaubert

Inspector Bucket - this character is the detective who discovers that an unscrupulous lawyer named Mr. Tulkinghorn has been murdered by Lady Dedlock's French maid, Mademoiselle Hortense, as he resisted a blackmail attempt; eventually, he is the one who is hired later by Mr. Tulkinghorn to investigate Lady Dedlock's hidden past in this Victorian Period novel (1852-1853).

4	**A Study In Scarlet** by Sir Arthur Conan Doyle
5	**Bleak House** by Charles Dickens
6	**The Mystery of Edwin Drood** by Charles Dickens

Hello-Central - this character is the young daughter of a skilled mechanic from New England who rises to the position of The Boss and his wife Alisande a/k/a Sandy; eventually, her illness and recuperation at the seashore is the precursor of the Battle of the Sand Belt in which Harry Morgan, Clarence and others take on a myriad of attackers in this Victorian Period novel (1889).

7	**Arrowsmith** by Sinclair Lewis
8	**A Connecticut Yankee In King Arthur's Court** by Mark Twain
9	**The Moonstone** by Wilkie Collins

1-5-8

Giovanelli - this character is the Italian gigolo whose public walks with a young unrefined American woman gets her in trouble with expatriates like Mrs. Walker; eventually, Frederick Winterbourne learns from this cad after this young woman dies in Rome from malaria that she would never had married him in this Victorian Period novel (1878).

1	The Marble Faun by Nathaniel Hawthorne
2	Daisy Miller by Henry James
3	Romola by George Eliot

Eugene Wrayburn - this character is the rash, energetic law partner of Mortimer Lightwood and the one who vies with a pretentious schoolmaster named Bradley Headstone for the hand of river man's daughter named Lizzie Hexam; eventually, he is almost drowned by Bradley and Roger Riderhood while Bradley is later actually drowned by "Rogue" Riderhood in this Victorian Period novel (1864-1866).

4	The Return of the Native by Thomas Hardy
5	Our Mutual Friend by Charles Dickens
6	Pendennis by William Makepeace Thackeray

Rawdon Crawley - this character is the charismatic English army officer who secretly marries an attractive, narcissistic scheming young woman named Becky Sharp only to be disinherited by his aunt and left with a spendthrift, flirting wife to support; eventually, his gambling debts, bankruptcy and discovery of his wife's liaison with the old, rich Lord Steyne prompt him to accept a military post abroad where he later dies of yellow fever on Coventry Island in this Victorian Period novel (1847).

7	Agnes Grey by Anne Bronte
8	Vanity Fair by William Makepeace Thackeray
9	Jude the Obscure by Thomas Hardy

2-5-8

<u>William Boldwood</u> - this character is the well-to-do farmer who is competing for Bathsheba Everdene's love with a wastrel sergeant from the dragoons named Francis Troy and a robust, young farm manager named Gabriel Oak; eventually, he is put into an   institution for fatally shooting Francis Troy while Gabriel Oak finally wins Bathsheba's hand in marriage in this Victorian Period novel (1874).

1	<u>Tess of the D'Umbervilles</u> by Thomas Hardy
2	<u>Far From the Madding Crowd</u> by Thomas Hardy
3	<u>Jude the Obscure</u> by Thomas Hardy

<u>George Radfoot</u> - this character is the unsavory fellow passenger on John Harmon's homeward voyage from South Africa to London to marry Bella Wilfer and the one who drugs him, robs him and dumps him into the Thames River; eventually, he is ironically murdered by his partner in crime and dumped into the Thames where he is mistakenly identified as John Harmon in this Victorian Period novel (1864-1866).

4	<u>Our Mutual Friend</u> by Charles Dickens
5	<u>A Study in Scarlet</u> by Sir Arthur Conan Doyle
6	<u>King Solomon's Mines</u> by H. Rider Haggard

<u>Emily Costigan</u> - this character is the coarse and attractive scheming English actress who is asked by her scrubby, libertine Irish father, Captain Costigan, to entertain the marriage proposal of a 16 year-old named Arthur who is twelve years her junior because of his future prospects; eventually, she is lured away from Arthur by his retired English Army major uncle with an acting job in London where she moves up in society in this Victorian Period novel (1848-1850).

7	<u>Vanity Fair</u> by William Makepeace Thackeray
8	<u>The Virginians</u> by William Makepeace Thackeray
9	<u>Pendennis</u> by William Makepeace Thackeray

2-4-9

<u>Fanny Cleaver (Jenny Wren)</u> - this character is the attractive, clever handicapped maker of doll's dresses whose apathetic, boozing father known as Mr. Dolls permits her to only have friends like   Mr. Riah and Lizzie Hexam; eventually, she delights in her friend Lizzie's marriage to Eugene Wrayburn after Bradley Headstone's murderous attack on him in this Victorian Period novel (1864-1866).

1	<u>A Tale of Two Cities</u> by Charles Dickens
2	<u>Our Mutual Friend</u> by Charles Dickens
3	<u>Great Expectations</u> by Charles Dickens

<u>Rev. Francis Arabin</u> - this character is the 40 year-old, erudite, High Churchman bachelor from Oxford who is offered the position of dean of the Cathedral over Archdeacon Grantly and the Rev. Obadiah Slope in a fictional cathedral town in the West of England where Dr. Proudie recently succeeded the late Dr. Grantly as bishop; eventually, he marries the wealthy, widowed daughter of the Rev. Septimus Harding, Mrs. Eleanor Bold in this Victorian Period novel (1857).

4	<u>Barchester Towers</u> by Anthony Trollope
5	<u>The Warden</u> by Anthony Trollope
6	<u>Orley Farm</u> by Anthony Trollope

<u>Edward Chester</u> - this character is the young, ambitious Protestant who challenges his father John's desire for him to marry a Protestant heiress and pursues the niece of a Catholic country squire named Emma Haredale instead; eventually, his heroism during the Gordon riots convinces Emma's sympathetic uncle, Geoffrey, to permit their marriage while bequeathing them   the rehabilitated estate known as <u>The Warren</u> in this Victorian Period novel (1841).

7	<u>Jane Eyre</u> by Charlotte Bronte
8	<u>Barnaby Rudge</u> by Charles Dickens
9	<u>Tom Jones</u> by Henry Fielding

2-4-8

<u>Ellis Duckworth</u> - this character is the enigmatic outlaw band leader known as John Amend-All who arrives at the church where Lawless and Richard Shelton (Dick) are disguised as priests to prevent the wedding between Lord Shoreby and Joanna Sedley; eventually, he kills Sir Daniel Brackley which allows Dick and Joanna to marry in this Victorian Period novel (1888).

1   <u>The Black Arrow</u> by Robert Louis Stevenson
2   <u>The Master of Ballantrae</u> by Robert Louis Stevenson
3   <u>Kidnapped</u> by Robert Louis Stevenson

<u>Durdles</u> - this character is the unusually strange English stonemason whose employment at Cloisterham Cathedral brings him in contact with an opium-addicted choirmaster named Jack Jasper who he later takes on a tour of the tombs beneath the old cathedral; eventually, he has a key to an underground tomb stolen from him one night while is asleep as a result of his excessive drinking in this unfinished Victorian Period novel (1870).

4   <u>A Study in Scarlet</u> by Sir Arthur Conan Doyle
5   <u>Barchester Towers</u> by Anthony Trollope
6   <u>The Mystery of Edwin Drood</u> by Charles Dickens

<u>Dinah Morris</u> - this character is the young Methodist preacher who accompanies her cousin, Hetty Sorrel to the scaffold after the latter had been convicted for the death of her illegitimate abandoned baby by Captain Arthur Donnithorne; eventually, she is romantically pursued by a young intelligent robust carpenter after her preaching dissuades the romantic advances of this carpenter's brother, Seth in this Victorian Period novel (1859).

7   <u>Adam Bede</u> by George Eliot
8   <u>Consuelo</u> by George Sand
9   <u>The Egoist</u> by George Meredith

1-6-7

<u>Sir Leicester Dedlock</u> - this character is the gullible husband of Lady Honoria Dedlock whose secret illicit affair with the libertine, Captain Hawson, a/k/a Nemo resulted in an illegitimate daughter named Esther Summerson; eventually, he loses his wife after she flees an unscrupulous, blackmailing lawyer named Mr. Turkington and dies at the gate where Captain Hawson is buried in this Victorian Period novel (1852-1853).

1	<u>Great Expectations</u> by Charles Dickens
2	<u>A Tale of Two Cities</u> by Charles Dickens
3	<u>Bleak House</u> by Charles Dickens

<u>Hilarion</u> - this character is the former disciple who appears to a despairing hermit who has lived in the mountains for 30 years and has 2nd thoughts about his life of denial and suffering while feeling nostalgia for his life as a monk; eventually, he reproaches this hermit for being ignorant and proceeds to defile him by laying open to him all the disconcerting heresies of the early Church and to all pseudo gods throughout history in this Victorian Period novel (1874).

4	<u>The Temptation of Saint Anthony</u> by Gustave Flaubert
5	<u>Camille</u> by Alexander Dumas, Jr.
6	<u>Under Two Flags</u> by Ouida (Marie Louise de la Ramee)

<u>Paul</u> - this character is the bright, frail little boy whose poor health prompts his austere father to send him from London to the healthy seaside town of Brighton along with his 12 year-old sister, Florence; eventually, his swift return to London after enduring the rigors of a stressful education in Brighton is unable to forestall the untimely death of this 6 year-old in this Victorian Period novel (1846-1848).

7	<u>Kidnapped</u> by Robert Louis Stevenson
8	<u>Dombey and Son</u> by Charles Dickens
9	<u>The Return of the Native</u> by Thomas Hardy

George Warrinton - this character is the impetuous, emotional twin whose initial allegiance with George Washington in the French and Indians War fades with the onset of the American Revolution; eventually, he travels to England after escaping a French Canadian prison, liberates his twin brother from an English debtor's prison, marries Theo Lambert and relinquishes any future claim to the estate known as Castlewood in the Colonies in this Victorian Period novel (1857-1859).

1	The Prisoner of Zenda by Anthony Hope
2	The American by Henry James
3	The Virginians by William Makepeace Thackeray

John Willet - this character is the stubborn, overbearing owner of the Maypole Inn near Epping Forest who is traumatized by the Gordon rioters Simon Tappertit, Hugh and Ned Dennis when the mob plunders his inn; eventually, he retires to Maypole Farm along with a half-wit, his talking raven, Grip, and the half-wit's mother while his son, Joe, marries Dolly Varden and runs Mapole Inn in this Victorian Period novel (1841).

4	Treasure Island by Robert Louis Stevenson
5	Barnaby Rudge by Charles Dickens
6	The Return of the Native by Thomas Hardy

Dr. Austin Sloper - this character is the brilliant physician father who lives with his dull, plain daughter named Catherine and his widowed sister, Lavinia Penniman, before the intrusion of a fortune hunting young man named Morris Townsend; eventually, he leaves his fortune to charity before dying so that his daughter would not be the heiress her suitor, Morris, had thought her in this Victorian Period novel (1881).

7	Washington Square by Henry James
8	The American by Henry James
9	The Ambassadors by Henry James

3-5-7

Tigg Montague - this character is the corrupt president of a non-existent loan and insurance company who blackmails a coarse hustler named Jonas into investing in worthless stock which drives a greedy flim-flam architecture teacher named Seth Pecksniff to purchase the same stock; eventually, his murder by Jonas is discovered by his investigator, Nadgett, and this leads to Pecksniff's ruination when David Crimple absconds with the company's funds in this Victorian Period novel (1843-1844).

1   **Martin Chuzzlewit** by Charles Dickens
2   **A Tale of Two Cities** by Charles Dickens
3   **Great Expectations** by Charles Dickens

George Osmond - this character is the egotistical aesthete who edges out Lord Warburton and Caspar Goodwood for the hand of a 23 year-old American heiress; eventually, his secret affair with Madame Merle and their ensuing child, Pansy, is exposed by his sister, Countess Gemini in this Victorian Period novel (1881).

4   **The Portrait of a Lady** by Henry James
5   **The Mayor of Casterbridge** by Thomas Hardy
6   **The Marble Faun** by Nathaniel Hawthorne

Old Harmon - this character is the deceased refuse collector who writes his will with the condition that his son John would only receive his inheritance if he marries Bella Wilfer; eventually, his son fakes his death and assumes the disguise of John Rokesmith, secretary to Mr. Boffin in this Victorian Period novel (1864-1866).

7   **A Tale of Two Cities** by Charles Dickens
8   **Dombey and Son** by Charles Dickens
9   **Our Mutual Friend** by Charles Dickens

1-4-9

<u>Kirsanoff</u> - this character is the elderly, music-loving liberal landowner who is visited by a nihilist doctor named Bazaroff along with the former's son, Arkady, after they complete their studies; eventually, he becomes a magistrate and marries his mistress, Fenichka, is joined on his farm by Arkady and Katya, and they learn that Bazaroff has died from typhus in this Victorian Period novel (1862).

1	<u>Dead Souls</u> by Nicholai V. Gogol
2	<u>Fathers and Sons</u> by Ivan Turgenev
3	<u>The Idiot</u> by Fyodor Dostoevski

<u>John Westlock</u> - this character is the ex-apprentice of a flim-flam teacher of architecture named Seth Pecksniff and the one who uses collaborating testimony from a young doctor named Lewsome and a cockney nurse named Mrs. Gamp to expose a scoundrel named Jonas of attempted murder of his father; eventually, he marries Tom Pinch's sister, a governess named Ruth, who had been rescued from an unpleasant job by her brother in this Victorian Period novel (1843-1844).

4	<u>Great Expectations</u> by Charles Dickens
5	<u>A Tale of Two Cities</u> by Charles Dickens
6	<u>Martin Chuzzlewit</u> by Charles Dickens

<u>Mr. Snagsby</u> - this character is the meek, wife-ridden law stationer who is directed by an unscrupulous lawyer named Mr. Tulkington to identify the handwriting in Lady Dedlock's letter; eventually, this identification leads Mr. Tulkinghorn to a junkyard dealer named Krook where a secretive boarder named Nemo is exposed as the Captain Hawson who left Lady Dedlock with an illegitimate daughter, Esther Summerson, in this Victorian Period novel (1852-1853).

7	<u>Barchester Towers</u> by Anthony Trollope
8	<u>Jude the Obscure</u> by Thomas Hardy
9	<u>Bleak House</u> by Charles Dickens

2-6-9

Tito Melema - this character is the young good-looking Greek who arrives in late 15th century post Medici Florence to sell a number of gems for his patron, Baldassare Calvo; eventually, his political deceptions, his treachery toward his patron and his marital infidelity come home to roost when he is run out of town and strangled by Calvo while his childless wife takes in his mistress, Tessa, and her two children in this Victorian Period novel (1863).

1	The Egoist by George Meredith
2	Consuelo by George Sand
3	Romola by George Eliot

Ada Clare - this character is the young, docile ward of the mellowing proprietor of an ancestral home named John Jarndyce and the one who secretly marries another of John Jarndyce's wards, Richard Carstone, to protect him from poverty; eventually, she ends up widowed with a son as a result of her new husband's unsuccessful attempts at various careers and his despair over a court case which lingers on for years in this Victorian Period novel (1852-1853).

4	Great Expectations by Charles Dickens
5	Bleak House by Charles Dickens
6	A Tale of Two Cities by Charles Dickens

Nicholas Bulstrode - this character is the rich, proselytizing sanctimonious banker who uses his religion and wealth to manipulate the goings on in an English town; eventually, his escape is blocked when he is confined to bed after a scandal reveals how his ill-gotten wealth had really stemmed from a marriage to his employer's widow rather than as a result of his own efforts in this Victorian Period novel (1871-1872).

7	Romola by George Eliot
8	Consuelo by George Sand
9	Middlemarch by George Eliot

3-5-9

Esther Summerson - this character is the orphaned companion for John Jarndyce's two wards, Ada Clare and Richard Carstone, and the one who is exposed as the illegitimate daughter of Lady Honoria Dedlock and Captain Hawson a/k/a Nemo; eventually, she is released from her promise to marry the aging John Jarndyce and marries a humane surgeon named Allan Woodcourt in this Victorian Period novel (1852-1853).

1	A Tale of Two Cities by Charles Dickens
2	Great Expectations by Charles Dickens
3	Bleak House by Charles Dickens

David Crimple - this character is the secretary of a non-existent company named the Anglo-Bengalee Disinterested Loan and Life Insurance Company which is run by a corrupt president named Tigg Montague, Esq. a/k/a Montague Tigg; eventually, his absconding with the company funds after learning of his employer's murder leads to the ruination of flim-flam teacher of architecture named Seth Pecksniff in this Victorian Period novel (1843-1844).

4	Bleak House by Charles Dickens
5	Martin Chuzzlewit by Charles Dickens
6	Great Expectations by Charles Dickens

Roger "Rogue" Riderhood - this character is the ruthless informer who slanders the reputation of his ex-partner, Gaffer Hexam, who was known for collecting rewards for retrieving corpses from the Thames River he had actually placed there after murdering them; eventually, he is drowned during a scuffle with a villain named Bradley Headstone after John Harmon exposes the slander in this Victorian Period novel (1864-1865).

7	Barnaby Rudge by Charles Dickens
8	Our Mutual Friend by Charles Dickens
9	Martin Chuzzlewit by Charles Dickens

3-5-8

<u>Camille</u> - this character is the Parisian courtesan whose meteoric rise from poor needleworker begins when a wealth Duke sees a strong resemblance between her and his dead daughter and introduces her to the high Parisian society where she incurs heavy gambling debts; eventually, her deception of making her true love, Armand Duval, believe that she would rather be the mistress of Count de Varville is finally revealed to Andre as lay dying of consumption in this Victorian Period novel (1852).

1	Alexander Dumas, Jr.
2	Alexander Dumas, Sr.
3	Gustave Flaubert

<u>Richard Carstone</u> - this character is the young ward of a mellowing proprietor, John Jarndyce, of an ancestral home and the one who secretly marries another ward of John Jarndyces's, Ada Clare; eventually, his unsuccessful pursuit of numerous careers coupled with his despair over a lingering court case that consumes his inheritance in legal fees culminates in his death in this Victorian Period novel (1852-1853).

4	<u>Bleak House</u> by Charles Dickens
5	<u>Great Expectations</u> by Charles Dickens
6	<u>A Tale of Two Cities</u> by Charles Dickens

<u>Mrs. Jarley</u> - this character is the obese, good-natured owner of a celebrated wax work museum and the one who hires a 14 year-old girl named Little Nell to explain the exhibits and her grandfather to dust them off after the these two had just left a traveling puppet show; eventually, she loses these two traveling companions after the grandfather's degenerate gambling forces them to move on in this Victorian Period novel (1848).

7	<u>The Old Curiosity Shop</u> by Charles Dickens
8	<u>Great Expectations</u> by Charles Dickens
9	<u>A Tale of Two Cities</u> by Charles Dickens

Rev. Septimus Harding - this character is the charitable new head of a cathedral who comes under attack by a young surgeon, John Bold, and a newspaperman, Tom Towers, over the large amount of money he receives for overseeing an almshouse known as Hiram's Hospital which regularly houses twelve old residents; eventually, he resigns his position against the protests of his future son-in-law, John Bold, who has fallen in love with his daughter, Elinor, in this Victorian Period novel (1855).

1   **The Temptation of Saint Anthony** by Gustave Flaubert
2   **The Master of Ballantrae** by Robert Louis Stevenson
3   **The Warden** by Anthony Trollope

Harry - this character is the young orphaned grandson of the Marquis of Monmouth and the one who comes of age during England's political turmoil of the 1830's and 1840's when the Whigs, Tories, and Conservatives were vying for power; eventually, he is disinherited by his grandfather because of political differences, marries Edith Millbank after winning her father's favor, and is ultimately left the family inheritance by his aunt, Flora in this Victorian Period novel (1844).

4   **Coningsby** by Benjamin Disraeli
5   **The Marble Faun** by Nathaniel Hawthorne
6   **The Prince and the Pauper** by Mark Twain

Henry Durie - this character is the younger Scottish brother of James who is constantly blackmailed financially and emotionally over a lifetime after James had ceded his birthright to him along with the love of Alison Graeme; eventually, he dies of fright and is buried next to James when Secundra Dass's trick of suspended animation turns awry because of the cold climate out in the American wilderness in the American wilderness in this Victorian Period novel (1889).

7   **The Black Arrow** by Robert Louis Stevenson
8   **The Master of Ballantrae** by Robert Louis Stevenson
9   **Kidnapped** by Robert Louis Stevenson

3-4-8

<u>Sergeant Dunham</u> - this character is the British soldier serving under Major Duncan and Lieutenant Davy Muir at the Fort Oswego garrison located near Lake Ontario during the French and Indian Wars; eventually, his mortal wounds after an ambush by the Iroquois Indians prevents him from seeing his daughter Mabel marry Jasper Western instead of his own friend, Natty Bumppo, in this third Leatherstocking Tale (1840).

1	<u>The Last of the Mohicans</u> by James Fenimore Cooper
2	<u>The Pathfinder</u> by James Fenimore Cooper
3	<u>The Pilot</u> by James Fenimore Cooper

<u>Mr. Mason</u> - this character is the brother-in-law of <u>Thornfield</u>'s arrogant, pensive owner, Edward Rochester, and the one who is wounded by his sister, Bertha Mason Rochester, on a business visit to that estate; eventually, he sends someone from Jamaica to England to prevent the marriage between Edward Rochester and the private governess of Edward's ward and illegitimate daughter, Adele Varens, on the grounds that a marriage already existed in this Victorian Period novel (1847).

4	<u>Wuthering Heights</u> by Emily Bronte
5	<u>Jane Eyre</u> by Charlotte Bronte
6	<u>Agnes Grey</u> by Anne Bronte

<u>Maggie Tulliver</u> - this character is the young woman whose devotion to her brother, Tom, prevents her from having a loving relationship with a deformed lawyer named Philip Nolan because he is considered an enemy of the family; eventually, she runs off with her cousin Lucy Dean's fiancé, Stephen Guest, has her reputation compromised and dies along with her brother when they are caught up in a flood in this Victorian Period novel (1859).

7	<u>Adam Bede</u> by George Eliot
8	<u>Consuelo</u> by George Sand
9	<u>The Mill of the Floss</u> by George Eliot

Francis Spenlow - this character is the established London lawyer who opposes the marriage of a young, aspiring clerk in his firm, <u>Spenlow and Jorkins</u>, to his naive, dependent daughter, Dora, because this young clerk's benefactress, Miss Betsy Trotwood, had lost her fortune; eventually, his death as a result of falling from a carriage and the discovery that he died penniless removed all obstacles from this marriage in this Victorian Period novel (1849-1850).

1	<u>Great Expectations</u> by Charles Dickens
2	<u>A Tale of Two Cities</u> by Charles Dickens
3	<u>David Copperfield</u> by Charles Dickens

Colonel Chateauroy - this character is the commanding officer of a French Foreign Legionnaire contingent in Algeria who provokes a Londoner named Bertie Cecil who is posing as Louis Victor to strike him which draws the sentence of a firing squad; eventually, his jealousy and hatred for Bertie are foiled when a French camp follower, Cigarette, steps in and blocks the bullets thereby allowing him to return to London, exonerate himself and marry Princess Corona d' Amague in this Victorian Period novel (1867).

4	<u>A Sentimental Education</u> by Gustave Flaubert
5	<u>Under Two Flags</u> by Ouida (Marie Louise de la Ramee)
6	<u>The Charterhouse of Parma</u> by Stendhal

Chuffey - this character is the elderly, deaf and visually-impaired clerk whose lifetime loyalty to his distrustful employer, Anthony, is proven when he saves this stingy boss from an attempted poisoning by the employer's son, Jonas; eventually, he can't prevent Anthony from dying of a broken heart while Jonas ironically poisons himself as he awaits prison in this Victorian Period novel (1843-1844).

7	<u>Martin Chuzzlewit</u> by Charles Dickens
8	<u>Great Expectations</u> by Charles Dickens
9	<u>Bleak House</u> by Charles Dickens

3-5-7

Hamilcar - this character is the third century country leader who must defend Carthage from his own mercenaries led by Matho and Spendius when the Council of Elders short changes them after their unsuccessful attempt to defeat the romans in Italy; eventually, his daughter commits suicide during her wedding ceremony to a Numidian chief name Narr' Havas after she witnesses a enormous Libyan chief named Matho die before her in this Victorian Period novel (1862).

1   Salummbo by Gaustave Flaubert
2   The Red and the Black by Stendhal
3   Les Miserables by Victor Hugo

Michael Henchard - this character is the wealthy corn merchant who swore an oath of sobriety after he sold his wife, Susan, and their daughter while intoxicated to an outspoken, exuberant sailor named Richard Newson; eventually, his arrogance toward his former manager, Donald Farfrae, and business competitor because the latter had stolen his lover, Lucetta (nee Le Sueur) Templeman, drives him into bankruptcy in this Victorian Period novel (1886).

4   Jude the Obscure by Thomas Hardy
5   The Mayor of Casterbridge by Thomas Hardy
6   Far From the Madding Crowd by Thomas Hardy

Reverend St. John's Rivers - this character is the young clergyman who wishes to marry a young woman named Jane Eliot after her impulsive flight from the Thornfield estate ends in the refuge of the Rivers household; eventually, he offers a platonic marriage wherein they can devote their lives to missionary work in India in this Victorian Period novel (1847).

7   Jane Eyre by Charlotte Bronte
8   Agnes Grey by Anne Bronte
9   Wuthering Heights by Emily Bronte

Matho - this character is the enormous Libyan chief of mercenaries who returns to Carthage after the Council of Elders shortchanges his army with regard to their back pay for following the Carthaginian leader, Hamilcar, in an unsuccessful attack on the Roman army; eventually, he is defeated by Hamilcar, dragged through the streets of Carthage and tortured to death in front of Hamilcar's daughter who takes poison at her weeding ceremony in order to join him in death in this Victorian Period novel (1862).

1	**Camille** by Alexander Dumas, Jr.
2	**Salammbo** by Gustave Flaubert
3	**The Charterhouse of Parma** by Stendhal

Mrs. Bread - this character is the old English family servant who leaves the Bellegarde family to become the servant of an American businessman named Christopher Newman; eventually, she reveals a deadly secret about Madame de Bellegarde to this American after her son Valentin's dying words in this Victorian Period novel (1877).

4	**Anthony Adverse** by Hervey Allen
5	**The Thirty-Nine Steps** by John Buchan
6	**The American** by Henry James

Richard Newson - this character is the outspoken, exuberant sailor who buys his wife, Susan Henchard-Newson, and her baby daughter at a village fair from a drunken young farmer named Michael Henchard and then moves from England to Canada; eventually, he returns to Wessex to claim his daughter, Elizabeth-Jane, and see her settled in marriage with a wealthy corn merchant named Donald Farfrae in this Victorian Period novel (1886).

7	**Jude the Obscure** by Thomas Hardy
8	**The Mayor of Casterbridge** by Thomas Hardy
9	**Far From the Madding Crowd** by Thomas Hardy

2-6-8

<u>Mrs. Pegler</u> - this character is the mysterious elderly woman seen in Stephen Blackpool's company the night that Josiah Bounderby's bank was robbed in Coketown; eventually, her identity as Bounderby's mother leads him to fire his elderly spying housekeeper, Mrs. Sparsit, eventhough the latter exposed his wife Laura's plan to elope with James Harthouse in this Victorian Period novel (1854).

1	<u>Hard Times</u> by Charles Dickens
2	<u>Great Expectations</u> by Charles Dickens
3	<u>A Tale of Two Cities</u> by Charles Dickens

<u>Berkeley Cecil</u> - this character is the forger of a promissary note that brings shame on his older brother, Cecil, until this innocent man flees London on his horse, Forest King, accompanied by his valet, Rake, and joins the French Foreign Legion in Algeria so that Lady Guenevere will not be compromised; eventually, he owns up to his crime which allows Bertie to return to London where he can rightfully claim his noble heritage and marry Princess Corona d' Amague in this Victorian Period novel (1867).

4	<u>Consuelo</u> by George Sand
5	<u>Romola</u> by George Eliot
6	<u>Under Two Flags</u> by Ouida (Marie Louise de la Ramee)

<u>Mr. Podsnap</u> - this character is the pompous and arrogant leader of a society in London which is the smug epitome of Philistinism; eventually, he and his majestic wife and his daughter named Georgiana join Mr. and Mrs. Lammle's and the Veneerings to make up a subplot in this last completed Victorian Period novel by an English author (1864-1866).

7	<u>Great Expectations</u> by Charles Dickens
8	<u>Our Mutual Friend</u> by Charles Dickens
9	<u>A Tale of Two Cities</u> by Charles Dickens

1-6-8

<u>Hanno</u> - this character is the obese, pretentious member of the Carthaginian Council of Elders who travels to Sicca to appease an   army of disgruntled mercenaries shortchanged pay after their unsuccessful attempt to destroy the Roman army in Italy; eventually, he barely escapes with his life after a former slave named Spendius misinterprets his message to go home and await their back pay from the third century leader of Carthage, Hamilcar, and the Council of Elders in this Victorian Period novel (1862).

1   <u>Under Two Flags</u> by Ouida (Marie Louise de la Ramee)
2   <u>Salammbo</u> by Gustave Flaubert
3   <u>Camille</u> by Alexander Dumas, Jr.

<u>Miss Flite</u> - this character is the astute, amiable Jarndyce relative who spends everyday attending a Chancery court case in the hopes of inheriting money in a prolonged suit; eventually, she realizes that the inheritance had been devoured in legal fees and raises birds for comfort and consolation after the settlement while assisting others in a similar predicament in this Victorian Period novel (1852-1853).

4   <u>Great Expectations</u> by Charles Dickens
5   <u>Bleak House</u> by Charles Dickens
6   <u>A Tale of Two Cities</u> by Charles Dickens

<u>Tom</u> - this character is the young American sailor who joins Toby when they desert their ship, the <u>Dolly</u>, at one of the Marquesas Islands where they are held captive by the cannibal tribal chief, Mehevi, the native servant, Kory-Kory, and an attractive native girl named Fayaway; eventually, his rescue off the island by an Australian vessel with the help of the taboo man, Marnoo, reunites him with Toby who had been shanghaied in this Victorian Period novel (1846).

7   <u>Salammbo</u> by Gustave Flaubert
8   <u>Typee</u> by Herman Melville
9   <u>Heart of Darkness</u> by Joseph Conrad

2-5-8

Murazov - this character is the shrewd, Russian lawyer who frees a young adventurer named Pavel Ivanovitch Tchitchikoff from jail after the latter had been charged with forgery while purchasing the names of deceased serfs to increase his mortgage with the Trustee Committee; eventually, he unscrupulously unearths so many buried town scandals that the townspeople welcome the quick departure of his client in this Victorian Period novel (1842).

1	**Fathers and Sons** by Ivan Turgenev
2	**The Idiot** by Fyodor Dostoevski
3	**Dead Souls** by Nikolai V. Gogol

Lucius Mason - this character is the son of Lady Mason who is the winner of two court trials spaced by 20 years regarding a forged will and codicil involving a large estate that draws the attention of such lawyers as Mr. Furnival, Mr. Aram, Mr. Chaffenbrass, Samuel Dockwrath and Felix Graham; eventually, he leaves Sophia Furnival and joins his mother on a trip to Germany to secure a farming career in Australia in this Victorian Period novel (1861).

4	**Barchester Towers** by Anthony Trollope
5	**Orley Farm** by Anthony Trollope
6	**The Warden** by Anthony Trollope

William Guppy - this character is the law clerk for the firm of John Jarndyce who noticed the likeness between Esther Summerson and Lady Honoria Dedlock; eventually, his rendezvous with a junkyard dealer named Krook which had to do with a packet of Nemo's letters that were to be returned to Lady Dedlock is aborted when Krook dies in a drunken state from spontaneous combustion in this Victorian Period novel (1852-1853).

7	**A Tale of Two Cities** by Charles Dickens
8	**Great Expectations** by Charles Dickens
9	**Bleak House** by Charles Dickens

3-5-9

Toby (Tommo) - this character is the young American sailor who joins another sailor named Tom when they desert their ship, the <u>Dolly</u>, at one of the Marquesas Islands where they are held captive by the cannibal tribal chief, Mehevi, the native servant, Kory-Kory, and an attractive native girl named Fayaway; eventually, he is shanghaied and ultimately reunited with Tom in this Victorian Period novel (1846).

1   **<u>Typee</u> by Herman Melville**
2   **<u>Lord Jim</u> by Joseph Conrad**
3   **<u>Two Years Before the Mast</u> by Richard Henry Dana, Jr.**

Cecilia "Sissy" Jupe - this character is the compassionate caring young daughter of a circus clown whose abandonment results in her attending Thomas Gradgrind's innovative school in Coketown and living with Louisa and Tom Gradgrind; eventually, she offers solace to Louisa, convinces James Harthouse to leave Coketown and assists in young Tom Gradgrind's escape from England in this Victorian Period novel (1854).

4   **<u>Great Expectations</u> by Charles Dickens**
5   **<u>A Tale of Two Cities</u> by Charles Dickens**
6   **<u>Hard Times</u> by Charles Dickens**

Doctor Long Ghost - this character is the ship's doctor who joins a young American seaman in a number of South Sea adventures after this seaman is rescued from a Marquesas Island cannibal tribe; eventually, he is denied passage by the Captain on a ship that will take the seaman home after they both are released from a stockade overseen by a good-humored jailor named Captain Bob in this Victorian Period novel (1847).

7   **<u>Omoo</u> by Herman Melville**
8   **<u>Two Years Before the Mast</u> by Richard Henry Dana, Jr.**
9   **<u>Lord Jim</u> by Joseph Conrad**

165

1-6-7

Mark Tapley - this character is the cheerful, individualistic stable manager at the Wiltshire Blue Dragon Inn who leaves his employ in order to join an aspiring architect on a journey to America to seek their fortunes; eventually, this friendly, people-person returns disillusioned to Wiltshire where he marries the landlady of the Blue Dragon Inn and changes its name to the Jolly Tapley in this Victorian Period novel (1843-1844).

1	A Tale of Two Cities by Charles Dickens
2	Great Expectations by Charles Dickens
3	Martin Chuzzlewit by Charles Dickens

Captain Bob - this character is the good-humored Tahitian jailor who oversees a group of mutineer from the ship, Julia, which includes the ship's doctor, Dr. Long Ghost, and an American seaman recently rescued from a Marquesas Island cannibal tribe; eventually, he releases his prisoners after the captain of the Julia sets sail with a new crew made up of beachcombers who were hanging around the island in this Victorian Period novel (1847).

4	Two Years Before the Mast by Richard Henry Dana, Jr.
5	Omoo by Herman Melville
6	Lord Jim by Joseph Conrad

Lady Mason - this character is the winner of two court trials spaced by 20 years regarding a forged will and codicil involving a large estate that draws the attention of such lawyers as Mr. Furnival, Mr. Aram, Mr. Chaffenbrass, Samuel Dockwrath and Felix Graham; eventually, she relinquishes the estate and joins her son, Lucius, as he travels to Germany so he can secure a farming career in Australia in this Victorian Period novel (1861).

7	Tess of the D'Umbervilles by Thomas Hardy
8	Jude the Obscure by Thomas Hardy
9	Orley Farm by Thomas Hardy

Narr Havas - this character is the Numidian chief who deserts an army of disgruntled mercenaries led by the enormous Libyan chief, Matho, to join the Carthaginian leader, Hamilcar, in protecting the third century city of Carthage with the promise of marrying Hamilcar's daughter as a reward for his efforts; eventually, his wedding ceremony ends when his bride-to-be decides to poison herself and join Matho in death after the latter is captured and tortured to death in front of her in this Victorian Period novel (1862).

1	**The Charterhouse of Parma** by Stendhal
2	**Les Miserables** by Victor Hugo
3	**Salammbo** by Gustave Flaubert

Lord Rockingham - this character is the London nobleman who mistakenly believes that a promissory note has been forged by his best friend, a young insolvent well-liked military officer named Bertie Cecil when in fact the guilty party was Bertie's younger brother, Berkeley; eventually, he intercedes to prevent Bertie from dying in front of a firing squad which allows Bertie to marry his sister, Princess Corona d' Amague in this Victorian Period novel (1886).

4	**Adam Bede** by George Eliot
5	**Consuelo** by George Sand
6	**Under Two Flags** by Ouida (Marie Louise de la Ramee)

Donald Farfrae - this character is the young Scottish corn merchant manager who incurs the wrath of his jealous boss, Michael Henchard, after he eclipses the latter in ability, popularity and prosperity and then marries the latter's ex-lover, Lucretta (nee Le Sueur) Templeman; eventually, this widower remarries daughter of a sailor named Elizabeth-Jane Newson in this Victorian Period novel (1867).

7	**Jude the Obscure** by Thomas Hardy
8	**The Mayor of Casterbridge** by Thomas Hardy
9	**Far From the Madding Crowd** by Thomas Hardy

3-6-8

<u>Bertie Cecil</u> - this character is the young, insolvent military officer who flees London on his horse, Forest King, along with Rake after being falsely accused of forging a promissory note signed by his younger brother, Berkeley; eventually, his life as Louis Victor in the French Foreign Legion ends when a patriotic French woman and mascot of the Legion, Cigarette, saves him from a firing squad   to return home and marry Princess Corona d' Amague in this Victorian Period novel (1867).

1	<u>Consuelo</u> by George Sand
2	<u>Under Two Flags</u> by Ouida (Marie Louise de la Ramee)
3	<u>Adam Bede</u> by George Eliot

<u>Ganya Ardalionovitch</u> - this character is the ambitious secretary of General Epanchin who is seeking to marry his employer's rich and beautiful daughter, Aglaya, while carrying on an illicit affair with a beautiful harlot named Natasya Filipovna; eventually, he learns that Natasya had jilted a young epileptic prince named Myshkin on their wedding day and was later found murdered by Parfen Rogozhin during a jealous rage in this Victorian Period novel (1868).

4	<u>The Possessed</u> by Fyodor Dostoevski
5	<u>The Idiot</u> by Fyodor Dostoevski
6	<u>The Gambler</u> by Fyodor Dostoevski

<u>Pip</u> - this character is the clever, carefree cabin boy aboard the whaling ship, <u>Pequod</u>, whose abandonment by the second mate, Stubb, when he falls overboard leaves him unbalanced and terrified after being rescued; eventually, he perishes when the ship's deranged captain, Abab, allows his delusional fixation to ultimately cause the death of his entire crew with the exception of a schoolmaster turned seaman named Ishmael in this Victorian Period novel (1851).

7	<u>Great Expectations</u> by Charles Dickens
8	<u>Captain Courageous</u> by Rudyard Kipling
9	<u>Moby Dick</u> by Herman Melville

168

2-5-9

<u>Arrowhead</u> - this character is the Tuscarora Indian who is joined by his wife Dew-of-June in guiding Mabel Dunham and her salt-water seaman uncle, Charles Cap, on a journey to the Oswego River where they rendezvous with a wilderness scout, Natty Bumppo, and Jasper Western; eventually, his treachery is exposed, he stabs Lt. Muir to death and is then killed by a Mochican chief named Chingachcook in this <u>Leatherstocking Tales</u> (1840).

1	<u>The Pathfinder</u> by James Fenimore Cooper
2	<u>Babbitt</u> by Sinclair Lewis
3	<u>Drums Along the Mohawk</u> by Walter Edmonds

<u>George Osborne</u> - this character is the gallant, young English army officer who marries Amelia Sedley after she attends Miss Pinkerton"s finishing school for girls where she becomes best friends with the scheming, narcissistic Becky Sharp; eventually, his death at Waterloo leads to an old time admirer of Amelia named Captain William Dobbin finally winning her hand in a marriage that produces a daughter named Jane in this Victorian Period novel (1847).

4	<u>Pendennis</u> by William Makepeace Thackeray
5	<u>The Virginians</u> by William Makepeace Thackeray
6	<u>Vanity Fair</u> by William Makepeace Thackeray

<u>Colonel Altamont</u> - this character is the drunk posing as a retired English army officer who lives at <u>Shepherd's Lane Inn</u> with Captain Edward Strong until his true identity is exposed by a retired English army major who had returned from India and recognized him as the supposedly dead Mr. Amory at dinner; eventually, he eludes the police after his previous marriage to Jemima Amory and her subsequent marriage to Sir Francis Claverings is not deemed bigamous because of his other earlier marriages in this Victorian Period novel (1848-1850).

7	<u>Vanity Fair</u> by William Makepeace Thackeray
8	<u>Pendennis</u> by William Makepeace Thackeray
9	<u>The Virginians</u> by William Makepeace Thackeray

1-6-8

Amy - this character is the little girl born and reared along with her older brother and sister, Fanny, in Marshaled debtors prison until she secures a daytime sewing job outside the prison with Mrs. Clennam where she meets her employer's son, Arthur Clennam; eventually, she and Arthur prosper and marry after Mrs. Clennam renounces a blackmailer, Monsieur Blandois, and confesses Arthur's real heritage and the money she had stolen from both of them over the years in this Victorian Period novel (1843-1844).

1   The Old Curiosity Shop by Charles Dickens
2   Martin Chuzzlewit by Charles Dickens
3   Little Dorrit by Charles Dickens

Mr. Krook - this character is the landlord whose tenant, Nemo, dies of a drug overdose and is buried in potter's field; eventually, this junk yard dealer and confirmed drunk dies of spontaneous combustion the very night he was supposed to give Captain Hawson's letters to William Guppy in this Victorian Period novel (1842).

4   A Tale of Two Cities by Charles Dickens
5   Great Expectations by Charles Dickens
6   Bleak House by Charles Dickens

Mrs. Eleanor Bold - this character is the wealthy, widowed daughter of the Warden of Hiram's Hospital, the Rev. Septimus Harding, in the fictional cathedral town until a new political appointee is made Bishop named Dr. Proudie; eventually, she marries the new Dean of the Cathedral, the Rev. Francis Arabin, after turning down the villainous Rev. Obadiah Slope and the immature Ethelbert Stanhope (Bertie) in this Victorian Period novel (1857).

7   The Warden by Anthony Trollope
8   Orley Farm by Anthony Trollope
9   Barchester Towers by Anthony Trollope

3-6-9

Mr. Barkis - this character is the timid wagon driver and bashful suitor of a corpulent, good-natured nurse and loyal servant named Peggotty who works for a young, naive widow named Clara and her sensitive boy; eventually, he marries Clara Peggotty after she is fired by her new, miserly and sadistic employer, Mr. Edward Murdstone, and his strict, stern sister, Jane, after her former employer, Clara, dies giving birth to another child while her young boy is being overworked and underfed at his stepfather's export business in this Victorian Period novel (1849-1850).

1   <u>Great Expectations</u> by Charles Dickens
2   <u>David Copperfield</u> by Charles Dickens
3   <u>A Tale of Two Cities</u> by Charles Dickens

Frederick Winterbourne - this character is the young American expatriate in Europe who joins another expatriate named Mrs. Walker in trying to make a nonconformist from Schenectady, New York more refined; eventually, he gets some feedback about her from an Italian cad named Giovanelli after she dies in Rome from malaria in this Victorian Period novel (1879).

4   <u>Consuelo</u> by George Sand
5   <u>Romola</u> by George Eliot
6   <u>Daisy Miller</u> by Henry James

Gabriel Oak - this character is the robust, young farmer who competes for beautiful Bathsheba Everdene's love with a wastrel named Sergeant Troy and a well-to-do, middle aged farmer named William Boldwood; eventually, he wins her over after Willaim Boldwood sentence of death is commuted to being institutionalized for fatally shooting Francis Troy in the chest when he appeared at a Christmas party in this Victorian Period novel (1874).

7   <u>Jude the Obscure</u> by Thomas Hardy
8   <u>The Return of the Native</u> by Thomas Hardy
9   <u>Far From the Madding Crowd</u> by Thomas Hardy

2-6-9

<u>Miriam Schaefer</u> - this character is the alluring, young femme fatale who is a member of a 19th century art colony in Rome that includes a sculptor named Kenyon, another female painter named Hilda and an Italian nobleman named Donatello who is known as the Count of Monte Beni; eventually, she becomes instrumental in causing Donatello being imprisoned for fatally throwing a Capuchin monk named Brother Antonio off <u>Tarpian Rock</u> in this Victorian Period novel (1860).

1	<u>The Marble Faun</u> by Nathaniel Hawthorne
2	<u>Daisy Miller</u> by Henry James
3	<u>Romola</u> by George Eliot

<u>Richard Swiveller (Dick)</u> - this character is the young, dissolute law clerk for an unethical lawyer named Sampson Brass and the   foil of a grotesque-looking deranged dwarf named Daniel Quilp; eventually, he exonerates Kit Nubbles of theft and rejects his old life when he marries the Brass's servant girl, Sophronia Sphynx in this Victorian Period novel (1848).

4	<u>A Tale of Two Cities</u> by Charles Dickens
5	<u>The Old Curiosity Shop</u> by Charles Dickens
6	<u>Great Expectations</u> by Charles Dickens

<u>Rachel Verinder</u> - this character is the young Englishwoman who inherit a Hindu diamond from her brutal, sadistic uncle, John Herncastle, and then becomes engaged to a handsome charity worker after seeing Franklin Blake stealing the precious gem; eventually, she marries Franklin once he is exonerated while Godfrey's dead body is found dressed as a sailor in a waterfront boarding house with clues that he was heading to Amsterdam in this Victorian Period novel (1868).

7	<u>The Mystery of Edwin Drood</u> by Charles Dickens
8	<u>The Moonstone</u> by Wilkie Collins
9	<u>A Study in Scarlet</u> by Sir Arthur Conan Doyle

1-5-8

<u>Donatello</u> - this character is the young Italian nobleman titled the Count of Monte Beni who is a member of a 19th century art colony in Rome which includes a sculptor named Kenyon and two female painters, Hilda and Miriam Schaefer; eventually, he is imprisoned for fatally throwing a Capuchin monk named Brother Antonio off <u>Tarpian Rock</u> in this Victorian Period novel (1860).

1   <u>The Rainbow</u> by D.H. Lawrence
2   <u>The Marble Faun</u> by Nathaniel Hawthorne
3   <u>The Invisible Man</u> by H.G. Wells

<u>Lord Royallieu</u> - this character is the old viscount who withholds his love from his son, Bertie Cecil, because he suspects that he not only looks like his wife's dead lover, but also carries part of his name - Cecil; eventually, the news of this viscount's death at ninety reaches young Bertie six months late because the latter had fled under the alias of Louis Victor to Algeria and the French Foreign Legion in this Victorian Period novel (1867).

4   <u>Far From the Madding Crowd</u> by Thomas Hardy
5   <u>Under Two Flags</u> by Ouida
6   <u>Moll Flanders</u> by Daniel Defoe

<u>John Bold</u> - this character is the young surgeon and reformer town politician who joins wit a newspaperman, Tom Towers, in exposing Rev. Septimus Harding as being overpaid for managing an almshouse known as Hiram's Hospital which regularly houses twelve elderly people; eventually, he reverses his position his position after falling in love with the Reverend's daughter, Elinor, whom he later marries after the Reverend resigns in this Victorian Period novel (1855).

7   <u>Barchester Towers</u> by Anthony Trollope
8   <u>The Warden</u> by Anthony Trollope
9   <u>Orley Farm</u> by Anthony Trollope

2-5-8

<u>Kory-Kory</u> - this character is the loyal native servant who is assigned along with an attractive young native girl named Fayaway by a cannibal tribal chief, Mehevi, to two young American sailors, Tom and Toby, who deserted the ship, the <u>Dolly</u>, at one of the Marquesas Islands; eventually, he is left behind after Toby is shanghaied and Tom is rescued by an Australian ship with the help of the taboo man, Marnoo in this Victorian Period novel (1846).

1	<u>Lord Jim</u> by Joseph Conrad
2	<u>Two Years Before the Mast</u> by Richard Henry Dana, Jr.
3	<u>Typee</u> by Herman Melville

<u>Princess Corona d'Amague</u> - this character is the lovely English widow whose husband had been injured saving the life of her brother, Lord Rockingham - also known as the Seraph; eventually, Bertie Cecil under the assumed name of Louis Victor falls in love with her and risks a firing squad in Algeria to defend her honor against Colonel Chateauroy in this Victorian Period novel (1852).

4	<u>Under Two Flags</u> by Ouida
5	<u>Adam Bede</u> by George Eliot
6	<u>The Egoist</u> by George Meredith

<u>Kenyon</u> - this character is the young American sculptor who belongs to an art colony in 19th century Rome which includes a young Italian nobleman named Donatello, a young painter named Miriam Schaefer and an American painter named Hilda; eventually, he reunites Miriam and Donatello only to see Donatello imprisoned for fatally throwing a Capuchin monk named Brother Antonio off <u>Tarpian Rock</u> in this Victorian Period novel (1860).

7	<u>Anthony Adverse</u> by Hervey Allen
8	<u>The Marble Faun</u> by Nathaniel Hawthorne
9	<u>The Ordeal of Richard Feveral</u> by George Meredith

3-4-8

Clara Middleton - this character is the 17 year-old, uneducated, middle-class Englishwoman whose failed engagement to Sir Willoughby Patterne which had been prearranged by her retired clergyman father, Rev. Dr. Middleton, allows her to marry a writer named Vernon Whitford and travel the Alps; eventually, her future role as Lady Patterne is filled by 27 year-old writer/tenant, Laetitia Dale, after this twice jilted nobleman accedes to her demands in this Victorian Period novel (1879).

1   The Egoist by George Meredith
2   Anthony Adverse by Hervey Allen
3   The Ordeal of Richard Feveral by George Meredith

Stepan Verhovensky - this character is the 53 year-old professor of history who is hired by Varvara Petrovna Stavrogin to tutor her tormented son, Nikolay; eventually, this sentimental scholar sees through his own illusions and realizes his own intellectual buffoonery after discovering that his son, Pyoty, had turned into a nihilistic terrorist who is bent on destruction in this Victorian Period novel (1867).

4   The Possessed by Fyodor Dostoevski
5   The Idiot by Fyodor Dostoevski
6   Crime and Punishment by Fyodor Dostoevski

Fyodor - this character is the lecherous, shrewd old businessman who fathered four sons named Dmitri, Ivan, Alexey and Smerdyakov and then deserted each one of them after their mothers died while keeping Smerdyakov on as his servant; eventually, his murderer, Smerdyakov, hangs himself after confessing to Ivan while Aloysha plans to accompany Dmitri to Siberia after the latter in unjustly convicted for the murder in this Victorian Period novel (1880).

7   The Idiot by Fyodor Dostoevski
8   The Brothers Karamazov by Fyodor Dostoevski
9   Crime and Punishment by Fyodor Dostoevski

1-4-8

Sir Austin - this character is the old master of <u>Raynham Abbey</u> whose overreaction to his wife's desertion for a failed poet named Diaper Sandoe is to strictly regulate his only son's education under the tutelage of his son's uncle, Adrian Harley; eventually, this misogynist's fails when his son rejects his cousin, Clare Forey, who loves him and marries the niece of a neighboring farmer, Lucy Desborough, who dies of brain fever in this Victorian Period novel (1859).

1   <u>The Ordeal of Richard Feverel</u> by George Meredith
2   <u>Anthony Adverse</u> by Hervey Allen
3   <u>The Egoist</u> by George Meredith

Samuel Dockwrath - this character is the disreputable attorney who unearths evidence which allows Joseph Mason, Esq. to reopen a 20 year old court case against his step-mother, Lady Mason, about whether a will and its codicil were forged; eventually, he is ruined when he attempts to recover a bonus owed to him by Joseph Mason after Lady Mason finally decides to relinquish the estate to her step-son in this Victorian Period novel (1861).

4   <u>Orley Farm</u> by Anthony Trollope
5   <u>The Warden</u> by Anthony Trollope
6   <u>Barchester Towers</u> by Anthony Trollope

Pavel Ivanovitch Tchitchikoff - this character is the young clerk who travels from one Russian estate to another with his coachman, Selifan, and valet, Petrushka, buying the names of deceased serfs to increase his mortgage standing; eventually, he is freed from jail for writing a forged will by a shrewd lawyer named Murazov who unearths so many buried town scandals that the townspeople welcome his client's swift departure in this Victorian Period novel (1842).

7   Nicholai V. Gogol
8   Ivan Turgenev
9   Fyodor Dostoevski

1-4-7

Littimer - this character is the depraved servant who joins his hypocritical employer, James Steerforth, in an attempt to dishonor Little Em'ly by marrying her in lieu of his employer; eventually, this plan backfires when Little Em'ly escapes to join her uncle, Mr. Daniel Peggotty, in emigrating to Australia and James Steerforth ironically drowns with her earlier intended finacee, Ham, in this Victorian Period novel (1849-1850).

1   Great Expectations by Charles Dickens
2   A Tale of Two Cities by Charles Dickens
3   David Copperfield by Charles Dickens

Thomas Hutter - this character is the former pirate turned trapper who lives in a cabin built on piles known as Muskrat Castle in the middle of Lake Glimmerglass with his adopted daughter, Judith, and her retarded sister, Hetty; eventually, he is killed and scalped during an ambush by a band of Iroquois Indians while the young woodsman, Natty Bumppo, is being held captive in this Victorian Period novel (1841).

4   Drums Along the Mohawk by Walter Edmonds
5   The Deerslayer by James Fenimore Cooper
6   Arrowsmith by Sinclair Lewis

Nicodemus Boffin (Noddy) - this character is the uneducated, kindly   clerk known as the Golden Dustman who inherits the Harmon fortune after young John Harmon is mistakenly reported dead from drowning on his voyage home from South Africa to marry Bella Wilfer; eventually, he hires this young man as a secretary under the guise of John Rokesmith until Bella Wilfer undergoes a necessary personality transformation in this Victorian Period novel (1864-1866).

7   Great Expectations by Charles Dickens
8   Our Mutual Friend by Charles Dickens
9   A Tale of Two Cities by Charles Dickens

3-5-8

Franklin Blake - this character is the young Englishman who almost loses Rachel Verinder to a handsome charity worker named Godfrey Applewhite after she sees him steal the Hindu diamond bequeated to her by her sadistic uncle, John Herncastle; eventually, his exoneration allows him to marry Rachel while Godfrey's dead body is found dressed as a sailor at a waterfront boarding house with clues that he was heading for Amsterdam in this Victorian Period novel (1868).

1   The Mystery of Edwin Drood by Charles Dickens
2   The Moonstone by Wilkie Collins
3   A Study in Scarlet by Sir Arthur Conan Doyle

Josiah Bounderby - this character is the rich old banker from Coketown whose friendship with a narrow-minded schoolmaster named Thomas Gradgrind leads him into a loveless marriage with latter's youthful daughter, Louisa; eventually, he mistakenly accuses one of his maltreated ex-employees, Stephen Blackpool, of bank theft until Thomas Gradgrind's son Tom is found guilty in this Victorian Period novel (1854).

4   Our Mutual Friend by Charles Dickens
5   Hard Times by Charles Dickens
6   Barnaby Rudge by Charles Dickens

Esther Lyon - this character is the superficial, attractive young presumed daughter of the local curate, Rufus Lyon, whose choice of a future husband lies between a watchmaker who works amongst the lower classes and the wealthy son of a Tory landowner named Harold Transome; eventually, she marries the watchmaker after her mature testimony helps him to receive a pardon for the accidental death of a worker while trying to prevent a riot in this Victorian Period novel (1859).

7   The Egoist by George Meredith
8   Adam Bede by George Eliot
9   Consuelo George Sand

<u>Bella Wilfer</u> - this character is the materialistic, young woman who is invited to live with the nouveau rich Nicodemus and Henrietta Boffin because of her engagement to the son of their benefactors, John Harmon, who was presumed drowned returning home from South Africa; eventually, she is tricked by the Boffins and John Harmon under the guise of John Rokesmith into rejecting her materialistic ways in this Victorian Period novel (1864-1866).

1   <u>Our Mutual Friend</u> by Charles Dickens
2   <u>Great Expectations</u> by Charles Dickens
3   <u>A Tale of Two Cities</u> by Charles Dickens

<u>Rake</u> - this character is the dedicated servant who joins a young, insolvent English military officer named Bertie Cecil when he flees London after being falsely accused of forging a promissory note signed by his younger brother, Berkeley Cecil; eventually, he is killed by Arabs while he and his master known under the alias, Louis Victor, are on a dangerous dispatch mission for the French Foreign Legion in this Victorian Period novel (1867).

4   <u>Under Two Flags</u> by Ouida (Marie Louise de la Ramee)
5   <u>Consuelo</u> by George Sand
6   <u>Silas Marner</u> by George Eliot

<u>Niccolo Antonio Porpora</u> - this character is the music teacher who watches as his talented goddaughter and student replaces a lead singer named Corilla at the theater of Count Zustiniani; eventually, his excessive doting on his goddaughter to further her career eliminates both her fiancé, a no-talent musician named Anzoleto and a count named Albert Rudolstadt in this Victorian Period novel (1842).

7   <u>Under Two Flags</u> by Ouida
8   <u>Consuelo</u> by George Sand (Mme. Aurora Dudevant)
9   <u>Silas Marner</u> by George Eliot (Mary Anne Evans)

1-4-8

<u>Cigarette</u> - this character is the illegitimate, young French patriotic dancer/singer who is the mascot of the French Foreign Legionnaire troops in Algeria under the commanding officer Colonel Chateauroy; eventually, she gives up her life when she protects her lover, Bertie Cecil posing as Louis Victor, when she blocks bullets intended for him by a firing squad in this Victorian Period novel (1867).

1   <u>Under Two Flags</u> by Ouida (Marie Louise de la Ramee)
2   <u>Consuelo</u> by George Sand
3   <u>Silas Marner</u> by George Eliot

The Post-Victorian Period
(1890-1920)

Some of the noted novelists of this period are as follows: Thomas Hardy, William Somerset Maugham, James Joyce, Joseph Conrad, Rudyard Kipling, Henry James, D.H. Lawrence, H.G. Wells, Edith Wharton, E.M. Forster and Anatole France.

Some of the factors that determined the mood and temper of this period are as follows: in the 1890's popular education allowed everyone to read and write while the hunger to devour written material grew at a phenomenal pace.   Book production and books in serialized form in local newspapers skyrocketed.   Soon supply and demand turned book production into a lucrative business.   Readership increased while profits soared.   Literature was no longer limited to an art form for only the landed gentry and the well-educated; it had finally become democratic.   From the beginning of this period until long after the turn of the century, the type of material covered by novelists expanded to the point that it had become eclectic.   Anything and everything came under their scrutiny.   All aspects of life were looked at and all experiences qualified as legitimate subject matter.   Contemporary themes took preference over content dealing with the past.

Some of the underlying concepts that help to describe what motivated the writers of this period have to do with the issues that affect modern day society. Popular works began to compete with literary works for sales.   Authors who chose to write for an educated, critical reading public vied with authors who wrote for direct popular appeal.   It created a tension where the struggle involved form versus content.   The main issue became one of literary legitimacy and like today no dominant school emerged.   As of today, this battlefield atmosphere exists between what are referred to as pot-boilers and legitimate fiction.

<u>1</u>

<u>Wolf Larsen</u> - this character is the unfeeling, pitiless captain of the sailing vessel, the <u>Ghost</u>, which is heading from California to the seal ranges off Alaska in the Bering Sea and the one who rescues a man from the Pacific Ocean named Humphrey (Hump) Weyden after the latter's ship sinks because of a collision at sea; eventually, he loses his crew who desert him, develops severe headaches that ultimately result in blindness and a coma and is buried at sea by Weyden and Maud Brewster in this Post-Victorian novel (1904).

1   <u>Captains Courageous</u> by Rudyard Kipling
2   <u>The Sea Wolf</u> by Jack London
3   <u>Two Years Before the Mast</u> by Richard Henry Dana, Jr.

<u>Disco Troop</u> - this character is the owner/captain of the <u>We're Here</u>, a fishing schooner whose dory rescues an immature 15 year-old named Harvey Cheyne while on a fishing expedition in the Great Banks off Newfoundland; eventually, he and his crew help
this millionaire's son grow into a self-reliant young man in this novel by a Nobel Prize winning author (1897).

4   <u>Captains Courageous</u> by Rudyard Kipling
5   <u>Two Years Before the Mast</u> by Richard Henry Dana Jr.
6   <u>The Sea Wolf</u> by Jack London

<u>Henry Fleming</u> - this character is the young farm hand turned volunteer recruit in the Union Army during the American Civil War who becomes unnerved awaiting his regiment's first engagement with the enemy to the point where he actually runs away when the fighting starts; eventually, his contact through fate and circumstances with such fellow soldiers as the tall Jim Conklin, the loud Wilson and a twice wounded soldier whose uniform is tattered causes his transition from cowardice to bravery in this Post-Victorian novel (1895).

7   <u>All Quiet on the Western Front</u> by Erich Maria Remarque
8   <u>Drums Along the Mohawk</u> by Walter Edmonds
9   <u>The Red Badge of Courage</u> by Stephen Crane

2-4-9

<u>Kimball O'Hara</u> - this character is the orphaned son of a soldier in an Irish regiment during British India's Raj whose horoscope by an old Tibetan lama is fulfilled when he finally envisions a red bull on a green field; eventually, his recruitment by Colonel Creighton and Mahbub Ali which is followed by instructions by a Babu named Hurree train him to successfully swipe crucial military plans from the Russians in the Himalayas in this Post-Victorian Nobel Prize winning novel (1901).

1	<u>Four Feathers</u> by Percival Wren
2	<u>The Prisoner of Zenda</u> by Anthony Hope
3	<u>Kim</u> by Rudyard Kipling

<u>Richard Hannay</u> - this character is the prosperous, retired mining engineer who is accused of murdering an American private investigator named Franklin Scudder while the latter was visiting his London flat; eventually, his plea that a plot exists whereby a German spy group known as the <u>Black Stone</u> plans to invade England believed by Sir Walter Bullivant when the Greek diplomat, Constantine Karolides, is assassinated in this Post-Victorian novel (1915).

4	<u>Kim</u> by Rudyard Kipling
5	<u>The Thirty-Nine Steps</u> by John Buchan
6	<u>The Prisoner of Zenda</u> by Anthony Hope

<u>George Willard</u> - this character is the sole, young newspaper reporter for a small Midwestern town's weekly paper whose gregarious life   in a family hotel with his parents permits him to become a magnet whereby numerous people confide in him about their intimate thoughts and lives; eventually, this aspiring writer who receives mixed signals regarding spirituality and sexuality from his former teacher, Kate Swift, and inspiration from the banker's daughter, Helen White, finally decides to leave town after his mother's death in search of a better life in this Post-Victorian novel (1919).

7	<u>The Titan</u> by Theodore Drieser
8	<u>The Jungle</u> by Upton Sinclair
9	<u>Winesburg, Ohio</u> by Sherwood Anderson

3-5-9

<u>Harvey Cheyne</u> - this character is the immature, 15 year-old who falls overboard from his millionaire father's ocean liner because of seasickness on a trip between the United States and Europe; eventually, his rescue by the crew of the fishing schooner, the <u>We're Here</u>, and the subsequent trials he endures become a right of passage to his manhood in this Post-Victorian novel by a Nobel Prize winning author (1897).

1	<u>The Sea Wolf</u> by Jack London
2	<u>Captains Courageous</u> by Rudyard Kipling
3	<u>Two Years Before the Mast</u> by Richard Henry Dana, Jr.

<u>Chadwick (Chad) Newsome</u> - this character is the immature, uneducated factory supervisor in Lycurgus, New York who impregnates his mistress, Roberta Allen, while social climbing so he can marry Sondra Finchley; eventually, he is electrocuted for Roberta's death by misadventure during a boating accident because the jury found it to be premeditated in this Post-Victorian novel (1903).

4	<u>The Turn of the Screw</u> by Henry James
5	<u>The Ambassadors</u> by Henry James
6	<u>Washington Square</u> by Henry James

<u>Mildred Rogers</u> - this character is the promiscuous London waitress at a London tea shop who becomes the obsessive love object of a neurotic clubfooted medical student whose advances are constantly rebuffed; eventually, she leaves with her baby after going ballistic and trashing his apartment only to later lose him when he marries his young unpretentious mistress, Susan Athelney in this Post-Victorian novel (1915).

7	<u>The Forsythe Saga</u> by John Galsworthy
8	<u>Of Human Bondage</u> by William Somerset Maugham
9	<u>Tess of the D'Urbervilles</u> by Thomas Hardy

2-5-8

<u>Jurgis Rudkus</u> - this character is the Lithuanian immigrant who travels to Packingtown in Chicago where he marries Ona and takes a job in meatpacking to support his wife and father, Antanas along with his extended family which includes Ona's stepmother, Elzbieta, Jonas, Marija and Elzbieta's six children; eventually, tragic setbacks like his wife's prostitution, her death in childbirth, being injured and jailed occur in succession until his utter despair is lifted when he embraces the Socialist's ideology in this muckraker Post-Victorian novel (1906).

1	<u>The Jungle</u> by Upton Sinclair
2	<u>The Pit</u> by Frank Norris
3	<u>The Octopus</u> by Frank Norris

<u>Jim Conklin</u> - this character is the tall, veteran soldier in the Union Army during the American Civil War who tries to reassure a young, volunteer unnerved recruit named Henry Fleming about the upcoming battle while arguing with another outspoken bragging recruit named Wilson; eventually, his predictions prove true and fear over the mortal wound he has suffered drive him to seek safe haven and ultimate death on an open field rather than fall under the wheels of an artillery wagon in this Post-Victorian novel(1895).

4	<u>Drums Along the Mohawk</u> by Walter Edmonds
5	<u>All Quiet on the Western Front</u> by Erich Maria Remarque
6	<u>The Red Badge of Courage</u> by Stephen Crane

<u>Caroline Meeber</u> - this character is the young Wisconsin girl whose travels to Chicago lead to affairs with a good-looking, shallow traveling salesman named Charles Drouet and a married Chicago saloon manager named G. W. Hurstwood; eventually, she travels to Europe under a different acting name after her success in New York City in this Post-Victorian novel (1900).

7	<u>Arrowsmith</u> by Sinclair Lewis
8	<u>Sister Carrie</u> by Theodore Dreiser
9	<u>Elmer Gantry</u> by Sinclair Lewis

1-6-8

Presley - this character is the 30 year-old Eastern poet whose journey out west during the 1870's ti the Los Muertos ranch in the San Joaquin Valley for health reasons puts him in the middle of a war between wheat farmers and the railroad; eventually, he sides with wheat farmers, Maggus Derick and Annixter, blacklisted railroad engineer and sheepherder, Vanamee against the railroad which is represented by banker, S. Behrman and railroad president, Mr. Shelgrim in this muckraker Post-Victorian novel (1901).

1	The Jungle by Upton Sinclair
2	Babbitt by Sinclair Lewis
3	The Octopus by Frank Norris

Curtis Jadwin - this character is the self-reliant speculator in the 1890's Chicago wheat market who makes a fortune while married to the former Laura Dearborn whom he won away from a painter named Sheldon Corthell, who was her long time suitor; eventually, he faces financial ruin when the relentless, unyielding wheat market turns on him shortly after his friend Charles Cressler's bankruptcy and suicide while neither man was ever aware that they were secret opponents in this muckraker Post-Victorian novel (1903).

4	The Jungle by Upton Sinclair
5	The Pit by Frank Norris
6	Sister Carrie by Theodore Dreiser

Mattie Silver - this character is the young, lovely girl who travels to rural Massachusetts to act as a companion for her sickly cousin, Zeena, who has trapped a 21 year-old into a seven year loveless marriage rather than let him become an engineer or chemist; eventually, her dismissal by Zeena over a broken pickle dish results in a string of events where she ends up being nursed by Zeena after she receives a permanent spine injury in a tragic snow sled accident that leaves this farmer with an incurable lameness in this Post-Victorian novel (1911).

7	My Antonia by Willa Cather
8	Ethan Frome by Edith Wharton
9	Penguin Island by Anatole France

3-5-8

<u>Tess Durbeyfield</u> - this character is the young, physically endowed   country girl who is seduced by a predatory young man named Alec d'Urberville which produces a daughter, Sorrow, who only lives a few days; eventually, she is deserted by her dairy farmer husband, Angel Clare, and is later arrested, convicted and sentenced to hang for fatally stabbing Alec while he slept in this Post-Victorian novel (1891).

1	Joseph Conrad
2	Victor Hugo
3	Thomas Hardy

<u>The Tattered Man</u> - this character is the twice wounded soldier in the Union Army during the American Civil War whose encounter with a young farm hand turned volunteer recruit named Henry Fleming and ensuing questions about the latter's wounds profoundly affect this recruit's future actions; eventually, he and this recruit observe a pitiful-looking fellow soldier, Jim Conklin, do a grotesque dance in an pe field before he falls dead, thereby avoiding being run over by he wheels of an artillery wagon in this Post-Victorian novel (1895).

4	<u>The Red Badge of Courage</u> by Stephen Crane
5	<u>Three Soldiers</u> by John Dos Passos
6	<u>All Quiet on the Western Front</u> by Erich Maria Remarque

<u>Dan Troop</u> - this character is the adolescent son of a fishing schooner's owner and captain, Disco Troop, and the one who accompanies him on annual fishing expeditions in the Great Banks off Newfoundland; eventually, he attains the position of mate aboard an ocean liner due to his youthful association and friendship with a millionaire's son, Harvey Cheyne, in this Post-Victorian novel by a Nobel Prize winning author (1897).

7	<u>Captains Courageous</u> by Rudyard Kipling
8	<u>The Sea Wolf</u> by Jack London
9	<u>Two Years Before The Mast</u> by Richard Henry Dana, Jr.

3-4-7

<u>Humphrey Van Weyden (Hump)</u> - this character is the ship passenger who is rescued off the coast of California when his ship sinks after a collision and the one who observes that brutality of Captain Wolf Larsen after he is pressed into service as a cabin boy aboard the <u>Ghost</u> as this sailing vessel heads for the seal ranges off Alaska; eventually, he and another rescued woman named Maud Brewster bury Captain Wolf Larsen at sea and sail a deserted and refitted <u>Ghost</u> until they meet up with a Unites States revenue cutter in this Post-Victorian novel (1904).

1	<u>Two Years Before the Mast</u> by Richard Henry Dana, Jr.
2	<u>The Sea Wolf</u> by Jack London
3	<u>Captains Courageous</u> by Rudyard Kipling

<u>Charles Strickland</u> - this character is the 40 year-old English stockbroker who abandons a comfortable humdrum, middle-class life with his dull wife and children and secretly travels to Paris to become an artist; eventually, his aloofness toward Blanche Stroeve after she deserts her husband, Dirk, drives her to commit suicide while his artistic compulsions compel him to travel to the island of Tahiti in this Post-Victorian novel(1919).

4	<u>The Moon and Sixpence</u> by William Somerset Maugham
5	<u>Cakes and Ale</u> by William Somerset Maugham
6	<u>Of Human Bondage</u> by William Somerset Maugham

<u>Wilson</u> - this character is the outspoken, bragging soldier in the Union Army during the American Civil War whose fear of death before the first engagement of his regiment causes him to turn over a packet of letters to a young farmhand turned volunteer recruit named Henry Fleming; eventually, his arguments before battle with a tall veteran soldier named Jim Conklin and his stability after the first attack clear away some of his brashness and boasting to where he asks for the return of his letters in this Post-Victorian novel (1895).

7	<u>Three Soldiers</u> by John Dos Passos
8	<u>The Red Badge of Courage</u> by Stephen Crane
9	<u>All Quiet on the Western Front</u> by Erich Maria Remarque

<u>Rudolf Rassendyll</u> - this character is the 29 year-old, aimless, red-bearded Englishman whose visit to Ruritania and contact with Fritz von Tarlenheim and Colonel Sapt results in his impersonation of King Rudolf to save the Ruritanian crown from Black Michael; eventually, his deception is exposed along with his attraction to Princess Flavia who honorably chooses to marry the king despite her personal feelings in this Post-Victorian novel by an English author writing under a nom de plume (1894).

1   <u>The Prisoner of Zenda</u> by Anthony Hope
2   <u>The Invisible Man</u> by H.G. Wells
3   <u>Jude the Obscure</u> by Thomas Hardy

<u>Zenobia Pierce (Zeena)</u> - this character is the sickly, nagging wife   who had trapped a 21 year-old into a seven year loveless marriage rather than let him become an engineer or chemist only to witness him fall in love with a young, lovely girl named Mattie Silver who has traveled to rural Massachusetts to be her companion; eventually, she is forced to nurse this young girl after a tragic snow sled accident leaves crippled from a permanent spine injury while leaving her husband with an incurable lameness in this Post-Victorian novel (1911).

4   <u>Ethan Frome</u> by Edith Wharton
5   <u>Little Women</u> by Louisa May Alcott
6   <u>The Lost Lady</u> by Willa Cather

<u>Sir Walter Bullivant</u> - this character is the government official who questions the veracity of a retired mining engineer concerning a German spy group known as the <u>Black Stone</u> and their involvement in a plot to invade England; eventually, he believes Richard Hannay did not kill a private investigator named Franklin Scudder after he receives notification that a Greek diplomat named Constantine Karolides had been assassinated in this Post-Victorian novel (1915).

7   <u>The Thirty-Nine Steps</u> by John Buchan
8   <u>The Invisible Man</u> by H.G. Wells
9   <u>Kim</u> by Rudyard Kipling

1-4-7

<u>Pennsylvania</u> - this character is the former preacher who tragically lost his entire family in the Johnstown flood; eventually, he is hired by Captain Disco Troop and joins the crew of a fishing schooner named the <u>We're Here</u> for annual expeditions looking for cod in the Great Banks off Newfoundland in this Post-Victorian novel by a Nobel Prize winning author (1897).

1	<u>Captains Courageous</u> by Rudyard Kipling
2	<u>Two Years Before the Mast</u> by Richard Henry Dana, Jr.
3	<u>The Sea Wolf</u> by Jack London

<u>Simon Dedalus</u> - this character is the glib, carefree drinking Irishman whose ineffectual life and admiration of the Irish patriot, Parnell, incurs the wrath of his son Stephen's aunt, Mrs. Dante Riordan, to the point where she is constantly contentious with him; eventually, his arguments about her provincial beliefs leave his son so disillusioned with his Catholicism and national heritage that he decides in order to leave Ireland to pursue his artistic goals on the Continent in this Post-Victorian novel (1916).

4	<u>A Portrait of the Artist As A Young Man</u> by James Joyce
5	<u>Ulysses</u> by James Joyce
6	<u>Finnegan's Wake</u> by James Joyce

<u>Alec d'Urberville</u> - this character is the sexual predator whose seduction of a simple country girl named Tess Durbeyfield produces   an illegitimate daughter, Sorrow, who only lives for a few days; eventually, he is stabbed to death while sleeping by Tess who is summarily arrested, convicted and hanged just after being reunited with her husband upon his return from Brazil in this Post-Victorian novel (1891).

7	Joseph Conrad
8	Victor Hugo
9	Thomas Hardy

1-4-9

<u>Mael</u> - this character is the naive, devout Breton monk on the island of Alca who is deceived by Kraken's mistress, Oberosia, into believing that she is the virgin sent to slay a dragon that is threatening the island's inhabitants; eventually, he is tricked again when Kraken jumps out from a prearranged spot and pretends to kill a fake dragon manufactured by Oberosia and him which then earns him an annual tribute from the island's inhabitants in this Post-Victorian novel by a Nobel Prize winning author (1908).

1	<u>Steppenwolf</u> by Herman Hesse
2	<u>Sanctuary</u> by William Faulkner
3	<u>Penguin Island</u> by Anatole France

<u>Lucien Gregory</u> - this character is the young, anarchistic poet   who desires to join the Central Anarchist Council which consists of the Secretary, Gogol, the Marquis de St. Eustache, Professor de Worms, Dr. Bull and its chairman who ultimately dresses up as the symbol of the Christian Sabbath; eventually, he loses his seat on the Council to Gabriel Syme and is exposed as an intellectual anarchist when the Council reveals that it is totally made up of spies from Scotland Yard in this Post-Victorian novel (1908).

4	<u>The Man Who Was Thursday</u> by G. K. Chesterton
5	<u>The Thirty-Nine Steps</u> by John Buchan
6	<u>Kim</u> by Rudyard Kipling

<u>Rima</u> - this character is the slim, young and delicate British Guayan female who compels a young Venezuelan rebel, Abel Guevez de Argensola, and an old hunter and adopted grandfather, Nuflo, to take her on a eighteen miles journey from a savannah to Mount Riolama; eventually, this chameleon-like, ethereal being is perceived as evil by neighboring savage-like natives and ordered burned to death by their leader, Managa, which brings about their destruction by Mr. Abel in this Post-Victorian novel (1904).

7	<u>Magnificent Obsession</u> by Lloyd C. Douglas
8	<u>Green Mansions</u> by W.H. Hudson
9	<u>Tono-Bungay</u> by H.G. Wells

3-4-8

<u>Mrs. Cuzak (nee Schimerda)</u> - this character is the young, innocent, Bohemian homesteader of simple passions and moral integrity in Nebraska who is seduced and impregnated by a dashing railroad conductor; eventually, her jilting by him in Denver, Colorado, allows to meet and finally marry the dependable and hard-working farmer, Cuzak, and have a large family in this Post-Victorian novel (1918).

1	<u>Ethan Frome</u> by Edith Wharton
2	<u>My Antonia</u> by Willa Cather
3	<u>Cat's Eye</u> by Margaret Atwood

<u>Black Michael</u> - this character is the King Rudolf of Ruritania's treacherous, half brother whose diabolical plans include killing the king and his impersonator, Rudolf Rassendyll, while seizing the throne and the king's betrothed, Princess Flavia, for himself; eventually, he is killed by an unfaithful aide named Rubert Hentzau during an assault on a hunting lodge to free the imprisoned king by Fritz von Tarlenheim and Colonel Sapt in this Post-Victorian novel by an English author writing under a pen name (1894).

4	<u>Anthony Adverse</u> by Hervey Allen
5	<u>The Prisoner of Zenda</u> by Anthony Hope
6	<u>Lord Jim</u> by Joseph Conrad

<u>Mrs. Grose</u> - this character is the simple minded, illiterate servant at a country estate, Bly, who becomes the companion and confidante of a 21 year-old governess for 2 orphaned children, 8 year-old Flora and her 10 year-old brother Miles; eventually, she relates to this governess the history of 2 late employees, a valet named Peter Quint and a governess named Miss Jessel, who may be appearing to the children in order to corrupt their innocence in this Post-Victorian novel (1898).

7	<u>Washington Square</u> by Henry James
8	<u>The Ambassadors</u> by Henry James
9	<u>The Turn of the Screw</u> by Henry James

2-5-9

<u>Antonie (Tony)</u> - this character is the late 19th century Germany woman who is the oldest child in a family consisting of Tom, Christian and younger sister, Clara, who have all inherited a successful grain-trading firm from their father, Jean, and grandfather, Johann; eventually, her two unsuccessful marriages to a Hamburg merchant, Bendix Grunlich, and a Munich brewer named Alois Permaneder which end in divorce reflects the decadence that plagues the entire family by a Nobel Prize winning author (1902).

1	<u>Buddenbrooks</u> by Thomas Mann
2	<u>Steppenwolf</u> by Herman Hesse
3	<u>The Magic Mountain</u> by Thomas Mann

<u>Weena</u> - this character is the young girl from the weak vegetarian people known as the Eloi who is saved from drowning by a stranger and ultimately becomes his friend and guide; eventually, the stranger awakens on a hill beyond the forest to discover that their fire is out, she has disappeared along with the matches and about 35 subterranean Morlocks have perished from an earlier fire in this Post-Victorian novel (1895).

4	<u>The Invisible Man</u> by H.G. Wells
5	<u>Tono-Bungay</u> by H.G. Wells
6	<u>The Time Machine</u> by H.G. Wells

<u>Blanche Stroeve</u> - this character is the half-baked Dutch artist's English wife who becomes the lover of a 40 year-old English stockbroker living in Paris who had abandoned his humdrum, middle class existence in England, his dull wife, Amy, and their children; eventually, she commits suicide by poisoning herself with oxalic acid after her new lover, Charles, finally deserts her in this Post-Victorian novel (1919).

7	<u>Cakes and Ale</u> by William Somerset Maugham
8	<u>The Moon and Sixpence</u> by William Somerset Maugham
9	<u>Of Human Bondage</u> by William Somerset Maugham

1-6-8

<u>Jim Burden</u> - this character is the young Harvard lawyer who becomes the legal counsel for a Western railroad with the aid of a brilliant but incompatible marriage; eventually, he nostalgically narrates about his earlier years and positive experiences upon the   prairie and in the town of Black Hawk, Nebraska in this Post-Victorian novel (1918).

1   <u>The Lost Lady</u> by Willa Cather
2   <u>Little Women</u> by Louisa May Alcott
3   <u>My Antonia</u> by Willa Cather

<u>Chief Doramin</u> - this character is the stern, old chieftain whose son, Dain Waris, leads other natives of the tribe in a siege of a renegade leader, Gentleman Brown, and his roving band of cutthroats on a Patusan island hilltop, thereby protecting the main protagonist's stronghold from plunder; eventually, he carries out native justice when he avenges his son's careless death by shooting the main protagonist through the breast in this Post-Victorian novel by a Nobel Prize winning author (1915).

4   <u>The Castle</u> by Franz Kafka
5   <u>Buddenbrooks</u> by Thomas Mann
6   <u>Lord Jim</u> by Joseph Conrad

<u>Angel Clare</u> - this character is the dairy farmer whose marriage to a young, simple country girl named Tess Durbeyfield ends in desertion when he learns that she had an illegitimate daughter, Sorrow, with a sexual predator named Alec d'Urberville; eventually, his return from Brazil gives him only a few days with Tess before she is hanged for stabbing Alec to death as he slept in this Post-Victorian novel (1892).

7   Joseph Conrad
8   Victor Hugo
9   Thomas Hardy

3-6-9

Gertrude Morel - this character is the mother of 4 whose shift of love from her drunken miner husband, William, to her artistic son, Paul, leads to Paul's dilemma between choosing idealistic Miriam Leivers or earthy Clara Dawes; eventually, her fatal morphine overdose by Paul to stop her terminal cancer pain allows Paul to reconcile Clara with her husband, Baxter, leave Miriam and start his life over again in this Post-Victorian novel (1913).

1   <u>How Green Was My Valley</u> by Richard LLewellyan
2   <u>Far From the Madding Crowd</u> by Thomas Hardy
3   <u>Sons and Lovers</u> by D.H. Lawrence

Vinicius - this character is the nephew of a wealthy, Roman patrician named Petronius who holds favor with the Emperor Nero and the one who is a returning military soldier who encounters Lygia who is the daughter of a barbarian king being held hostage; eventually, his love for this converted Christian results in his own conversion, their subsequent marriage and ultimate flight to the safety of Sicily along with her slave, Ursus, in this Post-Victorian novel written by a Nobel Prize winning Polish author (1895).

4   <u>Ben Hur: A Tale of the Christ</u> by Lewis (Lew) Wallace
5   <u>Quo Vadis</u> by Henryk Sienkiewicz
6   <u>Thaddeus of Warsaw</u> by Jane Porter

Herr Permaneder - - this character is the successful Munich beer merchant who is the second German businessman to marry a young German woman growing up in late 19th century Germany named Antonie (Tony) with a family who had inherited a successful grain-trading firm from their father, Jean, and grandfather, Johann; eventually, he ends up returning her dowrey after a divorce based on his drinking and sexual advances to their cook, Babette, in this Post-Victorian novel by a Nobel Prize winning author (1902).

7   <u>The Magic Mountain</u> by Thomas Mann
8   <u>Steppenwolf</u> by Herman Hesse
9   <u>Buddenbrooks</u> by Thomas Mann

3-5-9

<u>Col. Creighton</u> - this character is the director of the British Secret Service in India during the Raj who joins a horse trader named Mahbub Ali in recruiting a young Irish orphan boy named Kimball O'Hara into the spy business under the training of a Babu named Hurree; eventually, he directs an operation to swipe crucial military documents from the Russians by this street urchin who has finally envisioned a red bull in a green field as prophesied by a Tibetan lama in this Nobel Prize winning Post-Victorian novel (1901).

1	<u>The Thirty-Nine Steps</u> by John Buchan
2	<u>Kim</u> by Rudyard Kipling
3	<u>Captains Courageous</u> by Rudyard Kipling

<u>William Sylvanus Baxter</u> - this character is the flighty, inane young man from a small Midwestern town whose summer infatuation with the Parcher's new seasonal boarder, Miss Platt, is constantly undermined by his annoying younger sister, Jane; eventually, his numerous attempts to impress this lisping young woman who has a small dog, Flopit, ultimately prove frustrating whether they are at a dance, a tea party, a farewell party or at the train station when she leaves town in this Post-Victorian novel (1916).

4	<u>Little Women</u> by Louisa May Alcott
5	<u>The Lost Lady</u> by Willa Cather
6	<u>Seventeen</u> by Booth Tarkington

<u>Arcade</u> - this character is the culprit who is responsible when a valuable book and manuscript collection starts to disappear from the d'Esparvieu library run by a meticulous manager named Monsieur Julien Sariette, which are later found in Maurice D'Espanvieu's room because of this culprit's voracious appetite for learning; eventually, he fails to convince a sympathetic prince to lead him and others such as Prince Istar and Zita against Ialdabaoth with the prince explaining that they would all their sympathy for humanity in this Post-Victorian novel by a Nobel Prize winning French author (1914).

7	<u>Les Miserables</u> by Victor Hugo
8	<u>Madame Bovary</u> by Gustave Flaubert
9	<u>The Revolt of the Angels</u> by Anatole France

2-6-9

<u>The Governess</u> - this character is the new employee at a country estate in Bly whose charges are two orphaned children, 10 year-old, Miles, and his 8 year-old sister, Flora; eventually, she joins forces with the housekeeper, Mrs. Grose, to fight evil attempts by two apparitions named Peter Quint and Miss Jessel in this Post-Victorian novel (1898).

1	<u>The Turn of the Screw</u> by Henry James
2	<u>Washington Square</u> by Henry James
3	<u>The Wings of the Dove</u> by Henry James

<u>Mr. Kurtz</u> - this character is the smart, charismatic manager of an inland trading station in the Belgian Congo who excels in ivory exports while failing in his goal of civilizing the natives; eventually, his downward spiral of decline into savagery ends in death just after he gives a packet of letters to Marlow for his fiancee in Belgium in this Post-Victorian novel written by a Polish author (1902).

4	<u>Heart of Darkness</u> by Joseph Conrad
5	<u>Lord Jim</u> by Joseph Conrad
6	<u>Victory</u> by Joseph Conrad

<u>Griffin</u> - this character is the suspicious, mysterious stranger whose presence in the village of Burdock, England is made apparent when an argument ensues between him and the owner of the <u>Coach and Horses Inn</u> over an unpaid bill; eventually, his identity is abruptly revealed during a brawl involving a physician named Dr. Kemp right after he wounds the Village Police Chief, Colonel Ayde, and is summarily killed by a constable with a garden spade in this Post-Victorian novel (1987).

7	<u>The Invisible Man</u> by H.G. Wells
8	<u>The Time Machine</u> by H.G. Wells
9	<u>Tono-Bungay</u> by H.G. Wells

1-4-7

Kraken - this character is the opportunist who has his mistress, Oberosia, trick an overly pious naive Breton monk named Mael into believing that she is the virgin who had been sent to slay a dragon that is threatening the island of Alca's inhabitants; eventually, he jumps out from a prearranged spot and pretends to kill a fake dragon which he and Oberosia had manufactured which earns him an annual tribute from the island's inhabitants in this Post-Victorian novel by a French Nobel Prize winning author (1908).

1	**Steppenwolf** by Herman Hesse
2	**Sanctuary** by William Faulkner
3	**Penguin Island** by Anatole France

Axel Heyst - this character is the lifelong non-committal East Indies loner who rescues a young English violin player renamed Lena from the hotel owner Schomberg's lascivious advances and takes her   to his island bungalow; eventually, he and Lena burn together in his bungalow after a deadly confrontation with Martin Ricardo, Mr. Jones and a brute named Pedro in this Post-Victorian novel (1915).

4	**Victory** by Joseph Conrad
5	**Lord Jim** by Joseph Conrad
6	**Heart of Darkness** by Joseph Conrad

Mrs. Dante Riordan - this character is the overly jealous Catholic aunt of young Irish student named Stephen Dateless and the one who constantly attacks Stephen's ineffectual father, Simon, because of his admiration of the heretical Irish patriot, Parnell; eventually, her provincialism becomes a factor in Stephen's decision to question his Catholic background and national heritage to the point where he decides to leave Ireland and pursue his artistic goals on the Continent in this Post-Victorian novel (1916).

7	**Ulysses** by James Joyce
8	**A Portrait of the Artist as a Young Man** by James Joyce
9	**Finnegan's Wake** by James Joyce

Miss Emily Wilkinson - this character is the difficult, uptight governess on holiday in Blackstable, England from her job in Germany who meets and is seduced by the young, orphaned clubfooted nephew of William and Louisa Carey named Philip; eventually, she repulses Philip and he moves on to obsess over a promiscuous waitress named Mildred Rogers until he marries a young unpretentious woman named Sally Athelney in this Post-Victorian novel written by an English author (1915).

1	**Of Human Bondage** by William Somerset Maugham
2	**Cakes and Ales** by William Somerset Maugham
3	**The Moon and Sixpence** by William Somerset Maugham

Stephen - this character is the young Irish student whose acute awareness makes him question Catholicism, Ireland's political unrest and economic decline along with arguments between his ineffectual father, Simon, and his aunt, Mrs. Dante Riordan over the Irish patriot, Parnell; eventually, his discussions with the University College students Davin, Lynch and Cranly become a major factor in his decision to leave Ireland and follow his artistic goals on the Continent in this Post-Victorian novel (1916).

4	**A Portrait of the Artist as a Young Man** by James Joyce
5	**Ulysses** by James Joyce
6	**Finnegan's Wake** by James Joyce

Sue Bridehead - this character is the capricious, broad-minded artist turned teacher assistant whose marriage to a schoolteacher named Richard Phillotson goes sour when she is reunited with a stonemason at the funeral of the latter's Aunt Drusilla; eventually, she returns to her husband after she has a still-born child and that her stepson, Little Father Time, had hung himself along with his younger siblings in this Post-Victorian novel (1894).

7	**Jude the Obscure** by Thomas Hardy
8	**Far From the Madding Crowd** by Thomas Hardy
9	**Return of the Native** by Thomas Hardy

1-4-7

Jewel - this character is the native wife on the island of Patusan of a disgraced English ex-chief mate who was accused of deserting a passenger ship named the Patna; eventually, she is widowed when her husband is shot to death by Chief Doramin in retaliation for his son Dain Waris's murder by Gentleman Brown in this Post-Victorian novel by a Nobel Prize winning author (1900).

1	Lord Jim by Joseph Conrad
2	Omoo by Herman Melville
3	Mutiny on the Bounty by Charles Nordhoff and James Norman Hall

Charles Drouet - this character is the good-looking, shallow traveling salesman who is rejected by a young Wisconsin girl named Caroline Meeber after she is wooed by the manager of a Chicago saloon named G. W. Hurstwood; eventually, he informs Caroline about how Hustwood had robbed his employer's safe of several thousand dollars to avoid ruin from his divorce before running off with her in this Post-Victorian novel (1900).

4	The Financier by Theodore Dreiser
5	The Titan by Theodore Dreiser
6	Sister Carrie by Theodore Dreiser

Mr. Verloc - this character is the obese, slovenly unkempt foreign functionary who lives behind his secluded Soho shop along with his English wife, Winnie, and her moronic brother, Stevie; eventually, he is stabbed in the heart by Winnie after Steve is blown-up trying to bomb the Greenwich Observatory in this Post-Victorian novel written by a Polish author (1907).

7	The Thirty-Nine Steps by John Buchan
8	Secret Agent by Joseph Conrad
9	Kim by Rudyard Kipling

1-6-8

Franklin Scudder - this character is the American private investigator who is stabbed to death while waiting in the London flat of a prosperous mining engineer named Richard Hannay; eventually, his death and the assassination of the Greek diplomat, Constantine Karolides, become links in the chain of events that convince Sir Walter Bullivant of a German plot to invade England which involve a spy group known as the <u>Black Stone</u> in this Post-Victorian novel (1915).

1   **The Maltese Falcon** by Dashiell Hammett
2   **A Study in Scarlet** by Arthur Conan Doyle
3   **The Thirty-Nine Steps** by John Buchan

Dain Waris - this character is Chief Doramin's native son on the island Patsuan who befriends a young, disgraced ex-chief mate accused of deserting a passenger ship named <u>Patna</u>; eventually, his death by Gentleman Brown is vindicated when the responsible ex-chief mate dies from Chief Doramin's fatal shot to the breast in this Post-Victorian novel by a Nobel Prize winning author (1900).

4   **Lord Jim** by Joseph Conrad
5   **Omoo** by Herman Melville
6   **Victory** by Joseph Conrad

Monsieur Julien Sariette - this character is the old, meticulous French librarian hired by the wealthy d'Esparvieu family to oversee te large and valuable collection of books and manuscripts which subsequently starts to disappear under his charge due to Arcade's voracious appetite for reading; eventually, he retrieves these books from Maurice d'Espanvieu's room only to later completely lose his mind when a volume of <u>Lucretius</u> is lost forever in this Post-Victorian novel by a Nobel Prize winning French author (1914).

7   **The Red and the Black** by Stendhal
8   **The Revolt of the Angels** by Anatole France
9   **A Sentimental Education** by Gustave Flaubert

Gentleman Brown - this character is the sociopath who decides to rob the stronghold of an ex-chief mate who had been accused of deserting a passenger ship named the Patna; eventually, he is responsible for getting this same ex-chief mate shot to death by Chief Doramin as an act of retaliation for the murder of the chief's son, Dain Waris, eventhough he committed the murder himself in this Post-Victorian novel by a Nobel Prize winning author (1900).

1	A Sentimental Education by Gustave Flaubert
2	Omoo by Herman Melville
3	Lord Jim by Joseph Conrad

Frank A. Cowperwood - this character is the steadfast, self-reliant entrepreneur whose marriage to Lillian Semple 5 years his senior runs the gamut from economic ruin to more than a year in prison and back to being a multi-millionaire; eventually, he gets a divorce from her when he leaves Philadelphia for Chicago with his new young mistress and future wife, Aileen Butler in this Post-Victorian novel (1912).

4	The Titan by Theodore Dreiser
5	Sister Carrie by Theodore Dreiser
6	The Financier by Theodore Dreiser

Soames - this character is the wealthy husband whose peace offering of a large country place named Robin Hill cannot appease his beautiful wife, Irene, who finds him materialistic, sexually repellant and abhorrent after he rapes her; eventually, he lives to see his daughter, Fleur, who was from his second marriage to a French woman named Annette Lamotte, marry Michael Mont after Young Jolyon prevents her marriage to the son he had with Irene named Jon in this Nobel Prize winning Post-Victorian novel (1922).

7	Babbitt by Sinclair Lewis
8	Winesburg, Ohio by Sherwood Anderson
9	The Forsythe Saga by John Galsworthy

3-6-9

Charles Gould - this character is the South American, English-educated manager of the San Tome silver mine in Costagnana during a civil war led by such rebels as General Sotillo and Pedrito Montero; eventually, he outlives a Creole newspaper editor named Martin Decoud and the Italian waterfront leader, Gran Battista in this Nobel Prize winning Post-Victorian novel (1904).

1   **Heart of Darkness** by Joseph Conrad
2   **Victory** by Joseph Conrad
3   **Nostromo** by Joseph Conrad

Arabella Donn - this character is the uncouth country girl who tricks a stonemason into marriage two times and has a gifted but neurotic child, Little Father Time, who ultimately hangs himself after killing his younger siblings; eventually, she maliciously refuses to let the stonemason's second wife, Sue Bridehead, know about his fatal physical decline that has been precipitated as a result of life's failure and drinking in this Post-Victorian novel (1894).

4   **Far From the Madding Crowd** by Thomas Hardy
5   **Jude the Obscure** by Thomas Hardy
6   **The Return of the Native** by Thomas Hardy

Lena - this character is the young violin player who is rescued by Axel Heyst from Wilhelm Schomberg's lascivious advances and taken to Axel's East Indies island bungalow; eventually, she and Axel burn to death in his bungalow after a deadly confrontation involving Axel's Chinese servant, Wang, a psychopathic misogynist named Mr. Jones, his follower, Martin Ricardo and a brute named Pedro in this Post-Victorian novel written by a Nobel Prize winning author (1915).

7   **Lord Jim** by Joseph Conrad
8   **Heart of Darkness** by Joseph Conrad
9   **Victory** by Joseph Conrad

3-5-9

<u>Salters</u> - this character is one of the crew members aboard a fishing schooner known as the <u>We're Here</u> under its captain and owner, Disco Troop; eventually, this schooner sails out of Gloucester, Mass. and heads for the Great Banks off Newfoundland looking for cod along with a fleet of other fishing boats in this Post-Victorian novel by a Nobel Prize winning author (1897).

1   <u>Two Years Before the Mast</u> by Richard Henry Dana, Jr.
2   <u>Captains Courageous</u> by Rudyard Kipling
3   <u>The Sea Wolf</u> by Jack London

<u>Wang</u> - this character is the mysterious Chinese servant working for Axel Heyst in his East Indian island bungalow where three criminals named Mr. Jones, Martin Ricardo and a brute named Pedro make an unexpected visit; eventually, he survives after shooting Pedro to death, Mr. Jones kills Martin, Lena and Axel are burned to death and Mr. Jones later drowns in this Post-Victorian novel by a Nobel Prize winning author (1915).

4   <u>Nostromo</u> by Joseph Conrad
5   <u>Heart of Darkness</u> by Joseph Conrad
6   <u>Victory</u> by Joseph Conrad

<u>Ernest Pontifex</u> - this character is the naive clergyman turned clothes shop owner turned writer who ultimate enlightenment results from experiencing fraud, imprisonment and bigamy whereby his drunken wife, Ellen, is exposed to be the real wife of coachman named John who had employed by his father, Theobald Pontifex; eventually, he turns twenty eight and surprisingly receives an unexpected inheritance of seventy thousand pounds from a friend named Edward Overton who had been named trustee of the legacy by Alethea Pontifex in this English Post-Victorian novel (1903).

7   <u>The Way of all Flesh</u> by Samuel Butler
8   <u>Arrowsmith</u> by Sinclair Lewis
9   <u>Winesburg, Ohio</u> by Sherwood Anderson

2-6-7

G. W. Hurstwood - this character is the manager of a Chicago saloon who steals several thousand dollars from his employer's safe to avoid ruin from a divorce and runs off with a young Wisconsin girl named Caroline Meeber; eventually, his moral and financial decline in New York ends with a lonely suicide in a flop house followed by a burial in Potter's Field in this Post-Victorian novel (1900).

1   Sister Carrie by Theodore Dreiser
2   The Titan by Theodore Dreiser
3   The Financier by Theodore Dreiser

Miriam Leivers - this character is the young idealistic farm girl who finds herself in a three way competition for the affections of a young artist named Paul Morel, a separated married woman five years his senior named Clara Dawes and the artist's overindulgent, interfering mother, Gertrude; eventually, she is jilted by his young artist after he successfully intercedes between Clara and her estranged husband, Baxter, and mercifully kills his mother with an overdose of morphine to alleviate her suffering from terminal cancer in this Post-Victorian novel (1913).

4   Sons and Lovers by D. H. Lawrence
5   How Green Was My Valley by Richard Llewellyan
6   Cakes and Ale by William Somerset Maugham

Kate Swift - this character is the Midwestern small town schoolteacher who inadvertently sends mixed signals about spirituality and sexuality to a former student named George Willard who gregarious life in a family hotel with his parents makes him a success as the sole newspaper reporter for the town's weekly paper; eventually, she joins the banker's daughter, Helen White, in providing him the impetus to leave this small town after his mother dies so he can seek the writing job which he has been aspiring to all along in this Post-Victorian novel (1919).

7   Appointment in Samarra by John O'Hara
8   Babbitt by Sinclair Lewis
9   Winesburg, Ohio by Sherwood Anderson

1-4-9

<u>Dain Maroola</u> - this character is the young, good-looking Malayan son of a rajah who travels up river to trade for gunpowder from the rajah of Sambir, Lakamba and an unsuccessful Dutch trader named Kaspar; eventually, he and Kaspar's half-caste daughter become lovers and finally avoid the Dutch aboard Lakamba's hidden boat in this first Post-Victorian novel by a Polish Nobel Prize winning author (1895).

1	<u>Lord Jim</u> by Joseph Conrad
2	<u>The Trial</u> by Franz Kafka
3	<u>Almayer's Folly</u> by Joseph Conrad

<u>George Ponderevo</u> - this character is the 22 year-old ambitious scientist who experiences a roller coaster ride between poverty, wealth and poverty when he starts out with his uncle, Edward, in selling a relatively harmless patent medicine and finally merges with the Do-Ut Corporation presided over by the affluent Mr. Moggs; eventually, he makes a marriage proposal to the aristocratic Hon. Beatrice Normandy that is refused after he becomes divorced from a shrewish wife, a shop girl named Marion Ramboat, when she catches him in an affair with his sexy secretary, Effie Rink in this Post-Victorian novel (1908).

4	<u>The Ambassadors</u> by Henry James
5	<u>Tono-Bungay</u> by H. G. Wells
6	<u>The Wings of the Dove</u> by Henry James

<u>Stein</u> - this character is the owner/trader of a number of East Indies trading posts who defers to Charles Marlow's wishes and gives a disgraced chief mate from the passenger ship, the <u>Patna</u>, a job; eventually, he helped this seaman forgive himself and finally heroically face death by Chief Doramin for Dain Waris's senseless death at the hands of Gentleman Brown in this Post-Victorian novel of Post-Victorian novel by a Nobel Prize winner Polish author (1900).

7	<u>Lord Jim</u> by Joseph Conrad
8	<u>Victory</u> by Joseph Conrad
9	<u>Nostromo</u> by Joseph Conrad

3-5-7

Charles Marlow -   - this character is the intelligent sea captain who sits on a board of inquiry where the officers of an unworthy steamer called the Patna are accused of deserting their ship and leaving 800 Muslim trapped passengers with only 7 lifeboats aboard;   eventually, his sympathy compels him to help this ex-chief mate get a job with an owner/trader named Stein on the island of Patusan in this Post-Victorian novel by a Nobel Prize winning author (1900).

1	The Sea Wolf by Jack London
2	Captains Courageous by Rudyard Kipling
3	Lord Jim by Joseph Conrad

Sally Athelny -   - this character is the unpretentious Englishwoman who beats out a promiscuous London tea shop waitress turned prostitute named Mildred Rogers for the affections of a neurotic clubfooted doctor named Philip Carey; eventually, her confession to him that she is not pregnant does not stop Philip from marrying her and settling down in a small fishing village in this English Post-Victorian novel (1915).

4	Cakes and Ale by William Somerset Maugham
5	Of Human Bondage by William Somerset Maugham
6	The Moon and Sixpence by William Somerset Maugham

Aileen Butler Cowperwood - this character is the spirited daughter of an Irish, Philadelphian politician who marries a financial wizard named Frank only to learn that he has taken on a mistress named Stephanie Platow; eventually, her infidelity and his failure to control the Chicago Transit System wind up in their divorce and his relocation to Europe with a 17 year-old named Berenice Fleming in this Post-Victorian novel (1914).

7	The Titan by Theodore Dreiser
8	Arrowsmith by Sinclair Lewis
9	Sister Carrie by Theodore Dreiser

3-5-7

<u>Mildred Theale (Milly)</u> - this character is the terminally ill,   pretty New York young woman who visits London along with her older Bostonian writer friend, Mrs. Stringham, and a younger Susan Shepherd where they encounter Mrs. Lowder; eventually, she learns from Lord Mark in Venice of Merton Densher and Kate Croy's plot before she finally dies in this Post-Victorian novel (1902).

1	<u>Washington Square</u> by Henry James
2	<u>The Wings of the Dove</u> by Henry James
3	<u>The Turn of the Screw</u> by Henry James

<u>Richard Phillotson</u> -   - this character is the simple schoolteacher who is married to a new, bright and intelligent assistant, Sue Bridehead, until she leaves him for a stonemason; eventually, he takes her back when her affair ends in tragedy after her first child is stillborn and her stepson, Little Father Time, hangs himself along with his siblings   in this Post-Victorian novel (1894).

4	<u>Jude the Obscure</u> by Thomas Hardy
5	<u>The Return of the Native</u> by Thomas Hardy
6	<u>Far From the Madding Crowd</u> by Thomas Hardy

<u>Ursula Brangwen</u> - this character is the young English schoolteacher of Polish extraction whose rare privilege of attending college in the last decade of the 19th century allows her to have an affair with a young, blond British Lieutenant of Polish extraction named Anton Skrebensky after he returns from the Boer War; eventually, her shunning of him for lacking spirituality results in his marrying the regimental commander's daughter and departing for India in this Post-Victorian novel (1915).

7	<u>The Rainbow</u> by D. H. Lawrence
8	<u>Sons and Lovers</u> by D. H. Lawrence
9	<u>How Green Was My Valley</u> by Richard Llewellyan

Long Jack - - this character is one of the crew members aboard the fishing schooner known as the We're Here with Disco Troop as captain and owner; eventually, this schooner which sails out of Gloucester, Mass. and heads for the Great Banks off Newfoundland looking for cod along with a fleet of other fishing boats rescues a teenager thrown overboard from an ocean liner named Harvey Cheyne in this Post-Victorian novel by a Nobel Prize winning author (1897).

1   Captains Courageous by Rudyard Kipling
2   Lord Jim by Joseph Conrad
3   The Sea Wolf by Jack London

William Latch - this character is the sullen, uneducated servant girl who is seduced and becomes pregnant and is jilted by William Latch for Peggy Barfield, while they are both in the employment of Peggy's aunt and uncle at their racing stable known as the Woodview; eventually, she gives birth to a son, Jackie, reneges on her marriage plans with the dependable Fred Parsons and finally marries to William Latch whose addiction to gambling leads to financial ruin until he dies of tuberculosis in this Post-Victorian novel (1894).

4   Washington Square by Henry James
5   Esther Waters by George Moore
6   Sister Carrie by Theodore Drieser

Philip Carey - this character is the clubfooted orphan who is brought up in a Blackstable, England Vicarage by a religious, narrow-minded, hypocritical uncle named William and his intimidated wife, Louisa, until he pursues such careers as clerk, artist and medicine; eventually, his freedom from an unhealthy relationship with a neurotic waitress turned prostitute named Mildred Rogers allows him to settle down and marry his unpretentious mistress, Susan Athelney in this English Post-Victorian novel (1915).

7   Of Human Bondage by William Somerset Maugham
8   The Moon and Sixpence by William Somerset Maugham
9   Cakes and Ale by William Somerset Maugham

1-5-7

<u>Mahbub Ali</u> - this character is the horse trader who joins the director of the British Secret Service during the Raj in India, Colonel Creighton, in recruiting a young Irish orphan named Kimball O'Hara onto the spy business; eventually, his recruitment proves successful when crucial military plans of the Russians are swiped by this street urchin after he envisions a red bull in a green field as prophesied by a Tibetan lama in this Nobel Prize winning Post-Victorian novel(1901).

1	<u>Captains Courageous</u> by Rudyard Kipling
2	<u>Kim</u> by Rudyard Kipling
3	<u>The Thirty-Nine Steps</u> by John Buchan

<u>Little Father Time</u> - this character is the gifted neurotic child born of an uncouth country girl named Arabella Donn and a stonemason who is aspiring to be a religious scholar; eventually, he causes his bright and intelligent stepmother, Sue Bridehead, to have a still-born child after he carries out his decision to kill his younger siblings and then hang himself in this Post-Victorian novel (1894).

4	<u>The Return of the Native</u> by Thomas Hardy
5	<u>Jude the Obscure</u> by Thomas Hardy
6	<u>Far From the Madding Crowd</u> by Thomas Hardy

<u>Margaret Schlegel</u> -this character is the older son of a prosperous, widowed London businessman named Henry who had married the much younger Margaret Schlegel and the one who becomes obsessed with discovering who is responsible for the out-of-wedlock pregnancy of this step-mother's sister, Helen Schlegel; eventually, he is imprisoned for the manslaughter death of a destitute clerk named Leonard Bast after he discovers Leonard with the pregnant Helen in the family country home outside London which convinces him that Leonard is the responsible party in this Post-Victorian novel (1910).

7	<u>A Passage to India</u> by E.M. Forster
8	<u>Howards End</u> by E.M. Forster
9	<u>A Room with a View</u> by E.M. Forster

2-5-8

Henry Wilcox -   - this character is the prosperous London businessman who lives with his wife, Ruth, and three grown children, Charles, Paul and Evie at a country house outside London; eventually, he marries the much younger Margaret Schlegel and they watch as his   older son, Charles, is imprisoned for the manslaughter of a destitute married clerk, Leonard Bast, because this clerk is responsible for impregnating Margaret's sister, Helen Schlegel, in this Post-Victorian novel (1910).

1   Far From the Madding Crowd by Thomas Hardy
2   Cakes and Ale by William Somerset Maugham
3   Howards End by E. Forster

Lily Bart - this character is the young, scheming and ruthless fortune hunter whose only assets are her beauty and good family background as she travels in New York society at the start of the 20th century; eventually, she misses out on opportunistic marriages with both Percy Gryce and Mr. Rosedale, loses the respect of Lawrence Selden, and dies in a dingy boarding-house from an overdose of choral in this Post-Victorian novel (1905).

4   The Reef by Edith Wharton
5   The House of Mirth by Edith Wharton
6   The Age of Innocence by Edith Wharton

Young Jolyon - this character is the underwriter for Lloyds of London and aspiring watercolor painter who deserted his first wife and daughter, June, for a governess who bears him two children, Jolly and Holly, only to become a widower who marries a woman named Irene after being assigned her trustee; eventually, he writes a letter that prevents the marriage which is hastily being sought between Soames's daughter, Fleur, and Jon, who is his son with Irene, from ever happening in this Nobel Prize winning Post-Victorian novel (1922).

7   The Forsythe Saga by John Galsworthy
8   Main Street by Sinclair Lewis
9   Winesburg, Ohio by Sherwood Anderson

3-5-7

Charles Wilcox - - this character is the prosperous, widowed London businessman Henry's older son who becomes obsessed with out-of-wedlock pregnancy of this step-mother Margaret's older sister, Helen Schlegel; eventually, he is imprisoned for the manslaughter death of a destitute clerk named Leonard Bast after he discovers Leonard and her in the family country home outside London in this Post-Victorian novel (1910).

1	Far From the Madding Crowd by Thomas Hardy
2	Howards End by E.M. Forster
3	Cakes and Ale by William Somerset Maugham

Martin Ricardo - this character is the third member of a criminal trio that includes a psychopathic misogynist named Mr. Jones and a brute named Pedro who show up at Wilhelm Schomberg's East Indies hotel and turn it into a professional gambling house against his wishes; eventually, he is shot by Mr. Jones after seducing a young English violin player named Lena while both are in Axel Heyst's island bungalow in this Post-Victorian novel by a Nobel Prize winning author (1915).

4	Nostromo by Joseph Conrad
5	Victory by Joseph Conrad
6	Lord Jim By Joseph Conrad

Mugridge - - this character is the ship's cook aboard a sailing vessel named the Ghost under captain Wolf Larsen headed for the seal ranges in the Bering Sea who is assigned a cabin boy named Humphrey (Hump) Weyden rescued from a ship wreck; eventually, he loses part of a leg after being keelhauled and deserts the Ghost with the crew leaving Wolf Larsen to be buried at sea by Weyden and Maud Brewster in this Post-Victorian novel by an American author (1904).

7	The Sea Wolf by Jack London
8	Lord Jim by Joseph Conrad
9	Captains Courageous by Rudyard Kipling

2-5-7

Leonard Bast - this character is the destitute young clerk living with his older frowsy wife, Jacky, in a run-down London flat who is discharged from his job at an insurance company after acting on information given to him by the two Schlegel sisters, Margaret and Helen, received from a prosperous London businessman named Henry Wilcox; eventually, he accidentally suffers a fatal heart attack when assaulted by Charles Wilcox because Charles discovered that he guilty of impregnated Helen Schlegeli in this Post-Victorian novel (1910).

1	**Howards End** by E.M. Forster
2	**Far From the Madding Crowd** by Thomas Hardy
3	**Cakes and Ale** by William Somerset Maugham

Lucy Honeychurch - this character is the young Englishwoman who vacations in Italy with her cousin, Charlotte Barlett, where they both meet a clergyman named Mr. Beebe, the unmarried Allen sisters, a writer named Elinor Lavish, Mr. Emerson and his impulsive son, George; eventually, she breaks off her engagement with the snooty, elitist dilettante, Cecil Vyse, and honeymoons with George Emerson at the Pensione Bertolini in Florence, Italy where they first meet in this Post-Victorian novel (19).

4	**A Room with a View** by E. M. Forster
5	**Howards End** by E. M. Forster
6	**A Passage to India** by E. M. Forster

Wilhelm Schomberg -   - this character is the cruel East Indies hotel owner whose hotel becomes a gambling house under pressure by three new strangers made up of a psychopathic misogynist named Mr. Jones, his follower, Martin Ricardo and a brute named Pedro; eventually,   he sends these three to Axel Heyst's island bungalow under the pretext they were hoarding great wealth in this Post-Victorian novel written by a Nobel Prize winning author (1915).

7	**Nostromo** by Joseph Conrad
8	**Victory** by Joseph Conrad
9	**Lord Jim** by Joseph Conrad

The Pre-Atomic Period
(1920-1945)

Some of the noted novelists of this period are as follows: Thomas Hardy, Sinclair Lewis, Ernest Hemingway, William Faulkner, Theodore Dreiser, F. Scott Fitzgerald, John Dos Passos, John Steinbeck, Franz Kafka, Willa Cather, Richard Wright, Thomas Mann, Langston Hughes, C.S. Forester, Herman Hesse and Pearl Buck.

Some of the factors that determined the mood and temper of this period are as follows: political oppression reared its ugly head when Nazism arose in Germany, Fascism arose in Italy, absolutism arose in Japan, and Fascism appeared in Spain. The Great Depression befell the United States while the rest of the world suffered global depression. Ultimately, capitalism withstood the assault of collectivism and the United States emerged as a world power while the British Empire declined. Along with these political and economics events occurred, technological revolutions and advances were taking place in the areas of communications, transportation and industry.

Some of the underlying concepts that help to describe what motivated the writers of this period were the new role of the novelist and the even stronger role of the critic.

Novelist like Joyce, Lawrence and Conrad and the other authors before the 1930's responded to the global changes that had transpired by meeting them head on. These major conflicts and problems provided a backdrop for their novels and these efforts resulted in a revival of the Post-Victorian novel. Many novelists wrote their work using new ideas from such sciences as psychology, sociology and anthropology. A revival of the Post-Victorian novel was the result.

During this period, literature began to compete with religion as a provider of inspiration and spiritual refreshment. Novelists became the target of the newly exalted critic who held that literature should be differentiated into both good and bad literature. Soon these critics proliferated like new priests who were ordained to oversee the literary flock. When the Atomic Bombs were dropped on Japan, the nuclear age emerged.

1-4-9

Eugene Gant - this character is the youngest child of a North Carolina family made up of a hard-drinking stonecutter father, Oliver, his penurious mother, Eliza and his brothers Ben, Steve, Luke and Grover along with sisters, Daisy and Helen; eventually, he meets a girl 5 years his senior named Laura James at his mother's boarding house, the Dixieland, who throws him over for a previous boyfriend in this Pre-Atomic novel (1929).

1	The Web and the Rock by Thomas Wolfe
2	Sanctuary by William Faulkner
3	Look Homeward, Angel by Thomas Wolfe

Robert Jordan - this character is the young American expatriate schoolteacher turned explosives expert who joins Spanish Loyalist guerillas Pablo, Pilar and Maria on a mission to blow up a bridge that is strategic to Franco's Fascist forces; eventually, he volunteers to forfeit his life after Anselmo courageously dies so that Pablo, Pilar and Maria can escape the oncoming Fascists forces in this Pre-Atomic novel written by a Nobel Prize winning author (1940).

4	For Whom the Bell Tolls by Ernest Hemingway
5	The Sun Also Rises by Ernest Hemingway
6	Arms for the Man by Ernest Hemingway

Bernard Marx - this character is the unorthodox citizen in 632 After Ford who is joined by an Alpha worker named Lenina Crowne on a rocket ship trip to New Mexico and the Savage Reservation where they meet a savage named John whose mother, Linda, had been marooned there years earlier by Thomakin the Director of Hatcheries in London 632 After Ford; eventually, he returns to London with Linda and John where Thomakin resigns and Lenina is whipped to death by the savage when John goes into an emotional frenzy in this Pre-Atomic novel (1932).

7	Animal Farm by George Orwell
8	Brave New World by Aldous Huxley
9	Nineteen Eighty Four by George Orwell

3-4-8

<u>Julian English</u> - this character is the friendly 50 year-old owner of a Cadillac dealership in Gibbsville, PA whose public drunkenness and belligerence alienates him from his country club and drives his shallow wife, Caroline, to seek a divorce; eventually, his confrontation with Caroline's one-armed cousin, Froggy Ogden, and one night stand with a bootlegger named Ed Charney's mistress, Helene Holman, compels him to commit suicide by carbon monoxide in this Pre-Atomic novel (1934).

1   **<u>Arrowsmith</u> by Sinclair Lewis**
2   **<u>Appointment In Samarra</u> by John O'Hara**
3   **<u>Winesburg, Ohio</u> by Sherwood Anderson**

<u>Esther Jack</u> - this character is the successful, well-known New York set designer who is the mistress of a budding Southern writer from Libya Hill, North Carolina named George Webber who is 15 to 20 years her junior; eventually, her affair with George deteriorates into quarrels over her smothering his individuality and artistic ability until one final abusive scene where he abandons her and escapes to Europe in this Pre-Atomic novel(1939).

4   **<u>The Web and the Rock</u> by Thomas Wolfe**
5   **<u>Look Homeward, Angel</u> by Thomas Wolfe**
6   **<u>Of Time and the River</u> by Thomas Wolfe**

<u>Clyde Griffiths</u> - this character is the immature, uneducated factory supervisor in Lycurgus, New York who impregnates his mistress, Roberta Allen, while social climbing to marry Sondra Finchley; eventually, he is electrocuted for Roberta's death by misadventure during a boating accident because the jury found premeditation to exist in this Pre-Atomic novel (1925).

7   **<u>Sister Carrie</u> by Theodore Dreiser**
8   **<u>An American Tragedy</u> by Theodore Dreiser**
9   **<u>The Titan</u> by Theodore Dreiser**

2-4-8

Paul Riesling - this character is the frustrated violinist turned tar-roofing manufacturer in the fictional Midwestern town of Zenith who accompanies a prosperous real estate broker named George on a hunting and fishing trip to Maine while leaving their respective wives, Zilla and Myra, behind; eventually, he goes to prison for a near fatal shooting of his quarrelsome wife in this Pre-Atomic novel by a Nobel Prize winning author (1922).

1   **Arrowsmith** by Sinclair Lewis
2   **Babbitt** by Sinclair Lewis
3   **Elmer Gantry** by Sinclair Lewis

Joe Christmas - - this character is an Afro-American circus entertainer's illegitimate son who loses his father when he is killed by his grandfather, Doc Hines, and his white mother, Mary Hines, when Doc Hines allows her to die during his birth; eventually, he meets his end in Jefferson, Mississippi after slashing the throat of his Yankee spinster mistress, Joanna Burden, over domineering nature in this Pre-Atomic novel by a Nobel Prize winning author (1932).

4   **Absalom, Absalom!** by William Faulkner
5   **Light in August** by William Faulkner
6   **Sanctuary** by William Faulkner

Rosemary Hoyt - this character is the 18 year-old Hollywood actress whose dives into Venetian canals during the shooting of a movie lead to her recuperation in the south of France where she becomes infatuated with a 38 year-old research psychologist named Dick Diver in spite of the fact that he is married to Nicole and is the father of two children; eventually, she is pursued by him to Naples where she is making another motion picture until he ends up in jail over an unfair taxi fee and is beater severely for striking a policeman in this Pre-Atomic novel by an American author (1934).

7   **This Side of Paradise** by F. Scott Fitzgerald
8   **The Great Gatsby** by F. Scott Fitzgerald
9   **Tender is the Night** by F. Scott Fitzgerald

Curley - this character is the prizefighter who lives with his shameless wife on his father's barley farm in the Salinas Valley,   California with a group of seasonal, itinerant hired workers; eventually, he lies to a doctor about how his broken hand which had been crushed by an overgrown, simpleton worker named Lennie Small had occurred as the result of a machine accident in order to avoid humiliation regarding his masculinity in this Pre-Atomic novel by a Nobel Prize winning author (1937).

1	**Of Mice and Men** by John Steinbeck
2	**The Sun Also Rises** by Ernest Hemmingway
3	**Sanctuary** by William Faulkner

Joseph K. - this character is the 30 year-old successful junior bank manager whose uneventful hiring of an erratic and frustrating attorney named Huld is offset by the latter's promiscuous servant, Leni, who is full of kind instructions on how to get along with her boss; eventually, he is forcibly subdued at 9 o'clock on the eve of his 31st birthday by 2 strangers in top hats and frock coats, taken to a quarry and fatally stabbed in the heart in this   Pre-Atomic novel (1925).

4	**The Castle** by Franz Kafka
5	**The Magic Mountain** by Thomas Mann
6	**The Trial** by Franz Kafka

Mrs. Maximillian (Maxim) de Winter - this character is the young shy, sensitive and drab orphan whose travels about the continent as companion to a pushy American social climber, Mrs. Van Hopper, result in a marriage to the owner of a large estate known as **Mannerly**; eventually, she becomes embroiled in the mystery about the drowning death of her husband's first wife that involves a housekeeper named Mrs. Dancers and an lecherous in-law named Jack Favell in this Pre-Atomic novel (1938).

7	**The Wings of the Dove** by Henry James
8	**Rebecca** by Daphne du Mauier
9	**The Marble Faun** by Nathaniel Hawthorne

1-6-8

<u>Paul Baumer</u> - this character is the young, 19 year-old   soldier whose coming of age occurs abruptly when he experiences the first hand horrors of war along with a concurring indifference to emotions, pain and exhaustion while on the front line with his superior, Corporal Himmelstoss, and his closest comrades; eventually, after all his comrades have been killed off, his loneliness is finally put to an end when a stray bullet takes his life during October of 1918 in this Pre-Atomic novel (1928).

1   Stendhal
2   Erich Maria Remarque
3   Thomas Mann

<u>Catherine Barkley</u> - this character is the young British nurse whose assignment to a British hospital unit in Milan, Italy during World War I allows her to meet and fall in love with an American volunteer named Frederic Henry who is serving as a Lieutenant in an Italian ambulance unit; eventually, she dies in childbirth after delivering a stillborn baby in a Swiss hospital in Lausanne as Frederic looks on in this Nobel Prize winning Pre-Atomic novel (1929).

4   <u>For Whom the Bell Tolls</u> by Ernest Hemingway
5   <u>A Farewell to Arms</u> by Ernest Hemingway
6   <u>The Sun Also Rises</u> by Ernest Hemingway

<u>Slim</u> - this character is the barley ranch worker who gives a new born puppy to an overgrown simpleton named Lennie Small and convinces the owner's son, Curley, that he should blame a machine accident for the hand that Lennie has crushed; eventually, he joins in the search for Lennie after the latter accidently killed Curley's shameless wife that ends with George Milton killing his friend, Lennie in this Pre-Atomic novel by a Nobel Prize winning American author (1937).

7   <u>The Grapes of Wrath</u> by John Steinbeck
8   <u>Of Mice and Men</u> by John Steinbeck
9   <u>Travels with Charlie</u> by John Steinbeck

2-5-8

Gilbert (Gil) Martin - this character is the upstate New York farmer turned patriot whose militia participation during the Revolutionary War under General Herkimer and General Benedict Arnold constantly separates him from his beautiful wife, Lara, and his two young boys, Gilly and Joey; eventually, the War ends and he is able to return to his farm in Deerfield with his wife, two sons and a brand new baby daughter where he an settle down and begin a new life in this Pre-Atomic novel (1936).

1	The Pathfinder by James Fenimore Cooper
2	Drums Along the Mohawk by Walter D. Edmonds
3	The Scarlet Letter by Nathaniel Hawthorne

Baron de Charlus - this character is the degenerate French aristocrat whose concocted reputation as a womanizer is just a front for his hidden life of depravity where he has numerous perverted affairs with very young men; eventually, his sexual proclivities are the downfall that leads him into scandal while effecting his well-being by leaving him prematurely senile in this Pre-Atomic novel (1913-1927).

4	A Sentimental Education by Gustave Flaubert
5	Les Miserables by Victor Hugo
6	Remembrance of Things Past by Marcel Proust

Benjamin (Benji) Compson - this character is the Mississippi mentally retarded, youngest child of an alcoholic and hypochondriac and the brother of a depressed Harvard College student named Quentin along with a promiscuous sister nicknamed Caddy and a hate-filled brother named Jason; eventually, he is castrated for mistakenly fondling a local schoolgirl in this Pre-Atomic novel by a Nobel Prize winning author (1929).

7	The Sound and the Fury by William Faulkner
8	Sanctuary by William Faulkner
9	Absalom, Absalom! by William Faulkner

2-6-7

Buck Mulligan - this character is the Irish medical student who is pivotal to the parallel encounters which occur between a young 21 year-old Irish writer and teacher named Stephen Dateless and a middle-aged Jewish advertising salesman named Leopold Bloom on June 16, 1904; eventually, he leaves his roommate, Stephen, after they visit a pub which allows Stephen and Leopold the opportunity to visit a brothel and then go to Leopold's home in this Irish Pre-Atomic novel (1922).

1   Ulysses by James Joyce
2   Finnegan's Wake by James Joyce
3   A Portrait of the Artist as a Young Man by James Joyce

Cash Bundren - this character is the carpenter who gets the approval of his dying mother, Addie, on how well he is building her coffin when he shows her different pieces through a window where she is propped up in bed; eventually, he breaks his leg when the wagon carrying her dead body tips over crossing an old ford on the way to Jefferson City in this Pre-Atomic novel by a Nobel Prize winning author (1930).

4   Look Homeward, Angel by Thomas Wolfe
5   The Grapes of Wrath by John Steinbeck
6   As I Lay Dying by William Faulkner

Nicole Diver - this character is the wealthy, Chicagoan incest patient in a Zurich clinic who ends up marrying an upcoming handsome research psychologist named Dick, having two children with him and resettling in the south of France; eventually, her personal life is strengthened as she recuperates from her malady while Dick's drinking causes a spiral downturn to his life until they divorce, she begins a relationship with a war hero named Tommy Barban and Dick returns to America where practices medicine as a general practitioner in a small town in upstate New York in this American Pre-Atomic novel (1934).

7   This Side of Paradise by F. Scott Fitzgerald
8   The Last Tycoon by F. Scott Fitzgerald
9   Tender is the Night by F. Scott Fitzgerald

1-6-9

<u>Tehani</u> - this character is the alluring, attractive Tahitian princess whose first meeting with a linguistic British midshipman named Roger Byam ultimately leads to their marriage; eventually, her death becomes a major influence in Roger's decision not to acknowledge their surviving daughter after his return to Tahiti as captain of his own ship after being exonerated at a London court martial which involved Captain Bligh in this Pre-Atomic novel (1932).

1   <u>Captains Courageous</u> by Rudyard Kipling
2   <u>Mutiny on the Bounty</u> by Charles Nordholl and James Norman Hall
3   <u>The Sea Wolf</u> by Jack London

<u>Jester Leeter</u> - this character is the poor, shiftless Georgian father of seventeen children who encourages his 16 year-old son, Dude, to marry a middle-aged preacher woman named Bessie and his hare-lipped daughter, Ellie May, to replace her 15 year-old sister, Pearl, as the object of Love Bessie's affections; eventually, his attempts at manipulating people for materialistic reasons fail when he and his wife, Ada, perish in a fire that he carelessly set in this Pre-Atomic novel by an American author (1932).

4   <u>Tobacco Road</u> by Erskine Caldwell
5   <u>The Web and the Rock</u> by Thomas Wolfe
6   <u>The Sound and the Fury</u> by William Faulkner

<u>Roberta</u> - this character is the young, Kansas farmer's daughter who is seduced by a 23 year-old temperate, traveling salesman for a text book company in the Middle West; eventually, her marriage to him and subsequent life in a flat above a drug store allows her to experience his continual obnoxious behavior and constant vying for the affection of their adopted daughter, Elizabeth, to the point where she leaves him and takes Elizabeth back home to her parent's farm in this Pre-Atomic novel by an American author (1935).

7   <u>Heaven's My Destination</u> by Thornton Wilder
8   <u>Main Street</u> by Sinclair Lewis
9   <u>Elmer Gantry</u> by Sinclair Lewis

2-4-7

Lady Brett Ashley - this character is the promiscuous, war-widowed English woman whose present separation from Lord Ashley is a prelude to marrying Mike Campbell eventhough she is in love with an American expatriate newspaper correspondent named Jake Barnes; eventually, she seduces a bullfighter named Pedro Romero in Pamplona, Spain while on vacation with Jake, Mike, Bill Gorton and Robert Cohn in this Pre-Atomic novel by a Nobel Prize winning author (1926).

1	Tender is the Night by F. Scott Fitzgerald
2	Three Soldiers by John Dos Passos
3	The Sun Also Rises by Ernest Hemingway

Carol Kennicott - this character is the Minnesota college graduate with a degree in sociology and civic improvement who marries a well-respected doctor named Will and moves to the small town of Gopher Prairie; eventually, she sheds her eccentric ways and settles down with her husband into a conventional way of life with their young son, Hugh, in this Pre-Atomic novel by a Nobel Prize winning author (1920).

4	Elmer Gantry by Sinclair Lewis
5	Main Street by Sinclair Lewis
6	Arrowsmith by Sinclair Lewis

Tom Joad   - this character is the Oklahoman ex-convict whose return home from prison finds his family consisting of his parents, sisters Rose of Sharon Rivers (Rosasharn) and Ruthie, and brothers Noah, Al and Winfield evicted from their Dust Bowl property; eventually, he becomes a champion for the downtrodden after becoming a wanted man in California for avenging the brutal death of his preacher friend, Jim Casy, in this Pre-Atomic novel by a Nobel Prize winning author (1939).

7	The Red Pony by John Steinbeck
8	The Grapes of Wrath by John Steinbeck
9	Of Mice and Men by John Steinbeck

3-5-8

<u>Monroe Starr</u> -   - this character is the brilliant, self-made 35 year-old Hollywood film producer whose overwork results in his inability to deal with the death of his famous actress-wife, Minna Davis, and his efforts to defeat the Communists infiltrating his studio;   eventually, his death in a plane crash prevents him from aborting the premeditated gangland hit he had set up on his cold, calculating partner, Pat Brady, for blabbing about an affair involving Kathleen Moore in this unfinished Pre-Atomic novel (1940).

1	<u>The Last Tycoon</u> by F. Scott Fitzgerald
2	<u>This Side of Paradise</u> by F. Scott Fitzgerald
3	<u>The Great Gatsby</u> by F. Scott Fitzgerald

<u>Robert Cohn</u> - this character is the expatriate American novelist   in Paris after World War I whose title of Princeton ex-middleweight boxing champion coupled with his jealousy over Lady   Brett Ashley leads him to pulverize a bullfighter named Pedro Romero while vacationing in Pamplona, Spain with Jake Barnes, Bill Gorton, and Mike Campbell; eventually, he loses Brett to Mike Campbell eventhough she loves an American expatriate newspaper   correspondent, Jake Barnes, in this Pre-Atomic novel by a Nobel Prize winning author (1926).

4	<u>The Sun Also Rises</u> by Ernest Hemingway
5	<u>Tender Is the Night</u> by F. Scott Fitzgerald
6	<u>Three Soldiers</u> by John Dos Passos

<u>Addie Bundren</u> - this character is the worn out, exhausted wife of Anse Bundren and mother of Cash, Jewel, Darl, Vardaman and Dewey Dell; eventually, her reputation remains intact when Preacher Whitfield decides not to reveal that her high-spirited son, Jewel, is really illegitimate because of an early tryst between them in this Pre-Atomic novel by a Nobel Prize winner (1930).

7	<u>The Red Pony</u> byJohn Steinbeck
8	<u>As I Lay Dying</u> by William Faulkner
9	<u>The Sun Also Rises</u> by Ernest Hemingway

Brock Brewton - this character is the second oldest son of a beautiful, St. Louis woman named Lutie Cameron and Colonel James Brewton who is the taciturn, charismatic owner of the gigantic, arid ranch known as the Cross B Ranch in Salt Fork, Texas; eventually, he turns into a renegade outlaw who is finally hunted down by a group of deputies and ultimately killed by his own father who felt that he really was the son of his wife and a handsome district attorney named Brice Chamberlin in this Pre-Atomic novel (1936).

1   The Town by Conrad Richter
2   The Light in the Forest by Conrad Richter
3   The Sea of Grass by Conrad Richter

Temple Drake - this character is the young female collegiate whose date with the drunken Gowan Stevens involves her in both intrigue and murder with Lee Goodwin and Popeye; eventually, she ends up in Europe with her respected father, Judge Blake, after being forced by Popeye to stay in Reba Rivers's Memphis house of prostitution in this Pre-Atomic novel by a Nobel Prize winning author (1931).

4   Sanctuary by William Faulkner
5   The Sound and the Fury by William Faulkner
6   Absalom, Absalom! by William Faulkner

Brother Juniper - this character is the little, red-haired Spanish Franciscan friar whose total time is occupied examining the lives of five people who died together until he publishes a book showing how God had a reason for each of them to have died at that precise moment; eventually, his book is condemned by the Catholic Church, he is burned at the stake as a heretic and his book falls into the hands of this American author in this Pre-Atomic novel (1927).

7   The Power and the Glory by Graham Greene
8   The Bridge of San Luis Rey by Thornton Wilder
9   Green Mansions by W. H. Hudson

3-4-8

Horace Benbow - this character is the Southern attorney who defends the innocent moonshiner, Lee Goodwin, of a murder charge regarding the bootlegger, Tommy, who was really killed by a sociopath named   Popeye; eventually, his client is falsely convicted when the young female collegiate, Temple Blake, fingers him as the first man to attack her at an old plantation in this Pre-Atomic novel by a Nobel Prize winning author (1931).

1	The Web and the Rock by Thomas Wolfe
2	Sanctuary by William Faulkner
3	Tobacco Road by Erskine Caldwell

Kevin Porter - this character is the innkeeper's young son near Phoenix Park, Dublin who takes on numerous forms in an elaborate surrealistic dream that his father has when he falls asleep in the pub after closing time; eventually, he forms as Shem the Postman while Jerry becomes Shaun the Penman, his father and mother become Humphrey Climpden Earwicker and Anna Maria Plurabelle while Isobel becomes Issy   in this Pre-Atomic novel (1939).

4	Finnegan's Wake by James Joyce
5	A Portrait of the Artist as a Young Man by James Joyce
6	Ulysses by James Joyce

Tommy Barban - this character is the mercenary war hero who has a gun duel with Mr. McKisco in the south of France over Mrs. McKisco's not mentioning the hysterical behavior of Nicole Diver, the wife of a prominent 38 year-old research psychologist, Dr. Richard Diver; eventually, he seduces this former Zurich clinic patient after Nicole divorces Dick for drinking and philandering with a young actress half his age named Rosemary Hoyt in this Pre-Atomic novel written by an Irish-American author (1934).

7	The Last Tycoon by F. Scott Fitzgerald
8	Tender is the Night by F. Scott Fitzgerald
9	This Side of Paradise by F. Scott Fitzgerald

2-4-8

Blazes Boylan - - this character is the illicit paramour and road manager of a mediocre concert singer named Marion Tweedy Bloom who was born in Gibralter and is married to a middle aged Jewish salesman named Leopold; eventually, he is almost upstaged when she becomes aroused at the prospect of having a younger, 21 year-old boarder named Stephen Dedalus whom her husband had encountered a number of times on June 16, 1904 in this Irish Pre-Atomic novel (1922).

1	Finnegan's Wake by James Joyce
2	Ulysses by James Joyce
3	A Portrait of the Artist as a Young Man by James Joyce

Francis Starwick - this character is the amiable teaching assistant to a Harvard drama professor named Professor Hatcher and the one who begins a friendship with a promising young writer named Eugene Gant; eventually, his travels around Paris with two women from Boston named Elinor and Ann turns into an intrigue when Eugene becomes the third figure in an impossible love triangle involving him and Ann in this Pre-Atomic novel (1935).

4	The Web and the Rock by Thomas Wolfe
5	Look Homeward, Angel by Thomas Wolfe
6	Of Time and the River by Thomas Wolfe

Lady Barbara Wellesley - this character is the Duke of Wellington's aloof, cultured sister who requests passage from Panama to England aboard the frigate, the H.M.S. Lydia, before it engages in a sea battle with the Spanish ship, the Natividad, which is commanded by the prosperous Central American plantation owner, Don Alvarado (El Supremo); eventually, her unrequited love for the mature, married captain of the H.M.S. Lydia is later resolved when her husband, Admiral Leighton, dies in battle while her lover's wife, Maria, dies in childbirth in this historical Pre-Atomic novel (1937).

7	A Passage to India by E. M. Forster
8	Lord Jim by Joseph Conrad
9	Captain Horatio Hornblower by C. S. Forester

2-6-9

George Webber - this character is the zealous young Southern writer from the southern city of Libya Hill living in New York City whose first novel brings about the end of his illicit affair with a stage designer named Esther Jack; eventually, he returns to New York after leaving Else von Kohler behind in 1930's Nazi Germany and ends his longtime ties with his fatalistic, cynical editor, Foxhall Edwards, in order to pursue his lofty goals in this Pre-Atomic novel (1940).

1	You Can't Go Home Again by Thomas Wolfe
2	Look Homeward, Angel by Thomas Wolfe
3	Of Time and the River by Thomas Wolfe

Rosie Driffield - this character is the ex-barmaid and first wife of the late Victorian author who becomes the center of focus when a popular English novelist contacts an English writer named Ashenden and Driffield's widow, Amy, to write a biography about him; eventually, she contacts Ashenden when he travels to New York and explains that her true love was the contractor, George Kemp, whom she ran off with to New York before Driffield divorced her in this Pre-Atomic novel   (1930).

4	Cakes and Ale by William Somerset Maugham
5	Of Human Bondage by William Somerset Maugham
6	The Moon and Sixpence by William Somerset Maugham

Stephen Dedalus - this character is the 21 year-old perceptive Irish writer whose wanderings around Dublin on June 16, 1904 parallel the wandering of a Jewish advertising salesman named Leopold Bloom with subsequent meetings at a newspaper office, the National Library and a hospital where neither spoke; eventually, he accompanies a medical student and Bloom to a brothel after he leaves his roommate, Buck Mulligan, and others at a pub in this Irish Pre-Atomic novel (1922).

7	Ulysses by James Joyce
8	Finnegan's Wake by James Joyce
9	A Portrait of the Artist as a Young Man by James Joyce

Miles Archer - this character is the private detective who is murdered while secretly following a man named Floyd Thursby after his partner, Sam Spade, is retained by a young, sensuous woman client named Miss Wonderly thereby opening up an intrigue of deception and double crosses which had begun in Greece and ended up in San Francisco; eventually, his death is avenged by his partner after Miss Wonderly's true identity is revealed to be Brigid O'Shaughnessy while the gangster, Joel Cairo, and an older, stout man named Casper Gutman continue their search for the prize in this Pre-Atomic novel (1930).

1   <u>A Study in Scarlet</u> by Sir Arthur Conan Doyle
2   <u>The Maltese Falcon</u> by Dashiell Hammett
3   <u>The Thirty-Nine Steps</u> by John Buchan

Martin - this character is Dr. Max Gottlieb's medical doctor and researcher who jilts a graduate student named Madeline Fox to first marry a good-looking nurse named Leona Tozer and then a rich young widow named Joyce Lanyon; eventually, he turns down an assistant directorship to a rustic area of Vermont so that he can pursue a cure for pneumonia with Terry Wickett in this Pre-Atomic novel by a Nobel Prize winning author (1924).

4   <u>Arrowsmith</u> by Sinclair Lewis
5   <u>Elmer Gantry</u> by Sinclair Lewis
6   <u>Babbitt</u> by Sinclair Lewis

Robert Merrick - this character is the reckless, pampered, wealthy playboy whose selfish use of a medical instrument after a boating accident prevents its use by a renown unselfish, well-liked neurosurgeon named Dr. Wayne Hudson whose death from drowning leaves his second wife, Helen Brent Hudson, a disgusted widow; eventually, he finishes medical school and become a gifted neurosurgeon whose surgery restores sight to Dr. Hudson's widow whose ultimate forgiveness leads to their marriage in this Pre-Atomic novel (1929).

7   <u>Green Mansions</u> by W. H. Hudson
8   <u>Heavens My Destination</u> by Thornton Wilder
9   <u>Magnificent Obsession</u> by Lloyd C. Douglas

2-4-9

Daisy Buchanan - - this character is the wealthy, Long Island married woman whose shallow marriage to a Yale football player turned Wall Street millionaire named Tom is threatened when Jay mysteriously appears to pursue her hand; eventually, her carelessness results in the hit-and-run murder of Tom's mistress, Myrtle Wilson, and subsequent shooting death of Jay by Mytle's husband, George Mytle, who has been prodded by a jealous Tom in this Pre-Atomic novel (1935).

1	**The Last Tycoon** by F. Scott Fitzgerald
2	**The Great Gatsby** by F. Scott Fitzgerald
3	**This Side of Paradise** by F. Scott Fitzgerald

Joe Brown (a/k/a) Lucas Burch - this character is the brash, wishy-washy bootleg whiskey partner of an illegitimate son of a Afro-American circus entertainer and a white woman named Joe Christmas; eventually, he hops a freight train out of Jefferson, Mississippi rather than face Lena Grove and their new-born baby from his seduction of her in Alabama in this Pre-Atomic novel written by a Nobel Prize winning author (1932).

4	**The Sound and the Fury** by William Faulkner
5	**Sanctuary** by William Faulkner
6	**Light in August** by William Faulkner

Rutherford - this character is the old English schoolmate of a British consul, Hugh Conway, and the one who discovers his old friend in a Chinese mission hospital in an exhausted, disoriented condition; eventually, he is told an incredible story about being kidnaped and taken to an idyllic valley named Shangri-La in the Tibetan Himalayas along with another British consul, Captain Mallison, a missionary, Miss Roberta Brinklow and an American embezzler named Henry Barnard in this Pre-Atomic novel (1933).

7	**Lost Horizon** by James Hilton
8	**Goodbye, Mr. Chips** by James Hilton
9	**The Time Machine** by H. G. Wells

Philip Quarles - this character is the self-centered English novelist whose disregard of his wife, Elinor, drives her in a affair with a fascist named Everard Webley until Everard is murdered by a nihilist named Marice Spandrell; eventually, he returns abroad with his wife after their young son, Philip. dies from meningitis in this Pre-Atomic novel (1928).

1	**Point Counterpoint** by Aldous Huxley	
2	**Nineteen Eighty Four** by George Orwell	
3	**Brave New World** by Aldous Huxley	

Jimmy Herf - this character is the newspaper reporter who marries an accomplished Broadway actress after her marriage to an ineffectual actor named John Oglethorpe and love affair with Stan Emery that ends tragically when he dies in an apartment fire; eventually, he divorces her after their return from World War II Europe which permits her to enter an indifferent 3rd marriage with a lawyer named George Baldwin in this Pre-Atomic novel (1925).

4	**Manhattan Transfer** by John Dos Passos
5	**Three Soldiers** by John Dos Passos
6	**U. S. A. (Trilogy)** by John Dos Passos

Walter - this character is the Midwestern employee of a small town wholesale drug company whose immaturity and degenerate gambling result in directly in his theft of money from Lamb and Company and directly to his father Virgil's stroke and financial ruin at the hands of Mr. Lamb; eventually, his fantasizing sister's attempts to impress Arthur Russell turn nauseating and force her to make more realistic choices like entering a business school rather than college in this Pre-Atomic novel (1921).

7	**Alice Adams** by Booth Tarkington
8	**Little Women** by Louisa May Alcott
9	**Seventeen** by Booth Tarkington

1-4-7

<u>Dr. Richard Diver</u> -   - this character is the handsome, 38 year-old American promising research writer and psychologist in a Zurich clinic whose work with a wealthy Chicagoan patient, Nicole Warren, ends in marriage, 2 children and residence in the south of France; eventually, his drinking and brief affair with an actress half his age named Rosemary Hoyt ends in a divorce which allows Nicole to start an affair with a war hero named Tommy Barban in this Pre-Atomic novel (1934).

1	<u>This Side of Paradise</u> by F. Scott Fitzgerald
2	<u>The Great Gatsby</u> by F. Scott Fitzgerald
3	<u>Tender is the Night</u> by F. Scott Fitzgerald

<u>Gil Carter</u> - this character is the transient cowpuncher who is accompanied by a fellow cowpuncher, Art Croft, when he enters the northern Nevadan town of <u>Bridger's Wells</u> for a rendezvous with his girlfriend, Rose Mapen, unawares that she married someone else in San Francisco; eventually, this angry jilted cowboy allows his judgment to e clouded when he joins a posse led by Major Tetley which hangs 3 innocent men accused of killing a man named Kincaid and rustling his cattle in this Pre-Atomic novel (1940).

4	<u>Of Mice and Men</u> by John Steinbeck
5	<u>The Grapes of Wrath</u> by John Steinbeck
6	<u>The Ox-Bow Incident</u> by Walter Van Tilburg Clark

<u>Dr. Will Kennicott</u> - this character is the well-respected doctor from the small town of Gopher Prairie who marries a Minnesotan college graduate with a degree in sociology and civic improvement; eventually, his conventional life style wins out when he convinces his eccentric new wife, Carol, to adjust to their new life style with their young son, Hugh in this Pre-Atomic novel by a Nobel Prize winning author (1920).

7	<u>Main Street</u> by Sinclair Lewis
8	<u>Babbitt</u> by Sinclair Lewis
9	<u>Arrowsmith</u> by Sinclair Lewis

3-6-7

<u>Pilar</u> - this character is the tough, peasant leader of a Spanish Loyalist guerilla band consisting of her debauched husband, Pablo, Maria, Anselmo and an American expatriate schoolteacher turned explosive expert named Robert Jordan amongst others; eventually, she escapes the Fascist forces with Pablo and Maria while Robert Jordan volunteers to forfeit his life after Anselmo Courageously dies blowing up a bridge in this Pre-Atomic novel (1940).

1   <u>For Whom the Bell Tolls</u> by Ernest Hemingway
2   <u>The Sun Also Rises</u> by Ernest Hemingway
3   <u>Arms for the Man</u> by Ernest Hemingway

<u>Lenina Crowne</u> - this character is the London Alpha worker in 632 After Ford whose rocket ship trip to the Savage Reservation in New Mexico with Bernard Marx reveals a savage named John and his mother, Linda, who states she was marooned there years earlier by Thomakin, Director of Hatcheries; eventually, she returns to London with the group where she witnesses Thomakin's scandal and resignation only to be whipped to death during one of the savage, John's emotional frenzies in this Pre-Atomic novel (1932).

4   <u>Brave New World</u> by Aldous Huxley
5   <u>Nineteen Eighty Four</u> by Aldous Huxley
6   <u>Point Counterpoint</u> by Aldous Huxley

<u>Don Julian Alvarado (El Supremo)</u> - this character is the diminutive, dark-skinned and prosperous Central American plantation owner whose pact with England involves sending the 36 gun frigate <u>H. M. S, Lydia</u> to him with money and munitions so he can start a revolution with Spain; eventually, this domineering delusional despot forces the captain of the <u>H.M.S. Lydia</u> to yield her recent prize a 50 gun ship named the <u>Natividad</u> to him only to have it sunk under his command which leads to his capture and execution by the Spanish in this   Pre-Atomic novel (1937).

7   <u>Captain Horatio Hornblower</u> by C.S. Forester
8   <u>Lord Jim</u> by Joseph Conrad
9   <u>A Passage to India</u> by E. M. Forster

1-4-7

<u>Edouard</u> - this character is the aging French writer whose employment of a unprincipled and insolent 17 year-old, Bernard Profitendieu, as his personal secretary and disciple, evokes jealousy from his young, pensive, and reticent nephew, Olivier Moliner; eventually, he returns to writing as Olivier recovers from an suicide attempt, young George Moliner begins to mature after a fatal prank and his brother, Vincent Moliner, grieves over Lady Griffith's death in Africa in this Pre-Atomic novel (1925).

1	<u>The Counterfeiters</u> by Andre Gide
2	<u>The Red and the Black</u> by Stendhal
3	<u>The Charterhouse of Parma</u> by Gustave Flaubert

<u>Jerry Porter</u> - this character is the innkeeper's young son near Phoenix Park, Dublin who takes on numerous forms in an elaborate surrealistic dream that his father has when he falls asleep in the pub after closing time; eventually, he forms as Shem the Penman while Kevin becomes Shaun the Postman, his father and mother become Humphrey Climpden Earwicker and Anna Maria Plurabelle while Isobel becomes Issy in this Pre-Atomic novel (1939).

4	<u>Finnegan's Wake</u> by James Joyce
5	<u>A Portrait of the Artist as a Young Man</u> by James Joyce
6	<u>Ulysses</u> by James Joyce

<u>Frieda</u> - this character is the lithe, fair-haired, sad eyed, hollow-cheeked young barmaid who is the mistress of a plump, flabby-cheeked, chief with a pointed black mustache and a prince-nez; eventually, she jealously rejects K. because of his alleged interest in Olga and Amalia even though she has become his fiancee and stayed with him at the Bridge Inn and the schoolhouse in this   Pre-Atomic novel (1926).

7	<u>The Castle</u> by Franz Kafka
8	<u>Buddenbrooks</u> by Thomas Mann
9	<u>The Trial</u> by Franz Kafka

1-4-7

Michael Campbell (Mike) - this character is the   Lady Brett Ashley's hard-drinking English fiancé who vies with an American expatriate newspaper correspondent named Jake Barnes for her love; eventually, he travels to   Saint Jean de Luz after vacationing at the Pamplona bullfights with Jake Barnes, Bill Groton, Robert Cohn and Brett in this Pre-Atomic novel by a Nobel Prize winning author (1926).

1   A Farewell to Arms by Ernest Hemingway
2   For Whom the Bell Tolls by Ernest Hemingway
3   The Sun Also Rises by Ernest Hemingway

Hurd - this character is the erratic, old, bedridden lawyer known as the Advocate who is hired by 30 year-old successful junior bank manager, Joseph K., in order to extricate him from a legal mess that has assumed surrealistic proportions; eventually, he is fired by his client and his client winds up stabbed to death in the heart by two strangers dressed in top hats and frock coats at a quarry in this Pre-Atomic novel (1925).

4   The Castle by Franz Kafka
5   The Magic Mountain by Thomas Mann
6   The Trial by Franz Kafka

J. Ward Moorehouse - this character is the ambitious businessman whose two marriages to a rich immoral woman named Annabelle Strang and   Gertrude Staple helped him become a very successful advertising executive during the 1920's and 1930's despite his failure as a husband because of his illicit affairs; eventually, a wake-up call in the form of a heart attack gives him a wake-up call regarding his skirt chasing and workaholic life in this Pre-Atomic novel (1930).

7   U.S.A. (Trilogy) by John Dos Passos
8   Three Soldiers by John Dos Passos
9   Manhattan Transfer by John Dos Passos

3-6-7

<u>Jody Baxter</u> - - this character is the 12 year-old Florida boy who watches as his crippled young friend and next-door neighbor, Fodder-Wing Forrester, dies while having to put down his adopted fawn, Flag, when his mother Ora, fails to kill it; eventually, he runs away only to be found by a mail boat which returns him home where his coming of age prepares him for adulthood in this Pre-Atomic novel by an American authoress (1938).

1   <u>Of Time and the River</u> by Thomas Wolfe
2   <u>The Yearling</u> by Marjorie J. Rawlings
3   <u>Absalom, Absalom!</u> by William Faulkner

<u>Quentin Compson</u> - this character is the depressed Harvard College student from Mississippi whose dysfunctional family consists of an alcoholic father, a hypochondriacal mother, a mentally retarded brother named Benji, a promiscuous sister named Caddy and a hate-filled brother named Jason; eventually, he commits suicide by drowning in Boston's Charles River in this Pre-Atomic novel by a Nobel Prize winning author (1929).

4   <u>The Sound and the Fury</u> by William Faulkner
5   <u>Light in August</u> by William Faulkner
6   <u>Sanctuary</u> by William Faulkner

<u>Maria</u> - this character is the beautiful, young Spanish girl who joins a loyal guerilla group composed of a tough peasant leader, Pilar, her debauched, traitorous husband, Pablo, and an idealist named Anselmo; eventually, she meets and falls in love with an American expatriate schoolteacher turned explosive exert named Robert Jordan who watches as she escapes the oncoming the Fascist forces of Franco while he forfeits his life in this Pre-Atomic novel (1940).

7   <u>For Whom the Bell Tolls</u> by Ernest Hemingway
8   <u>The Sun Also Rises</u> by Ernest Hemingway
9   <u>Arms for the Man</u> by Ernest Hemingway

2-4-7

<u>Chang</u> - this character is the Chinese lama who serves a former Capuchin friar named Father Perrault in an idyllic valley named Shangri-La in the Tibetan Himalayas; eventually, he meets a wrecked plane carrying a group of kidnaped passengers consisting of two British consuls, Hugh Conway and Captain Mallison, a missionary, Roberta Brinklow and an American embezzler named Henry Barnard in this   Pre-Atomic novel (1933).

1	<u>Goodbye, Mr. Chips</u> by James Hilton
2	<u>Lost Horizon</u> by James Hilton
3	<u>Point Counterpoint</u> by Aldous Huxley

<u>Don Birnam</u> - this character is the sensitive, articulate, unsuccessful freelance fiction writer whose physical health deteriorates to the point where he is hospitalized becomes the victim of taunts from an aggressive male nurse named Bim; eventually, this well-dressed, down and out writer of fiction continues to deteriorate until an old girlfriend, Helen, takes him in and nurses him back to health out of pity in this Pre-Atomic novel (1944).

4	<u>The Last Tycoon</u> by F. Scott Fitzgerald
5	<u>The Sun Also Rises</u> by Ernest Hemingway
6	<u>The Lost Weekend</u> by Charles Jackson

<u>Roger Byam</u> - this character is the British midshipman assigned by Captain Bligh to study the Tahitian language so that all future shipments of the island's edible breadfruit tree would proceed expeditiously to cheaply feed West Indies slaves; eventually, he returns to the island as captain of his own ship after being exonerated at a London court martial and decides not to acknowledge a surviving daughter whom he had with an attractive native girl named Tehani in this Pre-Atomic novel (1932).

7	<u>Two Years Before the Mast</u> by Richard Henry Dana, Jr.
8	<u>Mutiny on the Bounty</u> by Charles Nordoff and James Norman Hall
9	<u>Captains Courageous</u> by Rudyard Kipling

<u>Candy</u> - this character is the old migrant bunkhouse cleaner on a barley ranch in Salinas Valley, California and the one who offers to join a short, wiry fellow worker named George Milton and his overgrown, simpleton friend, Lennie Small, in the future purchase of a farm; eventually, his dreams go up in smoke after George has to shoot Lennie because Lennie had accidently broke the neck of Curley's shameless wife in this Pre-Atomic novel by a Nobel Prize American author (1937).

1	<u>Of Mice and Men</u> by John Steinbeck
2	<u>The Grapes of Wrath</u> by John Steinbeck
3	<u>The Red Pony</u> by John Steinbeck

<u>Goodhue Coldfield</u> - this character is the reputable store owner in Jefferson, Mississippi whose docile daughter, Ellen, marries the overbearing plantation owner of <u>Sutpen's Hundred</u> named Thomas Sutpen; eventually, he barricades himself in the attic during the Civil War and is fed secretly by his daughter, Rosa, until he just dies alone one night in this Pre-Atomic novel by a Nobel Prize winning author (1936).

4	<u>Absalom, Absalom!</u> by William Faulkner
5	<u>Light in August</u> by William Faulkner
6	<u>The Sound and the Fury</u> by William Faulkner

<u>Sharon Falconer</u> - this character is the charming evangelist who builds a summer tabernacle on a New Jersey pier while seducing her assistant who is a shallow religious salesman devoid of any morality and ignorant of any theological dogma; eventually, she burns to death with a wooden cross in her hands when an accidental fire engulfs her and her congregation with the exception of her assistant in this Pre-Atomic novel by a Nobel Prize winning American author (1927).

7	<u>Heaven's My Destination</u> by Thornton Wilder
8	<u>Elmer gantry</u> by Sinclair Lewis
9	<u>death Comes for the Archbishop</u> by Willa Cather

1-4-8

Settembrini - this character is the Italian humanist and philosopher whose endless discussions with a Jesuit converted from Judaism, Leo Naphta, ultimately compel him to leave Davos-Platz and take rooms in the house where Leo is lodged; eventually, a duel between the two ends tragically when Leo commits suicide in this Pre-Atomic novel by a Nobel Prize winning author (1924).

1	Buddenbrooks by Thomas Mann
2	The Trial by Franz Kafka
3	The Magic Mountain by Thomas Mann

Ivy Peters - this character is the amoral, shyster Midwestern lawyer from Sweet Water, Colorado whose opportunistic and callous affair with the older Marian Forrester after the death of her honorable husband, Captain Daniel Forrester, offends the sensibilities of such townspeople as a law clerk named Neil Herbert and his uncle, Judge Pommeroy; eventually, he cons this older woman into shifting power of attorney away from the Captain's choice, Judge Pommeroy, to him   so that he ultimately gets possession of her home in this Pre-Atomic novel (1923).

4	A Lost Lady by Willa Cather
5	Little Women by Louisa May Alcott
6	Gone with the Wind by Margaret Mitchell

Antione Roquentin - this character is the 30 year-old, well-traveled French philosopher who spends 3 years in a French seaport named Bouville doing historical research about a Marquis whiled only socializing with a congenial and sexually active café owner named Francoise and Ogier P. whose goal is to read all the books in the library; eventually, his trip to Paris to revisit an old sweetheart named Anny proves futile except that he resolves to stop his research and return to Paris where he can write a Post-Victorian novel and deal with his affliction in this Pre-Atomic novel (1938).

7	The Stranger by Albert Camus
8	Nausea by Jean Paul Sartre
9	The Counterfeiters by Andre Gide

3-4-8

Melanie Hamilton - this character is the young, reserved, cultured, Southern belle from Clayton County, Georgia whose marriage to a tranquil, submissive idealist named Ashley Wilkes spurs another marriage between her head strong girlfriend and her brother, Charles Hamilton; eventually, she dies during miscarriage after her husband returns home from a Northern prisoner-of-war camp and goes to work with her sister-in-law in a sawmill located in Atlanta, Georgia in this Pre-Atomic novel (1936).

1	The Lost Lady by Willa Cather
2	Gone with the Wind by Margaret Mitchell
3	Little Women by Louisa May Alcott

Alroy Kear - this character is the English novelist whose plans to write a biography of the late Victorian author, Edward Driffield, leads him to join another English writer named Ashenden in collaboration with the dead author's widow, Amy; eventually, he appears dissatisfied with Ashenden's reminiscences and perspective about Driffield's first wife, Rosie, who is divorced after she runs off to New York with a contractor named George Kemp in this Pre-Atomic novel (1930).

4	Cakes and Ale by William Somerset Maugham
5	Of Human Bondage by William Somerset Maugham
6	The Moon and Sixpence by William Somerset Maugham

Joanna Burden - this character is the Yankee spinster in Jefferson, Mississippi who becomes the mistress of Joe Christmas born of a Afro-American circus entertainer who is killed by Doc Hines and a white woman named Mary Hines who is allowed to die in childbirth by the same Doc Hines; eventually, her attempts to control and rule him sexually causes him to slash her throat in a violent rage in this Pre-Atomic novel by a Nobel Prize winning author (1932).

7	Absalom, Absalom! by William Faulkner
8	Sanctuary by William Faulkner
9	Light in August by William Faulkner

<u>Jason Compson IV</u> - this character is the hardware store employee who comes from a dysfunctional Mississippian family consisting of an alcoholic father, a hypochondriacal mother, a mentally retarded brother nicknamed Benji, a promiscuous sister nicknamed Caddy and a suicidal brother named Quentin; eventually, he is robbed by his niece, Quentin, of money that is rightfully hers in this Pre-Atomic novel (1929).

1	<u>The Sound and the Fury</u> by William Faulkner
2	<u>Absalom, Absalom</u>! by William Faulkner
3	<u>Sanctuary</u> by William Faulkner

<u>Anthony</u> - this character is the illegitimate son whose noblewoman mother, Maria Bonnyfeather, dies in childbirth while her husband, the Marquis da Vincitata, Don Luis, kills her young Irish-French nobleman lover, Denis Moore;   eventually, his auspicious start in life at the bidding of a U.S. businessman from Leghorn, John Bonnyfeather, who turns out to be his maternal grandfather ends when he dies while cutting down a tree in this Pre-Atomic novel (1933).

4	John Dos Passos
5	Hervey Allen
6	Stephen Crane

<u>Jacob Barnes (Jake)</u> - this character is the American ex-patriate newspaper correspondent whose groin injury as an American Red Cross ambulance driver during World War I thwarts his relationship with promiscuous Lady Brett Ashley; eventually, he joins Bill Gorton, Mike Campbell, Robert Cohn and Brett in Pamplona, Spain to watch the bullfighter, Pedro Romero bullfight in this Pre-Atomic novel by a Nobel Prize winning author (1926).

7	<u>For Whom the Bell Tolls</u> by Ernest Hemingway
8	<u>The Sun Also Rises</u> by Ernest Hemingway
9	<u>A Farewell to Arms</u> by Ernest Hemingway

Byron Bunch - this character is the benevolent young sawmill worker in Jefferson, Mississippi who is approached by a young woman from Alabama named Lena Grove who is seeking the father of her unborn child; eventually, he joins Lena and her new-born baby as they scour the South searching for the brash and non-committal father, Joe Brown a/k/a Lucas Burch in this Pre-Atomic novel by a Nobel Prize winning author (1932).

1	**Light in August** by William Faulkner
2	**Sanctuary** by William Faulkner
3	**The Sound and the Fury** by William Faulkner

Ruby Lamar - this character is the common-law wife of the moonshiner named Lee Goodwin who is accused of killing the bootlegger, Tommy, and attacking a young female collegiate, Temple Blake; eventually, she testifies to his innocence and then she and his attorney, Henry Benbow, spend the night with him in a jail cell to prevent the sociopath, Popeye, from shooting him in this Pre-Atomic novel by a Nobel Prize winning author (1931).

4	**Absalom, Absalom!** by William Faulkner
5	**Sanctuary** by William Faulkner
6	**Light in August** by William Faulkner

George Milton - this character is the short, lean migrant worker who travels with an overgrown simpleton named Lennie Small into Salinas Valley, California to begin work on a barley ranch; eventually, he has to kill his friend, Lennie, after the latter unintentionally crushes Curley's hand, inadvertently kills a small puppy and accidently breaks the neck of Curley's shameless wife in this Pre-Atomic novel by a Nobel Prize winning American author (1944).

7	**Of Mice and Men** by John Steinbeck
8	**The Red Pony** by John Steinbeck
9	**Travels with Charlie** by John Steinbeck

Captain Mallison - this character is the young, high-strung British consul who is kidnaped along with another British consul, Hugh Conway, a missionary, Roberta Brinklow, and an American embezzler, Henry Barnard and taken to an idyllic valley named Shangri-La in the Tibetan Himalayas; eventually, he escapes from this paradise along with a Chinese woman named Lo-Tsen and Hugh Conway who ends up exhausted and disoriented in a Chinese mission hospital telling this incredible story to an old schoolmate named Rutherford in this Pre-Atomic novel(1933).

1	**Lost Horizon** by James Hilton
2	**Point Counterpoint** by Aldous Huxley
3	**Goodbye, Mr. Chips** by James Hilton

Bernard Profitendieu - this character is the 17 year-old unprincipled and insolent, illegitimate son who is hired as a secretary by an aging french writer named Edouard to the chagrin of this writer's young nephew, Olivier Moliner, who is jealous of his friend's new employment; eventually, he leaves Edouard and returns home to his foster father while Olivier recovers from a suicide attempt, young George Moliner matures and his brother, William Moliner grieves over Lady Griffith's death in Africa in this Pre-Atomic novel (1925).

4	**The Counterfeiters** by Andre Gide
5	**The Red and the Black** by Stendhal
6	**The Charterhouse of Parma** by Gustave Flaubert

Isobel Porter - this character is the young daughter of an Irish Protestant innkeeper and pub owner near Phoenix Park, Dublin who falls asleep after closing time and has an elaborate surrealistic dream; eventually, she is transformed in his dream into Issy while her father and mother respectively become Humphrey Climpden Earwicker and Anna Maria Plurabelle and her brothers, Kevin and Jerry, respectively become Shaun the Postmen and Shem the Penman in this Pre-Atomic novel (1939).

7	**Finnegan's Wake** by James Joyce
8	**A Portrait of the Artist as a Young Man** by James Joyce
9	**Ulysses** by James Joyce

1-4-7

Miss Roberta Brinklow - this character is the missionary who is kidnaped and taken to an idyllic valley named Shangri-La in the Tibetan Himalayas along with an American embezzler, Henry Barnard, and two British consuls, Captain Mallison and Hugh Conway; eventually, she decides to stay behind with Henry Barnard when the two British consuls decide to escape this paradise along with a Chinese woman named Lo-Tsen in this Pre-Atomic novel by an English author (1933).

1   **Lost Horizon** by James Hilton
2   **Point Counterpoint** by Aldous Huxley
3   **Goodbye, Mr. Chips** by James Hilton

James Gatz - this character is the mysterious rich newcomer on Long Island whose wild and extravagant parities at his newly acquired   mansion so that he can reunite with an old flame and neighbor named Daisy who is married to a Wall Street millionaire named Tom Buchanan and has a young daughter; eventually, his tragic shooting murder in own his swimming pool by an auto mechanic named George Wilson is engineered by Tom who has shifted the blame for an earlier hit-and-run of his mistress and George's wife, Myrtle Wilson, to this eternal optimist in this Pre-Atomic novel (1925).

4   **This Side of Paradise** by F. Scott Fitzgerald
5   **Tender is the Night** by F. Scott Fitzgerald
6   **The Great Gatsby** by F. Scott Fitzgerald

Helen - this character is the girlfriend of a down and out unsuccessful fiction writer named Don Birnam and the one whose love has turned to pity with regard to this sensitive , articulate, well-dressed free-lancer novelist who comes from a good family; eventually, her pity results in her taking him home to her apartment where she nurses him back to health and reassures his vacationing younger brother, Wick, that he is alright just as he is stealing her fur in order to pawn it in this Pre-Atomic novel (1944).

7   **The Last Tycoon** by F. Scott Fitzgerald
8   **The Lost Weekend** by Charles Jackson
9   **The Sun Also Rises** by Ernest Hemingway

Jim Casy - this character is the country preacher in the Dust Bowl who joins the Joad family as they make their way as Okies across the desert to California to become migrant workers in the promised land; eventually, he is killed after becoming a labor leader who tries to organize the migrant workers while Tom Joad becomes a wanted man for killing a deputy in this Pre-Atomic novel by a Nobel Prize winning author (1939).

1	**The Red Pony** by John Steinbeck
2	**The Grapes of Wrath** by John Steinbeck
3	**Of Mice and Men** by John Steinbeck

Mrs. Wickett - this character is the English landlady who watches over an 85 year-old school teacher at a school called **Brookfield**; eventually, she finds him dead in his bed after he spends a cold November day reminiscing about his students and his young wife, Kathie Bridges, whom he had married at 48 years of age and buried after she died in childbirth with his stillborn son in this Pre-Atomic novel (1933).

4	**Lost Horizon** by James Hilton
5	**Point Counterpoint** by Aldous Huxley
6	**Goodbye, Mr. Chips** by James Hilton

Rockyfeller - this character is the obese, repulsive fastidiously dressed Rumanian prisoner in the French prison known as **La Ferte** during World War I who causes a disturbance on his arrival; eventually, this former prosperous manager of a disreputable brothel alienates himself when he uses his large sums of money to buy special favors from the guards and hires a former hoodlum pimp known as the Fighting Sheeney for a bodyguard in this   Pre-Atomic novel (1922).

7	**Nausea** by Jean Paul Sartre
8	**The Enormous Room** by E. E. Cummings
9	**The Stranger** by Albert Camus

2-6-8

Lo-Tsen - this character is the Chinese woman who falls in love with a British consul named Captain Mallison after the latter has been kidnaped and taken to an idyllic valley named Shangri-La in the Tibetan Himalayas along with another British consul, Hugh Conway, a missionary, Roberta Brinklow, and an American embezzler named Henry Bernard; eventually, she decides to escape from this paradise along with the two British consuls while leaving behind Miss Roberta Brinklow ans Henry Barnard who have chosen to stay in this Pre-Atomic novel (1933).

1	**Goodbye, Mr. Chips** by James Hilton
2	**Point Counterpoint** by Aldous Huxley
3	**Lost Horizon** by James Hilton

Laura James - this character is the young girl who comes to a boarding house in North Carolina named **Dixieland** where she has an affair with a college student from Pulpit Hill 5 years her junior named Eugene Gant; eventually, she returns home to her parents and informs Eugene in a letter that she will marry a boy she had been engaged to for nearly a year in this Pre-Atomic novel (1929).

4	**Look Homeward, Angel** by Thomas Wolfe
5	**Of Time and the River** by Thomas Wolfe
6	**The Web and the Rock** by Thomas Wolfe

Leopold Bloom - this character is the middle-aged Jewish advertising salesman whose wanderings throughout Dublin on June 16, 1904 parallel the wanderings of a 21 year-old Irish writer and teacher named Stephen Dateless with subsequent meetings at a newspaper office, the National Library and a hospital where neither spoke to each other; eventually, he follows Stephen and a medical student to a brothel after Stephen leaves his roommate, Buck Mulligan, and others at a pub in this Irish Pre-Atomic novel (1922).

7	**Finnegan's Wake** by James Joyce
8	**A Portrait of the Artist as a Young Man** by James Joyce
9	**Ulysses** by James Joyce

3-4-9

<u>Nick Carraway</u> - this character is the young Midwestern who forsakes the family hardware business to sell bonds in New York City where he became involved in the lives and intrigues of wealthy Daisy and Tom Buchanan, George and Myrtle Wilson, a golfer named Jordan Baker and a mysterious gentleman gangster named Jay; eventually, he is the only other mourner to join Jay's father at his son's funeral after Jay is mistakenly murdered by George Wilson for the accidental hit-and-run murder of George's wife, Myrtle, in this Pre-Atomic novel (1925).

1	<u>Tender is the Night</u> by F. Scott Fitzgerald
2	<u>The Great Gatsby</u> by F. Scott Fitzgerald
3	<u>The Last Tycoon</u> by F. Scott Fitzgerald

<u>Marquesa de Montemayor</u> - this character is the wealthy, old, homely Peruvian mother of the beautiful Dona Clara and the one whose self-centered, thoughtless ways drove her daughter to marry a man who took her to Spain; eventually, intercepts a letter written by her unhappy maid, Pepita, to a former mistress, becomes contrite after realizing the hurt she has caused, and ironically dies a tragic death with her maid and three other people the next day in this   Pre-Atomic novel (1927).

4	<u>Heaven's My Destination</u> by Thornton Wilder
5	<u>The Bridge of San Luis Rey</u> by Thornton Wilder
6	<u>Sister Carrie</u> by Theodore Dreiser

<u>Lennie Small</u> - this character is the overgrown simpleton migrant worker who accompanies his short, lean friend named George Milton into Salinas Valley, California to begin working on a barley ranch; eventually, he is killed by George after unintentionally crushing Curley's hand, inadvertently killing a small puppy and accidently breaking the neck of Curley's shameless wife in this Pre-Atomic novel by a Nobel Prize winning American author (1937).

7	<u>The Grapes of Wrath</u> by John Steinbeck
8	<u>Of Mice and Men</u> by John Steinbeck
9	<u>Cannery Row</u> by John Steinbeck

2-5-8

Sidney Herbert Head - this character is the scoundrel who marries a promiscuous Southern woman named Caddy Compson after promising her brother, Jason, that he will reciprocate for the marriage with a job for Jason at his Southern bank; eventually, he rejects the child Caddy gives birth to as his own flesh and blood because of its premature birth, divorces Caddy and reneges on Jason getting the bank job in this Pre-Atomic novel by Nobel Prize winning author (1929).

1   <u>The Sound and the Fury</u> by William Faulkner
2   <u>Light in August</u> by William Faulkner
3   <u>As I Lay Dying</u> by William Faulkner

Father Jean Maria Latour - this character is the French Catholic clergyman who seeks refuge from a Southwestern American sleet storm in the cabin of a suspicious character named Buck Scales while touring his parish with his colleague, Father Vaillant; eventually, he and his friend's lives are saved when they are warded off from staying there by Buck's Mexican wife, Magdalena, they are saved by Buck's Mexican wife, Magdalena, who later takes up residence in the home of the famous American frontiersman, Kit Carson, when her husband is arrested and hanged in this Pre-Atomic novel (1927).

4   <u>Heaven's My Destination</u> by Thornton Wilder
5   <u>Elmer gantry</u> by Sinclair Lewis
6   <u>death Comes for the Archbishop</u> by Willa Cather

Red - this character is the young, favored customer of a particular prostitute named Temple Blake at Reba River's house of ill-repute in Memphis, Tenn.; eventually, he is killed by gang members under orders of their sociopathic leader, Popeye, to prevent his escape with this young female collegian forced into prostitution in this Pre-Atomic novel by a Nobel Prize winning author (1931).

7   <u>Light in August</u> by William Faulkner
8   <u>Sanctuary</u> by William Faulkner
9   <u>The Sound and the Fury</u> by William Faulkner

1-6-8

<u>Ellen Thatcher</u> - this character is the accomplished Broadway actress whose first marriage to inept, indolent actor named John Oglethorpe ends in divorce is followed by an affair with the love of her life, Stan Emery, until his death by misadventure in an apartment fie; eventually, her second marriage to newspaper reporter, Jimmy Herf, ends after Red Cross work in Europe during World War II and is followed by a third marriage to an indifferent lawyer named George Baldwin in this Pre-Atomic novel (1938).

1	<u>Manhattan Transfer</u> by John Dos Passos
2	<u>Three Soldiers</u> by John Dos Passos
3	<u>U. S. A. (Trilogy)</u> by John Dos Passos

<u>Ashenden</u> - this character is the English writer who is asked by the English novelist, Alroy Kear, to join in a collaboration with Amy Driffield to write a biography of the late Victorian author, Edward Driffield; eventually, his reminiscences and perspectives about Driffield's first wife, Rosie, whom Driffield divorced after she ran off to New York with a contractor named George Kemp do not meet with Kear's approval since they may prove embarrassing to Driffield's second wife in this Pre-Atomic novel (1930).

4	<u>Of Human Bondage</u> by William Somerset Maugham
5	<u>The Moon and Sixpence</u> by William Somerset Maugham
6	<u>Cakes and Ale</u> by William Somerset Maugham

<u>Popeye</u> - this character is the sociopathic leader of a gang of bootleggers from Memphis, Tenn. who kidnaps the young female collegian, Temple Blake, and forces her into prostitution at Reba River's house of ill-repute; eventually, justice is served when he is ironically executed for the murder of a Birmingham policeman that he did not commit in this Pre-Atomic novel by a Nobel Prize winning author (1931).

7	<u>Sanctuary</u> by William Faulkner
8	<u>Light in August</u> by William Faulkner
9	<u>As I Lay Dying</u> by William Faulkner

1-6-7

Pablo - this character is the   - this character is the Spanish Loyalist guerilla band leader Pilar's debauched, hard-drinking husband who returns after deserting to sell detonators and explosives to the opposing Fascist forces of Franco;   eventually, he escapes with Pilar and Maria while an American expatriate schoolteacher turned explosive expert named Robert Jordan forfeits his life after blowing up a bridge in this Pre-Atomic novel by a Nobel Prize winning author (1940).

1	A Farewell to Arms by Ernest Hemingway
2	The Sun Also Rises by Ernest Hemingway
3	For Whom the Bell Tolls by Ernest Hemingway

Daniel Fuselli - this character is the whining, groveling Californian Private First Class of the Medical Corps during World War I France who channels all his efforts into becoming a corporal; eventually, his final attainment of his goal is only realized after he has lost his French girlfriend, Yvonne, to his sergeant and his hometown girlfriend, Mabe, in San Francisco to a Naval Officer in this Pre-Atomic novel (1921).

4	Manhattan Transfer by John Dos Passos
5	Three Soldiers by John Dos Passos
6	U. S. A. (Trilogy) by John Dos Passos

Jewel Bundren - this character is the high-spirited, illegitimate son of Preacher Whitfield and Addie Bundren and the secret step-brother of Cash, Darl, Vardaman and Dewey Dell; eventually, he carries his mother on his back from a burning barn and ultimately allows his treasured spotted horse to be traded for mules in this Pre-Atomic novel by a Nobel Prize winning author (1930).

7	Light in August by William Faulkner
8	Absalom, Absalom! by William Faulkner
9	As I Lay Dying by William Faulkner

253

3-5-9

<u>Henry Sutpen</u> - this character is the pliable,   Mississippian college student who is unwittingly influenced by a sophisticated fellow student, Charles Bon, who is destined to be his future brother-in-law when he marries Henry's sister, Judith; eventually, he kills Charles at the gate of a plantation named <u>Sutpen's Hundred</u> when the Civil War ends because he discovers that Charles is part Afro-American in this Pre-Atomic novel by a Nobel Prize winning author (1936).

1	<u>Light in August</u> by William Faulkner
2	<u>Absalom, Absalom!</u> by William Faulkner
3	<u>Sanctuary</u> by William Faulkner

<u>Charles Ryder</u> - this character is the British army officer and former architectural painter whose nostalgic return to an old estate conjures up memories of his earlier days at Oxford with Sebastian Marchmain, the Marquis and Lady Marchmain, and Sebastian's siblings, Bridey, Julia, and Cordelia; eventually, he remembers how Sebastian finally sobers up and becomes a porter in a Carthage monastery, how the Marquis sees a Catholic priest on his deathbed after a life with his mistress, Cara, and how Julia returns to her husband, Rex Mothram, rather than divorce and marry him in this Pre-Atomic novel (1945).

4	<u>The Lost Lady</u> by Willa Cather
5	<u>Death Comes for the Archbishop</u> by Willa Cather
6	<u>Brideshead Revisited</u> by Evelyn Waugh

<u>Myra</u> - this character is the dull wife of a prosperous real estate broker name George and the mother of a pudgy daughter named Verona and a school hating son named Theodore (Ted) in the fictional Midwestern town of Zenith; eventually, her illness ends George's illicit affair with a widow named Mrs. Daniel "Tanis" Judique and his return to the conventional world of the Booster Club in this Pre-Atomic novel by a Nobel Prize winning author (1922).

7	<u>Babbitt</u> by Sinclair Lewis
8	<u>Elmer Gantry</u> by Sinclair Lewis
9	<u>Main Street</u> by Sinclair Lewis

2-6-7

<u>Virgil</u> - this character is the Midwestern employee of a small town wholesale drug outfit whose stroke is brought on by both the knowledge that his son, Walter, has embezzled money from Lamb and Company and the financial ruin that occurs when his old boss, Mr. Lamb, opens a glue factory across his new glue factory; eventually, his fantasizing daughter's attempts to impress Arthur Russell turn nauseating and force her to make more realistic choices like entering a business school rather than college in this Pre-Atomic novel (1921).

1	<u>Alice Adams</u> by Booth Tarkington
2	<u>Little Women</u> by Louisa May Alcott
3	<u>Seventeen</u> by Booth Tarkington

<u>Ned Beaumont</u> - this character is the lanky, cigar-smoking tough gambler turned amateur detective who discover's Senator Henry's son Tom's dead in the street and gets himself appointed special investigator by District Attorney, Michael Joseph Farr, whereby he questions a political boss named Paul Madvig, a gambler named Bernie Despain and a bootlegger named Shad O'Rory; eventually, he dismisses the Paul Madvig's confession, exposes the real murderer and leaves for New York with Janet Taylor which makes her Paul's unrequited love in this Pre-Atomic novel (1931).

4	<u>The Maltese Falcon</u> by Dashiell Hammett
5	<u>A Study in Scarlet</u> by Sir Arthur Conan Doyle
6	<u>The Glass Key</u> by Dashiell Hammett

<u>Charles Bon</u> - this character is the young, sophisticated college student at the university in Oxford, Mississippi who impresses fellow student, Henry Sutpen, and becomes engaged to the latter's sister, Judith; eventually, he is killed by Henry at the gate of the plantation known as <u>Sutpen's Hundred</u> at the end of the Civil War because Henry has learned his is part Afro-American in this Pre-Atomic novel by a Nobel Prize winning author (1936).

7	<u>Absalom, Absalom!</u> by William Faulkner
8	<u>Light in August</u> by William Faulkner
9	<u>Sanctuary</u> by William Faulkner

1-6-7

Eupheus Hines (Doc) - this character is the quick-tempered, old man who kills an Afro-American circus entertainer because of the latter's responsibility for an illegitimate son named Joe Christmas and the one who lets his daughter, Mary, die while bearing this child; eventually, he unsuccessfully attempts to have this grandson lynched after the latter kills Joanna Burden in this Pre-Atomic novel by a Nobel Prize winning author (1932).

1	Light in August by William Faulkner
2	As I Lay Dying by William Faulkner
3	Sanctuary by William Faulkner

Olivier Molinier - this character is the aging writer Edouard's young, reticent nephew whose jealousy becomes evident when his uncle employs an unprincipled and insolent 17 year-old named Bernard Pofitendieu as his personal secretary; eventually, he recovers from a failed suicide attempt while his uncle returns to writing, his young brother, George, starts to mature and his brother, William, grieves over Lady Griffith's death in Africa in this   Pre-Atomic novel (1925).

4	The Counterfeiters by Andre Gide
5	The Red and the Black by Stendhal
6	The Charterhouse of Parma by Gustave Flaubert

John Claggart - this character is the British Master-at-Arms aboard the H.M.S. Indomitable whose initial contact with a young, handsome and guileless seaman just impressed from the British merchant ship, the Rights of Man, stirs deep hostility and envy in him; eventually, his accidental death from this impulsive seaman's physical blow with Captain Vere as the only witness results in this seaman's court martial and ultimate hanging in this Pre-Atomic novel written by a Nobel Prize winning author (1924).

7	Captains Courageous by Rudyard Kipling
8	Two Years Before the Mast by Richard Henry Dana, Jr.
9	Billy Budd - Foretopman by Herman Melville

1-4-9

Dewey Dell Bundren - this character is the 17 year-old unmarried, pregnant, well-developed daughter of Addie and Anse Bundren and sister of Cash, Jewel, Darl and Vardaman; eventually, her secondary motive for accompanying Addie's coffin to Jefferson, Mississippi is to get drugs to cause a miscarriage in this Pre-Atomic novel written by a Nobel Prize winning author (1930).

1	**Absalom, Absalom!** by William Faulkner
2	**The Sound and the Fury** by William Faulkner
3	**As I Lay Dying** by William Faulkner

Lena Grove - this character is the country girl from Alabama who traces a brash, non-committal man named Joe Brown a/k/a Lucas Burch to the town of Jefferson, Mississippi because he had abandoned her after her seduction and impregnation; eventually, she is joined in her pursuit of him throughout the South by Byron Burch who had fallen in love with her in this Pre-Atomic novel written by a Nobel Prize winning author (1932).

4	**Sanctuary** by William Faulkner
5	**Light in August** by William Faulkner
6	**The Sound and the Fury** by William Faulkner

Roberta Alden - this character is the poor Lycurgus, New York factory worker who becomes the mistress of her immature, uneducated boss, Clyde Griffiths, while he social climbs to marry Sondra Finchley; eventually, her pregnancy compels her to accompany him on a boating trip where she is left to die after accidently falling overboard which leads to Clyde's trial, conviction and execution in this Pre-Atomic novel (1925).

7	**An American Tragedy** by Theodore Dreiser
8	**Sister Carrie** by Theodore Dreiser
9	**The Titan** by Theodore Dreiser

3-5-7

<u>Katey Macauley</u> - this character is the widowed mother of Marcus, Homer, Ulysses and daughter, Bess, in the small home town of Ithica, New York whose philosophy of life embodies the belief that war results from alienation and the lack of God's grace; eventually, her premonition of Marcus's death in the army is verified by a telegram at the same time that she accepts another soldier into her family as a substitute son and new member of the family in this Pre-Atomic novel by an American author (1943).

1	<u>The Human Comedy</u> by William Saroyan
2	<u>The Lost Lady</u> by Willa Cather
3	<u>Ethan Frome</u> by Edith Wharton

<u>Janey Williams</u> - this character is the embittered stenographer whose ambition and competency lands her a job with J. Ward Moorehouse who is a successful advertising executive and philanderer whose conquests outside marriage did not include her; eventually, her abilities earned her a high level of success in business during the 1920's and 1930's with only periodic embarrassments when her sailor brother, Joe, visited her bringing presents in this Pre-Atomic novel (1930).

4	<u>U.S.A. (Trilogy)</u> by John Dos Passos
5	<u>The Titan</u> by Theodore Dreiser
6	<u>Arrowsmith</u> by Sinclair Lewis

<u>Robert Weaver</u> - this character is the young student at Harvard from Altamont, North Carolina who shows up drunk and obnoxious at the room of a future writer named Eugene Gant only to end up on the cot of a mysterious Chinese student named Wang; eventually, his drunkenness causes future embarrassment to Eugene when they are jailed in South Carolina and when Robert must escape the wrath of an irate husband in New York City in this Pre-Atomic novel (1935).

7	<u>Of Time and the River</u> by Thomas Wolfe
8	<u>Look Homeward, Angel</u> by Thomas Wolfe
9	<u>The Web and the Rock</u> by Thomas Wolfe

1-4-7

Mr. Ramsay - this character is the professor of Philosophy who captivates his students with his metaphysics while his 8 children view his remarks as sarcastic; eventually, when his wife dies in her sleep and the war ends, he tries to take up where his family left off in earlier days and returns with surviving members of the family to a summer cottage in this Pre-Atomic novel (1927).

1	<u>To the Lighthouse</u> by Virginia Woolf
2	<u>Little Women</u> by Louisa May Alcott
3	<u>Seventeen</u> by Booth Tarkington

Hans Castorp - this character is the young German engineer whose future career with a shipbuilding firm in Hamburg is put on hold when tuberculosis forces him to spend 7 years in the International Sanatorium Bergh located in Switzerland; eventually, his acquaintance there with an Italian philosopher, Lodovico Settembrini, a Jew who became a Jesuit named Leo Naphta, a gay Russian named Clavdia Chauchat and the hedonistic Mynheer Peeperkorn does not deter him from seeking service when world War I breaks out in this Pre-Atomic novel by a Nobel Prize winning author (1924).

4	<u>The Magic Mountain</u> by Thomas Mann
5	<u>Steppenwolf</u> by Herman Hesse
6	<u>Buddenbrooks</u> by Thomas Mann

Dr. Aziz - this character is the caring and astute, young Muslim doctor in Chandapore, India, who extends himself to three newcomers from England named Cecil Fielding, Mrs. Moore and Adela Quested who are respectively the President of Government College, the mother of the City Magistrate, Ronny Heaslop, and Ronny's fiancé; eventually, his arrest, trial and acquittal for the alleged rape of Adela Quested at the Marabar Caves puts a crimp in his relations with Cecil Fielding when he returns to India with his new wife, Stella, in this Pre-Atomic novel (1924).

7	<u>A Passage to India</u> by E. M. Forster
8	<u>A Study in Scarlet</u> by Sir Arthur Conan Doyle
9	<u>Kim</u> by Rudyard Kipling

Foxhall Edwards - this character is the cynical, fatalistic editor for a prestigious New York publishing house who takes a young zealous Southern writer named George Webber under his wing while George has an illicit affair with a married stage designer named Esther Jack; eventually, he suffers the same fate as Esther when George severs all ties with him due to artistic differences and George's lofty goals for the future in this   Pre-Atomic novel (1940).

1	<u>The Web and the Rock</u> by Thomas Wolfe
2	<u>Look Homeward, Angel</u> by Thomas Wolfe
3	<u>You Can't Go Home Again</u> by Thomas Wolfe

Leora Tozer - this character is the good-looking, compassionate nurse who marries a yung medical doctor and researcher named Martin after he jilts a superficial graduate school student named Madeline Fox; eventually, she accompanies her husband and a Swedish secretary named Gustave Sondelius to the West Indies island of St. Hubert where she inadvertently contracts the bubonic plague and dies along with Gustave in this Pre-Atomic novel by an American Nobel Prize winning author (1924).

4	<u>Elmer Gantry</u> by Sinclair Lewis
5	<u>Arrowsmith</u> by Sinclair Lewis
6	<u>Main Street</u> by Sinclair Lewis

Adela Quested - this character is the pompous, immature young woman who sails from England with Mr. Moore to see the real India and visit Mrs. Moore's son, Ronny Heaslop, who is the City Magistrate of Chandrapore, India, and her fiancé; eventually, her accusations of alleged rape at the Marabar caves result in the arrest and trial of a young Muslim doctor named Dr. Aziz who is subsequently acquitted when she recants her testimony in this Pre-Atomic novel (1924).

7	<u>Kim</u> by Rudyard Kipling
8	<u>A Passage to India</u> by E. M. Forster
9	<u>A Study in Scarlet</u> by Sir Arthur Doyle

3-5-8

Willie Shrike - this character is the New York Post-Dispatch feature editor whose constant tormenting of a lovelorn column writer assists in his subordinate's deterioration into booze and illness eventhough the latter's girlfriend, Betty, tries to help by taking him away to her aunt's Connecticut farm; eventually, he loses this employee when a cripple named Peter Doyle fatally shoots him for allegedly raping his wife, Faye, in this Pre-Atomic novel (1933).

1	**Manhattan Transfer** by John Dos Passos
2	**Miss Lonelyhearts** by Nathaniel West
3	**The Last Tycoon** by F. Scott Fitzgerald

John Andrews (Andy) - this character is the young Harvard musical student who believes that his military life as a World War I private in France is corrupting his individuality and artistic talents even while attending the French University under falsified documents that recommended him for this assignment; eventually, his two desertions which earn him hard labor and a prison sentence confuse and sour a young Parisian Frenchwoman named Genevieve Rod who had originally applauded his piano talent and aesthetic appreciation in this Pre-Atomic novel (1921).

4	**All Quiet on the Western Front** by Erich Maria Remarque
5	**A Farewell to Arms** by Ernest Hemingway
6	**Three Soldiers** by John Dos Passos

Admiral Leighton - this character is the husband of the Duke of Wellington's cultured aloof sister, Lady Barbara, who is responsible for defeating a French squadron in the bay of the French town of Rosas where the real love of her life is imprisoned along with his fellow crew members, the First Lieutenant, Bush, and coxswain, Brown; eventually, he is fatally wounded at the Battle of Gilbraltar leaving his wife free to pursue her widowed lover after she adopts the latter's son in this Pre-Atomic novel(1937).

7	**Captain Horatio Hornblower** by C. S. Forester
8	**The Naked and the Dead** by Norman Mailer
9	**The Pilot** by James Fenimore Cooper

Thomakin - this character is the Director of Hatcheries in London during 632 After Ford whose attempts to dismiss Bernard Marx from the Hatchery are stymied when Bernard and Lenina Crowne produce Linda and John from the Savage Reservation; eventually, he resigns his directorship after a scandal reveals that he was responsible for fathering John after marooning a pregnant Linda on a vacation trip to New Mexico years earlier in this Pre-Atomic novel (1932).

1	Nineteen Eighty Four by George Orwell
2	Brave New World by Aldous Huxley
3	Lost Horizon by James Hilton

Henry Barnard - this character is the American embezzler who is kidnaped and taken to an idyllic valley named Shangri-La in the Tibetan Himalayas along with a missionary named Miss Roberta Brinklow and two British consuls, Captain Mallison and Hugh Conway; eventually, he opts to stay behind with Miss Roberta Brinklow when the two British consul's decide to escape this paradise along with a Chinese woman named Lo-Tsen in this Pre-Atomic novel(1933).

4	Lost Horizon by James Hilton
5	Brave New World by Aldous Huxley
6	Sister Carrie by Theodore Drieser

Captain Daniel Forrester - this character is the courteous, honorable retired Union Army Officer who is a pioneer in the growth of the railroad across the Northwest while accompanied by a wife twenty five his junior named Marian; eventually, a fall from a horse results in his retirement to the Midwestern town of Sweet Water, Colorado where he suffers both financial reverses and a stroke which leave him paralyzed in a wheelchair while Marian has an illicit affair with a despicable lawyer named Ivy Peters in this Pre-Atomic novel (1923).

7	A Lost Lady by Willa Cather
8	Heaven's My Destination by Thornton Wilder
9	Arrowsmith by Sinclair Lewis

2-4-7

<u>Congo</u> - this character is the French sailor who accompanies his brother, Emile, to New York City in search of their fortunes and the one who decides to return to the sea while his brother stays and marries a widowed Frenchwoman who owns a delicatessen; eventually, his affluence upon returning to New York City as a prosperous bootlegger when Prohibition began after World War I ended allows him to entertain old friends like Jimmy Herf, the newspaper reporter recently divorced from the accomplished Broadway actress, Ellen Thatcher in this Pre-Atomic novel (1925).

1   <u>Manhattan Transfer</u> by John Dos Passos
2   <u>U.S.A. (Trilogy)</u> by John Dos Passos
3   <u>Three Soldiers</u> by John Dos Passos

<u>Marion Tweedy Bloom</u> - this character is the Irish mediocre concert singer born in Gibraltar whose dull marriage to a middle-aged Jewish advertising salesman and drab life in Dublin drives her to have illicit affairs with such younger men as the manager of her concert tour, Blazes Boylan; eventually, she is aroused by the thought that a young Irish writer and teacher named Stephen Dateless whom Leopold had met on his wanderings about Dublin on June 16, 1904 might come and live with her and be her husband in this Pre-Atomic novel by an Irish author (1922).

4   <u>A Portrait of the Artist as a Young Man</u> by James Joyce
5   <u>Finnegan's Wake</u> by James Joyce
6   <u>Ulysses</u> by James Joyce

<u>Hermine</u> - this character is the young prostitute who teaches a greying middle-aged hermit living in an attic how to dance which ultimately brings him into contact with a young blue-eyed, blonde lover named Maria and a dark, handsome saxophonist named Pablo; eventually, her domination of this melancholy recluse is ended when he finds her and Pablo together on the floor of the <u>Magic Theater</u> and summarily kills her in this Pre-Atomic novel by a Nobel Prize winning author (1927).

7   <u>The Magic Mountain</u> by Thomas Mann
8   <u>Steppenwolf</u> by Herman Hesse
9   <u>Buddenbrooks</u> by Thomas Mann

1-6-8

<u>Bush</u> - this character is the loyal and Courageous First Lieutenant assigned to both <u>H.M.S. Lydia</u> which sails to South America from England to deliver money and munitions to Don Julian Alvarado (El Supremo) so the latter can start a revolution against Spain and the <u>H.M.S. Sutherland</u> where he loses a leg during a battle under the same captain; eventually, he is made captain of his own ship after he successfully escapes from France with a coxswain named Brown and his captain who is subsequently knighted, exonerated during a court martial and reunited with the Duke of Wellington's sister, Lady Barbara in this Pre-Atomic novel (1937).

1	<u>Captains Courageous</u> by Rudyard Kipling
2	<u>Two Years Before the Mast</u> by Richard Henry Dana, Jr.
3	<u>Captain Horatio Hornblower</u> by C. S. Forester

<u>Hugh Conway</u> - this character is the exhausted and disoriented British consul who is discovered in a Chinese mission hospital by an old schoolmate friend named Rutherford; eventually, he tells his old friends an incredible story about being kidnaped and taken to an idyllic valley named Shangri-La in the Tibetan Himalayas along with another British consul, Captain Mallison, a missionary, Miss Roberta Brinklow and an American embezzler named Henry Barnard in this Pre-Atomic novel (1933).

4	<u>Brave New World</u> by Aldous Huxley
5	<u>Lost Horizon</u> by James Hilton
6	<u>Animal Farm</u> by George Orwell

<u>Ashley Wilkes</u> - this character is the young, compassionate, urbane Southern gentleman whose marriage to a young, reserved, cultured Southern belle named Melanie Hamilton spurs another young Southern belle to impulsively marry Melanie's brother, Charles Hamilton; eventually, he returns home from a Northern prisoner-of-war and goes to work with his sister-in-law in a sawmill located in Atlanta, Georgia only to have his wife die of a miscarriage in this Pre-Atomic novel by an American writer (1936).

7	<u>Sanctuary</u> by William Faulkner
8	<u>Look Homeward, Angel</u> by Thomas Wolfe
9	<u>Gone with the Wind</u> by Margaret Mitchell

3-5-9

<u>Amory Blaine</u> - this character is the tall, light-haired, green-eyed Princeton student from the Midwest whose separation from his mother, Beatrice, allows him to interact with literary types like Thomas Park D'Ivelliers and have a romantic fling with Rosalind Connage who breaks off the affair to marry someone who can provide for her in the way she expects; eventually, he is discharged from the Army which he joined in Princeton and moves to New York City where he begins a new career just when his surrogate father, Monsignor Thayer Darcy, dies in this Pre-Atomic novel (1920).

1	<u>Tender is the Night</u> by F. Scott Fitzgerald
2	<u>This Side of Paradise</u> by F. Scott Fitzgerald
3	<u>The Last Tycoon</u> by F. Scott Fitzgerald

<u>Cadace (Caddy) Compson</u> - this character is the promiscuous young woman who comes from a Mississippian dysfunctional family consisting of an alcoholic father, a hypochondriacal mother, a mentally retarded brother named Benji, a hate-filled brother named Jason, and a suicidal brother named Quentin; eventually, she is evicted by the banker, Sydney Herbert Head, when she has a baby too prematurely in this Pre-Atomic novel by a Nobel Prize winning author (1929).

4	<u>The Sound and the Fury</u> by William Faulkner
5	<u>Absalom, Absalom!</u> by William Faulkner
6	<u>Sanctuary</u> by William Faulkner

<u>Frederic Henry</u> - this character is the American volunteer whose service as a Lieutenant in an Italian ambulance unit during World War I allows him to meet and fall in love with a British nurse named Catherine Barkley who is stationed with a British unit in Milan, Italy ; eventually, he tragically watches as Catherine dies in childbirth after delivering a stillborn baby in a Swiss hospital in Lausanne in this Pre-Atomic novel by a Nobel Prize winning American author (1929).

7	<u>For Whom the Bell Tolls</u> by Ernest Hemingway
8	<u>A Farewell to Arms</u> by Ernest Hemingway
9	<u>The Sun Also Rises</u> by Ernest Hemingway

2-4-8

<u>Tom Buchanan</u> - this character is the wealthy Wall Street millionaire who lives on Long Island with his wife, Daisy, and their young daughter while carrying on an affair with a vulgar woman named Myrtle Wilson whose husband is an auto mechanic named George; eventually, his growing jealousy over the attention being paid to his wife by a former flame named Jay drives him to con George into killing Jay while believing that he was the hit-and-run murderer of his wife which was really due to the carelessness of Daisy who was driving Jay's car at the time in this Pre-Atomic novel (1925).

1	<u>This Side of Paradise</u> by F. Scott Fitzgerald
2	<u>The Great Gatsby</u> by F. Scott Fitzgerald
3	<u>Tender is the Night</u> by F. Scott Fitzgerald

<u>George Marvin Bush</u> - this character is the 23 year-old temperate, traveling salesman for a text book company in the Middle West who seduces a Kansas farmer's daughter named Roberta; eventually, his marriage to her and subsequent living in a flat above a drug store allows her to experience his continual obnoxious behavior and constant vying for the affection of their adopted daughter, Elizabeth, to the point where she leaves him and takes Elizabeth back home to her parent's farm in this Pre-Atomic novel by an American author (1935).

4	<u>Babbitt</u> by Sinclair Lewis
5	<u>Heaven's My Destination</u> by Thornton Wilder
6	<u>Room at the Top</u> by John Braine

<u>George Kemp</u> - this character is the English contractor who runs off to New York with Rosa Driffield who is the first wife of a Victorian author named Edward Driffield; eventually, he is revealed to be the true love of her life when she talks to an English writer named Ashenden after he has collaborated with and English novelist in Writing Driffield's biography in this Pre-Atomic novel (1930).

7	<u>Of Human Bondage</u> by William Somerset Maugham
8	<u>Cakes and Ale</u> by William Somerset Maugham
9	<u>The Razor's Edge</u> by William Somerset Maugham

2-5-8

<u>Preacher Whitfield</u> - this character is the former lover of the sickly, worn out Addie Bundren and the one who appears while the Bundrens are on their journey so he can confess to Addie's husband, Anse, that their high-spirited son, Jewel, is illegitimate as opposed to the other Bundren children Cash, Darl, Vardaman and Dewey Dell; eventually, he decides that the difficulties of his journey are sufficient atonement for his sins and that a public confession is no longer needed in this Pre-Atomic novel by a Nobel Prize winning author (1930).

1	<u>As I Lay Dying</u> by William Faulkner
2	<u>The Sound and the Fury</u> by William Faulkner
3	<u>Light in August</u> by William Faulkner

<u>Huw Morgan</u> - this character is the Welsh carpenter who reminisces about the last 5 decades with his mining family that consisted of his mining superintendent father, Gwilym, his mother, Beth, his sister, Angharad and his 4 brothers named Owen, Gwilym, Iano and Davy; eventually, he remembers the strike that divided his family, how he saved his mothers life and how he watched as his father died when a collapsed mine became flooded in this Pre-Atomic novel (1940).

4	<u>Green Mansions</u> by W. H. Hudson
5	<u>Sons and Lovers</u> By D. H. Lawrence
6	<u>How Green Was My Valley</u> by Richard Llewellyn

<u>Thomas Sutpen</u> - this character is the owner of a Jefferson, Mississippi plantation named <u>Sutpen's Hundred</u> whose exvocable will and drive leads him to marry a docile woman named Ellen Coldfield who bears him 2 children, Henry and Judith; eventually, he is left without a male heir when Charles Bon is killed, Henry flees and Milly Jones has a girl in this Pre-Atomic novel by a Nobel Prize winning author (1936).

7	<u>Absalom, Absalom</u>! by William Faulkner
8	<u>As I Lay Dying</u> by William Faulkner
9	<u>Light in August</u> by William Faulkner

1-6-7

<u>Ann Porter</u> - this character is the wife of an Irish Protestant innkeeper who owns a pub near Phoenix Park, Dublin who falls asleep in his pub after closing time and has a surrealistic dream in which she and her 3 children are changed into archetypal forms; eventually, she evolves into Anna Livia Plurabelle while her husband becomes Humphrey Climpden Earwicker and her twin sons, Kevin and Jerry, respectively become Shaun the Postman and Shem the Penman and her daughter, Isobel, becomes Issy in this Pre-Atomic novel (1939).

1	<u>Finnegan's Wake</u> by James Joyce
2	<u>A Portrait of the Artist as a Young Man</u> by James Joyce
3	<u>Ulysses</u> by James Joyce

<u>Jinny Marshland</u> - this character is the working class woman in her twenties who marries a 41 year-old district Judge in Grand Republic, Minnesota, only to find his conventional life style stifling to her youthful desires after their baby is delivered still-born; eventually, her tryst with Bradd Criley in New York City which leaves her in a diabetic coma results in a happy reconciliation with her patient, understanding husband in this Pre-Atomic novel by a Nobel Prize winning author (1945).

4	<u>Magnificent Obsession</u> by Lloyd C. Douglas
5	<u>Green Mansions</u> by W. H. Hudson
6	<u>Cass Timberlane</u> by Sinclair Lewis

<u>Cecil Fleming</u> - this character is the principal of Government College who incurs the wrath of the City Magistrate, Ronald Heaslop, when he takes Mrs. Moore on a school tour and leaves Adela Quested alone with a young Moslem surgeon named Dr. Aziz; eventually, he is ostracized from a club when he takes the side of Dr. Aziz during a rape trial in which the young surgeon is exonerated in this Pre-Atomic novel (1924).

7	<u>Kim</u> by Rudyard Kipling
8	<u>A Passage to India</u> by E. M. Forster
9	<u>A Study in Scarlet</u> by Sir Arthur Conan Doyle

1-6-8

Jimboy - this character is the Afro-American itinerant husband of a Afro-American cook and housekeeper named Annjee working for a wealthy white family in fictional Stanton, Kansas while rearing his son, James "Sandy" Rogers along with her mother, Aunt Hagler, who takes in laundry six days a week; eventually, his wanderings during the early part of the 20th Century in search of dignified work take him to both Detroit where he is joined by Annjee and to Europe where he serves in World War I in this Pre-Atomic novel(1930).

1	<u>Not Without Laughter</u> by Langston Hughes
2	<u>Tambourines to Glory</u> by Langston Hughes
3	<u>I Wonder as I Wander</u> by Langston Hughes

Genevieve Rod - this character is the young Parisian Frenchwoman who applauds John Andrews for his piano talent an aesthetic appreciation while he is attending the French University under falsified documents that recommended him for this assignment; eventually, her feelings toward Andy turn cold ad detached when she becomes confused over his 2 desertions which earn him a prison sentence and hard labor in this Pre-Atomic novel (1921).

4	<u>Three Soldiers</u> by John Dos Passos
5	<u>U. S. A. (Trilogy)</u> by John Dos Passos
6	<u>Manhattan Transfer</u> by John Dos Passos

Ellie May - this character is the hare-lipped, dirt-poor, Georgian girl with 16 siblings who follows in the footsteps of her 16 year-old brother, Dude, who marries a middle-aged woman preacher named Bessie - when she replaces her 15 year-old sister, Pearl, as he object of Love Bessie's affections; eventually, she becomes an orphan after her father, Jester Leeter, and his wife, Ada, die in a fire in this Pre-Atomic novel by a Southern author (1932).

7	<u>The Grapes of Wrath</u> by John Steinbeck
8	<u>Sanctuary</u> by William Faulkner
9	<u>Tobacco Road</u> by Erskine Caldwell

1-4-9

<u>Aunt Tempy</u> - this character is the Afro-American well-fixed social climber in fictional Stanton, Kansas married to a railroad clerk named Mr. Siles who takes in her young nephew, Sandy, after her mother and his grandmother, Aunt Hagler, collapses and dies; eventually, this woman with bourgeois pretensions has to release this unhappy youth from her overbearing control after Annjee summons him to Chicago to join her since Jimboy has gone to Europe to serve in World War I in this Pre-Atomic novel(1930).

1	<u>Tambourines to Glory</u> by Langston Hughes
2	<u>I Wonder as I Wander</u> by Langston Hughes
3	<u>Not Without Laughter</u> by Langston Hughes

<u>Humphrey Crimpden Earwicker</u> - this character is the owner and bartender of an Irish pub just outside of Phoenix Park in Dublin who falls asleep after closing his pub and has an elaborate surrealistic dream until he is awoken at dawn; eventually, his dream becomes the collective psyche of myth and history and involves his wife, Ann Porter, as Anna Livia Plurabelle, his twin sons, Jerry and Kevin Porter as Shem the Penman and Shaun the Postman respectively, and his daughter Isobel as Issy in this Pre-Atomic novel (1939).

4	<u>Finnegan's Wake</u> by James Joyce
5	<u>Ulysses</u> by James Joyce
6	<u>A Portrait as an Artist as a Young Man</u> by James Joyce

<u>Raymond Courreges</u> - this character is the young adolescent whose obsession with unattainable love centers on a young, pretty, French widowed, sexually frigid mother named Maria Cross with a sick child at the   same time that she is seducing his middle-aged father, Doctor Paul Courreges; eventually, his encounter with her later in life permits him to view her dominant character in a different light when the new meeting engenders a mysterious sentiment instead of raking up unfulfilled passions representative of those earlier trouble times in this Pre-Atomic novel by a Nobel Prize winning author (1925).

7	<u>Woman of the Pharisees</u> by Francois Mauriac
8	<u>The Desert of Love</u> by Francois Mauriac
9	<u>The Kiss to the Leper</u> by Francois Mauriac

3-4-8

<u>Thomas Bigger</u> - this character is the sullen and angry 20 year-old, Afro-American Mississippi-born chauffeur with an eight grade education whose job with the wealthy Dalton family away from the Chicago slums of the 1930's results in his inadvertent murder of their daughter, Mary Dalton, by suffocation with a pillow; eventually, his scheme to cove up this death by misadventure by concocting a kidnaping ploy results in the murder of his girlfriend, Bessis Mears, his conviction and ultimate sentencing to death by electrocution in this Pre-Atomic novel(1940).

1	<u>Black Boy</u> by Richard Wright
2	<u>Native Son</u> by Richard Wright
3	<u>The Outsider</u> by Richard Wright

<u>Matthew Towns</u> - this character is the gifted young Afro-American whose exclusion from an internship in obstetrics at the renown New York City medical school, the University of Manhattan, compels him to sail to Europe where he meets a high-born woman named Kautilya who convinces him to join a third world radical group against white imperialism; eventually, he divorces Sara Andrews who is the assistant to a forceful Chicago politician named Samuel Scott who gets him released from prison so he could reunite with Kautilya and their new child in this Pre-Atomic novel (1928).

4	<u>Black Flame</u> by W. E. B. DuBois
5	<u>The Quest of the Silver Fleece</u> by W. E. B. DuBois
6	<u>Dark Princess: A Romance</u> by W. E. B. DuBois

<u>Doctor Paul Courreges</u> - this character is the middle-aged doctor in pre-World War I France who joins his son, Raymond, in an obsession with Maria Cross who is a lazy, young widowed sexually frigid mother of a sickly child; eventually, he is seduced by this pretty young woman whose character causes him to recklessly abandon his career for one last, desperate fling of sensuality in this Pre-Atomic novel by a Nobel Prize winning author (1925).

7	<u>Woman of the Pharisees</u> by Francois Mauriac
8	<u>The Desert of Love</u> by Francois Mauriac
9	<u>The Kiss to the Leper</u> by Francois Mauriac

2-6-8

<u>Mary Dalton</u> - this character is the young Chicagoan daughter of a wealthy family who is driven around a Chicago ghetto with her communist lover, Jan Erlone, by a newly hired Afro-American, Mississippi-born chauffeur named Thomas Bigger until she is returned home intoxicated; eventually, her inadvertent suffocation with a pillow case and his hurling his girlfriend, Bessie Mears, down an air shaft ultimately ends in this angry, sullen chauffeur's conviction and death sentence in this Pre-Atomic novel (1940).

1	<u>Black Boy</u> by Richard Wright
2	<u>Native Son</u> by Richard Wright
3	<u>The Outsider</u> by Richard Wright

<u>Sara Andrews</u> - this character is the light-skinned, Afro-American legal assistant to a forceful Afro-American Chicago politician named Samuel Scott and the one who marries a gifted young Afro-American aspiring politician named Matthew Towns; eventually, she becomes enraged when he deserts her at his nomination dinner for State legislature so that he can take a blue collar job while supporting a high born Indian woman named Kautilya and their new born child in this Pre-Atomic novel (1928).

4	<u>Black Flame</u> by W. E. B. DuBois
5	<u>The Quest of the Silver Fleece</u> by W. E. B. DuBois
6	<u>Dark Princess: A Romance</u> by W. E. B. DuBois

<u>Annjee</u> - this character is the Afro-American cook and housekeeper for a wealthy, white family in fictional Stanton, Kansan during the early part of the 20th century and the mother of James "Sandy" Rogers whose stay with his grandmother, Aunt Hager, is quickly followed with his stay with Aunt Tempy and Mr. Siles after Hager abruptly dies; eventually, she travels to Detroit to meet her wandering husband, Jimboy, which is followed by a trip to Chicago where she summons Sandy to join her after Jimboy ships out to Europe where he will serve in World War I in this Pre-Atomic novel (1930).

7	<u>Tambourines to Glory</u> by Langston Hughes
8	<u>I Wonder as I Wander</u> by Langston Hughes
9	<u>Not Without Laughter</u> by Langston Hughes

2-6-9

Bessie Mears - this character is the young girl friend of a sullen, angry 20 year-old Afro-American Mississippi-born chauffeur named Thomas Bigger who enlists her aid in a phony kidnaping scheme involving a young wealthy Chicagoan woman named Mary Dalton; eventually, she is frozen to death after being pushed down a air shaft by this boyfriend after he is exposed as the inadvertent murderer of Mary by suffocation which results in his ultimate conviction and death by electrocution in this Pre-Atomic novel (1940).

1	Native Son by Richard Wright
2	Black Boy by Richard Wright
3	The Outsider by Richard Wright

Kautilya - this character is the elegant, good-looking and high-born Indian woman who recruits a gifted Afro-American ex-medical student in a Berlin café into a third world radical group that is against white imperialism; eventually, she and their child together are reunited after he is released from prison through the efforts of a forceful Chicago politician named Samuel Scott and a divorce from Sara Andrews who is this politician's legal assistant in this Pre-Atomic novel (1928).

4	Black Flame by W. E. B. DuBois
5	The Quest of the Silver Fleece by W. E. B. DuBois
6	Dark Princess: A Romance by W. E. B. DuBois

Aunt Hager - this character is the Afro-American grandmother of a young boy named James "Sandy" Rogers, the mother of a Afro-American cook and housekeeper named Annjee Rogers and the mother-in-law of an itinerant named Jimboy in fictional Stanton, Kansas during the early part of the 20th century; eventually, this ex-slave who takes in laundry six days a week collapses and dies which forces Sandy to live with his well-fixed Aunt Tempy and railroad clerk uncle, Mr. Siles, because his mother, Annjee, is off pursuing Jimboy in this   Pre-Atomic novel (1930).

7	Tambourines to Glory by Langston Hughes
8	I Wonder as I Wander by Langston Hughes
9	Not Without Laughter by Langston Hughes

1-6-9

<u>Maria Cross</u> - this character is the young, French widowed sexually frigid mother with a sick child during Pre-World War I who becomes the unattainable first love of an adolescent boy named Raymond while tempting his respected father, Doctor Paul Courreges, to recklessly abandon his career for one last, desperate fling of sensuality; eventually, her dominant character is seen years later in a different light by these two admirers when this new encounter engenders a mysterious sentiment instead of raking up unfulfilled passions representative of those troubled times in this Pre-Atomic novel by a Nobel Prize winning author (1925).

1	<u>Woman of the Pharisees</u> by Francois Mauriac
2	<u>The Desert of Love</u> by Francois Mauriac
3	<u>The Kiss to the Leper</u> by Francois Mauriac

<u>James "Sandy" Rodgers</u> - this character is the quiet and observant young Afro-American youth living in fictional Stanton, Kansas during the early part of the 20th Century who lives with his mother, Annjee, and his grandmother, Aunt Hager while his father, Jimboy, travels for months at a time trying to find dignified work; eventually, he has to live in Stanton with his mother's well-off sister, Aunt Tempy, and her railroad mail clerk husband, Mr. Siles, until his mother summons him to Chicago because Jimboy has left for Europe to serve in World War I in this Pre-Atomic novel(1930).

4	<u>Tambourines to Glory</u> by Langston Hughes
5	<u>I Wonder as I Wander</u> by Langston Hughes
6	<u>Not Without Laughter</u> by Langston Hughes

<u>Gustav Von Aschenbach</u> - this character is the famous German novelist and critic from Munich during the early part of the 20th century who begins to obsess over the beauty of a 14 year-old boy   named Tadzio who is part of a governess's party of young Poles; eventually, this fixation proves fatal when the city authorities attempt to conceal an outbreak of cholera by silencing him backfires in this Pre-Atomic novel by a Nobel Prize winning author (1930).

7	<u>Buddenbrooks</u> by Thomas Mann
8	<u>Death in Venice</u> by Thomas Mann
9	<u>The Magic Mountain</u> by Thomas Mann

2-6-8

Brigid O'Shaughnessy - this character is the sensuous young woman whose first introduction as Miss Wonderly to a young rugged private detective named Sam Spade results in the deaths of Sam's partner, Miles Archer, and the man he was following, Floyd Thursby; eventually, her part in an intrigue involving Thursby reveals deceptions and double crosses between Thursby, a prissy gangster named Joel Cairo and an older stout man named Casper Gutman that began in Greece and moved from Constantinople to Hong Kong to San Francisco in this Pre-Atomic novel (1930).

1   Miss Lonelyhearts by Nathaniel West
2   The Glass Key by Dashiell Hammett
3   The Maltese Falcon by Dashiell Hammett

Lutie Cameron Brewton - - this character is the owner of the Cross B Ranch in Salt Fork who marries Lutie Cameron from St. Louis, Missouri during a range war and has 3 children; eventually, he is abandoned by Lutie for 15 years over her adultery with a handsome town district attorney, Brice Chamberlin, only to have her return to him when he chases down the son she had with Bruce named Brock and kill him as an outlaw in this Pre-Atomic novel by a Pulitzer Prize winning author (1936).

4   The Town by Conrad Richter
5   The Light in the Forest by Conrad Richter
6   The Sea of Grass by Conrad Richter

Wang Lung - this character is the Chinese farmer who successfully struggles to accumulate land while his former slave-girl wife, O-lan, bears him children and remains loyal eventhough he adds a mistress named Lotus Blossom to their household; eventually, his success over time permits him to happily return to his roots as a widower along with a simple young slave-girl named Pearl Blossom, his slow-witted daughter and some servants eventhough he is aware his sons don't respect the land as he does (NPWA) in this Pre-Atomic novel (1931).

7   Dragon Seed by Pearl Buck
8   A Bridge for Passing by Pearl Buck
9   The Good Earth by Pearl Buck

3-6-9

\Colonel James Brewton - this character is the owner of the Cross B Ranch in Salt Fork who marries Lutie Cameron from St. Louis, Missouri during a range war and has three children named Jimmy, Brock and Sarah Beth; eventually, he is abandoned by Lutie for fifteen years because of possible adultery with the handsome town district attorney, Brice Chamberlin, only for her to return in old age after the Colonel chases Brock and kills him as an outlaw in this Pre-Atomic novel by a Pulitzer Prize winning author (1936).

1	The Town by Conrad Richter
2	The Light in the Forest by Conrad Richter
3	The Sea of Grass by Conrad Richter

William "Studs" Lonigan - this character is the young Irish Catholic high school dropout in 19th century Chicago whose wild coming of age consists of shunning the priesthood, leading a street gang, messy drunken sprees and a shallow romantic relationship with Lucy Scanlan that fizzles; eventually, he settles down with Catherine Banahan, has his stock market investments turn sour, his father's business fail and his health flounder to the point where pneumonia brings on delusions where he faces his plight in this Pre-Atomic trilogy (1932;1934;1935).

4	Judgement Day by James T. Farrell
5	Ellen Rogers by James T. Farrell
6	Tommy Gallagher's Crusade by James T. Farrell

Harry Haller - this character is the 50 year-old German loner whose daily record in a journal of his ten month stay in an attic is later published by his landlady's nephew who is an editor; eventually, this schizoid-like tormented soul's life revolves around a blue-eyed, blond lover named Maria, a dark and handsome saxophonist known as Pablo who helps him enter the Magic Theater and a young prostitute, Hermine, whom he ultimately kills in this Pre-Atomic novel by a Nobel Prize winning author(1927).

7	Siddhartha by Herman Hesse
8	Demian by Herman Hesse
9	Steppenwolf by Herman Hesse

3-4-9

<u>Brice Chamberlain</u> - this character is the handsome district attorney of Salt Fork, Texas, who opposes the taciturn, charismatic owner of the gigantic Cross B Ranch, Colonel James Brewton, over who should control the ranges; eventually, his rumored affair with the Colonel's beautiful wife, Lutie Cameron Brewton, appears to account for her mysterious 15 year disappearance and the birth of her renegade outlaw son, Brock, in this Pre-Atomic novel (1936).

1	<u>The Town</u> by Conrad Richter
2	<u>The Light in the Forest</u> by Conrad Richter
3	<u>The Sea of Grass</u> by Conrad Richter

<u>Catherine Banahan</u> - this character is the thickset, loving young Irish woman in Chicago who replaces the virtuous Lucy Scanlon as the love interest of the young Irish Catholic gang leader of the Fifty-eight and Prairie Street Gang named William Studs Lonigan after he marries her in the early part of the 20th century; eventually, she becomes a widow with child after witnessing her husband's bad fortune when both his stocks and his father's paint business go south during the Depression and he contracts a fatal case of pneumonia complicated by concurrent heart problems in this Pre-Atomic trilogy (1932;1934;1935).

4	<u>Judgement Day</u> by James T. Farrell
5	<u>Ellen Rogers</u> by James T. Farrell
6	<u>Tommy Gallagher's Crusade</u> by James T. Farrell

The Nuclear Age
(1945 - Present)

Some of the noted novelists of this period are as follows: George Orwell, Carson McCullers, Gabriel Garcia Marquez, Eudora Welty, Heinrich Boll, Toni Morrison, Leon Uris, Gunter Grass, Thomas Pynchon, John Barth, Margaret Atwood, Vladimir Nabokov, Imre Kertesz, Ivo Andric and other Nobel and Pulitzer Prize winners.

Some of the factors that determined the mood and temper of this period are as follows: the advent of nuclear weapons at the end of World War II, coupled with the present-day threat of global warning have posed the realistic possibility of nuclear annihilation and future extinction. Every aspect and facet of civilization is overshadowed and influenced by these threats - and novels are by no means excluded.

Some of the underlying concepts that help to describe what is motivating the writers of this period are the same concerns with future survival, social progress and higher ideals that existed in past endeavors.

Up to now, the evolution of the "classical" Post-Victorian novel has been historically discussed and described by using the history of English Literature as a guideline. Initially, it was shown how fiction emerged out of its earlier forms (medieval fiction, English Renaissance fiction, and English fiction) during the 17th and 18th centuries. Then, the mood and underlying concepts of each subsequent periods (Romantic, Victorian, Post-Victorian, Pre-Atomic) were posited. Finally, the most difficult period of all - the Nuclear Age - must, of necessity come under our scrutiny.

This period presents a problem regarding selection. The word Classic presupposes that something has endured. When a novel has passed the test and endured for a minimum of fifty to a hundred years, it is usually ranked among the greats in literature. In order to objectively select classical novels from contemporary novels, some criteria must be established if one lacks a crystal ball. The criteria chosen is the following: continued works of authors who have received such noteworthy awards as the Nobel Prize in Literature or the Pulitzer Prize. Since this criteria is open to criticism, only the test of time will vindicate the choices.

<u>Winston Smith</u> - this character is the 39 year-old Ministry of Truth writer of newspeak in the society of Oceania who has the job of rewriting records; eventually, he falls in love with a bold, rebellious, dark-haired girl named Julia, his allegiance to Emmanuel Goldstein is unearthed by Mr. Charrington of the thought police and he is forced to renounce his love of Julia when threatened with rats in this Nuclear Age novel (1949).

1   <u>Animal Farm</u> by George Orwell
2   <u>Brave New World</u> by Aldous Huxley
3   <u>Nineteen Eighty Four</u> by George Orwell

<u>Santiago</u> - this character is the simple, old Cuban fisherman whose 84 day search for fish in the Gulf Stream off Havana ends successfully when he finally harpoons a 18 foot, over 1000 pounds marlin only to have sharks devour most of his prize before he can return to shore; eventually, he is consoled when he awakens in his beach shack the next morning after much needed sleep with coffee by a young Cuban boy named Manolin in this Nuclear Age novel by an American author (1952).

4   <u>Captains Courageous</u> by Rudyard Kipling
5   <u>The Old Man and the Sea</u> by Ernest Hemingway
6   <u>The Sea Wolf</u> by Jack London

<u>Jack Burden</u> - this character is the cynical, one-time journalist who acts as a factotum for a ruthless, dictatorial Governor named Willie Stark eventhough this demagogue has dropped Sadie Burke as a mistress and took up with this character's childhood sweetheart; eventually, he is sent by Willie to bribe Judge Irwin based on the evidence of Miss Littlepaugh which results in the Judge's suicide and the revelation by his mother that his father, Ellis, had really deserted her because he was really the son of the Judge in this Nuclear Age novel by a Pulitzer Prize winning author (1946).

7   <u>The Heart is a Lonely Hunter</u> by Carson McCullers
8   <u>The Power and the Glory</u> by Graham Greene
9   <u>All the King's Men</u> by Robert Penn Warren

3-5-9

<u>Julia</u> - this character is the bold, dark-haired and good-looking girl wearing a red chastity belt who becomes the mistress of a 39 year-old Minister of Truth named Winston Smith eventhough they are risking torture if apprehended by the thought police; eventually, her capture with Winston by Mr. Charrington of the thought police while they are reading the subversive treatise of Goldstein leads to their brainwashing and ultimate submission to the will of the Party in this Nuclear Age novel (1949).

1	<u>Brave New World</u> by Aldous Huxley
2	<u>Nineteen Eighty Four</u> by George Orwell
3	<u>Animal Farm</u> by George Orwell

<u>Harry Angstrom</u> - this character is the 36 year-old cynical, conservative linotype operator from a Pennsylvania suburb who invites a runaway teenager named Jill and a Afro-American fugitive named Skeeter into his home along with his son, Nelson, after his wife, Janice, moves in with her lover, Charles Stavros; eventually, his neighbors kill Jill when they burn down his house, he helps Skeeter to escape and finally reconcile with Janice eventhough she has accidently drowned their second child in this Nuclear Age novel by a Pulitzer Prize winning author (1971).

4	<u>From the Terrace</u> by John O'Hara
5	<u>Brave New World</u> by Aldous Huxley
6	<u>Rabbit Redux</u> by John Updike

<u>John Singer</u> - this character is the intelligent deaf-mute employee of a jeweler who loses his mute, feeble-minded roommate, Spiros Antonapoulos, when his obscene acts, assaults on people and bizarre behavior forces the latter's cousin, Charles Parker, to fire him from his fruit store and commit him to a mental institution; eventually, this tall, immaculate, soberly dressed young man shoots himself in his room when he learns that his ex-roommate of ten years named Spiro has died jobless in an insane asylum in this Nuclear Age novel by a Pulitzer Prize winning author (1940).

7	<u>The Member of the Wedding</u> by Carson McCullers
8	<u>The Heart is a Lonely Hunter</u> by Carson McCullers
9	<u>Reflections in a Golden Eye</u> by Carson McCullers

2-6-8

Holden Caufield - this character is the 17 year-old teenager whose boredom drives him to spend 2 aimless days in New York City where he breaks up with his longtime girlfriend, Sally Hayes, before going home to see his sister, Phoebe, and tell his parents about his dismissal from Pencey Prep; eventually, the reader learns that his story is being told from a psychiatric institution in that part of California where his older brother, D. B., is a successful screenwriter in this Nuclear Age novel (1951).

1	The Catcher in the Rye by J. D. Salinger
2	Saturday Night and Sunday Morning by Alan Sillitoe
3	Brave New World by Aldous Huxley

Frances "Frankie" Addams - this character is the lanky, naive, 12 year-old tomboy whose adolescent isolation and loneliness influences such people around her as her father, Royal Addams, the Afro-American cook who is her surrogate parent, Berenice Sadie Brown, and this character's younger cousin, John Henry "Candy" West; eventually, her coming of age begins with the alleged rejection by her brother and his wife, the death from meningitis of 6 year-old John Henry and her new home with her Aunt Pet and Uncle Eustace in this Nuclear Age novel by a Pulitzer Prize winning author (1946).

4	A Member of the Wedding by Carson McCullers
5	O Pioneers! by Willa Cather
6	The Optimist's Daughter by Eudora Welty

Don Fabrizio Corbera - this character is the aging Sicilian prince who lives long enough to see Garibaldi's red shirts under the Bourbon king, Francis II, and the corresponding unification of Italy and Sicily under the Piedmontese king, Victor Emanuel; eventually, this proud aristocrat has to endure the political marriage between his opportunistic nephew, Tancedi, and Angelica who is the daughter of an ambitious mayor named Don Calogera Sedara in this Nuclear Age novel (1960).

7	In Dubious Battle by John Steinbeck
8	The Leopard by Guiseppe Tomasi di Lampedusa
9	Nausea by Jean Paul Sartre

1-4-8

Susan Brown - this character is the good-looking, vacuous 19 year-old who joins a local acting group called the Warley Thespians where she meets Alice Aisgill and is attracted to an opportunistic 25 year-old accountant named Joe Lampton; eventually, her pregnancy and plans for marriage with Joe causes Alice Aisgill's death by misadventure when her speeding car crashes during a drinking binge in this Nuclear Age novel by one of the "angry young men" (1957).

1	Room at the Top by John Braine
2	Lie Down In Darkness by William Styron
3	The Reprieve by Jean-Paul Sartre

Laura McRaven - this character is the 9 year-old niece who journeys to a plantation named Shellmound owned by her cousins, the Fairchilds, where she encounters a well-knit family of relatives having a unique self-sufficiency coupled with a solid front that outsiders either love or hate; eventually, she observes Battle Fairchild's aloofness toward the career choices of his daughters, Shelley and Dabney, the elitism toward the plantation's manager, Troy Flavin, and Uncle George's wife, Robbie, and the warmth extended when she left to return to her father in this Nuclear Age novel (1972).

4	The Optimist's Daughter by Eudora Welty
5	Delta Wedding by Eudora Welty
6	Losing Battles by Eudora Welty

Moses - this character is the comical, 47 year-old unemployed twice-divorced Phd. Professor of History whose custody concerns of his daughter, June, leads him to almost kill his ex-wife, Madelaine, and his best friend, Valentine Gersbach; eventually, his aberrant behavior diminishes while communing with God and nature at a summer house with his successful, conventional older brother, William, and his girlfriend, Ramona, in this Nuclear Age novel by a Pulitzer Prize winner (1964).

7	Dangling Man by Saul Bellow
8	Humboldt's Gift by Saul Bellow
9	Herzog by Saul Bellow

1-5-9

Humbert Humbert - this character is the middle-aged Parisian teacher whose attempts at a conventional existence lead him to first marry Valeria in Paris who later abandons him for a White Russian former taxi driver and then marry Charlotte Haze;   eventually, his death before his murder trial for the brutal shooting of a perverted playwright Clare Quilty occurs before the death of his stepdaughter, Dorothy, while she is giving birth to a stillborn girl in this Nuclear Age novel (1955).

1   Dr. Zhivago by Boris Pasternak
2   Lolita by Vladimir Nabokov
3   Cancer Ward by Alexander Solzhenitsyn

Father Montez - this character is the assumed name of the old, alcoholic priest in Mexico during the 1930's who has a 7 year old illegitimate daughter named Brigida by a Mexican woman named Marcia;   eventually, his pursuit as a fugitive across Mexico for treason ends when he is captured in a trap, found guilty of treason and summarily shot without benefit of a confession by the cowardly Fr. Jose in this Nuclear Age novel (1940).

4   The Heart of the Matter by Graham Greene
5   The Old Man and the Sea by Ernest Hemingway
6   The Power and the Glory by Graham Greene

Patrice Meursault - this character is the young, apathetic Algerian clerk who spends the next day after his mother's funeral unemotionally attending a movie with his new Arabian lover, Marie Cardona, who is a traditional girl interested in marriage and a family; eventually, his association with a domineering Arab pimp named Raymond Sintes results in a sentence of death after his callous shooting of another Arab because of his lack of faith in God and disbelief in an afterlife in this existential Nuclear Age novel by a French Nobel Prize winning author (1946).

7   The Stranger by Albert Camus
8   Nausea by Jean-Paul Sartre
9   The Myth of Sisyphus by Albert Camus

<u>Caleb Trask</u> - this character is the moody, secretive twin son of Cathy Trask nee Ames who decides to desert her husband, Adam, and the other twin, Aron, right after giving birth so she can join a brothel under the new assumed name of Kate; eventually, he reveals his new mother's identity to Aron which results in the latter leaving his fiancé, Abra Bacon, enlisting in the Army and getting killed in World War I France in this Nuclear Age novel by a Nobel Prize winning author (1952).

1	<u>East of Eden</u> by John Steinbeck
2	<u>In Dubious Battle</u> by John Steinbeck
3	<u>The Pearl</u> by John Steinbeck

<u>Adrian Leverkuhn</u> - this character is the proud, frail musical genius who is lured from theological pursuits to a brilliant career as a composer for 24 years during which he endures numerous tragedies which culminate with his adored nephew, Nepomuk nicknamed Little Echo, fatally contracting meningitis; eventually, a paralytic stroke hurls him into madness for the next 10 years until his death in this Nuclear Age novel by a Nobel Prize winning author (1947).

4	<u>Buddenbrooks</u> by Thomas Mann
5	<u>Dr. Faustus</u> by Thomas Mann
6	<u>The Magic Mountain</u> by Thomas Mann

<u>Stingo</u> - this character is the readily affected, shrewd and scholarly 22 year-old Southern aspiring novelist who moves to New York City in order to develop as an author; eventually, his short-lived love affair with a lovely Polish survivor of Auschwitz ends tragically when she commits suicide wish her Jewish lover, Nathan Landau, in this Nuclear Age novel by an American author (1979).

7	<u>All the King's Men</u> by William Penn Warren
8	<u>Sophie's Choice</u> by William Styron
9	<u>Tortilla Flat</u> by John Steinbeck

1-5-8

<u>Peyton Loftis</u> - this character is the neurotic daughter of a Virginia lawyer named Milton and his wife, Helen, and the one who drops out of college, travels to New York and enters into an unsuccessful marriage to a Jewish artist named Harry Miller; eventually, she is exhumed from Potter's Field by Harry and returned to Virginia after committing suicide by jumping off a New York building naked in this   Nuclear Age novel by a Pulitzer Prize winning author (1951).

1	<u>The Power and the Glory</u> by Graham Greene
2	<u>A Confederacy of Dunces</u> by John Kennedy Toole
3	<u>Lie Down in Darkness</u> by William Styron

<u>Oleg Kostoglotov</u> - this character is the 34 year-old unmarried army Sergeant turned surveyor whose fiercely independent and rebellious nature lands him in a Stalinist labor camp where an illness occurs that transfers him to a hospital in the town of Ush-Terek; eventually, he moves to Ush-Terek with other political exiles to live a simple life and ends his relationships with a young nurse, Zoya, and an older doctor named Vera Gangart because the hormone therapy he is receiving causes impotence in this Nuclear Age novel (1968).

4	<u>Cancer Ward</u> by Alexander Solzhenitsyn
5	<u>Dr. Zhivago</u> by Boris Pasternak
6	<u>Lolita</u> by Vladimir Nabokov

<u>Willie Stark</u> - this character is the ruthless, dictatorial Governor who ruthlessly heads a powerful political machine while betraying his wife, Lucy, when he has affairs with both his clever, hard-bitten secretary, Sadie Burke, and a young welfare worker named Anne Stanton; eventually, his attempts to manipulate everyone around him results in his being fatally shot by Anne's idealistic surgeon brother, Adam Stanton, who is turn is killed by Willie's bodyguard, Sugar-Boy O'Sheean in this Nuclear Age novel by a Pulitzer Prize winning author   (1946).

7	<u>Sophie's Choice</u> by William Styron
8	<u>All the King's Men</u> by Robert Penn Warren
9	<u>The Naked and the Dead</u> by Norman Mailer

3-4-8

Joe Lampton - this character is the opportunistic 25 year-old accountant whose driving ambition compels him to join an acting group called the Warley Thespians where he meets a 34 year-old wife named Alice Aisgill and a gorgeous, vacuous 19 year-old named Susan Brown; eventually, his plans to marry a pregnant Susan results in Alice's death by misadventure when her speeding car crashes during a drinking binge in this Nuclear Age novel (1957).

1   The Naked and the Dead by Norman Mailer
2   The Power and the Glory by Graham Greene
3   Room at the Top by John Braine

Jay Follet - this character is the hardworking, practical father of a 6 year-old boy named Rufus and his younger sister, Catherine, and the husband whose irreligious, countrified ways of drinking, swearing and spitting constantly embarrass his urban, Catholic wife, Mary; eventually, his response to a false alarm by his younger brother, Ralph, that his father is dying results in his own death as his car does not escape a near miss and unfortunately hits another oncoming vehicle in this Nuclear Age novel published posthumously (1959).

4   Room at the Top by John Braine
5   A Death in the Family by James Agee
6   Lie Down in Darkness by William Styron

Alexandra Bergson - this character is the steadfast, intrepid, enterprising daughter of a Swedish immigrant homesteader on the Divide in Nebraska who overcomes the adversities farm life can throw at you and prospers along with her 3 bothers Oscar, Lou and Emil; eventually, she lives long enough to see her younger brother, Emil, shot to death along with Marie Shabata by Marie's jealous husband, Frank, which makes her aware of her own love for Carl Linstrum in this Nuclear Age novel by an American authoress (1949).

7   The Optimist's Daughter by Eudora Welty
8   A Member of the Wedding by Carson McCullers
9   O Pioneers! by Willa Cather

3-5-9

<u>Thomas (T.R.) Gray</u> - this character is the public defender for the Commonwealth of Virginia who represents a self-proclaimed preacher being tried for both the murder of Margaret Whitehead and as a leader who is responsible for violent acts committed in the name of   freedom; eventually, he requests better conditions for his client eventhough he implicitly agrees with prosecution regarding both his client's guilt and the necessity for his execution in this Nuclear Age novel (1967).

1	<u>A Death in the Family</u> by James Agee
2	<u>Lie Down in Darkness</u> by William Styron
3	<u>The Confessions of Nat Turner</u> by William Styron

<u>Manolin</u> - this character is the young Cuban boy who is told to switch boats by his father after spending 40 days in the Gulf Stream off Havana with a simple, old Cuban fisherman, Santiago, because of the old man's bad luck; eventually, this youngster consoles a well-rested Santiago with a cup of coffee in the old man's beach shack where he learns how sharks devoured the 18 foot, over a 1000 pound marlin that he finally harpooned after 84 days in this Nuclear Age novel by an American Nobel Prize winning author (1952).

4	<u>The Old Man and the Sea</u> by Ernest Hemingway
5	<u>The Pearl</u> by John Steinbeck
6	<u>The Giant</u> by Edna Ferber

<u>Ignatius J. Reilly</u> - this character is the 30 year-old, self-proclaimed genius out to reform the entire 20th century, which doesn't leave him much time for an ordinary 9 to 5 job; eventually, the reactionary female, Myrna Minkoff, helps him to escape psychiatric confinement by driving him from New Orleans to New York in this modern farce by a posthumously published American author in this Nuclear Age novel (1980).

7	<u>Tortilla Flat</u> by John Steinbeck
8	<u>Requiem for a Nun</u> by William Faulkner
9	<u>A Confederacy of Dunces</u> by John Kennedy Toole

3-4-9

<u>Dr. A. Herbert Bledsoe</u> - this character is the opportunistic president of an all-Afro-American college who admits both that he manipulated Afro-Americans and whites to achieve his present position and also that he feels very insignificant in the scheme of things in spite of his success; eventually, he joins a white Northern philanthropist, Mr. Norton, Brother Jack of the Brotherhood, the martyred idealist, Tod Clifton, the every-changing Rinehart and Ras the Destroyer in their influencing a young impressionable man in his journey to manhood in this Nuclear Age novel (1952).

1	<u>The Invisible Man</u> by Ralph Ellison
2	<u>King of the Bingo Game</u> by Ralph Ellison
3	<u>Flying Home</u> by Ralph Ellison

<u>Willie Chandran</u> - this character is the bitterly, unhappy young man in India who detests his Brahman father for marrying someone below his caste simply because of the teachings of Mahatma Gandhi that he doesn't love decides to leave his loving mother and sister when a scholarship to a second-rate London college comes along; eventually, he marries a small, thin, easy-going young woman named Ana who has a mixed African background and moves to her family estate in a Portugese colony in Africa where he is finally made aware that every place has a caste system in this Nuclear Age novel by a Nobel Prize winning author (2001).

4	<u>A House for Mr. Biswas</u> by V.S. Naipaul
5	<u>Half a Life</u> by V.S. Naipaul
6	<u>The Enigma of Arrival</u> by V. S. Naipaul

<u>Piggy</u> - this character is the scholarly, bespeckled, overweight young boy stranded on a remote island during World War II with a group of boys that includes their elected leader, Ralph, the spiritualistic Simon, the steadfast twins, Sam and Eric   known as Sameric and the anarchistic Jack; eventually, his and Simon's deaths tragically precede the arrival of a rescue operation spearheaded by a Naval Officer in this Nuclear Age novel by a Nobel Prize winning author (1954).

7	<u>The Inheritors</u> by William Golding
8	<u>Pincher Martin</u> by William Golding
9	<u>Lord of the Flies</u> by William Golding

1-5-9

Sethe - this character is the young, bold, independent slave woman whose escape from a Kentucky farm, Sweet Home, results in her getting help from a white woman named Amy when she takes along her 4 children to a rural house close to the Northern city of Cincinnati; eventually, her closure over the murder of one of these children allows her to move on in life with a fellow slave from Sweet Home named Paul D. in this Nuclear Age novel by a Nobel Prize winning author (1987). - this character is the undistinguished, friendless, and conscientious 50 year-old bachelor whose drab career as a nondescript clerk for the central registry leads him to research the life of an unknown 36 year-old woman;

1   The Bluest Eye by Toni Morrison
2   Jazz by Toni Morrison
3   Beloved by Toni Morrison

Senhor Jose - this character is the undistinguished, friendless, and conscientious 50 year-old bachelor whose drab career as a nondescript clerk for the central registry for births, marriages and deaths leads him for no apparent reason to research the life of an unknown 36 year old woman eventually, this awkward workaholic discovers that she was a divorced, mathematics teacher who committed suicide by overdosing on sleeping pills in this Nuclear Age novel by a Nobel Prize winning author (1997).

4   The Stone Raft by Jose Saramago
5   All the Names by Jose Saramago
6   Blindness by Jose Saramago

Laurel McKelva Hand - this character is the slender, stable mid-forties widow and successful fabric designer from Chicago who travels to New Orleans where her father, Judge McKelva, will die after an operation to repair a damaged retina; eventually, she returns home with the body to her roots in Mount Salus, Mississippi, accompanied by her father's uncouth 2nd wife and widow, Fay, where she gets closure over the death of her parents and her young husband during the War in this Nuclear Age novel (1969).

7   Delta Wedding by Eudora Welty
8   Losing Battles by Eudora Welty
9   The Optimist's Daughter by Eudora Welty

3-5-9

<u>Cesar Castillo</u> - this character is the young, handsome Cuban musician whose travels to New York City during the 1950's with his brother, Nestor, to seek success finds him ultimately working as a superintendent in a building after his brother is killed in a car accident; eventually, he registers for the night in a room at the Hotel Splendor so he can drink, reflect on his past and finally commit suicide in this Pulitzer Prize winning Nuclear Age novel (1989).

1   <u>Our House in the Last World</u> by Oscar Hijuelos
2   <u>The Fourteen Sisters of Emilio Montez O'Brien</u> by Oscar Hijuelos
3   <u>The Mambo Kings Play Songs of Love</u> by Oscar Hijuelos

<u>Tom Robinson</u> - this character is the young devout father of 4 from Maycomb County, Alabama whose false accusation   of rape by a young white woman named Mayella Ewell and finds him defended by a widowed lawyer named Atticus Finch;   eventually, he is found guilty by an all white jury even after Atticus's 2 children are rescued because Atticus proved that Bob Ewell and his daughter were lying in this Nuclear Age novel by a Pulitzer Prize winning author (1960).

4   <u>To Kill a Mockingbird</u> by Harper Lee
5   <u>The Web and the Rock</u> by Thomas Wolfe
6   <u>Sanctuary</u> by William Faulkner

<u>Hans Schnier</u> - this character is the traveling entertainer who leaves home because he detests the materialism that was accompying Post-War prosperity; eventually, he ends up as an ordinary beggar in a Bonn railway station after he loses   both his job and his live-in lover, Maria, because of his inability to commit both to marriage and rearing children as Catholics in this Nuclear Age novel penned by a Nobel Prize winning author (1963).

7   <u>Safety Net</u> by Heinrich Boll
8   <u>The Clown</u> by Heinrich Boll
9   <u>Billiards at Half-Past Nine</u> by Heinrich Boll

3-4-8

<u>John Yossarian</u> - this character is the 28 year-old Bombardier captain stationed with his Air Force squadron on the island of Pianosa off Italy at the end of World War II who believes that millions of people are out to kill him; eventually,   he refuses a discharge offer from Colonel Cathcart and Colonel Korn who use convoluted reasoning to keep raising his missions and decides to join a pilot named Orr who has already escaped to neutral Sweden in this Nuclear Age novel (1961).

1	<u>Good As Gold</u> by Joseph Heller
2	<u>Something Happened</u> by Joseph Heller
3	<u>Catch-22</u> by Joseph Heller

<u>Ling Jong</u> -   - this character is the young Chinese woman whosehidden art allows her to escape both a loveless promised marriage to Tyan-yu and the tyranny of his mother, Taitai, when she concocts a dream; eventually, she pays an American raised Chinese woman for a cheap apartment in San Francisco, a job in a cookie factory, and a marriage where her 2 sons are outshone by their sister, Waverly, who becomes national chess champion in this Nuclear Age novel (1989).

4	<u>The Hundred Secret Senses</u> by Amy Tan
5	<u>The Joy Luck Club</u> by Amy Tan
6	<u>The Kitchen God's Wife</u> by Amy Tan

<u>Dean Moriarty</u> - this character is the blue-eyed, handsome, sexually obsessed drifter who continually crisscrosses the United States encountering such fellow travelers as the brooding intellectual, Carlo Marx, Salvatore Paradise and   Stan Shephard while marrying Marylou and Camille with resulting children; eventually, his constant jaunts take their toll until he is tired, ravaged and subdued enough to try and patch up his 2nd marriage to Camille in this Nuclear Age novel (1955).

7	<u>The Dharma Bums</u> by Jack Kerouac
8	<u>On the Road</u> by Jack Kerouac
9	<u>Big Sur</u> by Jack Kerouac

3-5-8

<u>Kitty Fremont</u> - - this character is the American nurse whose loss of husband and daughter draws her to the Middle East where she encounters an undercover Zionist agent, Ari Ben Canaan, and a young girl named Karen Hansen Clement, who resembles her daughter; eventually,   she decides after Karen's death during an Arab raid on a kibbutz to accept Ari's proposal of marriage with their future plans interwoven with that of the future of Israel in this Nuclear Age novel (1958).

1	<u>Exodus</u> by Leon Uris
2	<u>Battle Cry</u> by Leon Uris
3	<u>Trinity</u> by Leon Uris

<u>Florentino Ariza</u>   - this character is the wealthy Colombian river boat magnate whose romantic pursuit of a widow named Fermina Daza is consummated 50 later years because her scheming father, Lorenzo, had married her off to a Parisian-educated doctor   named Juvenal Urbino; eventually, this doctor's accidental death recovering his pet parrot from a Mango tree allows these two lovers to reunite and rekindle their earlier affair   in this Nuclear Age novel by a Nobel Prize winning author (1986).

4	<u>One Hundred Years of Solitude</u> by Gabriel Garcia Marquez
5	<u>No One Writes to the Colonel</u> by Gabriel Garcia Marquez
6	<u>Love in the Time of Cholera</u> by Gabriel Garcia Marquez

<u>Macon Leary</u>   - this character is the divorced Baltimorean author of travel books whose broken leg requires him and a dog named Edward that is inherited from his murdered son,   Ethan, to move in with his eccentric family; eventually, Edward's unsocial behavior requires obedience training that triggers a romantic roller coaster ride between a kennel attendant named Muriel Pritchett and his ex-wife, Sarah, in this Nuclear Age novel (1985).

7	<u>Breathing Lessons</u> by Anne Tyler
8	<u>The Accidental Tourist</u> by Anne Tyler
9	<u>Dinner at the Homesick Restaurant</u> by Anne Tyler

1-6-8

<u>Jose Arcadio Buendia</u>   - this character is the driven patriarch of 6 future generations who entered an incestuous marriage with his cousin, Ursula Iguaran, founded an idyllic village named Macondo and violently killed Prudencio Aguilar in a quarrel over his wife and; eventually, he is frustrated in his attempts to free Macondo from the hold of magic spelled out by the mysterious gypsy, Melquiades in this Nuclear Age novel of magical realism by a Nobel Prize winning author (1967).

1	<u>One Hundred Years of Solitude</u> by Gabriel Garcia Marquez
2	<u>Love in the Time of Cholera</u> by Gabriel Garcia Marquez
3	<u>No One Writes to the Colonel</u> by Gabriel Garcia Marquez

<u>Gene Forrester</u>   - this character is the young, quiet, intellectual high school student at Devon School during World War II whose friendship with a handsome, self-confident athlete named Finny brings about a secret society; eventually, he returns to his old high school as a intelligent man in his thirties reflecting on his old classmates, Leper Lepellier, Brinker Hadley and Chet Douglas and administrators such as Mr. Patch-Withers, Dr. Stanpole and Mr. Ludsbury in this Nuclear Age novel (1959).

4	<u>Peace Breaks Out</u> by John Knowles
5	<u>A Separate Peace</u> by John Knowles
6	<u>Double Vision</u> by John Knowles

<u>Hamida</u>   - this character is the uncommonly beautiful, Egyptian girl who escapes her poverty-stricken village by becoming a prostitute for wealthy British soldiers until she finds herself in a Cairo ghetto as the foster daughter of a bath attendant   named Umm Hamida; eventually, her plan fails when she rejects a marriage proposal from a barber Abbas Huli to marry a wealthy businessman eventhough Abbas is willing to sell his shop in this Nuclear Age novel by a Nobel Prize winning author (1947).

7	<u>Midaq Alley</u> by Naguib Mahfouz
8	<u>Children of Gebelawi</u> by Naguib Mahfouz
9	<u>The Cairo Trilogy</u> by Naguib Mahfouz

1-5-7

Biff Brannon - this character is the owner of the New York Café where handicaps and people with disabilities are given special attention because he has a interest for their plight and an interest in human relationships; eventually, he is invited by a deaf-mute named John Singer to a gathering of John's other friends which consist of a female teenager named Mick Kelly, the alcoholic Jake Blount and a Afro-American physician named Dr. Copeland in this Nuclear Age novel by a Pulitzer Prize winning author (1940).

1	The Member of the Wedding by Carson McCullers
2	The Heart is a Lonely Hunter by Carson McCullers
3	Reflections in a Golden Eye by Carson McCullers

Bird - this character is the depressed, despairing father of a brain damaged newborn child and the one who tries to escape facing the truth about his child's deformity by turning to drink, taking a mistress and conniving with one of the child's doctors to let the boy die; eventually, he dismisses any ideas of abandoning his child to a clinic and decides to stop escaping reality and raise the child in this Nuclear Age novel by a Nobel Prize winning author (1964).

4	The Silent Cry by Oe Kenzaburo
5	A Personal Matter by Oe Kenzaburo
6	A Quiet Life by Oe Kenzaburo

Augustus McCrae - this character is the Kentuckian college graduate who joins the Texas Rangers where he meets taciturn Woodrow Call and the adventurous Jake Spoon; eventually, he accompanies them on a cattle drive to Montana on which his dilemma of choosing between a young whore named Lorena and an old flame named Clara Allen is resolved after the threat of having both his legs amputated leads to his death in this Nuclear Age novel by a Pulitzer Prize winning author (1985).

7	Terms of Endearment by Larry McMurtry
8	Lonesome Dove by Larry McMurtry
9	The Last Picture Show by Larry McMurtry

2-5-8

<u>Celie</u>   - this character is the poor, Afro-American rural teenager whose relationships include a stepfather who commits incest with her, 2 children who are taken away from her and a sister named Nettie, who escapes the lustful advances of an   of an unattractive suitor named Albert; eventually, she falls in love with Albert's mistress, Shug Avery, and returns home to be reunited with Shug, Nettie and her 2 grown children in this Nuclear Age novel by a Pulitzer Prize winning author (1982).

1   <u>The Color Purple</u> by Alice Walker
2   <u>The Third Life of Grange Copeland</u> by Alice Walker
3   <u>By the Light of My Father's Smile</u> by Alice Walker

<u>Lieutenant Robert Hearn</u>   - this character is the poor, Afro-American rural teenager whose relationships include a stepfather who commits incest with her, 2 children who are taken away from her and a sister named Nettie, who escapes the lustful advances of an   of an unattractive suitor named Albert; eventually, she falls in love with Albert's mistress, Shug Avery, and returns home to be reunited with Shug, Nettie and her 2 grown children in this Nuclear Age novel by a Pulitzer Prize winning author (1982).

4   <u>From Here to Eternity</u> by James Jones
5   <u>The Naked and the Dead</u> by Norman Mailer
6   <u>Catch-22</u> by Joseph Heller

<u>Catherine (Kay) Leiland Strong</u>   - this character is the young theater major graduate from Vassar College's Class of 1933 whose desire to become a director is put on hold while her husband, Harald, pursues his own career of playwright;   eventually, her funeral is attended by her 7 best friends from Vassar after she falls 20 floors from a window at the Vassar Club located in New York City in this Nuclear Age novel by a Pulitzer Prize winning author (1954).

7   <u>The Company She Keeps</u> by Mary McCarthy
8   <u>The Groves of Academe</u> by Mary McCarthy
9   <u>The Group</u> by Mary McCarthy

1-5-9

<u>General Ira "Bus" Beal</u> - this character is the youngest Air Force Major General following World War II whose assignment to a training installation begins ominously when his co-pilot, Lt. Col. Benny Carricker, is arrested for knocking out an Afro-American pilot;   eventually, he quells a mini protest involving other Afro-American aviators, protects old Colonel Pop Mowbray and diplomatically deals with a general who has been sent to evaluate his new assignment in this Nuclear Age novel (1948).

1   <u>The Just and the Unjust</u> by James Gould Cozzens
2   <u>Guard of Honor</u> by James Gould Cozzens
3   <u>By Love Possessed</u> by James Gould Cozzens

<u>Edgar Altschuler</u>   - this character is the young Jewish boy growing up in the Bronx during the late 1930's whose everyday normal life with his parents, his brother, Donald, and his maternal grandmother declines when his father's store business forces them to move;   eventually, his honorable mention in an essay contest allows his family to attend an outing where he is inspired to plant his own time capsule in a Nuclear Age novel by a Pulitzer Prize winning author (1986).

4   <u>Billy Bathgate</u> by E.L. Doctorow
5   <u>Ragtime</u> by E.L. Doctorow
6   <u>World's Fair</u> by E.L. Doctorow

<u>Major Victor Joppolo</u> - this character is the Italian-American officer during World War II in Italy whose initial encounters are with a man named Zito who informs him of current problems facing the townspeople such as a shortage of food and water and Guiseppe who becomes his interpreter; eventually, his roller coaster romance with the fisherman Tomasino's daughter, Tina, despite his stateside wife is finally resolved when he is reassigned to another location after he falls out of favor with his superior, General Marvin, for not following orders in this Nuclear Age novel by a Pulitzer Prize winning author (1944).

7   <u>Into the Valley</u> by John Hersey
8   <u>A Bell for Adano</u> by John Hersey
9   <u>Hiroshima</u> by John Hersey

2-6-8

<u>Rufus Scott</u>   - this character is the young, Afro-American musician born in Harlem whose tempestuous life with a Georgian white woman named Leona leads to her permanent commitment in a Souther institution; eventually, his fatal suicide jump off a the George Washington Bridge raises questions by his younger sister, Ida Jones, who is having a relationships with Vivaldo Moore and a white, married TV producer named Steve Ellis in this Nuclear Age novel by a Pulitzer Prize winning author (1962).

1   <u>Go Tell It On The Mountain</u> by James Baldwin
2   <u>Another Country</u> by James Baldwin
3   <u>Just Above My Head</u> by James Baldwin

<u>Lt. Col. Benny Carricker</u>   - this character is Ira "Bus" Neal's old friend and co-pilot of following World War II who is arrested for knocking a Afro-American pilot named Lt. Willis unconscious after a near air collision; eventually, he evades charges due to this Major General who also quells a mini protest involving the other Afro-American personnel on the base and protects an old colonel from charges of negligence while diplomatically neutralizing a general from Washington in this Nuclear Age novel (1948).

4   <u>The Just and the Unjust</u> by James Gould Cozzens
5   <u>Guard of Honor</u> by James Gould Cozzens
6   <u>By Love Possessed</u> by James Gould Cozzens

<u>Tomasino</u>   - this character is the crusty old Italian fisherman who owns a fishing fleet in a small Italian town held by Major Victor Joppolo during World War II after an American invasion displaces the Fascists; eventually, his blond daughter, Tina's roller coaster romance with this married Major is contingent on her P. O. W. boyfriend's plight ends when the Major falls out of favor with General Marvin in this Nuclear Age novel by a Pulitzer Prize winning author (1944)

7   <u>Into the Valley</u> by John Hersey
8   <u>A Bell for Adano</u> by John Hersey
9   <u>Hiroshima</u> by John Hersey

2-5-8

<u>Francis Whelan</u> - this character is the ex-ballplayer whose aimless drifting around the United States in order to escape his tragic, death-ridden past finally leads him and his girlfriend, Helen Archer, back to Albany where he reconciles with his family eventhough he is still hounded by the ghosts of his past such as his infant son, Gerald; eventually, he breaks the back of a ruthless raider from the American Legion at a riverside encampment, finds Helen dead from illness in a cheap hotel room and hops a train out of town only to jump off and return to the strange peace his family can offer him in this Nuclear Age novel (1983).

1	<u>Legs</u> by William Kennedy
2	<u>Ironweed</u> by William Kennedy
3	<u>Bill Phelan's Greatest Game</u> by William Kennedy

<u>Heinrich Faehmel</u> - this character is the 80 year old patriarch of a German family in Cologne whose birthday on September 6th, 1958 provides the opportunity to reflect on three generations of family architects including his son, Robert, and his grandson, Joseph, with regard to the building, destruction and restoration of St. Anthony's Abbey; eventually, his interest lies not with Robert's protest against the Catholic Church for their role in Nazi Germany but in whether his grandson condones demolition over construction in this Nuclear Age novel by a Nobel Prize winning author (1959).

4	<u>The Clown</u> by Heinrich Boll
5	<u>Billiards at Half Past Nine</u> by Heinrich Boll
6	<u>The Train Was On Time</u> by Heinrich Boll

<u>Willie Keith</u> - this character is the pampered, affluent, Princeton graduate who is trapped between loving a poor Italian singer named May Wynn and a domineering mother until he is drafted into the Navy and serves upon a dilapidated destroyer under respective Captains de Vriess and Philip Francis Queeg; eventually, his coming of age involves a court martial involving mutiny and Courageous actions during a kamikaze plane that result in freeing himself from his mother's control, marrying May and setting out on a new career teaching comparative literature in this Nuclear Age novel by a Pulitzer Prize winning author (1951).

7	<u>Marjorie Morningstar</u> by Herman Wouk
8	<u>Aurora Dawn</u> by Herman Wouk
9	<u>The Caine Mutiny</u> by Herman Wouk

2-5-9

<u>Peter Kien</u> - this character is the 40 year-old scholarly recluse whose loveless marriage to an illiterate, greedy old housekeeper named Therese Kummolz allows her to steal the immense library he is obsessed with by throwing him out of his apartment; eventually, he becomes so overwhelmed by this robbery which was abetted by a fascist-like caretaker named Benedict Pfaff that his psychiatrist brother, George, is helpless in preventing him from burning to death in the fire he sets to destroy his library in this Nuclear Age novel by a Nobel Prize winning author (1935).

1	<u>The Tower of Babel</u> by Elias Canetti
2	<u>Crowds and Power</u> by Elias Canetti
3	<u>The Agony of Flies</u> by Elias Canetti

<u>Vera Stark</u> - this character is the white civil rights lawyer and political activist in tumultuous South Africa during the final days of the Apartheid whose family consists of a husband named Ben, a London based banker son named Ivan and a gay South African doctor named Anne; eventually, she is reunited with friends, Didymus Maqoma and his wife, Sibongile, along with their half-Zulu, half-Xhosa, all Londoner teenage daughter, Mho, when these Afro-American revolutionaries return to South Africa after 20 years of exile in this Nuclear Age novel by a Nobel Prize winning author (1994).

4	<u>Guest of Honor</u> by Nadine Gordimer
5	<u>None to Accompany Me</u> by Nadine Gordimer
6	<u>The House Gun</u> by Nadine Gordimer

<u>Esteban Trueba</u> - this character is the cruel patriarch who, in the late 1930's, claws his way out of the working class to become a wealthy, Chilean landowner, marries the psychic beauty, Clara, and has a daughter named Blanca while caring for his persecuted spinster sister, Ferula; eventually, he begins to realize that everything he believed in must be reassessed based on Chile's new social and political atmosphere starting with the rage he felt over Blanca's running off with a revolutionary peasant named Pedro in this Nuclear Age novel (1985).

7	<u>The Infinite Plan</u> by Isabel Allende
8	<u>The House of the Spirits</u> by Isabel Allende
9	<u>A Discreet Miracle</u> by Isabel Allende

1-5-8

<u>Clara Trueba</u> - this character is the beautiful, clairvoyant wife   married to the cruel patriarch named Esteban whose early years in the late 1930's were spent clawing his way out of the working class to become a self-made wealthy, Chilean landowner; eventually, her marriage takes an unusual turn when she decides to punish her husband by never speaking to him again after he tries to destroy their daughter's love for a young revolutionary named Pedro Tercero Garcia in this Nuclear Age novel (1985).

1	<u>The House of the Spirits</u> by Isabel Allende
2	<u>The Infinite Plan</u> by Isabel Allende
3	<u>A Discreet Miracle</u> by Isabel Allende

<u>Jean "Scout" Finch</u> - this character is the young, observant, sensitive daughter of a widowed lawyer named Atticus and the one whose life in Maycomb County, Alabama during the 1930's takes on new proportions when her father defends a Afro-American man named Tom Robinson falsely accuse of raping a white woman named Mayella Ewell; eventually, she and her older brother, Jem, are saved from an attack by Mayella's father, Bob Ewell, by Boo Radley, an all white jury convicts an innocent Tom Robinson and life goes on for her and Jem under the guidance of their Afro-American cook, Calpurnia in this Nuclear Age novel by a Pulitzer Prize winning author (1960).

4	<u>To Kill a Mockingbird</u> by Harper Lee
5	<u>The Web and the Rock</u> by Thomas Wolfe
6	<u>Sanctuary</u> by William Faulkner

<u>Guy Montag</u> - this character is the 36 year-old fireman in the 24th century whose meeting with a new 17 year-old neighbor, Clarisse McClellan, makes him conscious of his mounting indifference to his job and how vacuous his wife, Millie, really is; eventually, he kills his Fire Chief boss, Captain Beatty, with a flamethrower to protect an old English professor named Faber and joins the rebels led by Granger in this Nuclear Age novel (1950).

7	<u>Fahrenheit 451</u> by Ray Bradbury
8	<u>The Martian Chronicles</u> by Ray Bradbury
9	<u>Something Wicked This Way Comes</u> by Ray Bradbury

1-4-7

<u>Oskar Matzarath</u> - this character is the illegitimate son resulting from a love triangle between a German grocery store owner of lower middle class background named Alfred Matzarath, an ethnic Pole named Jan Bronski and his mother, Agnes Matzarath, who dies from compulsively ingesting eels; eventually, this eccentric dwarf writes a fictitious autobiography in a mental hospital where he spends two years after being falsely accused of murdering the nurse, Sister Dorothea, while suffering no remorse over indirectly killing Jan and directly the causing the death of Alfred in this Nuclear Age novel by a Nobel Prize winning author (1959).

1	<u>Dog-Years</u> by Gunther Grass
2	<u>The Tin Drum</u> by Gunther Grass
3	<u>Cat and Mouse</u> by Gunther Grass

<u>Yakov Bok</u> -this character is the unemployed, 30 year-old Jewish handyman living in early 12th century Russia whose journey to Kiev for a better life involves him in reviving a rich man named Nikolai Lebedev who has passed out in the snow; eventually, he is rewarded by Nikolai when the latter gives him a job as overseer at a brick factory which results in his being falsely accused of the brutal murder of a gentile child followed by 2 years of solitary confinement in prison before the start of his trial in this Nuclear Age novel by a Pulitzer Prize winning author (1966).

4	<u>The Assistant</u> by Bernard Malamud
5	<u>The Tenants</u> by Bernard Malamud
6	<u>The Fixer</u> by Bernard Malamud

<u>Charles "Charlie" Citrine</u> - this character is the Fuller Brush salesman turned Pulitzer Prize winning author whose close bonding with a bipolar balladeer named Fleischer results in a Broadway hit for him and commitment to Bellevue Hospital for Fleischer; eventually, he loses his fortune to his divorcing wife, Denise, goes to Europe where he is abandoned by his frustrated girlfriend, Renata and becomes a loser until he wins a large plagiarism settlement in this Nuclear Age novel by a Pulitzer Prize winning author (1973).

7	<u>Herzog</u> by Saul Bellow
8	<u>The Dangling Man</u> by Saul Bellow
9	<u>Humbolt's Gift</u> by Saul Bellow

Clarisse McClellan - this character is the 17 year-old young woman living in the 24th century who tells a fireman neighbor   named Guy Montag about how firemen in the past would put out fires instead of starting them; eventually, her death in a hit and run accident leaves Guy filled with apathy toward his job, his society and his vacuous wife, Millie, to the extent that he kills his abrasive, patronizing Fire Chief boss, Captain Beatty, with a flamethrower and joins a group of rebels who are led by a man named Granger in this Nuclear Age novel (1950).

1	Something Wicked This Way Comes by Ray Bradbury
2	The Martian Chronicles by Ray Bradbury
3	Fahrenheit 451 by Ray Bradbury

Neil Klugman - this character is the young, bookish graduate of Newark Colleges of Rutger University whose presence at the Green Lane Country Club one summer day initiates a summer romance when he meets a young, beautiful free-spirited Radcliffe undergraduate named Brenda Pitamkin and her Montclair family which is upwardly mobile due to her father's prosperous Kitchen-and Bathroom-Sinks Enterprise; eventually, his is summoned to Boston by Brenda the following fall at Radcliffe only to find that there wouldn't be a marriage like her brothers but rather a breakup after her family discovered her diaphragm in this Nuclear Age novel (1959).

4	Letting Go by Philip Roth
5	Goodbye, Columbus by Philip Roth
6	Portnoy's Complaint by Philip Roth

Yithak Kummer - this character is the Jewish pathfinder who travels from Europe to Palestine during the wave of immigration to Palestine between 1907 and 1913 which anticipated the emergence of Israel out of the Holocaust; eventually, his journey's parallel with the wanderings of a dog named Balak takes on mystical significance as a contrast between the old and new ways of Jewish life after Kummer dies in Palestine of rabies from a fatal bite by Balak in this Nuclear Age novel by a Nobel Prize winning author (1945).

7	A Guest for the Night by Shmuel Agnon
8	The Day Before Yesterday by Shmuel Agnon
9	The Bridal Canopy by Shmuel Agnon

<u>Charles Arrowby</u> - this character is the tyrannical director, playwright and bright beacon of England's theatrical set who retires from glittering London to an isolated home by the seashore where he can write a memoir about his great love affair with his professional and personal mentor, Clemont Makin; eventually, he encounters this worn-out childhood sweetheart after forty years, bullies her without being able to change and then starts an affair with an equally monstrous 18 year-old girl named Lizzie in this Brooks Prize winning Nuclear Age novel (1978).

1	<u>Under the Net</u> by Iris Murdoch
2	<u>An Accidental Man</u> by Iris Murdoch
3	<u>The Sea, The Sea</u> by Iris Murdoch

<u>Mr. Jones</u> - this character is the decent, caring farmer whose ongoing cruelty toward his livestock reaches a climax one night when he neglects to feed them because of drunkenness; eventually, his inability to subdue those who overthrew him leads to his eviction from his own property while all future attempts to reclaim his land are repeatedly rebuffed in this Nuclear Age novel (1945)

4	<u>Brave New World</u> by Aldous Huxley
5	<u>Animal Farm</u> by George Orwell
6	<u>Nineteen Eighty Four</u> by George Orwell

<u>Tyrone Slothrop</u> - this character is the paranoid, unpredictable Lieutenant stationed in England during World War II who shares an office with British Lieutenant Oliver "Tantivy" Mucher-Maffick and reveals to him his odd predicament involving sexual arousement when he psychically nears a point where a rocket will strike; eventually, an agent forces Slothrop to run amok across Europe where he falls in with various bizarre underground organizations in this Nuclear Age novel (1973).

7	<u>The Crying of Lot 49</u> by Thomas Pynchon
8	<u>Gravity's Rainbow</u> by Thomas Pynchon
9	<u>Vineland</u> by Thomas Pynchon

3-5-8

<u>Oedipa Maas</u> - this character is the decent, lovable 28 year-old housewife from suburbia between Berkeley and Los Angelos whose world includes a disc jockey husband named Wendall (Mucho) Maas, a neurotic psychiatrist named Hilarius, a late tycoon named Pierce Inveranty and a former lover named Metzger; eventually, this hapless young woman loses her husband to LSD, Hilarius to madness, Metzger to a depraved 15 year-old girl and Pierce when he dies in this Nuclear Age novel (1966).

1   <u>The Crying of Lot 49</u> by Thomas Pynchon
2   <u>Gravity's Rainbow</u> by Thomas Pynchon
3   <u>V.</u> by Thomas Pynchon

<u>Ebenezer Cooke</u> - this character is the egotistical, chaste 17th century poet and tobacco peddler who inherits a tobacco plantation and has the delusion that he has been commissioned by the third Lord Baltimore to write an epic; eventually, he finds his life in constant jeopardy from political conspiracies of Henry Burlingame who was at sometime both tutor and suitor to him and his twin sister, Anna in this ludicrous mock-heroic Nuclear Age novel (1960).

4   <u>Giles Goat-Boy</u> by John Barth
5   <u>Sabbatical</u> by John Barth
6   <u>The Sot-Weed Factor</u> by John Barth

<u>Nick Shay</u> - this character is the ex-lover of an artist named Karla and former hoodlum whose early Roman Catholic education in the Bronx ends with reform school for murder while his father mysteriously disappears over possible gambling debts; eventually, this quiescent middle aged married man who relocates to the Southwest with a well-paying job in waste analysis possesses the game winning baseball from the 1951 Giant-Dodger World Series in this Nuclear Age novel (1997).

7   <u>Americana</u> by Don DeLillo
8   <u>Underworld</u> by Don DeLillo
9   <u>Mao II</u> by Don DeLillo

1-6-8

Rachel Owlglass - this character is the 4'10" tall, redhead Bennington College student whose dates with an aimless drifter named Benny Profane end when he sees her sick love for her MG eventhough he later asks her to roommate with Paola Maijstral; eventually, her job at the Space/Time Employment Agency affords her the opportunity to place an ex-boyfriend named Benny Profane in a security job with the Anthro-Research Associates laboratory in this Nuclear Age novel (1961).

1   The Crying of Lot 49 by Thomas Pynchon
2   Gravity's Rainbow by Thomas Pynchon
3   V. by Thomas Pynchon

Tancedi - this character is the nephew of an aging Sicilian prince who has lived long enough to see the ouster of Garibaldi's red shirts under the bourbon king, Francis II, and the corresponding unification of Italy and Sicily under the Piedmontese king, Victor Emanuel; eventually, this opportunist breaks tradition when he enters a political marriage with Angelica who is the daughter of an ambitious mayor named Don Calogera Sedara in this Nuclear Age novel (1960).

4   The Name of the Rose by Umberto Eco
5   The Leopard by Guiseppe Tomasi di Lampedusa
6   The Island of the Day Before by Umberto Eco

William of Baskerville - this character is the lanky, reflective middle-aged Franciscan Brother who embarks on an mission in 1337 with an assigned Benedictine novice named Adso from Melk, Germany to locate a heretic at an Italian Benedictine abbey; eventually, he is directed by Abbot Abo to catch a serial killer while he represents the Holy Roman Emperor and his adversary, a Dominican inquisitor named Bernard Gui, represents the corrupt pope, Pope John XXII who is seated in France in this Nuclear Age novel (1980).

7   The Island of the Day Before by Umberto Eco
8   The Name of the Rose by Umberto Eco
9   Foucault's Pendulum by Umberto Eco

Eudixia-Eddie-Eadith - this character is the bisexual Australian man whose confusions over his sexual and spiritual identity and struggles with a dual existence that occurs in the French riviera, Australia and London at various times between the World Wars; eventually, Eadith reveals to his mother that he his really her daughter and dies lying next to a soldier in the street dressed as a man with makeup of a madam   in this Nuclear Age novel written by a Nobel Prize winning author (1979).

1	**The Tree of Man** by Patrick White
2	**The Twyborn Affair** by Patrick White
3	**The Eye of the Storm** by Patrick White

Goldstein - this character is the fictional leader of a conspiracy against the Society of Oceania whose book is really a Party production written in part by an Inner Party member named O'Brien; eventually, he is exposed as bait for the thought police to nab such people as the newspeak revisionist named Winston Smith and his rebellious co-conspirator and mistress, Julia, in this Nuclear Age novel (1949).

4	**Animal Farm** by George Orwell
5	**Brave New World** by Aldous Huxley
6	**Nineteen Eighty Four** by George Orwell

George -this character is the foster child of an old Jewish herdsman ad the one whose birth is the possible result of a computer accident between a lecherous computer named WESCAC and a suitable virgin; eventually, he and Max are convinced that his destiny entails entering New Tammany University as the Grand Tutor during the Quiet Riots where he would oppose the False Tutor, Harold Bray, in this   Nuclear Age novel (1966).

7	**Giles Goat-Boy** by John Barth
8	**Sabbatical** by John Barth
9	**The Sot-Weed Factor** by John Barth

2-6-7

<u>Kunta Kinte</u> - this character is the West African youth born in 1750 of Omoro and Binta who is shanghaied onto a slave ship to America where he is renamed Toby, married, and becomes the father of a slave girl named Kizzy; eventually, his present day descendent traces the family history back to Africa where he encounters an oral historian who gives credence to his existence and verifies the circumstances of how he was enslaved   in this Nuclear Age novel by a Pulitzer Prize winning author (1976).

1   <u>Queen</u> by Alex Haley
2   <u>Roots</u> by Alex Haley
3   <u>The Gift</u> by Alex Haley

<u>Madelaine</u> - this character is the blue-eyed, dark haired second wife of a divorced Phd. professor of History named Moses who takes custody of their daughter, June, and proceeds to have an affair with his friend, Valentine (Val) Gersbach; eventually, she and Val escape being shot by Moses because of their treatment of June in the Nuclear Age novel by a Nobel Prize winning author (1964).

4   <u>Dangling Man</u> by Saul Bellow
5   <u>Humboldt's Gift</u> by Saul Bellow
6   <u>Herzog</u> by Saul Bellow

<u>Elaine Risley</u> - this character is the celebrated and provocative artist whose trip to Toronto for a review of her book awakens youthful nostalgia involving her and her two best friends from youth, Cordelia and Grace; eventually, she realizes that she has finally overcome her inner demons through her art and that those early years endured are not only the source of her drawings but also the source of her income in this Nuclear Age novel (1988).

7   <u>The Handmaid's Tale</u> by Margaret Atwood
8   <u>Cat's Eye</u> by Margaret Atwood
9   <u>The Edible Woman</u> by Margaret Atwood

2-6-8

<u>Mick Kelly</u> - this character is the precocious pre-adolescent whose fantasies of being a great composer attract her to a deaf mute boarder named John Singer in her family's boardinghouse; eventually, this gangling teen who always dresses in shorts, a shirt and tennis shoes feels cheated when this boarder, John Singer, fatally shoots himself in this Nuclear Age novel by a Pulitzer Prize winning author (1940).

1	<u>The Heart is a Lonely Hunter</u> by Carson McCullers
2	<u>The Member of the Wedding</u> by Carson McCullers
3	<u>Reflections in a Golden Eye</u> by Carson McCullers

<u>Offred</u> - this character is the 33 year-old fertile woman assigned to a high-ranking government official, Fred, and his wife, an ex-evangelist named Serena Joy, to bear them a child at the risk of death in the Republic of Gilead where decadence ruled until a theocracy was formed; eventually, she joins a chauffeur named Nick in a mock arrest so she could escape to Canada to reunite with her husband, Luke, and daughter in this Nuclear Age novel (1985).

4	<u>The Handmaid's Tale</u> by Margaret Atwood
5	<u>Cat's Eye</u> by Margaret Atwood
6	<u>Surfacing</u> by Margaret Atwood

<u>Alice Aisgill</u> - this character is the disappointed, unfulfilled 34 year old wife who joins a local acting group, the <u>Warley Thespians</u>, where she meets Susan Brown and is attracted to an opportunistic 25 year old accountant named Joe Lampton; eventually, her death by misadventure occurs when her speeding car crashes during a drinking spree after she learns of Susan's pregnancy and impending marriage in this Nuclear Age novel (1957).

7	<u>The Naked and the Dead</u> by Norman Mailer
8	<u>The Power and the Glory</u> by Graham Greene
9	<u>Room at the Top</u> by John Braine

1-4-9

Frenesi Gates - this character is the student activist and cameraperson for a guerilla movie outfit during the 1960's who spies for a federal agent named Brock Vond, participates in a murder of a prominent student leader and ends up in the Witness Protection Program; eventually, her two marriages to an amateur rock guitarist/house painter named Zoyd Wheeler and Fletcher respectively yield a daughter named Prairie and a son named Justin in this Nuclear Age novel (1990).

1	The Crying of Lot 49 by Thomas Pynchon
2	Gravity's Rainbow by Thomas Pynchon
3	Vineland by Thomas Pynchon

Georges - this character is the ex-prisoner of war whose sexual involvement after World War II with a beautiful woman named Corrine is juxtaposed with him relating about a scene of him lying in a field after being captured; eventually, the story he tells her as told to Blum shifts back to a scene involving the death of a calvary officer on a country road during the Battle of the Meuse in 1940 Nuclear Age novel by a Nobel Prize winning author (1960).

4	The Wind by Claude Simon
5	The Grass by Claude Simon
6	The Flanders Road by Claude Simon

Shug Avery - this character is the beautiful, elegant passionate blues singer whose romantic relationships involve her with Albert and his wife, Celie, along with her husband, Grady, who is distracted by Squeak and a band flute player named Germaine; eventually, her successes on tour which earn her fancy clothes, a car and a mansion in Memphis cannot prevent her from returning to Celie and Albert in this Nuclear Age novel by a Pulitzer Prize winning author (1982).

7	The Third Life of Grange Copeland by Alice Walker
8	The Color Purple by Alice Walker
9	By the Light of My Father's Smile by Alice Walker

<u>Elizabeth Hunter</u> - this character is the wealthy, elegant, self-centered woman who has her deathbed attempts at achieving a serene death interfered with by her selfish daughter, Dorothy aka the Princess de Las Cabanas and her famous egocentric actor-son, Sir Basil Hunter; eventually, her memories of being stranded on Bumbry Island off Queensland Coast are also interfered with by attending nurses and her housekeeper, Mrs. Lotte Lippmann, in this Nuclear Age novel by a Nobel Prize winning author (1973).

1	<u>The Tree of Man</u> by Patrick White
2	<u>The Twyborn Affair</u> by Patrick White
3	<u>The Eye of the Storm</u> by Patrick White

<u>Battle Fairchild</u> - this character is the patriarch whose family includes wife, Ellen, daughters, Shelley and Dabney, and the owner of a plantation named <u>Shellmound</u> where 9 year-old Laura McRaven attends the wedding of younger Dabney to the plantation manager, Troy Flavin; eventually, his paternal reluctance to let Dabney marry into an inferior social position hampers his feelings about missing her until they return and settle into an estate known as <u>Marmion</u> in this Nuclear Age novel (1972).

4	<u>The Optimist's Daughter</u> by Eudora Welty
5	<u>Delta Wedding</u> by Eudora Welty
6	<u>Losing Battles</u> by Eudora Welty

<u>Radisav</u> - this character is the Christian serf whose attempt to sabotage the Grand Vizier's construction project in Bosnia is prevented by the tyrannical, brutal overseer, Abidaga, after several nights of heightened security; eventually, his noble suffering and slow death and martyrdom from being impaled on a stake leads to the replacement of Abidaga by a more diplomatic overseer who finishes the job that unites Bosnia with the East in this Nuclear Age novel by a Nobel Prize winning author (1945).

7	<u>The Woman from Sarajevo</u> by Ivo Andric
8	<u>The Bridge on the Drina</u> by Ivo Andric
9	<u>The Bosnian Story</u> by Ivo Andric

3-5-8

<u>Sadie Burke</u> - this character is the hard-bitten, profane secretary and mistress of a ruthless Governor who has the Governor's Lieutenant Governor, Tiny Duffy, tell a noted surgeon named Adam Stanton about Stark's extra-marital affair with Stanton's sister, Anne; eventually, her jealousy over Willie Stark's return to his wife, Lucy, causes Willie's death by Adam Stanton whose subsequent murderer is Sugar-Boy O'Sheean in this Nuclear Age novel by a Pulitzer Prize winning author (1946).

1   <u>Sophie's Choice</u> by William Styron
2   <u>All the King's Men</u> by Robert Penn Warren
3   <u>The Naked and the Dead</u> by Norman Mailer

<u>Charlotte Haze</u> - this character is the conventionally, middle-class, religious widow with a daughter, Dorothy, from a small Northeastern town who becomes the second wife of a 37 year-old sexually obsessed, Parisian ex-schoolteacher; eventually, she is killed while frantically crossing a street to reach a mailbox after reading the diary of her new husband, Humbert Humbert, which spells out his sexual obsession with her daughter in this Nuclear Age novel (1955).

4   <u>Dr. Zhivago</u> by Boris Pasternak
5   <u>Lolita</u> by Vladimir Nabokov
6   <u>Cancer Ward</u> by Alexander Solzhenitsyn

<u>Janice Angstrom</u> - this character is the middle-aged suburban wife   whose job at her father's Pennsylvanian Toyota dealership is interrupted when she abandons her husband, Harry, and their teenage son, Nelson, to start a brief affair with Charles Stavros; eventually, she reconciles with Harry and Nelson who have witnessed the death of a runaway teenager named Jill when neighbors burned down their home in this Nuclear Age novel by a Pulitzer Prize winning author (1971).

7   <u>From the Terrace</u> by John O'Hara
8   <u>Rabbit Redux</u> by John Updike
9   <u>Brave New World</u> by Aldous Huxley

2-5-8

John Henry "Candy" West - this character is the delicate, fair-haired, sunburned 6 year-old cousin of a lanky, naive, 12 year-old tomboy named Frankie Addams who endures all the tribulations that Frankie experiences with her adolescent isolation and loneliness; eventually, he dies unexpectedly of meningitis at 7 years-old while a stout, motherly Afro-American cook named Berenice Sadie Brown consoles Frankie in this Nuclear Age novel by a Pulitzer Prize winning author (1946).

1	A Member of the Wedding by Carson McCullers
2	O Pioneers! by Willa Cather
3	The Optimist's Daughter by Eudora Welty

Agnes Matzarath - this character is the woman in an odd love triangle between her, her Polish postal clerk cousin, Jan Bronski, and her German grocery store owner husband, Alfred, that yields an eccentric dwarfish son named Oskar; eventually, her inability to cope with her son's behavior along with the guilt from her adultery drives her to commit suicide by compulsively ingesting eels in this Nuclear Age novel by a Nobel Prize winning author (1959).

4	Dog-Years by Gunther Grass
5	The Tin Drum by Gunther Grass
6	Cat and Mouse by Gunther Grass

Colonel Parrales Sonriente - this character is the army officer whose taunting of a mute idiot named el Pelele brings about the former's murder by the idiot only to allow a despotic dictator to accuse a lawyer named Carvagal and a General named Canales to be blamed for his death; eventually, his death results in Carvagal's arrest and shooting, General Canales's dying of heart failure and Cara de Angel (Angel Face)'s dying in prison in this Nuclear Age novel of magical realism by a Nobel Prize winning author (1946).

7	Mulata by Miguel Angel Asturias
8	The President by Miguel Angel Asturias
9	Strong Wind by Miguel Angel Asturias

1-5-8

<u>May Wynn</u> - this character is the poor, Italian, middle class   Catholic singer named Marie Minotti who falls in love with a wealthy, pampered piano player named Willie Keith from Princeton University with a domineering mother; eventually, she marries this future English professor after he acquitted during a Navy court martial involving his Captain, Philip Francis Queeg, in this Nuclear Age novel by a Pulitzer Prize winning author (1951).

1	<u>Marjorie Morningstar</u> by Herman Wouk
2	<u>Aurora Dawn</u> by Herman Wouk
3	<u>The Caine Mutiny</u> by Herman Wouk

<u>Brenda Pitamkin</u> - this character is the young, beautiful, desirable Radcliffe undergraduate who lives an affluent part of Short Hills, New Jersey, because of her father Ben's recent success in founding <u>Kitchen-and-Bathroom-Sinks Enterprise</u>; eventually, her presence at a country club sparks a summer romance with a smug, self-righteous middle class librarian named Neil Klugman which causes tensions within the Pitamkin family in this modern Nuclear Age novel (1959).

4	<u>Portnoy's Complaint</u> by Philip Roth
5	<u>Goodbye, Columbus</u> by Philip Roth
6	<u>The Ghost Writer</u> by Philip Roth

<u>Cara de Angel</u> - this character is the debonair, young man who is the favorite of a despotic dictator until his new task of setting   up General Canales for assassination finds him falling in love with the General's sickly daughter, Camila; eventually, his love is seen by the dictator as an act of treason which results in torture, imprisonment, and death after being falsely told of Camila's indiscretions with the dictator's in this Nuclear Age novel of magical realism by a Nobel Prize winning author (1946).

7	<u>Mulata</u> by Miguel Angel Asturias
8	<u>The President</u> by Miguel Angel Asturias
9	<u>Strong Wind</u> by Miguel Angel Asturias

3-5-8

<u>Nikolai Lebedev</u> - this character is the rich businessman in early 20th century Kiev, Russia who rewards a poor Jewish handyman with a supervisor's job in a non-Jewish section of the city for reviving him after he faints in the snow; eventually, this supervisor, Yakov Bok, is falsely accused of brutally murdering and blood draining a local gentile youth which results in two years of prison time before he is finally tried in this Nuclear Age novel by a Pulitzer Prize winning author (1966).

1	<u>The Assistant</u> by Bernard Malamud
2	<u>The Tenants</u> by Bernard Malamud
3	<u>The Fixer</u> by Bernard Malamud

<u>Renata</u> - this character is the girlfriend who travels to Europe with a young, sharp ex-Fuller Brush salesman turned Pulitzer Prize winning author after his wife's Denise divorce leaves her his entire fortune; eventually, her abandonment of him in Europe without a penny since he won't propose to her forces him to move into a cheap rooming house with her son in this Nuclear Age novel by a Pulitzer Prize winning author (1973).

4	<u>Herzog</u> by Saul Bellow
5	<u>The Dangling Man</u> by Saul Bellow
6	<u>Humbolt's Gift</u> by Saul Bellow

<u>Jan Bronski</u> - this character is the clerk who works at the Free City of Danzig Polish Post Office who is part of a love triangle involving a lower middle class German grocery store owner named Alfred Matzarath and Agnes Matzarath whose guilt compels her to commit suicide by compulsively ingesting eels; eventually, he is killed when the Germans capture and shoot him after he spends the night playing cards with Oskar and a dying Polish man in this Nuclear Age novel by a Nobel Prize winning author (1959).

7	<u>Dog-Years</u> by Gunther Grass
8	<u>The Tin Drum</u> by Gunther Grass
9	<u>Cat and Mouse</u> by Gunther Grass

3-6-8

Helen Archer - this character is the alcoholic woman from Albany, New York whose 9 year association with a fellow ex-ballplayer alcoholic also from Albany named Francis Whelan during the 1930's began in a New York bar; eventually, she returns to Albany with Francis only to die in a cheap hotel room after experiencing past memories of her past career and hopes in this Nuclear Age novel by a Pulitzer Prize winning author (1983).

1   Legs by William Kennedy
2   Ironweed by William Kennedy
3   Bill Phelan's Greatest Game by William Kennedy

Faber - this character is the old retired English professor in a   24th century totalitarian society where his exposure as a conspirator for reading books is thwarted when a fireman named Guy Montag intervenes and kills his coarse, condescending Fire Chief boss, Captain Beatty, with a flamethrower; eventually, his exposure is traced back a two-way radio planted in Guy Montag's ear in this Nuclear Age novel (1950).

4   Something Wicked This Way Comes by Ray Bradbury
5   The Martian Chronicles by Ray Bradbury
6   Fahrenheit 451 by Ray Bradbury

Therese Kummholz - this character is the illiterate, greedy old housekeeper whose loveless marriage to a 40 year-old scholarly recluse named Peter Kien allows her to join a fascist-like caretaker named Benedict Pfaff in the theft of Peter's immense library after she evicts him; eventually, her theft overwhelms that he burns himself to death in the fire he sets to destroy his library in this Nuclear Age novel by a Nobel Prize winning author (1935).

7   Crowds and Power by Elias Canetti
8   The Tower of Babel by Elias Canetti
9   The Agony of Flies by Elias Canetti

2-6-8

Balak - this character is the dog whose wanderings parallel those of the Jewish would-be pioneer named Yithak Kummer who travels from Europe to Palestine during the wave of immigration between 1907 and 1913 for the founding of the State of Isreal; eventually, this parallel journey is viewed as a mystical contrast between the old and new ways of Jewish life after Kummer dies in Palestine of rabies received from a bite by this dog in this Nuclear Age novel by a Nobel Prize winning author (1945).

1	**A Guest for the Night** by Shmuel Agnon
2	**The Day Before Yesterday** by Shmuel Agnon
3	**The Bridal Canopy** by Shmuel Agnon

Joseph Fahmel - this character is the German architect from Cologne who attends the 18th birthday party of patriarch Heinrich Fahmel on September 6th, 1958 along with his architect father, Robert; eventually, he is questioned by his grandfather about St. Anthony's Abbey future status after 1945 since the latter was responsible for its initial construction while his son, Robert, destroyed it during World War II in this Nuclear Age novel by a Nobel Prize winning author (1959).

4	**The Clown** by Heinrich Boll
5	**Billiards at Half Past Nine** by Heinrich Boll
6	**The Train Was On Time** by Heinrich Boll

Calpurnia - this character is the Afro-American housekeeper who supports her employer, Atticus Finch, in raising his widowed children, Scout and Jem; eventually, she is joined in her instruction of Scout and Jem by the intrusion of Atticus's aunt, Alexandria, during a trial where a Afro-American man named Tom Robinson falsely accused of rape and battery by a white woman named Mayella Ewell in this Nuclear Age novel by a Pulitzer Prize winning author (1960).

7	**The Web and the Rock** by Thomas Wolfe
8	**To Kill a Mockingbird** by Harper Lee
9	**Sanctuary** by William Faulkner

2-5-8

<u>Aunt Alexandra</u> - this character is Atticus Finch's proper Southern sister who maintains a strict code about which people she and her family should associate; eventually, her move into the Atticus household where she joins his children, Jem and Jean, during the rape trial of a Afro-American man named Tom Robinson puts pressure on Scout who is forced to wear dresses in this Nuclear Age novel by a Pulitzer Prize winning author (1960).

1   <u>The Web and the Rock</u> by Thomas Wolfe
2   <u>To Kill a Mockingbird</u> by Harper Lee
3   <u>Sanctuary</u> by William Faulkner

<u>Ivan Stark</u> - this character is the London based banker son of South Africans, Ben and Vera Stark, who are respectively a prestige luggage salesman and civil rights lawyer/political activist and brother of a gay South African doctor named Annie; eventually, his parents reunite with 2 Afro-American revolutionaries, Didymus and Sibongile (Sally) Maqoma and their half-Zulu, half-Xhosa, daughter, Mho, after years of exile in this Nuclear Age novel by a Nobel Prize winning author (1994).

4   <u>Guest of Honor</u> by Nadine Gordimer
5   <u>None to Accompany Me</u> by Nadine Gordimer
6   <u>The House Gun</u> by Nadine Gordimer

<u>Miles Roby</u> - this character is the intelligent, 40 year-old manager of a diner in an imaginary, tarnished Maine town whose sad sack existence centers around the diner's wealthy owner, Mrs. Francine Whiting, and his bright, sensitive teenage daughter, Tick; eventually, his vain, humorless wife, Janine, leaves him for the hideous barroom blowhard, Walt Comeau, when she sheds 50 pounds and becomes an aerobics instructor in this Nuclear Age novel by a Pulitzer Prize winning author (2001).

7   <u>Nobody's Fool</u> by Richard Russo
8   <u>Empire Falls</u> by Richard Russo
9   <u>Mohawk</u> by Richard Russo

2-5-8

Francine Whiting - this character is the conniving widow whose ownership of most of an imaginary tarnished Maine town centers around a deteriorating diner managed by a sad sack named Miles Roby; eventually, her refusal to make improvements to the profitless diner doesn't deter Miles from leaving because of her promise to will the diner to him which will ultimately benefit his teenage daughter, Tick, in this Nuclear Age novel by a Pulitzer Prize winning author (2001).

1   Empire Falls by Richard Russo
2   Nobody's Fool by Richard Russo
3   Mohawk by Richard Russo

Atticus Finch - this character is the widowed lawyer from Alabama who defends a young Afro-American man, Tom Robinson, falsely accused of raping a young white woman named Mayella Ewell; eventually, he loses the case to an all white jury while his Afro-American cook, Calpurnia, joins him in rearing Scout and Jean with the belief that they are born with an instinct for justice (1960).

4   The Web and the Rock by Thomas Wolfe
5   To Kill a Mockingbird by Harper Lee
6   Sanctuary by William Faulkner

Ben Stark - this character is the sculpturer turned prestige luggage salesman in South Africa at the end of Apartheid whose wife is a civil right's lawyer/political activist named Vera, his son, Ivan, a London based banker, and his daughter, Annie, a gay South African doctor; eventually, he and Vera reunite with old friends Didymus Maqoma and his wife, Sibongile, along with their half-Zulu, half-Xhosa daughter, Mpho, in this Nuclear Age novel by a Nobel Prize winning author (1994).

7   Guest of Honor by Nadine Gordimer
8   None to Accompany Me by Nadine Gordimer
9   The House Gun by Nadine Gordimer

1-5-8

Jem Finch - this character is the son of a widowed lawyer from   Alabama named Atticus whose defense of a young Afro-American man named Tom Robinson accused of raping a young white woman named Mayella Ewell proves that she and her father, Bob, are lying; eventually, he and his sister, Jean nicknamed Scout, come under attack by Bob Ewell only to be defended by Boo Radley in this Nuclear Age novel by a Pulitzer Prize winning author (1960).

1	**The Web and the Rock** by Thomas Wolfe
2	**To Kill a Mockingbird** by Harper Lee
3	**Sanctuary** by William Faulkner

Annie Stark - this character is the gay South African doctor in   South Africa at the end of the Apartheid whose parents, Ben and Vera Stark, are a prestige luggage salesman and civil rights lawyer/political activist while her brother, Ivan, is a London based banker; eventually, her parents reunite with 2 Afro-American revolutionaries, Didymus and Sibongile (Sally) Maqoma and their half-Zulu, half-Xhosa, daughter, Mho, when they return from exile in this Nuclear Age novel by a Nobel Prize winning author (1994).

4	**Guest of Honor** by Nadine Gordimer
5	**None to Accompany Me** by Nadine Gordimer
6	**The House Gun** by Nadine Gordimer

Walt Comeau - this character is the hilarious, fiancé of a vain, humorless aerobics instructor named Janice and the one who regularly torments her ex-husband, Miles Roby, who leads a sad sack existence as the manager of a deteriorating diner in an imaginary, tarnished Maine town owned by Francine Whiting; eventually, this preening, blowhard owner of a health club who helped Janine both shed her husband and 50 pounds in this Nuclear Age novel by a Pulitzer Prize winning author (2001).

7	**Nobody's Fool** by Richard Russo
8	**Empire Falls** by Richard Russo
9	**Mohawk** by Richard Russo

2-5-8

<u>Tick Roby</u> - this character is the bright, sensitive teenage daughter of a sad sack operator of a deteriorating diner named Miles and his vain, humorless, divorced wife, Janine; eventually, she has to deal with an odd, menacing ex-boyfriend named John Voss whose deeply troubled personality sends him on a shooting rampage at his high school in this Nuclear Age novel by a Pulitzer Prize winning author (2001).

1	<u>Nobody's Fool</u> by Richard Russo
2	<u>Empire Falls</u> by Richard Russo
3	<u>Mohawk</u> by Richard Russo

<u>Arthur "Boo" Radley</u> - this character is the town loner of Maycomb County, Alabama whose reputation formed by local gossip makes him out to be a demented monster to the neighborhood children; eventually, he protects 2 children, Jem and Jean, from a attack by Bob Ewell because their father, a widowed attorney named Atticus Finch had proven Bob and his daughter, Mayella, to be liars in this Nuclear Age novel by a Pulitzer Prize winning author (1960).

4	<u>The Web and the Rock</u> by Thomas Wolfe
5	<u>To Kill a Mockingbird</u> by Harper Lee
6	<u>Sanctuary</u> by William Faulkner

<u>Oupa</u> - this character is the South African Afro-American co-worker of a white civil rights activist/lawyer named Vera Stark and the one who just has been released as a prisoner from Robben Island; eventually, this political activist bursting with hopes and future plans for South Africa is killed during an ambush where bullets go through Vera allowing her to survive in this Nuclear Age novel by a Nobel Prize winning author (1994).

7	<u>Guest of Honor</u> by Nadine Gordimer
8	<u>None to Accompany Me</u> by Nadine Gordimer
9	<u>The House Gun</u> by Nadine Gordimer

2-5-8

Sibongile (Sally) Maqoma - this character is the Afro-American mother of Mho and wife of Didymus who overshadows her husband when she is surprisingly elected to the Movement Executive Committee in tumultuous South Africa at the end of Apartheid; eventually, she and her husband are reunited with old friends, Ben and Vera Stark, who are respectively a prestige luggage salesman and civil rights lawyer/political activist after a 20 year exile in this Nuclear Age novel by a Nobel Prize winning author (1994).

1	Guest of Honor by Nadine Gordimer
2	None to Accompany Me by Nadine Gordimer
3	The House Gun by Nadine Gordimer

Janine - this character is the vain, humorless, shallow aerobics instructor who is divorced from a sad sack manager of a deteriorating diner named Miles Roby, the mother of a teenager named Tick and the fiancee of an odious, blowhard, Walt Comeau; eventually, her daughter Tick's whole world becomes shattered when an odd ex-boyfriend named John Voss shoots up the local high school in a Nuclear Age novel by a Pulitzer Prize winning author (2001).

4	Empire Falls by Richard Russo
5	Nobody's Fool by Richard Russo
6	Mohawk by Richard Russo

Bob Ewell - this character is the father of 8 in Maycomb County, Alabama who lives behind the county dump where he spends most of his family's welfare check on drinking instead of properly feeding his children; eventually, he is thwarted by Boo Radley in his attempts to harm two young children, Jem and Jean, after their attorney father, Atticus Finch, proves he and his 19 year-old daughter, Mayella, to be liars in this Nuclear Age novel by a Pulitzer Prize winning author (1960).

7	The Web and the Rock by Thomas Wolfe
8	To Kill a Mockingbird by Harper Lee
9	Sanctuary by William Faulkner

1-5-8

<u>Mayella Ewell</u> - this character is the 19 year-old female with 7 siblings who lives in poverty in Alabama behind the Maycomb County dump with her father, Bob, who spends the family's welfare check on drinking rather than properly feed his family; eventually, she falsely accuses a young, Afro-American man, Tom Robinson, of rape and is proven a liar by a widowed lawyer named Atticus Finch in this Nuclear Age novel by a Pulitzer Prize winning author (1960).

1	<u>The Web and the Rock</u> by Thomas Wolfe
2	<u>To Kill a Mockingbird</u> by Harper Lee
3	<u>Sanctuary</u> by William Faulkner

<u>Didymus Maqoma</u> - this character is the Afro-American husband of Sibongile (Sally) and father of a teenage daughter named Mho; eventually, his return at the end of the Apartheid reunites him and his wife with old friends, Ben and Vera Stark, who are respectively a prestige luggage salesman an a civil rights lawyer/political activist who have London based banker son. Ivan, and a gay South African doctor daughter, Annie, in this Nuclear Age novel by a Nobel Prize winning author (1994).

4	<u>Guest of Honor</u> by Nadine Gordimer
5	<u>None to Accompany Me</u> by Nadine Gordimer
6	<u>The House Gun</u> by Nadine Gordimer

<u>Tina</u> - this character is the fickle, blond daughter of a crusty old Italian fisherman, Tomasino, whose romance with the ruling American officer, Major Victor Joppolo, heats up and cools down depending on the status of her P.O.W. boyfriend; eventually, her roller coaster romance with this married Major ends when the Major is reassigned by General Marvin in this Nuclear Age novel by a Pulitzer Prize winning author (1944).

7	<u>Into the Valley</u> by John Hersey
8	<u>A Bell for Adano</u> by John Hersey
9	<u>Hiroshima</u> by John Hersey

2-5-8

<u>Ida Scott</u> - this character is the young, Afro-American woman and aspiring professional singer whose brother Rufus' suicide jump off the George Washington Bridge involves her with his friends, Vivaldo Moore, Rich and Cass Silenski and Eric Jones; eventually, her relationship with Vivldo survives her anger and grief, Vivaldo's affair with Eric Jones and her own affair with a white television producer named Steve Ellis in this Nuclear Age novel (1962).

1	<u>Go Tell It On The Mountain</u> by James Baldwin
2	<u>Another Country</u> by James Baldwin
3	<u>Just Above My Head</u> by James Baldwin

<u>Mpho Maqoma</u> - this character is the half-Zulu, half-Xhosa, all Londoner teenage daughter of 2 Afro-American revolutionaries, Didymus and Sibongile (Sally) who return to South Africa at the end of the Apartheid; eventually, she and her parents are reunited with Ben and Vera Stark who are a prestige luggage salesman and civil rights lawyer and political activist respectively in this Nuclear Age novel by a Nobel Prize winning author (1994).

4	<u>None to Accompany Me</u> by Nadine Gordimer
5	<u>Guest of Honor</u> by Nadine Gordimer
6	<u>The House Gun</u> by Nadine Gordimer

<u>Pedro Tecero Garcia</u> - this character is the Chilean revolutionary and lifelong lover of Blanca who comes from a strong-willed family called the Truebas made up of the self-made wealthy landowner and patriarch, Esteban, his psychic, beautiful wife, Clara, and Rosa the beautiful; eventually, this idealistic peasant impregnates Blanca who subsequently makes a marriage of convenience with a fortune hunter named Count Jean De Satigny in this Nuclear Age novel of magical realism (1985).

7	<u>The Infinite Plan</u> by Isabel Allende
8	<u>The House of the Spirits</u> by Isabel Allende
9	<u>A Discreet Miracle</u> by Isabel Allende

Philip Francis Queeg - this character is the incompetent, cowardly Reserve Officer during World War II put in command of a dilapidated destroyer-minesweeper with Lieutenant Steve Maryk as the Executive Officer and Willie Keith as Communications Officer; eventually, his maniacal behavior warrants a court martial that relieves him of his command and acquits Willie Keith in this Nuclear Age novel by a Pulitzer Prize winning author (1951).

1	**Marjorie Morningstar** by Herman Wouk
2	**Aurora Dawn** by Herman Wouk
3	**The Caine Mutiny** by Herman Wouk

General Canales - this character is the hated enemy of a despotic dictator who is falsely accused by this dictator along with a lawyer, Carvagal, for the murder of Colonel Parrales Sonriente who was really killed by a mute idiot by the name of el Pelele; eventually, he escapes after being warned by Cara de Angel only to die of heart failure caused by a false newspaper report about his daughter with this dictator in this Nuclear Age novel of magical realism by a Pulitzer Prize winning author (1946).

4	**Mulata** by Miguel Angel Asturias
5	**The President** by Miguel Angel Asturias
6	**Strong Wind** by Miguel Angel Asturias

Bibikov - this character is the Russian magistrate who is sympathetic toward a 30 year-old Jewish handyman named Yakov Bok who has been held in solitary confinement for 2 years awaiting trial for the brutal murder of a gentile child; eventually, he, like Yakov, is falsely arrested under the accusation of missing government funds and thrown into Yakov's adjoining cell where he is tortured until he hangs himself in this Nuclear Age novel by a Pulitzer Prize winning author (1966).

7	**The Assistant** by Bernard Malamud
8	**The Tenants** by Bernard Malamud
9	**The Fixer** by Bernard Malamud

3-5-9

<u>Alfred Matzarath</u> - this character is the German grocery store owner whose marriage to Agnes Bronski makes him the presumed father of an old dwarfed boy, Oskar, along with Jan Bronski who is a clerk for the h Post Office across the German border; eventually, he joins the German Nazi Party because of their uniforms and their feeling of identity which allows Oskar to finger him as a collaborator and cause his death in this Nuclear Age novel by a Nobel Prize winning author (1959).

1	<u>The Tin Drum</u> by Gunther Grass
2	<u>Dog-Years</u> by Gunther Grass
3	<u>Cat and Mouse</u> by Gunther Grass

<u>Ari Ben Canaan</u> - this character is the agent whose undercover work for a Zionist organization seeking to make Israel a State compels him to go to an American nurse named Kitty Fremont to have a bullet removed from his leg obtained during a prison breakout; eventually, his repeated proposals to her finally lead to marriage after they learn that a young woman named Karen Hansen Clement had been killed during an Arab raid on a kibbutz in this Nuclear Age novel (1958).

4	<u>Battle Cry</u> by Leon Uris
5	<u>Exodus</u> by Leon Uris
6	<u>Trinity</u> by Leon Uris

<u>General Marvin</u> - this character is the American Army officer during World War II whose invasion of an Italian town results in his assignment of a Major named Victor Joppolo to take charge of the occupation; eventually, he becomes infuriated upon learning that Major Joppolo had rescinded his request to prevent mule carts on the road to the town and orders him returned to the States in this wartime Nuclear Age novel by a Pulitzer Prize winning author (1944).

7	<u>Into the Valley</u> by John Hersey
8	<u>A Bell for Adano</u> by John Hersey
9	<u>Hiroshima</u> by John Hersey

Blanca De Satigny - this character is the young Chilean daughter of a self-made, domineering wealthy landowner whose attraction to a revolutionary peasant named Pedro Tecero Garcia results in an out-of-wedlock daughter named Alba; eventually, her marriage of convenience to a fortune hunter, Count Jean De Satigny, finally ends when her reformed father helps her escape prison and reunite with Pedro in this Nuclear Age novel of magical realism (1985).

1	**The Infinite Plan** by Isabel Allende
2	**The House of the Spirits** by Isabel Allende
3	**A Discreet Miracle** by Isabel Allende

Oliver "Tantivy" Mucher-Maffick - this character is the British Lieutenant during World War II who works in a London office with the unpredictable American Lieutenant Tyrone Slothrop; eventually, he is told by this paranoid American about his odd predicament involving sexual arousement when he psychically nears a point where a rocket will strike in this Nuclear Age novel (1973).

4	**The Crying of Lot 49** by Thomas Pynchon
5	**Gravity's Rainbow** by Thomas Pynchon
6	**Vineland** by Thomas Pynchon

Dr. Hilarius - this character is the crazed psychiatrist of a decent, lovable, 28 year-old suburban housewife named Oedipa Maas whom she loses to madness; eventually, he becomes the cause of the alienation between her and her used car salesman husband named Wendell "Mucho" Maas when the latter participates in an LSD experiment with him while she joins Metzer as the joint executor of Pierce Inveranty's estate in this Nuclear Age novel (1966).

7	**The Crying of Lot 49** by Thomas Pynchon
8	**Gravity's Rainbow** by Thomas Pynchon
9	**V.** by Thomas Pynchon

Herbert Stencil - this character is the son of British Foreign Office man whose drowning leaves him nothing but journals that identify an enigmatic woman as a young girl at the start of the century that leads him to pursue her; eventually, this young adventurer follows a clue to Malta with Benny Profane and Paola Maijstral and discovers her disguised as a Manichaean priest being dismembered by children while trapped under a beam in a World War II bombing raid in this Nuclear Age novel (1961).

1	The Crying of Lot 49 by Thomas Pynchon
2	Gravity's Rainbow by Thomas Pynchon
3	V. by Thomas Pynchon

Bernard Gui - this character is the relentless Dominican inquisitor who travels to an Italian Benedictine abbey to vie with a middle-aged Franciscan Brother, William of Baskerville, and his disciple, Adso, about locating heretics; eventually, he watches as the Abbot Abo directs Brother William to investigate 7 grotesque murders committed by a serial killer at this abbey in this Nuclear Age novel (1980).

4	The Island of the Day Before by Umberto Eco
5	The Name of the Rose by Umberto Eco
6	Foucault's Pendulum by Umberto Eco

Mr. Charrington - this character is the determined 35 year-old member of the thought police who disguises himself as an old man running an antique shop in order to uncover conspirators against the society of Oceania; eventually, he gains the confidence of a Minister of Truth named Winston Smith and his dark-haired mistress, Julia, and then apprehends them in the apartment of an Inner Party member named O'Brien in this Nuclear Age novel (1949).

7	Animal Farm by George Orwell
8	Brave New World by Aldous Huxley
9	Nineteen Eighty Four by George Orwell

3-5-9

<u>Kizzy</u> - this character is the slave girl who is taken from her parents, Toby and Bell, for helping her lover, Noah, try to escape and sold to Tom Lea whose repeated rapes of her result in a child later called Chicken George; eventually, her present day descendent traces the family history back to her father, a West African youth named Kunta Kinte in 1750 in Juffure, The Gambia, Africa in this Nuclear Age novel by a Pulitzer Prize winning author (1976).

1   <u>Queen</u> by Alex Haley
2   <u>Roots</u> by Alex Haley
3   <u>The Gift</u> by Alex Haley

<u>Nick</u> - this character is the chauffeur for a Commander named Fred and his ex-evangelist wife, Serena Joy, who has been recruited by the latter to have a liaison with a legal concubine named Offred in order to bear children; eventually, he concocts a plan where the repressed Offred in a Republic named Gilead is able to escape to Canada and rejoin her husband, Luke, and their daughter in this Nuclear Age novel of psychological realism (1985).

4   <u>The Handmaid's Tale</u> by Margaret Atwood
5   <u>Cat's Eye</u> by Margaret Atwood
6   <u>Surfacing</u> by Margaret Atwood

<u>Dr. Copeland</u> - this character is the Afro-American physician who watches his idealism compromised after his son, William, is sentenced to hard labor and his devout daughter, Portia, works as a maid; eventually, he is dumbfounded when a young deaf-mute named John Singer invites him to a gathering with a teenage girl named Mick Kelly, an alcoholic liberal, Jake Blount, and the owner of the <u>New York Café</u>, Biff Brannon, in this Nuclear Age novel by a Pulitzer Prize winning author (1940).

7   <u>The Member of the Wedding</u> by Carson McCullers
8   <u>The Heart is a Lonely Hunter</u> by Carson McCullers
9   <u>Reflections in a Golden Eye</u> by Carson McCullers

2-4-8

Brock Vond - this character is the notoriously evil FBI federal agent whose seduction of Frenesi Gates leads her to murder a student protest leader and abandon her husband, Zoyd Wheeler, and her daughter, Prairie, for 16 years when she enter a Witness Protection program; eventually, he wants her back again after Reagonomic cutbacks have left her and her new family bankrupt in this Nuclear Age novel (1990).

1	The Crying of Lot 49 by Thomas Pynchon
2	Gravity's Rainbow by Thomas Pynchon
3	Vineland by Thomas Pynchon

Jack Wales - this character is the up-and-coming, young son of a rich industrialist and the one who vies with an opportunistic 25 year old accountant named Joe Lampton for the hand of a good-looking, vacuous 19 year old woman named Susan Brown; eventually, this collegiate war hero loses out when Joe succeeds in getting Susan pregnant in this Nuclear Age novel of social realism (1957).

4	The Naked and the Dead by Norman Mailer
5	The Power and the Glory by Graham Greene
6	Room at the Top by John Braine

Robbie - this character is the contrite and humble wife whose short desertion from her marriage to George ends when she arrives unannounced at her brother-in-law Battle Fairchild's plantation, Shellmound, to attend Dabney Fairchild's marriage to plantation manager, Troy Flavin; eventually, Dabney Fairchild's wedding party has a last minute substitute when 9 year old niece, Laura McRaven, becomes a participant in this Nuclear Age novel (1972).

7	The Optimist's Daughter by Eudora Welty
8	Delta Wedding by Eudora Welty
9	Losing Battles by Eudora Welty

3-6-8

<u>Clare Quilty</u> - this character is the playwright at the Bearsdsley School whose awkward relationship with an adolescent named Dolores Haze exists because she is also involved sexually with her middle-aged stepfather, Humbert Humbert; eventually, his cross country pursuit of Humbert and Dolores results in Dolores's escape with him, Dolores's escape from him and his ultimate murder by Humbert in this Nuclear Age novel (1955).

1	<u>Lolita</u> by Vladimir Nabokov
2	<u>Dr. Zhivago</u> by Boris Pasternak
3	<u>Cancer Ward</u> by Alexander Solzhenitsyn

<u>Camila</u> - this character is the young daughter of the at-large General Canales who has been falsely accused of murdering Colonel Parrales Sonriente and the one who falls gravely ill of pneumonia while being escorted by a young debonair man named Cara de Angel; eventually, she recovers, falls in love with this escort who is later tortured and dies in prison and bears him a baby son in the Nuclear Age novel of magical realism by a Nobel Prize winning author (1946).

4	<u>Mulata</u> by Miguel Angel Asturias
5	<u>The President</u> by Miguel Angel Asturias
6	<u>Strong Wind</u> by Miguel Angel Asturias

<u>Millie</u> - this character is the unrealistic, pill-popping vacuous wife of a 24th century fireman named Guy Montag whose job is to both burn books and the houses of their owners because books   condone free thought; eventually, she turns her husband in for holding books to his coarse, condescending Fire Chief boss, Captain Beatty, in this Nuclear Age novel (1950).

7	<u>Something Wicked This Way Comes</u> by Ray Bradbury
8	<u>The Martian Chronicles</u> by Ray Bradbury
9	<u>Fahrenheit 451</u> by Ray Bradbury

1-5-9

<u>Vivaldo Moore</u> - this character is the Irish-Italian novelist whose intervention between his best friend who is a Afro-American Jazz musician named Rufus Scott and a white woman from Georgia named Leona prevents her any severe harm; eventually, his affair   with Rufus's younger sister, Ida, after Rufus commits suicide by jumping off the George Washington Bridge survives her affairs in this Nuclear Age novel by a Pulitzer Prize winning author (1962).

1   <u>Go Tell It On The Mountain</u> by James Baldwin
2   <u>Another Country</u> by James Baldwin
3   <u>Just Above My Head</u> by James Baldwin

<u>Alba</u> - this character is the recorder of the eccentric Chilean family, the Truebas, beginning with her domineering, possessive grandfather, Esteban, her clairvoyant grandmother, Clara, her mother, Blanca de Satigny and her peasant revolutionary father, Pedro Tecero Garcia; eventually, her luminous personality helps her grandfather to lose his rage so that he even helps Blanca and Pedro escape imprisonment in this Nuclear Age novel of magical realism (1985).

4   <u>The Infinite Plan</u> by Isabel Allende
5   <u>The House of the Spirits</u> by Isabel Allende
6   <u>A Discreet Miracle</u> by Isabel Allende

<u>Teddy Bloat</u> - this character is the employee of PISCES who first notices the correlation between Slothrop's encounters with women and German's rocket bombardment of London; eventually, an agent   headquartered at an insane asylum called the <u>The White Visitation</u>, wants Slothrop to become so paranoid and focused on rockets that all his other thoughts and behavior will be inhibited in this Nuclear Age novel (1973).

7   <u>The Crying of Lot 49</u> by Thomas Pynchon
8   <u>Gravity's Rainbow</u> by Thomas Pynchon
9   <u>Vineland</u> by Thomas Pynchon

2-5-8

<u>Spiro Antonapoulous</u> - this character is the fat, dreamy, slovenly, mute feeble-minded roommate of an intelligent, deaf-mute named John Singer who is finally fired from the fruit-store owned by his cousin, Charles Parker, and institutionalized; eventually, his death causes John to become so depressed that he fatally shoots himself in this Nuclear Age novel by a Pulitzer Prize winning author (1940).

1	<u>The Member of the Wedding</u> by Carson McCullers
2	<u>The Heart is a Lonely Hunter</u> by Carson McCullers
3	<u>Reflections in a Golden Eye</u> by Carson McCullers

<u>Serena Joy</u> - this character is the ex-evangelist wife of a Commander named Fred in the Republic of Gilead who follows the Protestant fundamentalist concept where Rachel commanded Jacob to sleep with her maid Bilhah; eventually, her overwhelming desire for a child prompts her to arrange a liaison between a legal concubine named Offred and her chauffeur, Nick, in this Nuclear Age novel of psychological realism (1985).

4	<u>The Handmaid's Tale</u> by Margaret Atwood
5	<u>Cat's Eye</u> by Margaret Atwood
6	<u>Surfacing</u> by Margaret Atwood

<u>Mr. Brown</u> - this character is the most influential politician in the English town of Warley and the father of a good-looking, vacuous 19 year old named Susan whose rejection of war hero Jack Wales leaves her pregnant by a 25 year old opportunistic accountant named Joe Lampton; eventually, his failure to bribe Joe with an offer to stay away from Susan forces him to finally accept this young man into his family in this Nuclear Age novel (1957).

7	<u>The Naked and the Dead</u> by Norman Mailer
8	<u>The Power and the Glory</u> by Graham Greene
9	<u>Room at the Top</u> by John Braine

2-4-9

<u>Max</u> - this character is the old Jewish herdsman and foster father of George who is the possible result of a computer accident by a lecherous computer named WESCAC and a suitable virgin; eventually, he is convinced that George should enter New Tammany University as Grand Tutor during the Quiet Riots and oppose the False Tutor, Harold Bray, in this Nuclear Age novel (1966).

1	<u>Giles Goat-Boy</u> by John Barth
2	<u>Sabbatical</u> by John Barth
3	<u>The Sot-Weed Factor</u> by John Barth

<u>Ramona Donsell</u> - this character is the flower shop owner in her late thirties who is left in New York while her lover, Moses, travels to Chicago to kill his ex-wife, Madelaine, and her lover Val, over the custody of his daughter, June; eventually, she joins Moses and his prosperous older brother, William, in Massachuttes in this Nuclear Age novel by a Nobel Prize winning author (1964).

4	<u>Dangling Man</u> by Saul Bellow
5	<u>Humbolt's Gift</u> by Saul Bellow
6	<u>Herzog</u> by Saul Bellow

<u>Abidaga</u> - this character is the domineering, amoral overseer assigned by the Grand Vizier to Visegrad, Bosnia to lead the Muslims, enslave the Christian serfs and tyrannize anyone who interferes with the Vizier's timetable in joining Bosnia with the East; eventually, his unwise decision to torture and brutally impale a Christian leads to a more diplomatic replacement in this Nuclear Age novel by a Nobel Prize winning author (1945).

7	<u>The Woman from Sarajevo</u> by Ivo Andric
8	<u>The Bridge on the Drina</u> by Ivo Andric
9	<u>The Bosnian Story</u> by Ivo Andric

<u>Leona</u> - this character is the white woman from Georgia whose stormy relationship with a young Afro-American Harlem jazz musician named Rufus Scott results in increasing violence; eventually, she is permanently hospitalized in the South by her brother while Rufus takes a fatal plunge off the George Washington Bridge in this Nuclear Age novel by a Pulitzer Prize winning author (1962).

1	<u>Go Tell It On The Mountain</u> by James Baldwin
2	<u>Another Country</u> by James Baldwin
3	<u>Just Above My Head</u> by James Baldwin

<u>The Commander</u> - this character is the high level bureaucrat and husband of an ex-evangelist named Serena Joy in the new Republic of Gilead which replaced a disintegrating, decadent U.S.A.; eventually, he breaks the laws of this newly founded country when he invites his mistress, Offred, to clandestine meetings in his study where he allows her to read books officially forbidden and even tries to kill her in this Nuclear Age novel (1985).

4	<u>The Handmaid's Tale</u> by Margaret Atwood
5	<u>Cat's Eye</u> by Margaret Atwood
6	<u>Surfacing</u> by Margaret Atwood

<u>Robert Faehmel</u> - this character is the German architect from Cologne who joins his son Joseph at the 80th birthday party of patriarch Heinrich Faehmel on September 6th, 1958; eventually, his destruction of St. Anthony Abbey during World War II is placed in perspective between his architect father who built it and his architect son who will be working on its restoration after 1945 in this Nuclear Age novel by a Pulitzer Prize winning author (1959).

7	<u>The Clown</u> by Heinrich Boll
8	<u>Billiards at Half Past Nine</u> by Heinrich Boll
9	<u>The Train Was On Time</u> by Heinrich Boll

2-4-8

<u>Captain Beatty</u> - this character is the coarse, condescending Fire Chief living in the 24th century who burns books and book owner's homes because books encourage free thought; eventually, he is killed with a flamethrower by a fireman named Guy Montag to stop him from exposing an old retired English professor named Faber in this Nuclear Age novel (1950).

1   <u>Something Wicked This Way Comes</u> by Ray Bradbury
2   <u>The Martian Chronicles</u> by Ray Bradbury
3   <u>Fahrenheit 451</u> by Ray Bradbury

<u>George Koves</u> - this character is the 15 year old Hungarian Jew who is arrested by the Nazis and interned in a camp where he learns to survive eventhough he is ostracized by the other Jews because he doesn't know either Hebrew or Jewish; eventually, he survives because he rationalizes that it would be normal not to protest the indignities that he suffers in this Nuclear Age novel by a Pulitzer Prize winning author (1975).

4   <u>The Fixer</u> by Bernard Malamud
5   <u>Fateless</u> by Imre Kertesz
6   <u>The Bridge on the Drina</u> by Ivo Andric

<u>Billy Pilgrim</u> - this character is the innocent person whose fate of being unstuck in time has him skipping from the present to the past to the future which assigns him the grim duty of witnessing monumental tragedies like the fire bombing of Dresden; eventually, he has the happy task of mating with a film star named Montana Wildhack on the planet Trafamadore in this Nuclear Age novel (1975).

7   <u>Breakfast of Champions</u> by Kurt Vonnegut, Jr.
8   <u>Slaughterhouse-Five</u> by Kurt Vonnegut, Jr.
9   <u>Cat's Cradle</u> by Kurt Vonnegut, Jr.

Index of Characters

A

Anzoleto, 143
Arabella, 15
Arabella Allen, 65
Arabella Donn, 205
Arabella Wilmot, 10
Arcade, 198
Ari Ben Canaan, 326
Arrowhead, 169
Arthur, 141
Arthur "Boo" Radley, 321
Arthur Compeyson, 103
Arthur Dimmesdale, 88
Arthur Gride, 51
Ashenden, 252
Ashley Wilkes, 264
Atticus Finch, 319
Augustus McCrae, 295
Augustus Snodgrass, 67
Aunt Alexandra, 318
Aunt Hager, 273
Aunt Polly, 82
Aunt Tempy, 270
Axel Heyst, 200

B

Bailie Nichol Jarvie, 77
Balak, 317
Baron de Charlus, 223
Battle Fairchild, 311
Bathsheba everdene, 140
Bazaroff, 127
Becky Sharp, 87
Becky Thatcher, 89
Bella Wilfer, 179
Ben Gunn, 129
Benjamin (Benji) Compson, 223
Ben Stark, 319
Berkeley Cecil, 160
Bernard Gui, 328
Bernard Marx, 218
Bernard Profitendieu, 246
Berta Mason rochester, 117
Bertie Cecil, 168
Bessie Leaven, 120
Bessie Mears, 273

Beth, 105
Bibikov, 325
Biff Brannon, 295
Bill Bones, 104
Bill Sikes, 45
Billy Pilgrim, 336
Bird, 295
Black Dog, 84
Black Michael, 191
Blanca De Satigny, 327
Blanche Stroeve, 195
Blazes Boylan, 230
Blind Pew, 93
Bob Ewell, 322
Brenda Pitamkin, 314
Brice Chamberlain, 274
Brigid O'Shaughnessy, 275
Brock Brewton, 228
Brock Vond, 330
Brother Juniper, 228
Buck Mulligan, 224
Bush, 264
Byron Bunch, 245

C

Cacambo, 13
Cadace (Caddy) Compson, 265
Caleb Trask, 285
Calpurnia, 317
Camila, 331
Camille, 156
Candy, 241
Captain Ahab, 83
Captain Beatty, 336
Captain Bob, 166
Captain Bob Singleton, 19
Captain Booth, 16
Captain Cuttle, 135
Captain Daniel Forrester, 262
Captain Mallison, 246
Captain William Dobbin, 138
Cara de Angel, 314
Carathis, 28
Cardinal Richelieu, 129
Carol Kennicott, 226

Colonel James Brewton, 273
Colonel Morgan, 133
Colonel Parrales Sonriente, 313
Colonel Pyncheon, 95
Colonel William Morden, 31
Commodore Hawser Trunnion, 12
Congo, 263
Conrad, 17
Corilla, 129
Corporal Trim, 24
Cosette, 105
Countess Anastasie De Restaud, 68
Count Morano, 19
Count Mosca, 60
Count Vronsky, 82
Curley, 221
Curtis Jadwin, 188

D

Dain Maroola, 208
Dain Waris, 203
Daisy Buchanan, 233
Damon Wildeve, 98
Daniel Fuselli, 253
Dan Troop, 189
David Balfour, 121
David Crimple, 155
Dean Moriarty, 292
Dewey Dell Bundren, 257
Didymus Maqoma, 323
Diggory Venn, 92
Dinah Morris, 149
Dirk Hatteraick, 76
Disco Troop, 184
Dmitri, 88
Doctor Livesey, 135
Doctor Long Ghost, 165
Doctor Paul Courreges, 271
Donald Farfrae, 167
Donald Bean Lean, 54
Donatello, 173
Don Birnam, 240
Don Fabrizio Corbera, 282
Don Julian Alvarado (El Supremo), 236
Don Rodrigo, 30

Dough-boy, 116
Dounia, 126
Dorothea Brooke (Dodo), 123
Dousterswivel, 72
Dr. A. Herbert Bledsoe, 289
Dr. Austin sloper, 151
Dr. Aziz, 259
Dr. Copeland, 329
Dr. Harrison, 22
Dr. Hilarius, 327
Dr. Max Gottlieb, 229
Dr. Pangloss, 4
Dr. Primrose, 8
Dr. Richard Diver, 235
Dr. Slammer, 54
Dr. Slop, 23
Dr. Strong, 118
Dr. Tertius Lydgate, 143
Dr. Vesey Stanhope, 103
Dr. Will Kennicott, 235
Durdles, 149

E

Ebenezer Cooke, 305
Edie Ochiltree, 66
Edgar Altschuler, 297
Edgar Linton, 80
Edith Granger, 043
Edward, 68
Edward Chester, 148
Edward Dantes, 90
Edward Ferrars, 62
Edward Leeford (Monks), 57
Edward Murdstone, 111
Edward Rochester, 80
Edward Tressilian, 63
Edwards, 35
Edouard, 237
Elaine Risley, 308
Elbis, 29
Elinor Dashwood, 63
Elizabeth Bennet, 45
Elizabeth Harris, 26
Elizabeth Hunter, 311
Elizabeth Matthew, 25

Ellen Thatcher, 252
Ellie May, 269
Ellis Duckworth, 149
Emily Costigan, 147
Emily Jervois, 38
Emily St. Aubert, 13
Emir Fakreddin, 36
Emma Haredale, 113
Emma rouault, 130
Eppie (Heplizibah), 97
Ernest Pontifex, 206
Esmerelda, 53
Esteban Trueba, 300
Estella , 91
Esther Jack, 219
Esther Lyon, 178
Esther Summerson. 155
Eudixia-Eddie-Eadith, 307
Eugene de rastignac, 53
Eugene Gant, 218
Eugene Wrayburn, 146
Eupheus Hines (Doc), 256
Eustacia Vye, 87

F

Faber, 316
Fabrizio, (64)
Fagin, 44
Falkland, 111
Fanny Cleaver (Jenny Wren), 148
Fanny Goodwill, 23
Fanny Price, 60
Fanny Robin, 141
Father Ambrosio, 15
Father Jean Maria Latour, 251
father Jerome, 31
Father Montez, 284
Fathom, 18
Fedallah, 99
Fergus MacIvor, 76
Flask (King-Post), 104
Florence, 102
Florentino Ariza, 293
Foxhall Edwards, 260
Frances "Frankie" Addams, 282

Francine Whiting, 316
francis Spenlow, 159
Francis Starwick, 230
Francis Whelan, 299
Frank A. Cowperwood, 204
Franklin blake, 178
Franklin Scudder, 203
Frank Osbaldistone, 42
Frederic Henry, 265
Frederic Moreau, 145
Frederick Winterbourne, 171
Frenesi Gates, 310
Frieda, 237
Fyodor, 175

G

Gabriel John Utterson, 112
Gabriel Oak, 171
Ganya Ardalionovitch, 168
Gene Forrester, 294
General Butzon, 72
General Canales, 325
General Ira "Bus" Beal, 297
General Marvin, 326
Genevieve Rod, 269
Gentleman Brown, 204
Geordie Robertson, 75
George, 307
George Dennison, 22
George Kemp, 266
George Knightly, 63
George Koves, 336
George Marvin Bush, 266
George Milton. 245
George Osborne, 169
George Osmond, 152
George Ponderevo, 208
George Radfoot, 147
Georges, 310
George Warrinton, 151
George Webber, 231
George Willard, 185
Gertrude Morel, 197
Giaour, 27
Gilbert (Gil) Martin, 223

Gil Blas, 35
Gil Carter, 235
Gina Pietranera, 52
Giovanelli, 146
Godrey Cass, 128
Goldstein, 307
Goodhue Coldfield, 241
Governor Bellingham, 130
Gracie Poole, 86
Griffin, 199
Gringiore, 57
Grizzle, 36
Grushenka, 132
Gulchenerouz, 34
Gustav Von Aschenbach, 274
Guy Montag, 301
G. W. Hurstwood, 207

H

Hamilcar, 160
Hamida, 294
Hank Morgan, 97
Hanno, 163
Hans Castorp, 259
Hans Schnier, 291
Hard-Heart, 74
Harriet Byron, 30
Harriet Smith, 77
Harry, 157
Harry Angstrom, 281
Harry Haller, 276
Harvey Cheyne, 186
Hayraddin Maugrabin, 76
Heathcliff, 84
Heinrich Faehmel, 299
Helen, 247
Helena Landless, 137
Helen Archer, 316
Hello-Central, 145
Henry Barnard, 262
Henry Durie, 157
Henry Fleming, 184
Henry Sutpen, 254
Henry Wilcox, 213
Herbert Pocket, 100

I

J

M

Miles Roby, 318
Millie, 331
Mlle. Cunegonde, 7
Miriam Leivers, 207
Miriam Schaefer, 172
Miss Andrews, 9
Miss Anville, 15
Miss Atkins, 38
Miss Betsy Trotwood, 126
Miss Beverley, 17
Miss Broadhurst, 70
Miss Emilia, 35
Miss Emily Wilkinson, 201
Miss Flite, 163
Miss Havisham, 90
Miss Melinda Goosetrap, 23
Miss Pross, 128
Miss Rachel Wardle, 52
Miss Roberta Brinklow, 247
Miss Snapper, 21
Miss Walton, 24
Mlle. Nioche, 140
M. Nioche, 132
Monroe Starr, 227
Monsieur Grandet, 69
Monsieur Homais, 131
Monsieur Julien Sariette, 203
Monsieur The Marquis St. Evremonde, 118
Monsieur Vautrin, 70
Mortimer Delvile, 18
Mortimer Lightwood, 119
Moses, 283
Mpho Maqoma, 324
Mr. Barkis, 171
Mr. Brown, 333
Mr. Bumble, 49
Mr. Burchell, 6
Mr. Charrington, 328
Mr. Creakle, 128
Mr. Crisparkle, 139
Mr. Gray, 61
Mr. Harley, 14
Mr. Holgrave, 127
Mr. Jaggers, 105
Mr. Jones, 304
Mr. Krook, 170

Paul Riesling, 220
Pedro Tecero Garcia, 324
Pembroke Somerset, 66
Pennsylvania, 192
Peter Kien, 300
Peyton Loftis, 286
Philip Carey, 211
Philip Francis Queeg, 325
Philip Nolan, 88
Philip Pirrip, 84
Philip Quarles, 234
Pierre Bezuhov, 91
Piggy, 289
Pilar, 236
Pip, 168
Popeye, 252
Porfiry, 100
Preacher Whitfield, 267
Presley, 188
Prince Myshkin, 80
Professor Bhaer, 122
Prof. Pierre Aronimax, 136
Pyotr Verhovensky, 134

Q

Quasimodo, 42
Quentin Compson, 239
Quilp, 124

R

Rachel Owlglass, 306
Rachel Verinder, 172
Radisav, 311
Rake, 179
Ramona Donsell, 334
Rashleigh Osbaldistone, 65
Rawdon Crawley, 146
Raymond Courreges, 270
Red, 248
Renata, 315
Rev. Arthur Villars, 5
Rev. Edward Casaubon, 137
Rev. Francis Arabin, 148
Rev. Septimus Harding, 157

Reverend Obadiah Slope, 99
Reverend St. John's Rivers, 160
Richard, 83
Richard Carstone, 156
Richard Hannay, 185
Richard Newson, 161
Richard Phillotson, 210
Richard Swiveller (Dick), 172
Richard Varney, 60
Rima, 193
Robbie, 330
Roberta, 225
Roberta Alden, 257
Robert Cohn, 227
Robert Dudley, 69
Robert Faehmel, 335
Robert Jordan, 218
Robert Lovelace, 33
Robert Merrick, 232
Robert Walton, 52
Robert Weaver, 258
Robin, 16
Robinson, 5
Rockyfeller, 248
Rodion Raskolnikov, 81
Rodolphe Boulanger, 115
Roger Byam, 240
Roger Chillingworth, 86
Roger "Rogue" Riderhood, 155
Roger Solmes, 32
Rosa Bud, 140
Rosa Dartle, 144
Rosemary Hoyt, 220
Rosie Driffield, 231
Ruby Lamar, 245
Rudolf Rassendyll, 188
Rufus Scott, 298
Rutherford, 233

S

Sadie Burke, 312
Sally Athelny, 209
Salters, 206
Samuel Dockwrath, 176
Sam Weller, 66

Tomasino, 298
Tom Buchanan, 266
Tom Faggus, 122
Tommy Barban, 229
Tommy Traddles, 108
Tom Pinch, 108
Tom Pipes, 8
Tom Robinson, 291
Tracy Tupman, 56
T. Sobieski, 65
Tyrone Slothrop, 304

U

Uncas, 44
Uncle Toby, 22
Uriah Heep, 97
Ursula Brangwen, 210

V

Valancourt, 30
Vathek, 14
Vera Stark, 300
Virgil, 255
Vinicius, 197
Vivaldo Moore, 332

W

Wackford Squeers, 42
Walt Comeau, 317
Walter, 234
Walter Cay, 101
Wang, 206
Wang Lung, 275
Weena, 195
Widow Bardell, 51
Widow Wadman, 20
Wilfred, 48
Wilhelm Schomberg, 215
Wilkins Micawber, 92
William Boldwood, 147
William Latch, 211
William of Baskerville, 306

William "Studs" Lonigan, 276
William Sylvanus Baxter, 198
Willie Chandran, 289
William Guppy, 164
Willie Keith, 299
Willie Stark, 286
Willie Shrike, 261
Wilson, 190
Winifred Jenkins, 32
Winston Smith, 280
Wolf Larsen, 184

Y

Yakov Bok, 302
Yithak Kummer, 303
Young Jolyon, 213

Z

Zenobia Pierce (Zeena), 191

Index of Titles

A

Absalom, Absalom! by William Faulkner
    Goodhue Coldfield (241), Henry Sutpen (254), Charles Bon (255), Thomas Sutpen (267)
The Absentee by Maria Edgeworth
    Miss Broadhurst (70), Nicholas Garraghty (69), Lord Clonbrony (67)
The Accidental Tourist by Anne Tyler
    Macon Leary   (293)
Adam Bede by George Eliot (Mary Anne Evans)
    Hester Sorrel (Hetty) (142), Dinah Morris (149), Esther Lyon (178)
Agnes Grey by Anne Bronte
    Agnes (100)
Alice Adams by Booth Tarkington
    Walter (234), Virgil (255)
Alice in Wonderland by Lewis Carroll
    The Duchess (95)
All the King's Men by Robert Penn Warren
    Jack Burden (280), Willie Stark (286), Sadie Burke (312)
All the Names by Jose Saramago
    Senhor Jose (290)
All Quiet on the Western Front by Erich Maria Remarque
    Paul Baumer (222)
Almayer's Folly by Joseph Conrad
    Dain Maroola (208)
The Ambassadors by Henry James
    Chadwick (Chad) Newsome (186)
Amelia by Henry Fielding
    Captain Booth (16), Dr. Harrison (22), Elizabeth Matthews (25), Elizabeth Harris (26)
The American by Henry James
    Mr. Tristram (107), Claire de Cintre, nee Bellegarde (107), Christopher Newman (114), M. Nioche (132), The Marquis de Bellegarde (Urbain) (139), Mlle. Nioche (140), Mrs. Bread (161)
An American Tragedy by Theodore Dreiser
    Clyde Griffiths (219), Roberta Alden (257)
Animal Farm by George Orwell (Eric Blair)
    Mr. Jones (304)
Anna Karenina by Count Leo Tolstoy
    Count Vronsky (82), Alexei Karenin (94)

The Bridge of San Luis Rey by Thornton Wilder
    Brother Juniper (228), Marquesa de Montemayor (250)
The Bridge on the Drina by Ivo Andric
    Radisav (311), Abidaga (334)
The Brothers Karamazov by Fyodor Dostoevski
    Dmitri (88), Ivan (98), Grushenka (132), Smerdyakov (134), Fyodor (175)
Buddenbrooks by Thomas Mann
    Antonie (Tony) (195), Herr Permaneder (197)

C

The Caine Mutiny by Hermnan Wouk
    Willie Keith (299), May Wynn (314), Philip Francis Queeg
    (325)
Cakes and Ale by William Somerset Maugham
    Rosie Driffield (231), Alroy Kear (243), Ashenden (252), George Kemp (266)
Caleb Williams by William Godwin
    Ferdinando Falkland (11)
Camille by Alexander Dumas, Jr.
    Camille (156)
Cancer Ward by Alexander Solzhenitsyn
    Oleg Kostoglotov (286)
Candide by Voltaire
    Dr. Panglossc(4), Mlle. Cunegonde (7), Cacambo (13)
Captain Horatio Hornblower by C.S. Forester
    Lady Barbara Wellesley (230), Don Julian Alvarado (El Supremo)(236), Admiral
    Leighton (261), Bush (264)
Captains Courageous by Rudyard Kipling
    Disco Troop (184), Dan Troop (189), Harvey Cheyne (186), Pennsylvania (192),
    Salters (206), Long Jack (211)
Captain Singleton by Daniel Defoe
    Captain Bob Singleton (19)
Cass Timberlane by Sinclair Lewis
    Jinny Marshland (268)
The Castle by Franz Kafka
    Frieda (237)
The Castle of Otranto by Horace Walpole
    Conrad (17), Father Jerome (31), Theodore (32), Isabella (33), Manfred (37), Matilda
    (38)
Castle Rackrent by Maria Edgeworth
    Isabella (75), Honest Thady Quirk (73), Jason (74)
Catch-22 by Joseph Helloer
    John Yossarian (292)
The Catcher in the Rye by J.D. Salinger
    Holden Caufield (282)

G

H

Hard Times by Charles Dickens
> Steven Blackpool (109), Mrs. Sparsit (110), Thomas Gradgrind (112), Mrs. Pegler (162), Cecilia "Sissy" Jupe (165), Josiah Bounderby (178)

The Heart is a Lonely Hunter by Carson McCullers
> John Singer (281), Biff Brannon (295), Mick Kelly (309), Dr. Copeland (329), Spiro Antonapoulous (333)

The Heart of Midlothian by Sir Walter Scott
> Jeanie Deans (73), Meg Murdockson (74), Geordie Robertson (75)

Heart of Darkness by Joseph Conrad
> Mr. Kurtz (199)

Heaven's My Destination by Thornton Wilder
> Roberta (225), George Marvin Bush (266)

Herzog by Saul Bellow
> Moses (283), Madelaine (308), Ramona Donsell (334)

The House of Mirth by edith Wharton
> Lily Bart (213)

The House of the Seven Gables by Nathaniel Hawthorne
> Colonel Pyncheon (95), Matthew Maule (102), Mr. Holgrave (127)

The House of the Spirits by isabel Allende
> Esteban Trueba (300), Clara Trueba (301), Pedro Tecero Garcia (324), Blanca De Satigny (327), Alba (332)

Howards End by E.M. Forster
> Margaret Schlegel (212), Henry Wilcox (213), Charles Wilcox (214), Leonard Bast (215)

How Green Was My Valley by Richard Llewellyn
> Huw Morgan (267)

Huckleberry Finn by Mark Twain (Samuel Longhorn Clemens)
> Judge Thatcher (99), Jim (133), Pap (136)

The Human Comedy by william Saroyan
> Katey Macauley (258)

Humbolt's Gift by Saul Bellow
> Charles "Charlie" Citrine (302), Renata (315)

Humphrey Clinker by Tobias George Smollett
> Matthew Bramble (11), Lt. Obadiah Lismahago (13), Tabitha Bramble (20), George Dennison (22), Lydia Melford (25), Jerry Melford (31), Winifred Jenkins (32)

The Hunchback of Notre Dame by Victor Hugo
> Quasimodo (42), Claude Frollo (44), Esmerelda (53), Gringiore (57)

I

The Idiot by Fyodor Dostoevski
> Prince Myshkin (80), Natasya Filipovna (139), Parfen Rogozhin (144), Ganya Ardalionovitch (168),

Magnificent Obsession by Lloyd C. Douglas
  Robert Merrick (232)
Main Street by Sinclair Lewis
  Carol Kennicott (226), Dr. Will Kennicott (235)
The Maltese Falcon by Dashiell Hammett
  Miles Archer (232), Brigid O'Shaughnessy (275)
The Mambo Kings Play Songs of Love by Oscar Hijuelos
  Cesar Castillo (291)
Manhattan Transfer by John Dos Passos
  Jimmy Herf (234), Ellen Thatcher (252), Congo (263)
Mansfield Park by Jane Austen
  Lieutenant Price (47), Mrs. Norris (56), Sir Thomas Bertram
  (58), Fanny Price (60)
The Man Who Was Thursday by G. K. Chesterton
  Lucien Gregory (193)
The Man Without a Country by Edward Everett Hale
  Philip Nolan (88), Colonel Morgan (133)
The Marble Faun by Nathaniel Hawthorne
  Miriam Schaefer (172), Donatello (173), Kenyon (174)
Martin Chuzzlewit by Charles Dickens
  Seth Pecksniff (86), Mercy (Merry) Pecksniff (104), Chastity
  (Cherry) Pecksniff (106), Tom Pinch (108), Mrs. Sarah Gamp
  (117), Nadgett (142), Tigg Montague (152), John Westlock (153),
  David Crimple (155), Chuffey (159), Mark Tapley (166)
The Master of Ballantrae by Robert Louis Stevenson
  James Durie (113), Secundra Dass (142), Henry Durie (157)
The Mayor of Casterbridge by Thomas Hardy
  Michael Henchard (160), Richard Newson (161), Donald Farfrae
  (167)
A Member of the Wedding by Carson McCullers
  Frances "Frankie" Addams (282), John Henry "Candy" West (313)
Midaq Alley by Naguib Mahfouz
  Hamida   (294)
Middlemarch by George Eliot (Mary Anne Evans)
  Dorothea Brooke (Dodo) (123), Rev. Edward Casaubon (137), Dr.
  Tertius Lydgate (143), Nicholas Bulstrode (154)
The Mill of the Floss by George Eliot (Mary Anne Evans)
  Maggie Tulliver (158)
Miss Lonelyhearts by Nathaniel West
  Willie Shrike (261)
Moby Dick by Herman Melville
  Captain Ahab (83), Starbuck (92), Ishmael (93), Fedallah (99),
  Stubb (102), Flask (King-Post) (104), Dough-Boy (116), Pip
  (168),
Moll Flanders by Daniel Defoe
  Jeremy E. (6), Robin (16)

O

Abriham White (73), Hard-Heart (74), Ishmael Bush (75)
Pride and Prejudice by Jane Austen
Elizabeth Bennet (45), Mr. Bingly (49), Fitzwilliam Darcy (51)
The Prisoner of Zenda by Anthony Hope
Rudolf Rassendyll (191), Black Michael (194)

Q

Quentin Durward by Sir Walter Scott
Ludovic Lesley (Le Balafre) (68), Hayraddin Maugrabin (76)
Quo Vadis by Henryk Sienkiewicz
Vinicius (197)

R

Rabbit Redux by John Updike
Harry Angstrom (281), Janice Angstrom (312)
The Rainbow by D.H. Lawrence
Ursula Brangwen (210)
Rasselas by Dr. Samuel Johnson
Nekayah (12)

Reebecca by Daphne du Mauier
Mrs. Maximillian (Maxim) de Winter (221)
The Red and the Black by Stendhal (Marie Henri Beyle)
Julien Sorel (43), M. De Renal (49), Mathilde de la Mole (62)
The Red Badge of Courage by Stephen Crane
Henry Fleming (184), Jim Conklin (187), The Tattered Man (189)
Wilson (190)
Remembrance of Things Past by Marcel Proust
Baron de Charlus (223)
The Return of the Native by Thomas Hardy
Clym Yeobright (81), Eustacia Vye (87), Diggory Venn (92), Damon
Wildeve (98), Johnny Nonsuch (127), Thomasin Yeobright (132)
The Revolt of the Angels by Anatole France (Jacques Anatole Tribault)
Arcade (198), Monsieur Julien Sariette (203)
Rip Van Winkle by Washington Irving
Judith (46)
Robinson Crusoe by Daniel Defoe
Robinson (5)
Rob Roy by Sir Walter Scott
Frank Osbaldistone (42), Macgregor Campbell (46), Rashleigh
Osbaldistone (65), Bailie Nichol Jarvie (77)
Roderick Random by Tobias George Smollett
Strap (7), Narcissa (10), Miss Snapper (21), Miss Melinda
Goosetrap (23) Tom Bowling (25), Lieutenant Hatchway (29), Don

Index of Authors

Boll, Heinrich
    Billiards at Half Past Nine
        Heinrich Faehmel (299), Joseph Faehmel (317), Robert Faehmel (335)
    The Clown
        Hans Schnier (291)

Bradbury, Ray
    Fahrenheit 451
        Guy Montag (301), Clarisse McClellan (303), Faber (316), Millie (331), Captain Beatty (336)

Braine, John
    Room at the Top
        Susan Brown (283), Joe Lampton (287), Alice Aisgill (309), Jack Wales (330), Mr. Brown (333)

Bronte, Anne
    Agnes Grey
        Agnes (100)

Bronte, Charlotte
    Jane Eyre
        Edward Rochester (80), Gracie Poole (86), Jane (103), Adele Varens (114), Berta Mason Rochester (117), Bessie Leaven (120), Mrs. Fairfax (131), Mr. Mason (158), Reverend St. John's Rivers (160)

Bronte, Emily
    Wuthering Heights
        Edgar Linton (80), Heathcliff (84), Mr. Lockwood (98), Nelly Dean (101)

Buchan, John
    The Thirty-Nine Steps
        Richard Hannay (185), Sir Walter Bullivant (191), Franklin Scudder (203)

Buck, Pearl
    The Good Earth
        Wang Lung (275)

Bunyan, John
    The Pilgrim's Progress
        Christian (39)

Burney, Frances (Fanny)
    Cecelia
        Miss Beverley (17), Mortimer Delvile (18)
    Evelina
        Rev. Arthur Villars (5), Miss Anville (15), Lady Howard (26), Sir John Belmont (27), Sir Clement Willoughby (28), Lord Orville (29)

Butler, Samuel
The Way of all Flesh
Ernest Pontifex (206)

C

Caldwell, Erskine
Tobacco Road
Jester Leeter (225), Ellie May (269)
Camus, Albert
The Stranger
Patrice Meursault (284)
Canetti, Elias
The Tower of Babel
Peter Kien (300), Therese Kummholz (316)
Carroll, Lewis
Alice in Wonderland
The Duchess (95)
Cather, Willa
A Lost Lady
Ivy Peters (242), Captain Daniel Forrester (262)
My Antonia
Mrs. Cuzak (nee Schimerda) (194), Jim Burden (196)
O Pioneers!
Alexandra Bergson (287)
Death Comes for the Archbishop
Father Jean Maria Latour (251)
Cervantes, Miguel
Don Quixote
Aldonza Lorenzo (16)
Chesterton, G. K.
The Man Who Was Thursday
Lucien Gregory (193)
Clark, Walter Van Tilburg
The Ox-Bow Incident
Gil Carter (235)
Collins, Wilkie
The Moonstone
Rachel Verinder (172), Franklin Blake (178)
Conrad, Joseph
Almayer's Folly
Dain Maroola (208)
Heart of Darkness
Mr. Kurtz (199)
Lord Jim
Chief Doramin (196), Jewel (202), Dain Waris (203),

Delillo, Don

    <u>Underworld</u>

        Nick Shay (305)

Dickens, Charles

    <u>A Tale of Two Cities</u>

        Sidney Carton (89), Jarvis Lorry (95), Madame Defarge (106), Monsieur The Marquis St. Evremonde (118), Mr. Stryver (120), Jerry Cruncher (121),   Solomon Pross (125), Miss Pross (128)

    <u>Barnaby Rudge</u>

        Emma Haredale (113), Edward Chester (148), John Willet (151)

    <u>Bleak House</u>

        Nemo (85), Lady Honoria Dedlock (96), Mr. Tulkinghorn (119), John Jarndyce (126), Inspector Bucket (145), Sir Leicester Dedlock (150), Mr. Snagsby (153), Ada Clare (154), Esther Summerson (155),Richard Carstone (156),
        Miss Flite (163), William Guppy (164), Mr. Krook (170)

    <u>David Copperfield</u>

        Mealy Potatoes (85), Wilkins Micawber (92), Uriah Heep (97), Agnes Wickfield (107), Tommy Traddles (108), James Steerforth (110), Edward Murdstone (111), Dr. Strong (118), Clara Peggotty (122), Miss Betsy Trotwood (126), Mr. Creakle (128), Rosa Dartle (144), Francis Spenlow (159), Mr. Barkis (171), Littimer (177)

    <u>Dombey and Son</u>

        Walter Cay (101), Florence (102), James Carker (134), Captain Cuttle (135), Edith Granger (143), Paul (150)

    <u>Great Expectations</u>

        Philip Pirrip (84), Miss Havisham (90), Estella (91), Joe Gargery (93), Herbert Pocket (100), Arthur Compeyson (103), Mr. Jaggers (105), Abel Magwitch (Mr. Provis) (108)

    <u>Hard Times</u>

        Steven Blackpool (109), Mrs. Sparsit (110), Thomas Gradgrind (112), Mrs. Pegler (162), Cecilia "Sissy" Jupe (165), Josiah Bounderby (178)

    <u>Little Dorrit</u>

        Amy (170)

    <u>Martin Chuzzlewit</u>

        Seth Pecksniff (86), Mercy (Merry) Pecksniff (104), Chastity (Cherry) Pecksniff (106), Tom Pinch (108), Mrs. Sarah Gamp (117), Nadgett (142), Tigg Montague (152), John Westlock (153), David Crimple (155), Chuffey (159), Mark Tapley (166)

The Sound and the Fury
Benjamin (Benji) Compson (223), Quentin Compson (239), Jason Compson IV (244), Sidney Herbert Head (251), Cadace (Caddy) Compson (265)

Fielding, Henry
Amelia
Captain Booth (16), Dr. Harrison (22), Elizabeth Matthews (25), Elizabeth Harris (26)
Jonathan Wild
Jonathan Wild   (12)
Joseph Andrews
Mrs. Slipslop (6), Lady Booby (7), Parson Adams (17), Fanny Goodwill (23), Squire Wilson (24)
Tom Jones
Squire Allworthy (4), Jenny Jones (8), Squire Western (10), Sophia Western (19), Lady Bellaston (20), Mr. Partridge (21), Master Blifil (34)

Fitzgerald, F. Scott
Tender is the Night
Rosemary Hoyt (220), Nicole Diver (224), Tommy Barban (229), Dr. Richard Diver (235)
The Great Gatsby
Daisy Buchanan (233), James Gatz (247), Nick Carraway (250), Tom Buchanan (266)
The Last Tycoon
Monroe Starr (227)
This Side of Paradise
Amory Blaine (265)

Flaubert, Gustave
A Sentimental Education
Frederic Moreau (145)
Madame Bovary
Leon Dupuis (111), Rodolphe Boulanger (115) Emma Rouault (130), Monsieur Homais (131)
Salammbo
Hamilcar (160), Matho (161), Hanno (163), Narr Havas (167)
The Temptation of Saint Anthony
Hilarion (150)

Forester, C. S.
Captain Horatio Hornblower
Lady Barbara Wellesley (230), Don Julian Alvarado (El Supremo)(236), Admiral Leighton (261), Bush (264)

Grass, Gunther
    <u>The Tin Drum</u>
        Oskar Matzarath (302), Agnes Matzarath (313), Jan Bronski (315), Alfred Matzarath (326)

Greene, Graham
    <u>The Power and the Glory</u>
        Father Montez (284)

<u>H</u>

Haggard, H. Rider
    <u>King Solomon's Mines</u>
        Allan Quartermain (121)

Hale, Edward Everett
    <u>The Man Without A Country</u>
        Philip Nolan (88), Colonel Morgan (133)

Haley, Alex
    <u>Roots</u>
        Kunta Kinte (308), Kizzy (329)

Hall, James Norman & Charles Nordhoff
    <u>Mutiny on the Bounty</u>
        Tehani (225), Roger Byam (240)

Hammett, Dashiell
    <u>The Glass Key</u>
        Ned Beaumont (255)
    <u>The Maltese Falcon</u>
        Miles Archer (232), Brigid O'Shaughnessy (275)

Hardy, Thomas
    <u>Far From the Madding Crowd</u>
        Bathsheba Everdene (140), Fanny Robin (141), William Boldwood (147) Gabriel Oak (171)
    <u>Jude the Obscure</u>
        Sue Bridehead (201), Arabella Donn (205) Richard Phillotson (210), Little Father Time (212)
    <u>The Mayor of Casterbridge</u>
        Michael Henchard (160), Richard Newson (161), Donald Farfrae (167)
    <u>The Return of the Native</u>
        Clym Yeobright (81), Eustacia Vye (87), Diggory Venn (92), Damon Wildeve (98), Johnny Nonsuch (127), Thomasin Yeobright (132)

401

Morrison, Toni
    <u>Beloved</u>
        Sethe (290)
Murdoch, Iris
    <u>The Sea, The Sea</u>
        Charles Arrowby (304)
Muriac, Francois
    <u>The Desert of Love</u>
        Raymond Courreges (270), Doctor Paul Courreges (271), Maria Cross (274)

N

Nabokov, Vladimir
    <u>Lolita</u>
        Humbert Humbert (284), Charlotte Haze (312), Clare Quilty (331)
Naipaul, V. S.
    <u>Half a Life</u>
        Willie Chandran (289)
Nordhoff, Charles & James Norman Hall
    <u>Mutiny on the Bounty</u>
        Tehani (225), Roger Byam (240)
Norris, Frank
    <u>The Octopus</u>
        Presley (188)
    <u>The Pit</u>
        Curtis Jadwin (188)

O

O'Hara, John
    <u>Appointment In Samarra</u>
        Julian English (219)
Orwell, George (Eric Blair)
    <u>Animal Farm</u>
        Mr. Jones (304)
    <u>Nineteen Eighty Four</u>
        Winston Smith (280), Julia (281), Goldstein(307), Mr. Charrington (328)
Ouida (Marie Louise de la Ramee)
    <u>Under Two Flags</u>
        Colonel Chateauroy (159), Berkeley Cecil (162), Lord
        Rockingham (167), Bertie Cecil (168), Rake (179), Cigarette (180)

Stendhal (Marie Henri Beyle)
      <u>The Charterhouse of Parma</u>
               Gina Pietranera (52), Marietta Valsera (59), Count Mosca (60), Clelia Conti (62), Fabrizio (64)
      <u>The Red and the Black</u>
           Julien Sorel (43), M. De Renal (49), Mathilde de la Mole (62)
Sterne, Laurence
      <u>Tristram Shandy</u>
           Susannah (4), Widow Wadman (20), Uncle Toby (22), Dr. Slop (23), Corporal Trim (24)
Stevenson, Robert Louis
      <u>Dr. Jekyll and Mr. Hyde</u>
           Gabriel John Utterson (112)
      <u>Kidnapped</u>
           Alan Breck Stewart (117), David Balfour (121)
      <u>The Black Arrow</u>
           Ellis Duckworth (149)
      <u>The Master of Ballantrae</u>
           James Durie (113), Secundra Dass (142), Henry Durie (157)   <u>Treasure Island</u>
           Black Dog (84), Jim Hawkins (90), Blind Pew (93), Bill Bones (104), Squire Trelawney (115),, Ben Gunn (129), Doctor Livesey (135), Long John Silver (136)
Stowe, Harriet Beecher
      <u>Uncle Tom's Cabin</u>
           Simon Legree (89)
Styron, William
      <u>Lie Down in Darkness</u>
           Peyton Loftis (286)
      <u>Sophie's Choice</u>
           Stingo (285)
      <u>The Confessions of Nat Turner</u>
           Thomas (T.R.) Gray (288)
Swift, Jonathan
      <u>Gulliver's Travels</u>
           Lemuel (21)

<u>T</u>

Tan, Amy
      <u>The Joy Luck Club</u>
           Ling Jong (292)

Tarkington, Booth
    <u>Alice Adams</u>
        Walter (234), Virgil (255)
    <u>Seventeen</u>
        William Sylvanus Baxter (198)

Thackeray, William Makepeace
    <u>Pendennis</u>
        Laura Bell (124), Arthur (141), Emily Costigan (147)   Colonel Altamont
        (169)
    <u>The Virginians</u>
        George Warrinton (151)
    <u>Vanity Fair</u>
        Becky Sharp (87), Amelia Sedley (96), Sir Pitt Crawley (111), Joseph (Jo)
        Sedley (137), Captain William Dobbin (138) Rawdon Crawley (146), George
        Osborne (169)

Tolstoy, Count Leo
    <u>Anna Karenina</u>
        Count Vronsky (82), Alexei Karenin (94)
    <u>War and Peace</u>
        Pierre Bezuhov (91), Andrey Bolkonsky (116), Natasha Rostov (125)

Toole, John Kennedy
    <u>A Confederacy of Dunces</u>
        Ignatius J. Reilly (288)

Trollope, Anthony
    <u>Barchester Towers</u>
        Reverend Obadiah Slope (99), Dr. Vesey Stanhope (103), Mrs. Proudie (120),
        Mr. Quiverful (138), Rev. Francis Arabin (148), Mrs. Eleanor Bold (170)
    <u>Orley Farm</u>
        Lucius Mason (164), Lady Mason (166), Samuel Dockwrath (176)
    <u>The Warden</u>
        Rev. Septimus Harding (157), John Bold (173)

Turgenev, Ivan
    <u>Fathers and Sons</u>
        Bazaroff (127), Kirsanoff (153)

Twain, Mark (Samuel Langhorne Clemens)
    <u>A Connecticut Yankee In King Arthur's Court</u>
        Hank Morgan (97), Hello-Central (145)
    <u>Huckleberry Finn</u>
        Judge Thatcher (99), Jim (133), Pap (136)

BIBLIOGRAPHY

Aarmour, Richard.   Classics Redefined.   New York: McGraw-Hill Book   Co.,
     Inc.,1980.

Becjiffm, Samuel Phd., Monarch College Outlines: English Literature   I (450 - 1798 A.D.)
     New York: Simon and Schuster, 1971.S

Becjiffm, Samuel Phd., Monarch College Outlines: English Literature   I (1798 - Present).
     New York: Simon and Schuster, 1971.

Drew, Elizabeth.   The Novel (A Modern Guide to Fifteen English
     Masterpieces).   New York: Dell Publishing Co, , Inc., 1983.

Grozier, Edwin A., ed.   Everyday Handbooks: Plot Outlines of   101Best Novels.
New York: Barnes & Noble, Inc., 1962.

Hopper, Vincent F., and Grebanier, Bernard D. N., Essentials of   European English
     Literature (A Guide to Great Books).   New York: Barrons Educational Seriers, Inc.,
     1952.

Hornstein, Lillian herlands. Ed.   The Readers Companion to World   Literature.   New
     York: The New American Library of World Literature, 1962.

Lass, Abraham H., and Brooks Wright, eds. A Students Guide to   50Great European
Novels. A Students Guide to 50 Great Anerican   novels. New York: Washington Square
Press, 1967; 1973.

McGill, Fank Nothern.   Cyclopedia of Literary Characters.   New York: Salem Press, Inc.,
     1963.

McGill, Fank Nothern.   Masterpieces of World Literature In Digest   Form.   New York:
Harper, Inc., [1952 - 1969].

Wynne-Davies, Marion, ed.   The Bloomsbury Guide to English   Literature.   New
York: Prentice Hall General Reference, 1990.
NY

Printed in Great Britain
by Amazon